D1631939

Pl

-4.

06467822

Fundamentals of Skill

Fundamentals of Skill

A. T. WELFORD

M.A., Sc.D.
Professor of Psychology in the University
of Adelaide

METHUEN & CO LTD
11 New Fetter Lane London EC4

First published 1968
Reprinted with corrections 1971
First published as a University Paperback 1971

Hardback SBN 416 03000 9
University Paperback SBN 416 70020 9

© 1968 *A. T. Welford*

Printed and bound in Great Britain
by Butler & Tanner Ltd
Frome and London

This book is sold subject to the condition that it shall not, by way of trade or otherwise, be lent, re-sold, hired out, or otherwise circulated without the publisher's prior consent in any form of binding or cover other than that in which it. is published and without a similar condition including this condition being imposed on the subsequent purchaser.

Distributed in the USA
by Barnes & Noble Inc.

190,391

Contents

Tables:

Acknowledgements

The author would also like to thank all authors and publishers who have given permission to quote copyright material from journals and books: *American Journal of Psychology, British Journal of Psychology,* Butterworth & Co. Ltd., *Ergonomics,* Ergonomics Research Society, H.M.S.O., *Journal of Experimental Psychology, Mind, Nature, Philips Technical Review, Psychology Review, Quarterly Journal of Experimental Psychology, Soc. Sci. Fennica Commentationes Humanorum Litterarum,* John Wiley and Sons, Inc.

Preface

Studies of human performance made during the past twenty-five years have profoundly affected thought and practice in experimental psychology both in the laboratory and in many fields of application. The present volume attempts a broad survey and appraisal of the main ideas which have emerged from this work. In writing it, three points especially have been borne in mind: firstly, although the research surveyed did not aim at establishing a 'grand theory' of human behaviour, certain principles seem to recur in several contexts so that different facets of performance can be linked together more closely than they have been hitherto. Secondly, much of the work has involved mathematical treatments which have been difficult to master for those whose mathematical education, like the author's, stopped at the age of fifteen or sixteen. It was felt to be essential to discuss some of these treatments, but an effort has been made to do so in a way that requires no mathematical knowledge beyond O-level in the British General Certificate of Education together with an elementary course on statistics as usually taken by psychology students. Thirdly, many of the studies surveyed have been of interest not only to psychologists but also to those engaged in various branches of operational research and industrial work study, for whom psychological terms are often a barrier to understanding. Technical terminology has therefore been kept, as far as possible, within the bounds of that which is common to any broad scientific training.

The amount of work published in the areas with which this book is concerned has increased very greatly during the last decade, and the task of surveying it has proved a formidable one. I am well aware that much has been omitted and that some treatments will be regarded as controversial. I hope that anyone whose work has been inadequately represented will accept my apologies, and will get in touch with me to point out my shortcomings.

This book owes a great deal to discussion with colleagues too numerous to mention. Especial thanks are, however, due to C. G. Cameron, E. R. F. W. Crossman, B. Fowler, D. A. Kassum, A. A. Knight, D. McNicol, J. Ryan and D. Vickers for permission to cite unpublished data for the first time, and to W. E. Hick for help in checking the derivation of Table A5. Thanks are also due to Mrs A. K. Copeman for her unusually competent translation of manuscript into typescript. Drafting was begun in 1964 while I was holding a Commonwealth Visiting Professorship at the University of Adelaide, and the book was finished shortly before returning there from Cambridge in a more permanent capacity.

A. T. WELFORD

St John's College,
Cambridge
24 November 1967

I

Introduction

The scientific study of skill may perhaps be taken as dating from 1820 when the astronomer Bessel began to examine the differences between his colleagues and himself in the recording of star-transit times. The observer had to note the time on a clock accurately to a second and then to count seconds by the ticks of the pendulum while he watched the star cross the graticule line of a telescope, estimating the time of crossing to the nearest tenth of a second. It was a complex task and it is not surprising that errors were made or that some observers were more skilful than others in avoiding them, so that substantial differences appeared when one was compared with another. Important pioneering studies of various aspects of skilled performance continued through the nineteenth century and in the early years of the present one. Every student of psychology has heard of the psychologist Bryan and his engineer collaborator Harter whose studies (1897, 1899) of learning Morse code still make interesting reading. The researches on movement by Woodworth (1899), the mathematical teacher who turned psychologist, are still fundamental. The intensive work by Book (1908) on typewriting, although less known is nevertheless classical.

During the 1920s and 1930s this type of study was swamped by other lines of interest. The work on skill that continued was usually done outside psychological laboratories as a part of industrial 'work study'. Its separation from the main stream of psychology was unfortunate, leaving work-study without theoretical foundations and depriving experimental psychology of some stimulating lines of research.

The Second World War, however, brought a resurgence of interest. Just as in Bessel's era perfection of the chronoscope and the improvement it brought in the measurement of time focused attention on human errors of observation, so in the early 1940s technical developments of weapons, high-speed aircraft, radar and other devices reached a point at which the limitations of man and machine working together were no longer mainly in the machine but in the human operator. The full potentialities of the machine could sometimes be realised if the operator was rigorously selected and highly trained, but often it was clear that no amount of selection or training could ensure adequate performance. The need was therefore imperative for an understanding of the factors making for ease or difficulty in the operation of elaborate equipment, and this in its turn called for knowledge of many facets of human capacity and performance. It was thus that experimental psychologists came, together with physiologists and anatomists, to take up work alongside the engineers responsible for developing equipment.

The partnership was destined to be of far-reaching importance to both sides. The engineers came to recognise the necessity of considering the potentialities and limitations of the human operator if their machines were to be used to best advantage, and their psychological colleagues set new criteria of adequacy in design which, although not always convenient for the engineer, were clearly important. The lessons did not end with the war but have continued for service equipment since, and have gradually been gaining currency in industry both in the design of work, machinery and machine tools and also in the design of products such as cars and household equipment.

On the psychological side it was significant that much of the initial research was done by people who came from their university laboratories to play their part in the war effort. These men brought to their studies an interest in fundamentals, and recognised at once that a great deal of *ad hoc* research on particular pieces of equipment could be by-passed if the essential 'key' features of human skill shown by expert operators could be understood. Previous psychological theory turned out on the whole to be of little help, but the application of certain mathematical and engineering concepts proved remarkably fruitful, and has wrought something of a revolution in thought about many aspects of human performance. There are, indeed, few important developments of theory in post-war experimental psychology which do not owe something to this type of approach.

The researches made have come to be called studies of *skill*, but the word is not used in quite the same sense as it is in industry. An industrial worker is said to be skilled when he is qualified to carry out trade or craft work involving knowledge, judgment and manual deftness, usually acquired as a result of long training, whereas an unskilled man is not expected to do anything that cannot be learnt in a relatively short time. The industrial definition of skill is thus a formal one in terms of training. The psychological use of the term is wider, concerned with all the factors which go to make up a competent, expert, rapid and accurate performance. Skill in this sense thus attaches, to a greater or lesser extent, to *any* performance and is not limited to manual operations but covers a wide range of mental activities as well.

An early and influential sign of the developing thought of the war years was the insistence by Craik (1943) that the brain should not be conceived either as a vast telephone exchange of reflex arcs or as a vaguely defined field of interacting forces. Rather, he urged, it must be thought of as a computer receiving inputs from many sources and combining them to produce an output which is unique to each particular occasion although nevertheless lawful. The effects of this thinking might have been far less, however, had not three books appeared at the end of the forties. The first was Wiener's *Cybernetics* (1948) which set out ideas, clothed with appropriate mathematics, for considering man as a self-regulating mechanism, and which outlined the basic concepts of 'information theory'. The second was Shannon and Weaver's *The Mathematical Theory of Communication* (1949) which gave an expanded treatment of information theory including a set of theorems. The third was Wald's *Statistical Decision Functions* (1950) which paved the way for the application in recent years of statistical decision theory to human performance. These ways of thinking have not been without their critics, but it seems fair to claim that, whether or not they have provided significant answers to psychological questions, they have given a vigorous impetus to the treatment of psychological processes in precise, quantitative terms, and have brought together many areas of study previously thought to be unrelated.

The aim of this book is to sketch some of the main lines of this thinking. We shall in the rest of the present chapter consider, as examples, three areas of research each of which illustrates a fundamental principle of the general approach and emphasizes certain features of capacity which have come in for intensive study. In subsequent chapters we shall take up these several features one by one in more detail.

SENSORY-MOTOR SKILL AND THE CYBERNETIC APPROACH

One of the lines of work developed in the forties was the tracking of moving targets – a problem derived from gunlaying. Tracking in many ways epitomises sensory-motor performance and is similar to various everyday tasks such as steering a vehicle. Precise study is, however, difficult in real-life situations so that the task was incorporated into a number of laboratory experiments aimed at the study of its essential features and designed to ascertain some of the important characteristics of the human link in systems where man and machine interact. Let us look at one of these experiments by way of example.

A track, drawn on a strip of paper, passes vertically downwards past a window as shown in Fig. 1.1. The track moves irregularly from side to side of the paper and the subject attempts to follow it by moving a pen from side to side by means of a steering wheel. He observes any discrepancy between the positions of track and pen and takes action to bring the two into alignment. Any remaining discrepancy due to the correction not being adequate or to subsequent movement of the track leads to further action, and so on. Subject and machine together thus form a closed-loop, error-actuated servo system in which misalignments

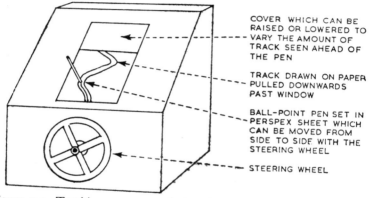

COVER WHICH CAN BE RAISED OR LOWERED TO VARY THE AMOUNT OF TRACK SEEN AHEAD OF THE PEN

TRACK DRAWN ON PAPER PULLED DOWNWARDS PAST WINDOW

BALL-POINT PEN SET IN PERSPEX SHEET WHICH CAN BE MOVED FROM SIDE TO SIDE WITH THE STEERING WHEEL

STEERING WHEEL

Figure 1.1. Tracking apparatus designed by A. E. Earle and used in experiments by Welford (1951, 1958), Griew (1958a, 1959) and Crossman (1960a).

lead to corrections and are in turn modified by them. Here is at once a contrast to much classical experimental psychology: performance is not being studied as discrete, isolated responses to particular perceived signals, but as an activity serial in time and involving a constant, interplay between signal and response. Although it may often be necessary, in order to simplify problems, to study discrete reactions, these are abstractions which leave out of account many significant features of the continuous performances that are normal in most real-life situations.

A number of interesting attempts were made to apply to tracking tasks the mathematical techniques developed for non-human servo mechanisms; for example to calculate 'transfer functions' to describe the human link between signals displayed and control actions (e.g. Tustin, 1947, Henderson, 1959, McRuer and Krendel, 1959, see also

Poulton, 1966). These equations, although essentially empirical, emphasised certain key features of human performance such as latency, stability and anticipation which were taken up in further experiments to yield indications of importance not only for tracking but for sensorimotor performance in general.

Reaction time and intermittency

If the track in Fig. 1.1 is hidden from view until it reaches the pen, the subject almost inevitably tracks a little late due to a reaction time between a stimulus entering the eye and the beginning of the responding action, which represents the time taken by various sensory, central and motor mechanisms to act. Craik (1947, 1948) raised the question of whether in a continuous task such as tracking the lag could be explained on the basis of nerve impulses having to traverse a long chain of synapses in the brain, but found evidence that this view was too simple. Close scrutiny of the trace made by the subject's pen reveals a number of minor wanderings first to one side of the track and then to the other. If reaction time were due simply to the time required for signals to pass through the various sensory, central and motor mechanisms, these irregularities should not occur: signals could be received and action initiated continuously, and the subject would quickly attain a smooth reproduction of the track. Instead he seems to initiate corrections only at intervals of about ·5 sec: in other words the servo acts discontinuously.

Broadly speaking, the subject behaves as if somewhere in the brain he has a computer which periodically samples the incoming data and calculates 'orders' to the motor mechanism. This then runs off the response 'ballistically' while the computer is taking in and processing the next sample leading to the next response. The response so triggered may be complex, embracing several detailed muscular actions in a phased and co-ordinated sequence. They are to some extent monitored by feedback from muscles, joints and tendons – in other words the motor mechanism itself is a servo-mechanism – but overall monitoring seems to involve the visual mechanism and 'computer' and to take time in these in the same way as do signals which initiate new action. The ·5 sec intervals between successive corrections appear to represent the sum of a reaction time of about ·3 sec and a monitoring time of about ·2 sec.

If this is so, the times taken to process data and to monitor action set an upper limit to the amount of data that can be handled in a given time. Further evidence from this view comes from the effects of speeding up the track. At low speeds the total movement of the subject's pen is, owing to the minor irregularities already mentioned, a little greater than the minimum required to follow the excursions of the track precisely. As speed rises above a critical level, however, the subject swings shorter and shorter, so that although the correct amount of movement rises, the amount actually made remains practically constant as shown in Fig. 1.2. The fact that movement falls short of what is required cannot

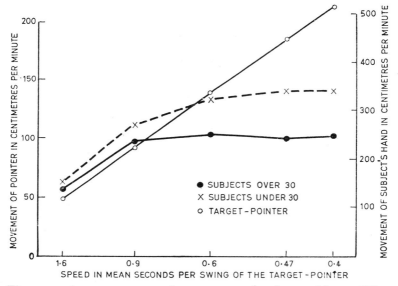

Figure 1.2. Average amounts of movement made when tracking at different speeds. (From Welford, 1951, p. 76, 1958, p. 88.) The apparatus was somewhat simpler than that shown in Fig. 1.1 and the task consisted of keeping a pointer moved by a lever in line with a target-pointer which swung irregularly from side to side. Each point is the mean for 25 subjects tracking for at least 1 min. Note that the older subjects make less movement: this was not accompanied by any consistent change of accuracy and thus implies a lowering of capacity with age.

be due to sheer inability to make the necessary movements as such, since the subject can move his wheel to-and-fro without regard for the track, very much faster than he does. It seems clearly to be due to the high speeds not allowing enough time for the necessary control to be exercised. We are thus led to view the human mechanisms mediating between sensory input and motor output as a *communication channel of limited capacity* and reaction time as a potentially valuable measure of this capacity.

Other sources of limitation

Performance can, of course, be limited by the motor mechanisms if the actual response is made sufficiently laborious. For example, the steering wheel shown in Fig. 1.1 took about half a turn to bring the pen from one extreme position to the other. If it had required, say, 10 times this amount of movement, sheer motor factors would have been a serious limitation at high speeds of the track. It is clearly idle to argue that one or other factor *always* limits performance: rather the stimulating possibility is raised of manipulating experimental conditions in order to determine *how many* mechanisms, and of *what kind*, are involved in the chain from sense organ to muscles.

Following this line we can say at once that *sensory* limitations have not normally entered into tracking experiments, although they could do so if the excursions of the target and of the subject's pen were sufficiently reduced in size or if the illumination was very low. The importance of several *perceptual* factors has, however, been demonstrated. For example, if the track can be seen for a short distance before it reaches the pen – that is if the cover shown in Fig. 1.1 is raised – the time lag due to reaction time is eliminated. So much is, perhaps, obvious: the subject looks ahead and responds to the track before it reaches the pen although how he manages thus to adapt the 'strategy' of his performance is not at present easy to say. Less obviously when the track can be seen ahead, the amount of movement by the subject's pen no longer falls short of that required as speed increases, or does so only at very much higher speeds than it did with the cover down (Welford, 1958, Crossman, 1960). The maximum effect of raising the cover is not obtained until the whole of one 'swing' of the track is revealed (Poulton, 1964), which suggests that the advantage of being able to see ahead lies in being able to observe the track in larger 'units': instead of having to observe each acceleration and deceleration separately, both can be seen together and form the basis of a single co-ordinated movement. In consequence fewer 'messages' or 'decisions' have to be passed through the central mechanisms in a given time. Those that are passed may, because they are more complex, take longer, but there is nevertheless a net saving, so that the speed at which the 'load' exceeds the available capacity is raised.

Similar results are obtained with the subject *un*able to seek the track ahead if it follows a simple, regular pattern instead of swinging irregularly. The subject can, on the basis of what he sees of the track, learn its regularity and thus predict its course (Poulton, 1966). He is able, in other words, to respond in larger units because his central computer can combine present data with constants extracted during previous experience. The process is by no means always deliberate or conscious, but the use of regularities observed in sequences to predict events and deal with larger units of data and action is one of the most fundamental features of skill. The ability to predict and anticipate makes for 'smoothness' and co-ordination of action, and the time saved by dealing in larger units can often lead to the timing of actions being more flexible and less hurried (Bartlett, 1947). The size and nature of the units that can be handled are at present little known and pose challenging questions for future research.

The formation of such larger units is perhaps only one aspect of a much more pervasive process. One of the most marked characteristics of many highly skilled performances is that details of the task are seen not only as present and immediate problems, but are placed in a wider setting, and actions are not designed as individual units but as parts of an extended activity demanded by the task as a whole.

The chain of mechanisms

During the forties it was commonly believed that the central control mechanisms could be adequately described in terms of two divisions – perceptual and motor. It gradually became clear, however, that performance depended not only upon these but also upon the *relationships* between them. The time required to respond to a signal depends very greatly upon the directness and the familiarity of the relationship between signal and response. For example, it seems 'natural' that turning the wheel of Fig. 1.1 clockwise should move the pen to the right, and this arrangement yields more accurate tracking than steering which works the other way or when the wheel is replaced by, say, a handle moving up and down. It seems, in short, that the time the central computer requires to operate depends on the amount of 'work' needed to relate the data from the signal to the responding action. The *translation* from signal to action appears to be an important stage which incorporates the traditionally recognised *choice of response*, but also emphasises the complex mediating processes that may be involved.

The disadvantages of unusual relationships can be largely overcome with practice, and this fact argues that very well-learnt relationships are somehow 'built into' the brain and enable the computer to be bypassed for routine actions. The establishment of such connections can be regarded as another mark of skill akin to the extraction of constants, the constancies being between display and control rather than in changes of the display alone.

We may represent the mechanism of sensory-motor performance

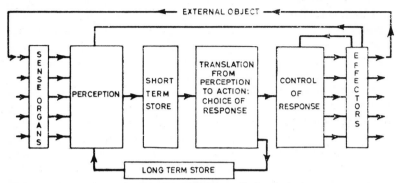

Figure 1.3. Hypothetical block diagram of the human sensory-motor system. Only a few of the many feedback-loops which exist are shown. (From Welford, 1965, p. 6.)

sketched so far in the block diagram of Fig. 1.3. Most of the researches on skill we shall be surveying in later chapters can be regarded as attempts to refine and extend this diagram, to understand the working of its various parts and to determine their capacities.

SIGNAL DETECTION, VIGILANCE AND DECISION

A different area of research was opened up in the forties by problems of watchkeeping, especially with operators of Asdic and Radar equipment Both required the detection of faint, infrequent signals, and it was found that many were missed even by the best watchkeepers. The attempt to find out why led to two lines of work, both with implications far beyond the situations that gave rise to them.

The first was concerned with the fact that the proportion of signals detected usually fell from the beginning to the later stages of a watch (Mackworth, 1950). The fall seemed often to be associated with drowsiness and lack of interest, and questions were thus raised about the conditions under which attention could be maintained and its relation to motivation, fatigue, boredom, monotony and state of arousal. Many laboratory studies made during the last 20 years have built up a complex, but reasonably coherent, picture of the association between, on the one hand, sensitivity and responsiveness as measured by behaviour, and on the other, physiological variables such as level of autonomic activity, and of the relationships of both to various environmental conditions. Ideas in this field have grown in parallel with those in some other areas of psychological enquiry, particularly emotion, motivation and personality, and it seems clear that the concepts which have been developed apply over a wide field. At the same time they are leading to a radical re-appraisal of concepts of fatigue, boredom and environmental stress, and have emphasised the importance of studying *continued performance as a function of time*.

The second line of work that arose from the problem of signal detection was a new approach to sensory thresholds. It had been known since the beginnings of classical psychophysics in the nineteenth century that the minimum strength of signal which can be detected varies in an apparently random manner from moment to moment, but the reasons why it does so had not been understood. A breakthrough was achieved, however, in the application by Tanner and his associates (Tanner and Swets, 1954, Swets *et al.*, 1961) of statistical decision theory. They argued that signals have to be detected against a certain amount of background noise: Asdic signals have to be distinguished from various unwanted sounds; the Radar watchkeeper has to observe flashes on his tube against other irrelevant flashes, or as they came to be termed 'visual noise'. Besides these external sources of noise, internal 'neural noise' arises from random firing in the sensory pathways and brain. The noise level, whether external or internal, varies from moment to moment, so that if the level of the signal greatly exceeds that of the noise the two will be clearly distinguishable, but if the signal level is relatively low, this will no longer be so and errors may occur. The signal level required to secure any given degree of accuracy will increase with the noise level so that the discriminability of a signal can be specified in terms of *signal-to-noise ratio*.

This approach has provided a powerful conceptual tool and metric for quantitative studies not only of sensory thresholds but of a wide variety of decision-making tasks including discrimination, guessing, betting, risk-taking and, more recently, recovery of data from memory. The concept of neural noise has been a stimulus to the formulation of physiological models and has emphasised the possibility of a much closer tie-up than hitherto between the two disciplines in the study of many sensory and behavioural phenomena.

The idea that performance is a function of signal-to-noise ratio in the brain leads to a concept of capacity parallel to, but different from, that derived from the study of reaction times. It is exemplified in the findings summarised by Miller (1956) that if a subject is given a series of stimuli to classify, the number of different classes he can distinguish accurately is limited and errors are made if this number is exceeded. Such a finding is understandable if the classification involves the identification of different signal levels and there is a maximum level that the system can handle: the presence of noise means that a certain separation must be preserved between classes if identification is to be accurate, and only a limited number of such separations can be fitted into the available range. Capacity in this case does not depend on the speed with which signals can follow each other along a single channel, but on the number of distinct states the brain mechanism concerned can assume at any one instant. The importance of this type of capacity as setting limits to skilled performance has not been at all thoroughly explored, but it seems likely to enter not only into discrimination and classification, but into the storage of data in memory, especially short-term memory.

More generally, the concept of neural noise blurring or distorting signals provides a plausible way of accounting for certain types of variability in performance. If signals in the brain are in the form of trains of nerve impulses – as they obviously are – and messages are conveyed by their patterning, the occurrence of random impulses could well transform one message into another upon occasion, and thus lead to errors. After effects of previous activity in the brain or the neural effects of insistent thoughts and interests can also, perhaps, act as noise in this way, leading to slips of the tongue and other minor confusions of everyday life.

MENTAL SKILL AND CONCEPTUAL FRAMEWORKS

Although a distinction is commonly drawn between sensory-motor and mental skills, it is very difficult to maintain completely. All skilled performance is mental in the sense that perception, decision, knowledge and judgment are required. At the same time all skills involve some kind of co-ordinated, overt activity by hands, organs of speech or other effectors. In sensory-motor skills the overt actions clearly form an essential part of the performance, and without them the purpose of the activity as a whole would disappear. In mental skills overt actions play a more incidental part, serving rather to give expression to the skill than forming an essential part of it. There are thus many features common to both sensory-motor and mental skills, while each serves to emphasize and illustrate some features more than others.

Let us consider, as an example of a mental skill, performance at a problem-solving task used in experiments by Bernardelli (see Welford, 1958, pp. 202–204). The apparatus consisted of a number of small boxes each with a row of six electrical terminals on top connected underneath by resistances. Each subject was given a box, together with a resistance meter and a circuit diagram which showed the connections between the terminals on the box, but did not indicate which terminals on the diagram corresponded to which on the box. The subject's task was to deduce which terminals corresponded to which, by means of readings taken on the meter. A modified version of the task, designed to avoid the need for subjects to understand electrical circuit diagrams, consisted of boxes with a row of six buttons on top and a diagram of the type shown in Fig. 1.4. When any two buttons were pressed the

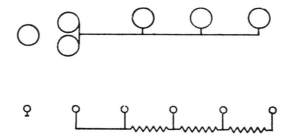

Figure 1.4. Diagram given to subjects in a problem-solving task (a), and its electrical equivalent (b). (From Welford, 1958, p. 205.)

The experiment was designed by Miss H. M. Clay and was based on a type of electrical-circuit problem originated by Carpenter (1946).

connections and distance between them on the diagram were indicated on a meter. The subject's task was to deduce which buttons corresponded to which circles on the diagram.

The performances of different subjects varied widely. Some took a large number of readings, many of them several times and, if they arrived at a solution at all, did so laboriously and haltingly. Others proceeded in a much more purposeful and effective manner: each reading appeared to be taken with some clear aim, either of obtaining systematic information or of testing some hypothesis. We can see here the operation of a 'strategy' of performance such as was implied by looking ahead in the tracking task, but in a very much more elaborate form. Such strategies develop rapidly with practice, becoming much clearer cut and more systematic in the later members of a series of problems. The formulation of an hypothesis may, perhaps, be thought of as the counterpart in a problem-solving task of the ballistic movements made in sensory-motor performance: in both the subject makes a move ahead of his data, and in both skill can be said to be shown in the extent to which these moves are made without the need subsequently to correct for errors.

Strategies varied from one individual to another. Some systematically took all possible readings, wrote them down and then tried to think out a solution. Others took readings until they had identified one terminal, then went on to another until all had been found. There were further more subtle variations between the performances of the same individual on different boxes. All these variations, between and within individual performances, emphasise that the same task may be done in many different ways and that if, therefore, we measure only overall achievement, such as success or failure in arriving at a solution or time taken or number of errors made, we miss some of the most important data available in the performance. For example, the strategies adopted by people of different ages, or under different conditions of fatigue, differ far more than do their overall achievements. There seem often to be compensatory shifts in the method and manner of performance under adverse conditions or in states of impairment, which serve to optimise the performance as a whole and to make the best use of capacities and conditions available at the time (Welford, 1958). If, therefore, performances of these kinds are to be studied adequately, it is essential to look not only at *overall achievement* but also at the *manner in which it was attained*.

Viewed from a different angle, this principle is a re-statement of the point made in the context of tracking tasks, that in skilled performance particular signals and actions are placed in a wider setting determined by the task as a whole, and larger units of performance exert an organising control over the smaller details of perception and response. The attainment of this wider co-ordination appears to depend on two capacities. Firstly, pieces of data arriving at different times may require to be combined, or a series of actions may have to be taken over a period of time. In these cases there is a need for *short-term retention* to hold some pieces of data while others are gathered and to keep a 'tally' upon action so that the subject knows what has been done and what remains to be done. Intensive experimental studies of short-term retention during recent years have indicated that more than one storage system is involved. Their identification and the measurement of their capacities are challenging questions for the future.

As anyone faced with a problem-solving task knows to his sorrow, however, possession of all the relevant facts does not ensure insight.

Short-term retention may often be a necessary element in problem-solving, but something more is also required. Just what this is seems to have eluded precise definition, but an important lead was given by Craik when he suggested that 'the fundamental feature of neural machinery' is 'its power to parallel or model external events' (1943, p. 52). He had in mind that the brain's computer is able to extrapolate from present data and thus test the consequences of various lines of action or sequences of events, without their having to be acted out. In one sense this way of looking at the problem merely re-states it in a different form. It does, however, imply that thought consists of a number of definable computer-operations and that a much clearer picture of thinking would be obtained if these operations could be identified – in other words if we could spell out the 'computer programme'.

We can at present do this to only a very limited extent but we can recognise a number of categories as important. Arithmetical calculations and other mathematical and logical procedures are an obvious case in point, so are 'sets' and expectancies based on previous events in either the immediate or the more remote past, temporal and spatial relationships giving rise to perception of causality (Michotte, 1946, 1963), and certain types of 'simplicity' or 'economy' in the grouping or 'coding' of events which enable the maximum data to be accounted for in the minimum terms. Perhaps the most promising lead into the problem from an experimental point of view is to regard thinking as an elaborate version of the translation process from perception to action mentioned in relation to tracking. Some progress, which we shall review in Chapter 6, has been made in analysing 'indirectness', and thus difficulty, of relation between display and control in terms of spatial rotations, distortions and translations into different symbols. It seems plausible to regard these as simple prototypes of the more elaborate and recondite operations of thinking.

THE PRESENT RESEARCH POSITION

The study of skill in its various forms has not led to the formation of any all-embracing 'grand theory' with a label such as attaches to Gestaltism or to the various schools of Learning Theory. These broad generalisations are really a sign of immaturity: they do less than justice to the complexity of the organism and of its functioning, so that they are inevitably either incomplete or so broad as to be of trivial explanatory value. Instead there has been an attempt to build smaller-scale theories which, as far as possible, are scrutinised to see that they are not obviously inconsistent, but are left for the future to link together into a more coherent structure. Present achievements can, perhaps, be broadly summarised under four headings:

1. It has been clearly recognised that sophisticated self-regulating machines can carry out many operations closely analogous to those performed by human beings and that, in turn, it is an important aid to clear thinking about human behaviour to consider the type of machine that would have the same characteristics. It is a not unfair test of a psychological theory to challenge its author to design a machine that would behave in the same way as his theory would predict for a human being.

2. Substantial progress has been made towards a psychology which is truly quantitative, and thus towards the removal of what had previously been a serious deficiency. A physiologist can speak of human performance in terms of body-temperatures and pulse-rates and relate these to foot-pounds, calories and heat-loads. Hitherto a psychologist has been virtually unable to measure performance in ways which transcend the particular cases concerned. His ability to do so now is still fragmentary, but treatments of reaction-times and the detectability of signals using probability as a metric, avoid much of the criticism often levelled at psychometric procedures in the past – that they 'measured the unknown in units of uncertain magnitude'.

3. This quantitative emphasis has given fresh impetus to the detailed analysis of the various mechanisms which go to make up the sensory-motor chain. Two kinds of approach have been tried at this level, both potentially very important. The first, which we may term a 'microbehavioural' approach, is to consider extremely detailed behaviour by regarding, for example, the choice of response in a choice-reaction task as containing a series of sub-choices carried out according to a particular strategy. These details are seldom observable directly but can often be inferred by fitting mathematical models or by comparing performances at subtly different versions of a task. The second approach considers capacity neurologically in terms of the functioning of nerve cells either singly or, more important, in large masses to which statistical concepts can be applied. This has, perhaps, been particularly prominent in Britain where there has been a long and honoured tradition of close contact between experimental psychology and physiology. In the present state of knowledge both these approaches have their part to play, and each can be a valuable supplement to the other.

4. Finally there has been a much fuller recognition than ever before that performance cannot be adequately studied in terms of discrete,

isolated reactions. Behaviour typically involves a stream of signals and responses each in part dependent on those that have gone before and influencing those that come after. Even the simplest activity involves a complex, phased and co-ordinated set of detailed actions. Serious attempts have been made, and many more are needed, to grapple with the complexity that this implies, to study the basic components of performance without removing them from the wider context of the performance as a whole, to identify the main functional divisions of central processes, to show how each contributes to performance in any given circumstances, and to understand how the various contributions change with time.

II

Simple Decisions

It is traditional to begin the study of experimental psychology with a treatment of *psychophysics* – the relating of sensory experience to physical measures. The tradition is sound because, although the pursuit of psychophysics for its own sake is indeed an arid academic exercise, the judgments involved in psychophysical experiments represent a form of simple *decision-making* which is amenable to relatively precise measurement and mathematical formulation. Analogies of these simple decisions are found in other areas of psychological function and in the more complex decisions of everyday life, so that the theories developed in the psychophysical field provide a framework for thought which has an application far beyond the experiments on which they are based.

WEBER'S LAW, THRESHOLDS AND DISCRIMINATION

It was recognised in the nineteenth century that amounts of sound or of light that were physically measurable might nevertheless fail to be heard or seen even though the subject was fully alerted to detect them. To account for this, there grew up the concept of a 'threshold' or minimum quantity above which a stimulus had to rise in order to enter the subject's perceptual mechanism. It was also early recognised that the stimulus level required to pass this threshold was not completely fixed, but varied from instant to instant in an apparently random manner so that several measurements were required to establish its mean value. Just why this was so was not clear although it was reasonably argued that the central effect of a given physical stimulus may vary from one moment to another (Cattell, 1893, Solomons, 1900, Oldfield, 1955).

It is commonly assumed, following Thurstone (1927a, b) that the central effect of a stimulus, such as the frequency of nerve impulses generated, is proportional to the logarithm of the physical intensity, although the site and mechanism of the transformation are not generally clear in physiological terms. Such a logarithmic transformation provides what is probably the simplest and most elegant explanation for the constancy of the Weber Fraction

$$\frac{\delta S}{S} = \text{a constant} \tag{2.1}$$

where δS is the least noticeable increase of stimulus intensity from a given level S measured in physical units. This traditional way of stating that the least noticeable increase is a constant *ratio*, may also be written

$$\frac{S_G}{S_L} = \text{a constant} \tag{2.2}$$

where S_G and S_L are the greater and lesser respectively of two quantities compared, or alternatively

$$\log S_G - \log S_L = \text{a constant} \tag{2.3}$$

The implication of this last equation, taken with Thurstone's assumption is, of course, that the discriminability of two stimuli depends upon a constant difference between their central effects, whatever their absolute magnitudes.

It can be argued that this holds even though the Weber Fraction rises substantially at low values of S. It has been noted since the time of Fechner and Helmholtz that the rise can be abolished if a small constant (r) is added to S so that in place of Eq. 2.1 we write

$$\frac{\delta S}{S + r} = \text{a constant} \tag{2.4}$$

and in place of Eq. 2.3,

$$\log (S_G + r) - \log (S_L + r) = \text{a constant} \tag{2.5}$$

The quantity r is small so that it affects the Weber Fraction substantially only when S is small and can normally be neglected when S is large. It is commonly assumed to represent spontaneous activity in the sense organ so that it does in a very real sense add to S. Its relation to S and δS and a method of measuring it graphically in the same units as S is shown in Fig. 2.1.

The attempt to tie discrimination down into such central effects as frequencies of nerve impulses is obviously plausible for simple sensory magnitudes, but is perhaps more questionable when made in relation to complex perceptual quantities such as lengths of line or numbers of objects. Such quantities must, however, somehow be represented centrally, so that although the precise mode of representation is not clear, treating perceptual magnitudes in this way is not far-fetched. There is, however, need for caution in specifying S: for instance Ross and Gregory (1964) showed that the least noticeable difference between weights was greater for a set of small weights than for a set of larger which, although they weighed the same, appeared lighter in accordance with the size-weight illusion. The subjects in this case

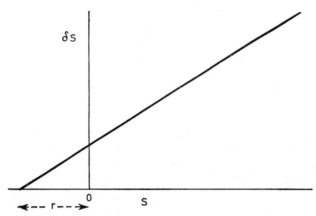

Figure 2.1. Plotting δS against S to measure the small random component r. Based on a diagram by Gregory (1956).

seemed not to have been judging in terms of weight alone, but of some integration of weight and size such as density.

There is an obvious extension of Eqs. 2.3 and 2.5 to above-threshold discrimination: if we can for practical purposes neglect r in these cases, we should be able to write, following Eq. 2.3,

$$\text{Discriminability} = (\log S_G - \log S_L) \times \text{a constant} \qquad (2.6)$$

This point was recognised by Fechner in the mid-nineteenth century but its main use and testing have come into prominence only recently with the work of Crossman (1955) and of Murdock (1960a). Crossman proposed as an index of confusability (C) between two quantities

$$C = \text{a constant}/(\log_2 S_G - \log_2 S_L) \qquad (2.7)$$

The use of logarithms to base 2 makes the *unit* of confusability the measure of confusion between two signals, one half the magnitude of the other. A table of C is given in the Appendix. Crossman tested his formula with studies of *times* taken to discriminate and found that time was linearly related to C. We shall consider these results in more detail later in this chapter. He extended his treatment to cases in which there are more than two quantities by suggesting that the average confusability of any one quantity with the others can be measured by taking the mean C for that quantity with each of the others.

Murdock adopted essentially the same type of approach. He suggested that the distinctiveness of a quantity from several others may be measured by taking the total of the log differences between it and each of the others and expressing this sum as a percentage of the total sum for all the quantities. This measure he termed $D\%$, i.e.

$$D\% = \frac{\sum_{j=1}^{n} (\log S_i - \log S_j)}{\sum_{i=1}^{n} \sum_{j=1}^{n} (\log S_i - \log S_j)} \tag{2.8}$$

He tested his formula against accuracy in categorising sound intensities and applied it to previous results by Eriksen and Hake (1957) on categorising areas of squares. Reasonable matches between theory and observation were obtained, especially when it is recognised that other factors such as biases against using extreme categories may also be operating. A method of correcting for such biases is suggested by Doherty (1966) who found that, after correction, Murdock's D scale provided a good fit for data on categorising lines of different lengths. Both Crossman and Murdock also proposed that the well-known tendency for recall to be more accurate at the ends of a list of items learnt by rote can be explained by the greater discriminability of serial positions at the ends of the list than in the middle. Table 2.1 sets out a sample of Murdock's results obtained by working out $D\%$ for each serial position on the assumption that distinctiveness can be measured in terms of log ordinal position. Very fair fits were obtained by this method with two samples of rote-learning data.

TABLE 2.1 *Percentage distinctiveness ($D\%$) for the several positions in a series of eight items, measured in terms of log ordinal position. From Murdock (1960a).*

Serial position	1	2	3	4	5	6	7	8
$D\%$	22.9	14.0	10.4	9.2	9.2	10.0	11.4	12.9

THE DECISION-THEORY APPROACH

It was commonly assumed until recent years in psychophysical studies that if the threshold was not passed but the subject had nevertheless to respond, he guessed at random, and methods of correcting data for such chance guessing were advocated. There were, however, two facts which called into question the idea and the procedure based on it. The first was that the measured threshold depended very much upon the degree of confidence required of the subject: his threshold was higher if he had to report a signal only when sure, than if he could do so even when somewhat doubtful. The second fact was that if he was not sure but was nevertheless forced to guess whether a signal had been given or not, his guesses over a number of trials were substantially better than chance, implying that the signal had to some extent been perceived even though the subject had no confidence that it had occurred.

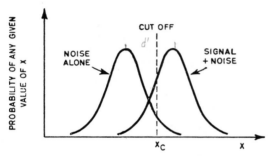

Figure 2.2. The basic signal-detection model. Based on a diagram by Tanner and Swets (1954).

Several groups seem to have arrived at similar methods of accounting for these facts round about the same time (e.g. Smith and Wilson, 1953, Munson and Karlin, 1954), but the approach most thoroughly worked out has been that of Tanner, Swets and their associates working on the detection of faint sounds against background noise or faint visual signals on an illuminated background constituting 'visual noise' (Tanner and Swets, 1954, Swets, 1959, 1964, Swets, Tanner and Birdsall, 1961, Green and Swets, 1966).

They consider as a basic situation one in which the subject is given a series of trials in each of which there is a brief presentation of either the background noise plus a signal, or the background noise alone. The subject's task is to decide whether or not a signal was present. Alternatively a series of two to eight presentations is made and the subject has to say in which one a signal occurred. The authors argue that at each presentation the subject observes a quantity x which, because of the noise, is liable to vary randomly in magnitude from trial to trial. We can represent the magnitude of x observed over a series of trials in which no signal was present by a distribution such as that shown for 'Noise Alone' in Fig. 2.2. The noise may be either *external* due to variability of the stimulation presented to the subject or *internal* due to randomness in the activity of the sense organ, neural pathways and brain. Such internal noise could arise from several sources such as spontaneous random firing in any of the sensory or central mechanisms concerned, from tonic neural activity in the brain (Pinneo, 1966) or from the after-effects of previous stimuli (Welford, 1965). Its presence means that signals can be conceived as having to be distinguished from noise even when external sources of noise are excluded. Any random variability in the sensitivity of any of the mechanisms involved could also be, for many purposes at least, taken as part of the internal noise since the essential result of both variations of sensitivity and of noise is to add a random component to the central effect of a signal (Atkinson, 1963). The shape of the noise distribution will depend on the distributions of the various components making up the noise and on any transformations of physical quantities that take place in the sense-organs or brain, but for purposes of our present discussion they can be tentatively regarded as normal.

The quantity x for presentations in which a signal is present is taken as having a similar distribution to the noise, but with each observation increased by the amount of the signal, as shown in the 'Signal-plus-Noise' curve of Fig. 2.2. The subject is assumed to establish a cut-off point x_c and to treat any level of x above this point as 'Signal' and any point below it as noise alone or rather as 'No Signal'. If the signals are strong enough for the distributions to be well separated the discrimination of 'Signal' from 'No Signal' can be virtually complete. If, however, the signal strength is weaker so that there is overlap between the distributions, discrimination cannot always be accurate: part of one or other distribution or of both will inevitably be on the wrong side of x_c so that errors will be made.

The model represented in Fig. 2.2 treats discrimination in terms of two parameters d' and β. The former is the distance between corresponding points – say the means – of the two curves measured in standard deviation units. We can thus write

$$d' = \frac{\bar{x}_{SN} - \bar{x}_N}{\sigma} \tag{2.9}$$

The second parameter β is the *likelihood ratio* that a central effect of the magnitude represented by x_c is due to signal-plus-noise as opposed to noise alone. In other words it is the ratio of the frequencies (f) – that is the heights of the ordinates – at x_c so that we write

$$\beta = \frac{f_{SN}}{f_N} \text{ at } x_c \qquad (2.10)$$

If the distributions of Signal-plus-Noise and Noise Alone are known or can be assumed, d' and β can be calculated from the proportions of the two possible classes of correct response thus:

(*a*) YES when a signal is present – represented by the area of the Signal-plus-Noise distribution to the right of x_c in Fig. 2.2. We may refer to the proportion of responses in the distribution falling into this category as $p\text{YES}_{SN}$.

(*b*) NO when a signal is not present – represented by the area of the Noise Alone distribution to the left of x_c. We may refer to this proportion of the Noise Alone distribution as $p\text{NO}_N$.

If, for example the distributions are normal, the distance from x_c to the mean of the Signal-plus-Noise distribution measured in standard deviation units can be found from a table of the normal probability integral, such as Fisher and Yates' (1938) Table I or IX, by noting the deviation required to produce $p\text{YES}_{SN}$. Similarly the distance from x_c to the mean of the Noise Alone distribution can be found by noting the deviation required to produce $p\text{NO}_N$. Assuming the two distributions are of equal variance, the value of d' will be the sum of these two deviations. To take a practical example, suppose $p\text{YES}_{SN} = \cdot 90$ and $p\text{NO}_N = \cdot 95$, the two deviations would be 1·28 and 1·64 respectively and d' would be 2·92.

The same result could have been obtained using the proportions of the two possible classes of error:

(*a*) 'Misses' – that is responses of NO when a signal is in fact present, represented by the area of the Signal-plus-Noise distribution to the left of x_c ($p\text{NO}_{SN}$).

(*b*) 'False Positives' – that is replies of YES when no signal is present, represented by the area of the Noise Alone distribution to the right of x_c ($p\text{YES}_N$).

The value of β can be calculated, when the distributions are normal, from a table of the ordinates of a normal distribution such as Fisher and Yates' Table II. For the example just quoted these are ·176 and ·103 respectively so that $\beta = 1\cdot71$. The value of β diminishes as x_c is moved to the left.

A table to find d' and β for different values of $p\text{NO}_{SN}$ and $p\text{YES}_N$ is given in the Appendix.

Although we have dealt so far with the absolute detection of signals, the model is obviously applicable to situations in which a signal is an increase or a decrease from a given reference value: the distributions of Signal-plus-Noise and of Noise Alone become respectively S_G (or S_L)-plus-noise and S_R-plus-noise with S_G (or S_L) and S_R the changed and the original signal values respectively.

The value of d' is the measure of true discriminability in terms of the ratio between, in the absolute case signal strength or in the comparative case difference between signal strengths, and the *variability* of the noise level. On the other hand β, as a measure of the cutoff point x_c, can vary independently of d'. It can be thought of as a measure of the caution exercised by the subject or of the confidence with which his judgments are made. For example a large value of β, implying a high cutoff well to the right in Fig. 2.2 means that he is being cautious about recognising signals and demanding a high degree of confidence before saying YES. The result will, of course, be that the proportion of occasions on which a YES response is given ($p\text{YES}_{SN}$ plus $p\text{YES}_N$) will be relatively low and the proportion of NO responses ($p\text{NO}_N$ plus $p\text{NO}_{SN}$) will be correspondingly high. There will thus be few false positives and a relatively large number of misses.

The subject is able to vary his cutoff to some extent at will, and indeed to make judgments in terms of more than one cutoff by defining different levels of confidence (e.g. Pollack and Decker, 1958, Swets, 1959, Swets, *et al.*, 1961, Broadbent and Gregory, 1963a). For example, Broadbent and Gregory presented their subjects with short bursts of noise during which there might or might not occur a pure tone of 1,000 cycles. Subjects had to rate their confidence as to whether or not a tone was present on a five-point scale: 'Sure; Not quite sure; Uncertain; Not quite sure not; Sure not'. These can be regarded as a series of five cutoff points of progressively decreasing severity, and there was in fact a clear trend for the proportion of misses to decrease and of false positives to increase from 'Sure' through the successive categories to 'Sure not'. If $p\text{YES}_{SN}$ is plotted against $p\text{YES}_N$ the points obtained for a range of criteria lie on a curve of the form shown in Fig. 2.3a, known as a *receiver-operating-characteristic* or ROC curve. When $d' = 0$ the ROC curve is a straight diagonal from the bottom left to the top right corner. As d' increases, the curve is bowed more and more into the top left corner. When the distributions are normal and of equal variance, the ROC curve plotted on double-probability paper becomes a straight line as shown in Fig. 2.3b.

It should be recognised that the 'noise' need not be noise in the literal sense but any random disturbance which may affect the signal. For example Winnick *et al.* (1967) have shown that the detectability of words shown briefly with a background of random letters in a tachistoscope can be accounted for in signal-detection terms if the random letters are regarded as 'noise' and the word as signal.

There is now an impressive array of experiments on signal detection in which this model and its assumptions seem to be valid although there are also cases (e.g. Hohle, 1965) in which they do not, indicating that

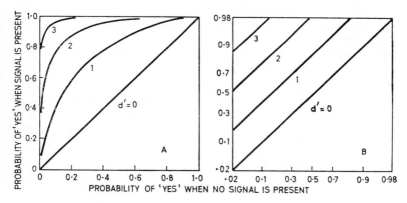

Figure 2.3. Receiver-Operating-Characteristic (ROC) curves. (A) with linear axes, (B) with normal probability axes.

there is further work to be done to determine its range of application. What has been achieved so far, however, makes it clear that the approach is a powerful one with, as we shall see in later chapters, widespread implications.

Placing the cutoff point

Although analysis of discrimination in terms of d' and β enables the effects of caution to be distinguished from those of true discriminability, it does not really solve the problem of thresholds but merely shifts it to the question of how the cutoff is fixed. Clearly the cutoff point can be affected by instructions to the subject to be cautious or otherwise, in other words by the relative importance of the two types of correct response and the two types of error. The objectively optimum cutoff point can be calculated if the rewards attached to each of the correct responses and the costs of the two types of error are known and are measurable in the same units:

$$\text{Optimum } \beta = \frac{\text{Probability of NO-SIGNAL}}{\text{Probability of SIGNAL}}$$
$$\times \frac{\text{Value of correct NO} + \text{Cost of incorrect YES}}{\text{Value of correct YES} + \text{Cost of incorrect NO}} \quad (2.11)$$

In order to fix his cutoff optimally, however, the subject would have to know or to be able to assess all these quantities, and also to relate them together. The evidence from a number of experiments on discrimination (e.g. Ulehla, 1966) and on guessing and betting (e.g. Edwards, 1961) makes it clear that the optimum is seldom if ever achieved. At least part of the reason probably lies in the fact that the limited span of short-term retention makes it impossible to assess accurately the way in which sequences of signals have been constructed: the subject tends to give undue weight at each point in the series to the three or four items presented just before. Part of the reason also may lie in a well marked tendency to overestimate the probability of rare events and to underestimate the probability of frequent ones (Howard, 1963). Part again may lie in subjects' inability to adjust their strategies to take full account of values and costs: for example Pitz and Downing (1967) in a guessing task found that performance was near optimum when the values of different guesses were equal, but departed markedly from optimum when they were not.

Knowledge and experience of the signal sequences, rewards and punishments can, however, affect the setting of cutoff points to some extent (e.g. Taub and Myers, 1961, Katz, 1964). A good example of the effect of knowledge is mentioned by Laming (1962) who required his subjects to sort packs of cards into two piles according to whether they bore a longer or shorter line on the face. The numbers of longer and shorter were varied in different packs from 24 of each to 30 shorter with 18 longer or 36 shorter with 12 longer. The proportions of errors in which longer was mistaken for shorter and *vice versa* were about equal when the pack containing equal frequencies came first, but when this followed a pack containing a preponderance of shorter lines, the mistaking of longer for shorter became much commoner than the mistaking of shorter for longer. The same was true in the packs with larger numbers of short lines and was more marked as the unbalance increased. Subjects appeared to be adjusting their cutoff point in a direction which reduced the errors made in responding to the more frequent signal. Swets and Sewall (1963) using a task in which subjects detected tones in short bursts of noise, showed that changes due to offering monetary rewards for improved performance left d' unchanged, implying that any changes in the proportions of different types of response were indeed due to a shift of β rather than to any genuine improvement of detection.

In the absence of any knowledge of the signal sequence or other considerations the subject must base his cutoff on his knowledge of the noise distribution alone. In this case he presumably sets it at a level which will give a tolerable – usually very low – likelihood of making false positives.

What is x?

The exponents of *signal-detection theory*, as this model has come to be called, have been at pains to stress that much of the usefulness of the model does not depend on being able to specify the quantity x which the observer uses as a basis of his decisions. It is clear, however, that x must in some way increase monotonically with increase of (a) the strength of the physical signal or difference between two signal levels, (b) central effects in the brain, such as the frequencies of nerve impulses generated and (c) confidence on the subject's part that a signal has arrived or that S_G has occurred rather than S_L. x cannot, however, be a linear function of all these. For instance, any logarithmic or other transformation between physical stimulus and central effect will preclude linearity with both (a) and (b) simultaneously.

The idea of scaling x in terms of confidence derives from a consideration of the fact that any point on the x axis can be specified in terms of a likelihood ratio f_{SN}/f_N. We have already noted one such value, β, at the cutoff point x_c and that the value of β diminishes as the cutoff point is moved to the left in Fig. 2.2. If the observer can use different cutoff points implying different degrees of confidence it is reasonable to suppose that he can somehow scale the whole x axis in the same way, either linearly with the likelihood ratio or linearly with some function of it such as its logarithm. Such a scale must presumably be correlated with level of neural activity, but need not be a linear function of it. For those who object to introducing the subjective term 'confidence' into the discussion, essentially the same point can be made by arguing that the likelihood ratio or some transformation of it can act as a functional quantity in the decision process.

It becomes necessary, however, to give x a measure, in terms of physical signal strength or neural effect, if we want to relate d' to

signal strength in any quantitative way. If Eq. 2.6 holds, the straightforward assumption is that

$$d' = (\log S_G - \log S_L)/\sigma_{\log S} \qquad (2.12)$$

so that x is a linear function of central activity, but if this is so the distributions cannot possibly be normal and are probably of unequal
variance. They cannot, for example, extend from minus infinity to plus
infinity as strictly normal distributions would have to do, but from zero

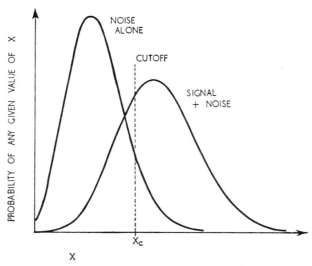

Figure 2.4. The basic signal-detection model assuming Poisson-like
distributions.

to some maximum set by the capacity of the brain mechanism concerned. If the noise is conceived as consisting of random neural impulses occurring within a brief period of time, the distributions would
be approximately of Poisson form with a variance equal to the mean
and would look like those shown in Fig. 2.4. This difficulty is, however,
not always serious. For example, all our discussion so far has been in
terms of the proportions of the four possible responses – YES or NO
either when a signal was or was not present, and these proportions
would remain the same if the measure along the x axis was transformed,
for example by taking the logarithm of the number of nerve impulses
concerned. We are thus in the position of an experimenter wishing to
perform a *t*-test or analysis of variance on data of non-normal distributions and unequal variances, and can follow the procedure recommended

in that case of transforming the measure so as to make the distributions normal and variances equal. Doing so will in no way invalidate the test or, in our case, the computation of d', and so long as we work in terms of our four proportions we do not need to specify the actual transformation.

The relation of signal-detection measures to those used in traditional psychophysics has been discussed by M. Treisman (1964) and by Treisman and Watts (1966). In particular they outline a way of treating data obtained by the Constant Method in signal-detection terms.

Multiple discrimination

Several attempts has been made to extend Signal-detection Theory to cases where more than one signal has to be discriminated. The cases

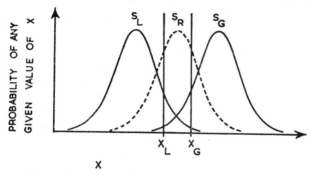

Figure 2.5. Extension of the signal-detection model to cases where a decision is required as to whether a signal is greater or less than a standard. The area between x_G and x_L represents judgments of 'equal'.

involved may be divided broadly into four types which we shall deal with in turn. The treatments are often somewhat speculative, but serve to indicate the potential range of usefulness of the approach.

1. *Two quantities presented simultaneously, or nearly so.* The most straightforward example of this type is when a standard reference signal is presented with a second signal which may be either greater or less. The corresponding signal-detection model is represented in Fig. 2.5 in which distributions are shown for the reference signal (S_R) and for greater and lesser signals (S_G and S_L) and there are two cutoff points (x_G and x_L).

It is not so clear what model is appropriate for cases in which, say, two lines are presented simultaneously one on the left and one on the right (e.g. Henmon, 1906, Vickers, 1967) and the subject has to say which is longer. In this case S_G and S_L are in effect presented without S_R. We may perhaps assume that one of three procedures is followed: firstly the subject may take one of the lines as S_R and decide whether the other is longer or shorter; secondly he may imagine some inter-mediate value between S_G and S_L as S_R and judge both differences from this simultaneously; thirdly he might simultaneously judge S_G with S_L as a reference and S_L with S_G as a reference. Of these three possibilities the first appears to be the simplest as it requires only one decision pro-cess whereas the second and third involve two.

2. *Several values of a single variable presented one at a time.* In the dis-criminations we have discussed so far the quantities to be distinguished have been present either simultaneously or nearly so. It has, therefore, been possible to make closely comparative judgments, and under these conditions very fine differences can be recognised accurately. When, however, the quantities are presented separately at different times – in other words when they have to be judged *absolutely* – the minimum differences which can be reliably distinguished are substantially greater. Lipsitt and Engen (1961), for example, found their subjects were about equally accurate at judging which was the longer of two lines presented simultaneously or separated by an interval of 1 sec, but less accurate when the two lines were presented 5 sec apart. Again, Pollack (1952), presenting subjects with tones of varying pitches equidistant on a logarithmic scale ranging from 100 to 8,000 c.p.s. and requiring them to classify the tones by assigning numbers, found that only about five or six classes could be reliably distinguished.

As already mentioned in Chapter 1 (p. 21) Miller (1956) has surveyed data which indicates that comparatively small numbers of distinguish-able classes are also found for judgments of other quantities such as loudness (about six), tastes (about four) and points on a line (about nine) (see also Spitz, 1967). In short, capacity for absolute judgment appears to be severely limited. It is, of course, true that individuals possessing 'absolute pitch' can recognise accurately a very much larger number of tones (Carpenter, 1951) and similarly fine discriminations can be made by expert industrial workers when judging colours or other sensory qualities in the course of their work, but how they do this is at present a mystery.

If we envisage classification on a single dimension as taking place in a system such as that of Fig. 2.2, we must assume that the quantity to be classified will produce an amount of activity in the system which ranges from a level indistinguishable from noise up to some maximum representing saturation of the system. If so, the number of discriminable classes will be the number of Signal-plus-Noise distributions that can be fitted in between minimum and maximum with acceptably low overlap, as shown in Fig. 2.6.

It is at first sight tempting to assume that this discriminable range is directly related to the sensory mechanism and its central projection, for example in the case of pitch, to the signalling from different portions

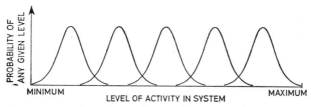

Figure 2.6. Extension of the signal-detection model to cases where absolute judgments are required of several values on a single 'dimension'.

of the basilar membrane and the representation of pitch in the auditory projection area. Adrian (1947, p. 50) cites Tunturi (1944) as having reported that in the dog equal octaves are represented by approximately equal intervals in this area so that discriminability might depend on neurological distance. In other cases we have already suggested that discriminability is likely to depend on frequency of nerve impulses in such a way that equal increases in frequency represent equal increments of discriminability. Such views in their crude form, however, are un-tenable because they imply that discriminability depends upon the total range of stimuli that can be perceived and should be independent of the range actually presented in any given circumstances. Pollack (1952, 1953a) has shown that this is clearly not so: the number of discriminable pitches remains about the same whether the stimuli are presented over a wide range of frequencies or concentrated within a narrow one. The same is true whether the frequencies are all towards one or other end of the range. Similar results have been obtained for different loudness levels (Hodge and Pollack, 1962): the information transmitted in classi-fying eight loudness levels was essentially the same whether they were spread over a range of 28, 14, 7 or 3·5 db.

The implication is that the decision axis is in some way capable of adjustment in such a way as to make the whole of its capacity available for the range of stimuli actually presented. How this is done is not clear, but one simple possibility is to assume firstly, as we have already done,

Fundamentals of Skill

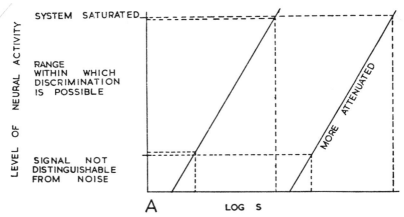

Figure 2.7. Effects on the decision axis of attenuating the signal (A)
before and (B) after a logarithmic transformation. In (A) the effect of
attenuation is to increase the *absolute* values of log S over which discrimination can be made while leaving the range of values unaffected.
In (B) the main effect of attenuation is to increase the *range* of values of
log S over which discrimination can be made.

that somewhere between the physical stimulus and its central effect
there is a logarithmic transformation; and secondly that the signal can
be attenuated either before or after this transformation has taken place.
Attenuation before the transformation would essentially subtract a constant amount from log S, and different levels of attenuation would produce a series of relationships between log S and its central effect as
shown in Fig. 2.7A. The effect would be to determine the *portion* of the
total range of stimuli over which the decision mechanism operated,
without affecting its extent – for example it might shift from low pitches
to high. Attenuation after the logarithmic transformation would alter
the slope of the relation between log S and its central effect as shown
in Fig. 2.7B, and affect the *range* over which the decision mechanism
operated – for example it would determine whether discriminative
capacity was spread over a wide range of pitches from high to low or
was confined to one part of the scale. The fine discriminations attained
in comparative judgments might on this view be due to the possibility, when both quantities are present together, of concentrating
the whole discriminative capacity on a very narrow band of stimulus
values.

   The mechanism postulated is not without its difficulties. For example,
Pollack (1952) noted that the number of classes discriminated was the

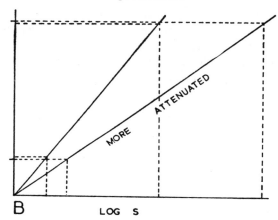

same whether the frequencies were spread at regular logarithmic intervals over a range or whether they were divided into two groups, half at the high end and half at the low. Such a finding implies some more complex adjustment of the decision axis; it might, for example, be accounted for on the assumption that *some* adjustment of the range takes place whenever a signal is presented so that when, say, one of the high group is presented the subject adjusts his scale towards the high end and when one of the low group, to the low end. If so, experiments such as Pollack's could be linked to those in which subjects, when asked to classify quantities, adjust their judgments to the range of quantities presented (e.g. Tresselt and Volkman, 1942) and to those of Helson (e.g. 1947, 1964) and others who have shown that a given quantity tends to be judged greater when preceding quantities have been small than when they have been large. The term 'adaptation' used to describe such adjustments could fairly be applied also to those we have postulated.

A second difficulty lies in understanding what is adjusted. Hodge and Pollack (1962) have produced evidence that it is not the discriminability of signals so much as the assignment of responses that is affected by a change in the range of quantities presented, and Parducci (1965) has suggested that adjustment tends to be such as to make the *frequencies* of the various categories of judgment equal. We cannot attempt to meet these difficulties here; it seems fair to remark however, firstly that some mechanism of adjustment has to be postulated, and secondly that this might reasonably be taken to operate on the decision axis mediating between signal and response.

44 Fundamentals of Skill

3. *Quantities varying in more than one dimension simultaneously.* The number of distinguishable categories is greater if the quantities do not lie along a single stimulus 'dimension' but along two or more dimensions simultaneously, such as pitch *and* loudness or if points have to be identified in a square instead of along a line (Klemmer and Frick, 1953, Pollack, 1953a, Pollack and Ficks, 1954, see also Miller, 1956).

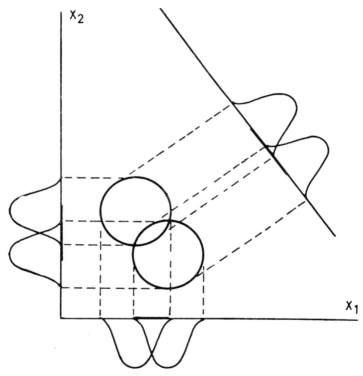

Figure 2.8. Extension of the signal-detection model to cases where signals vary on two independent 'dimensions'. Based on a diagram by Rodwan and Hake (1964). The separation of the two distributions on the oblique axis is greater than on either of the others.

The total number of categories is, however, considerably less than the product of the number for each dimension separately. For example Pollack, who found that about six pitches and five degrees of loudness could be discriminated, found that only about nine simultaneous diffferences of both pitch and loudness could be reliably distinguished instead of the 30 (i.e. 6 × 5) which might have been expected.

Several studies have indicated that when subjects make judgments in terms of two or more characteristics or 'dimensions' they detect differences of each independently and that the total amount of differentiation they achieve results from a combination of these. It is therefore possible to predict the accuracy of discrimination for two or more dimensions together from the accuracy attained on each separately. The overall result will, of course, depend on whether the dimensions are correlated and on whether accurate response requires correct judgment on all dimensions simultaneously, or on any one or more alone, or whether

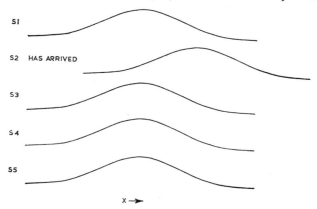

Figure 2.9. Extension of the signal-detection model to cases where there are several possible signals each on an independent 'dimension'.

some more complex synthesis is required such as when judging personal characteristics from faces.

Rodwan and Hake (1964) have suggested, on the basis of their experiments, that synthetic two-dimensional discrimination can be conceived as in Fig. 2.8: they assume that subjects combine the discriminations on the two dimensions with an overall result as indicated by the circular 'distributions' and by the oblique decision axis on to which the other two are projected. The angle of this new axis depends on the relative weights given to the two dimensions in the joint decision. The authors found that different subjects behaved as if they placed the oblique axis at substantially the same angle, implying that they weighted different dimensions in roughly similar ways. This model can, of course, be extended to discriminations involving three or more dimensions.

4. *Several signals each on a different 'dimension'*. When one of several possible signals, each independently liable to be disturbed by noise, is presented, the situation can be represented as in Fig. 2.9. Of the total

number of items one is correct and has a signal strength of d', while all the others have a signal strength of 'noise alone', i.e. zero level. For simplicity all the distributions are assumed to be of equal variance and normal although in practical cases this would almost certainly not be exactly true. This kind of model has been suggested by Green and Birdsall (1964) for words in a vocabulary, and would seem applicable to cases where stimuli may arrive over different sensory channels. The

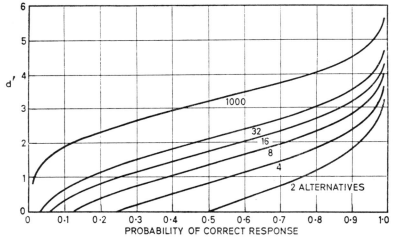

Figure 2.10. Value of d' required to produce a given proportion of correct responses from the type of case represented in Fig. 2.9. Based on a table by Elliot (1964).

subject's task is to decide which of the possible signals has occurred. At least two methods of doing this seem plausible:

(*a*) Green and Birdsall suggest that the subject in effect examines the strengths of all the alternatives at a particular instant and chooses the largest. If so, the greater the number of alternatives, the greater the chance that one of the noise levels will, at the moment concerned, exceed the signal level of the correct item and lead to an error being made. If accuracy is to be kept constant, d' must therefore rise with the number of alternatives. The values of d' for various proportions of correct response with numbers of alternatives from 2 to 1,000 have been tabulated by Elliot (1964), and are shown graphically in Fig. 2.10.

(*b*) An alternative method would be to set a criterion x_c and having done so to examine the alternatives until one was found which exceeded it. With this procedure, the greater the number of alternatives the greater the number that would, on average, have to be examined before one exceeding the criterion was found, and the greater the chance that the criterion would be exceeded by a reading from one of the 'noise alone' distributions so that a false positive would occur. Taking p as the probability of a false positive from any one 'noise alone' distribution,

Total probability of false positive from m samples $= 1 - (1 - p)^m$

$$(2.13)$$

where m is the number of incorrect alternatives sampled. A table of $1 - (1 - p)^m$ for various values of p and m has been provided by Wiener (1965).

If the subject is to keep his false positive rate constant, he will have to raise his criterion level progressively more and more as the number of alternatives increases. For example, if he wishes to maintain the rate at 1%, he would have to set his criterion level at 2·33 standard deviation units above the mean of the 'noise alone' distribution if he had to examine only one possible signal, at 2·57 if he had to examine two signals and at 2·81 if he had to examine four. We may note that the effect of increase in the number of alternatives is greater for relatively low or 'risky' criteria than for strict or 'cautious' ones. For example if the false positive rate had been 10%, the criterion would have had to be set at 1·28 standard deviation units with only one signal, at 1·63 units with two and at 1·94 with four. The difference between two and four signals is ·48 standard deviation units for the 1% criterion and ·66 for the 10%. The difference might in practice be greater since the absolute change in the false positive rate if no change of criterion was made would be much more noticeable and serious with a low criterion than with a high one: the changes from one to four signals would be from 1% to just under 4% and from 10% to just over 33%.

This kind of procedure could explain a finding by Broadbent and Gregory (1963b) which is otherwise difficult to understand. Their subjects watched three fluorescent tubes flashing rhythmically and had to report when one flashed brighter than usual, grading their responses into five categories of confidence. The most cautious criterion was found to change little as between relatively quiet conditions and loud ambient noise, whereas the most risky criterion rose so that the two criteria came closer together.

If, as appears to be the case, d' increases with the duration of a signal (Green *et al.*, 1957, Egan *et al.*, 1959, Swets, 1959) the same procedure can also explain results obtained by John (1966). His subjects had to respond by pressing a key to a light which came on at irregular intervals, while ignoring occasional sounds presented over earphones. The reaction time to the light was longer when the sounds were relatively loud than when they were softer. We may suppose that subjects raised their cutoff level to exclude the louder noise and had therefore to attain a greater d' in order to be sure of responding to the light.

THE TIME REQUIRED FOR DISCRIMINATION

It has been known from the early days of the study of reaction times that the time taken to discriminate between two signals tends to rise as they come to resemble one another more closely. Thus, for example, Henmon (1906) found that the time required to indicate which of two lines exposed on a screen was the longer, increased over a series of differences ranging from 10 and 13 mm to 10 and 10·5. The same author found similar results for pairs of tones of different pitches sounded one immediately after the other, and for patches of different colours. Parallel results have been obtained by Slamecka (1963) whose subjects had to decide which of two words was the more similar in meaning to a third word. Results which may perhaps be regarded as falling within the same area have been obtained by Wallace (1956) who found that the accuracy with which patterns and pictures of objects were identified rose with the time for which they were exposed, and by several authors (e.g. Barry, 1964, Carterette and Cole, 1963, Haber and Hershenson, 1965) that accuracy of discrimination or identification increases when the stimuli or messages are presented more than once. We may note in passing that both Wallace and Haber and Hershenson found that several brief exposures were less effective than one longer one of the same total duration. A tie-up with the signal-detection theory approach exists directly in the findings already mentioned that d' rises with increased duration or repetition of signals, and by implication in results obtained by Pierrel and Murray (1963) who found that the time required to discriminate weights from a standard increased, and at the same time both accuracy and confidence fell, as the difference from the standard became less.

Attempts to work out a quantitative relationship between reaction time and discriminability seem to date from a pioneering attempt by Crossman (1955) who conducted a series of experiments in which subjects sorted specially prepared packs of cards according to numbers of spots on the cards. Each pack contained equal numbers of cards with each of two different numbers of spots, and the time taken to sort packs was noted and related to the differences between the numbers. Crossman began by confirming a result obtained by Henmon, that equal *ratios* are discriminated in approximately equal time – packs containing cards with 1 and 2, 2 and 4, 3 and 6, 4 and 8, 5 and 10 spots all took about the same time to sort. Any formula or law relating reaction time to fineness of discrimination must therefore provide for time to rise as the ratio between the quantities concerned becomes smaller but to be little affected by changes in absolute magnitude. In other words, the time taken for discrimination appears to be a function of the Weber Fraction between the two quantities. Crossman considered three possible functions and associated models which we shall discuss in turn using, however, slightly different terms from his.

1. Statistical sampling

According to this approach, the brain is regarded as taking a series of brief samples of the data presented and averaging them. The samples are conceived as having a variance due to noise which causes the distributions for the two quantities to overlap. According to well-known statistical theorems we should expect the standard deviation of the mean of a series of samples to narrow at a rate proportional to the square root of the number of samples thus:

$$\sigma_N = \frac{\sigma_1}{\sqrt{N}} \qquad (2.14)$$

where σ_1 is the standard deviation for a single observation and σ_N that of the mean of N observations. If all samples take the same time we can write for the distribution associated with each of the quantities to be discriminated:

$$\sigma_T = \frac{\sigma_1}{\sqrt{T}} \times \text{a constant} \qquad (2.15)$$

when σ_T is the standard deviation of the mean of a sample obtained after time T. We may suppose the subject to go on taking samples until the distributions have reached a critical separation, say when the overlap is small enough to produce an acceptably low frequency of errors.

This approach has an obvious affinity to signal-detection theory: we can write

$$d'_T = d'_1 \sqrt{T} \times \text{a constant} \qquad (2.16)$$

or

$$\sqrt{T_c} = \frac{d'_c}{d'_1} \times \text{a constant} \qquad (2.17)$$

where T_c is the time required to achieve a critical separation of the distributions and d'_c is the value of d' at time T_c. Evidence in support of this formulation comes from results by Green *et al.* (1957) and Swets *et al.* (1959). The former found that d' rose linearly with $\sqrt{T}$ when T exceeded about 100 msec. The latter, using brief tones presented in external noise and allowing subjects to observe them several times found that d' rose linearly with the square root of the number of observations. Further supporting evidence comes from an analysis by Taylor *et al.* (1967) of data obtained by Schouten and Bekker (1967) from a two-choice reaction task in which the subject had to decide which of two lights had appeared. Taylor *et al.* calculated from the relationship between error frequencies and reaction time that d'^2 rose linearly with T.

If Eq. 2.12 holds we can write,

$$\sqrt{T_c} = \frac{d'_c \, \sigma_1}{\log S_G - \log S_L} \times \text{a constant} \qquad (2.18)$$

which implies that if error rate is held the same for different degrees of discrimination,

$$\text{Mean discrimination time} = \frac{1}{(\log S_G - \log S_L)^2} \times \text{a constant} \quad (2.19)$$

The treatment outlined here assumes that both S_G and S_L are presented together, but it can be extended to the case where only one is present at a time by assuming that the subject carries traces of both quantities in memory, or a trace of some average of them (cf. Hughes, 1964).

A somewhat similar result is reached by a different route with a type of model based on Wald's (1947) Sequential Probability Ratio Test, introduced by Stone (1960) and developed by Laming (1962) and by Shallice and Vickers (1964). The model deals with the case in which the subject is presented with only one quantity at a time and is required to state whether it is the larger or smaller of two possible alternatives. He is assumed to take a series of samples of the input data, each taking an equal time and liable to be added to or subtracted from by random noise. He makes a running total of the samples, and when this reaches a pre-assigned value of probability that the samples came from S_G, he decides for S_G. Similarly if the total reaches a pre-assigned probability that they came from S_L he decides for that. The procedure envisaged is illustrated in Fig. 2.11: the running total approaches the criterion by a so-called 'random-walk'.

Laming assumes that the central correlate of the signal, on the basis of which the decision must be made, is normally distributed with constant variance. As Shallice and Vickers point out, if the model is to be used to relate reaction time to different degrees of discrimination, it is necessary to make an assumption about how the central processes are related to the physical input, and they assume in accordance with Eq. 2.6 and with Crossman's and Henmon's findings, that the mean of the central activity varies as log S. On this basis they produce the following equation:

Mean discrimination time

$$= \frac{t2\sigma^2(1 - a - b) \log \frac{(1 - a)(1 - b)}{ab}}{(\log S_G - \log S_L)^2} \qquad (2.20)$$

where t is the time for any one sample and a and b are the proportions of errors on S_G and S_L. If errors do not vary from one discrimination to

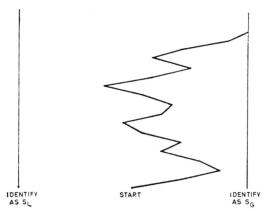

IDENTIFY AS S_L START   IDENTIFY AS S_G

Figure 2.11. 'Random-walk' model for decision between two alternatives.

another, Eq. 2.20 reduces to Eq. 2.19, although the constant has, of course, a different meaning.

The model might perhaps be extended to the case in which two quantities are presented at a time by assuming that both are sampled simultaneously.

We have spelt these models out in some detail as they are attractive in many ways and are enjoying a considerable vogue. Unfortunately, however, Eqs. 2.19 and 2.20 do not fit the experimental facts. In a few cases plotting reaction time against them gives a reasonable fit to the data, but in these cases alternative functions derived from other models do equally well. In other cases the alternative functions clearly fit better. Either the models or some of the assumptions made in applying them must be wrong.

2. An information-theory model

Crossman considered but rejected a model based on information-measurement which proposed that discrimination time was proportional to the logarithm of the reciprocal of the Weber Fraction thus:

$$\text{Mean discrimination time} = \log \frac{S_G}{S_G - S_L} \times \text{a constant} \qquad (2.21)$$

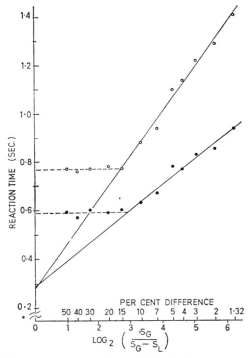

Figure 2.12. Times taken to decide which is the longer of two lines shown simultaneously, plotted against Eq. 2.21. Data obtained by Birren and Botwinick (1955). Open circles, subjects aged 61–91: filled circles subjects aged 19–36. Each point is the mean of the medians of 43 older or 30 younger subjects. The medians were each based on at least four readings.

The differences between the intercept of the two regression lines and the intercepts of the two dotted lines are approximately the times to be expected for a two-choice reaction by subjects in the age groups concerned. The results therefore suggest that reaction time was the time taken by discrimination or by choice, whichever was longer. The additional ·275 sec from zero to the intercept of the regression lines was probably due to a time delay either in the apparatus or in the execution of the reponse. (After Welford, 1960c.)

Eq. 2.21 does in fact provide a strikingly good fit to Henmon's data for lines and tones, and also to results obtained by Birren and Botwinick (1955) and Botwinick *et al.* (1958) who presented pairs of vertical lines and required subjects to say whether the longer was on the left or on the right. Birren and Botwinick's results are shown in Fig. 2.12: the linearity is good if it is assumed that there is a lower limit to the reaction times concerned, determined perhaps by a minimum time required to choose which of the two responses – 'left' or 'right' – to make.

However, Eq. 2.21 does not fit further data obtained by Crossman or any of the data on discrimination times obtained by other authors.

3. Crossman's Confusion Function

Crossman's third, and favoured, suggestion was that the time taken for discrimination was, as we have already mentioned, linear with his Confusion Function so that

$$\text{Mean discrimination time} = \frac{1}{\log S_G - \log S_L} \times \text{a constant} \quad (2.22)$$

or in other words, discrimination time is inversely proportional to the Weber Fraction between S_G and S_L and d' increases linearly with time. Eq. 2.22 gave a good fit to two experiments by Crossman himself. In one, subjects sorted packs containing equal numbers of cards with one of two numbers of spots: 10/1, 10/5, 12/8, 12/9, 10/8 and 12/10. In the other they sorted 16 small canisters by weight – eight lighter and eight heavier arranged in random order – with, in different trials, the ratios of 2/12, 4/12, 5/10, 6/9 and 6/8. The card-sorting results are shown in Fig. 2.13.

The good fit of Eq. 2.22 has been confirmed by McCoy (1963) for diameters of circles and shades of grey as defined by reflectance values, presented either as a card-sorting task or with each card shown separately and exposed until the subject responded by pressing one of two microswitches. In these experiments, unlike Crossman's, two quantities were always presented simultaneously. Further confirmatory evidence was obtained by Shallice and Vickers (1964) using card-sorting tasks with either one or two lengths of line on each card. These experiments were undertaken in an attempt to reproduce some of the essential features of the experiments by Birren and Botwinick and Botwinick *et al.* in a card-sorting form in the hope of discovering why the Information Theory model fitted some results and the Confusion Function others. They were followed by a substantial series of experiments by Vickers (1967) using pairs of lines projected on a screen. In all cases

Fundamentals of Skill

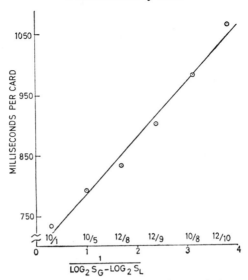

Figure 2.13. Crossman's (1955) data for sorting cards into two categories plotted in terms of Eq. 2.22. Each point is the mean time per card for four subjects each sorting 80–120 cards.

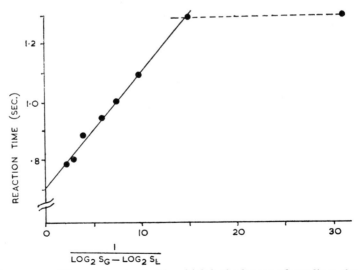

Figure 2.14. Times taken to decide which is the longer of two lines shown simultaneously in the presence of visual noise, plotted against Eq. 2.22. Data obtained by Vickers (1967). Each point is the mean of 16 readings obtained from each of 18 subjects.

the Confusion Function gave a much better fit except with some very fine discriminations, for which the observed times were much shorter than predicted by Eq. 2.22. An example of Vickers' results showing this effect is given in Fig. 2.14. These fine discriminations were, however, associated with substantial numbers of errors whereas the frequencies of errors in cases where Eq. 2.22 fitted well were low.

The simplest way of accounting for these results is to assume that data are accumulated, or some central state builds up, linearly with $(\log S_G - \log S_L)$ until a critical level is reached. The model envisaged can be represented as in Fig. 2.11 except that the progress is in a straight line towards one criterion or the other. Thus stated, however, the model takes no account of noise and makes no allowance for errors: if data from the signal are accumulated over time, ought not the noise also to be accumulated, and would this not lead to Eq. 2.19 or 2.20 rather than 2.22? Of various possible methods of overcoming this difficulty we may briefly consider three:

(*a*) In many cases the random variations which constitute the noise might well be the same for both S_G and S_L when they are presented together, or for both signal and remembered reference standard when S_G and S_L are presented separately. If so, any noise which accumulated would do so equally for both, and an accumulated *difference* would be free of noise.

(*b*) It is usually assumed that the main sources of noise occur prior to the accumulation of data, but as regards internal noise this is not necessarily so: it might be that the main source of noise was subsequent to the store: accumulation might take place in the perceptual mechanism of Fig. 1.3 (p. 19) while the main source of internal noise was in the translation mechanism. Both these possibilities may perhaps enable Crossman's and subsequent results where the noise was mainly internal, to be reconciled with those of Green *et al.* (1957) and of Swets *et al.* (1959) who found d' to rise as the square-root of time, since in their case the noise was mainly external.

(*c*) Before dealing with our third possibility we need to consider what sets the limit to discrimination. If Eq. 2.22 holds without qualification there should be no limit, given sufficient time, to the fineness with which discrimination can be made. Clearly this is not so, and the question arises of why not? It cannot be due to a constant such as r in Eqs. 2.4 and 2.5 because although this would slow discriminations of very small absolute magnitudes (Steinman, 1944) it would leave discrimination of larger magnitudes virtually unaffected. Nor is it likely to be due to a time-limit beyond which data cannot be effectively accumulated, because any such limit would have to differ widely from one experiment to another to account for various results which have been obtained (Hughes, 1963, Green *et al.*, 1957, Vickers, 1967).

A more promising line has been suggested by Vickers following experiments in which he superimposed on his projected lines a randomly varying pattern of spots by means of a cine-film running at

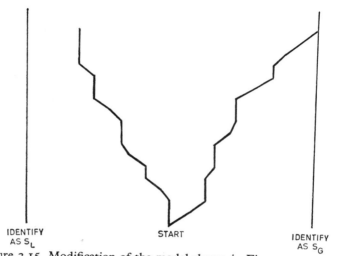

Figure 2.15. Modification of the model shown in Fig. 2.12 proposed by Vickers (1967).

16 frames per sec. The film has been described by MacKay (1965). The effect was to reduce the black lines on white ground to somewhat ill-defined areas of darker spots within a larger area of lighter spots, all on a white ground. The numbers of spots making up each line varied from frame to frame producing a distribution for each line. Vickers counted the actual spots in the line areas for samples of frames with each of several differences between the lines, and showed that Eq. 2.22 broke down at the point where substantial numbers of frames showed more spots in the shorter line than in the longer. One plausible suggestion is that the subject adds up the positive and negative quantities taking their sign and magnitude into account, until a critical total in favour of one decision or the other is reached, but this would imply a model like that of Fig. 2.11 and that the data should fit Eq. 2.19, which they do not. Vickers' alternative suggestion was that the subject accumulates positive and negative quantities separately, deciding in favour of whichever attains a critical total first, as indicated in Fig. 2.15.

If this is so Eq. 2.22 no longer applies strictly for two reasons which, however, partly offset each other. Firstly, the attainment of the criterion is slowed owing to time lost when data are accumulating in the 'wrong' store. Secondly, the rate of accumulation in the 'correct' store is faster than the mean ($\log S_G - \log S_L$) would suggest. The reason is indicated in Fig. 2.16, and is due to the fact that the average rate for

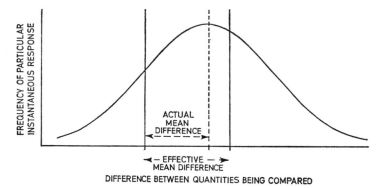

Figure 2.16. Diagram illustrating how, when two quantities to be discriminated are disturbed by noise, the effective mean difference between them may be increased according to the model illustrated in Fig. 2.15. The distribution is of the momentary differences between the quantities being compared. Zero difference is indicated by the leftmost of the three vertical lines which cut the distribution.

moments when the difference between the numbers of spots in the two lines is 'correct' is based on instances on one side only of the zero difference point. The net effect of these two factors is to produce a levelling off of discrimination time when substantial numbers of errors are made. We may note that Figs. 2.15 and 2.16 imply that even if S_G and S_L are exactly alike, some decision will eventually be reached since the average rate of accumulation will still be appreciable – it will, if the distribution in Fig. 2.16 is normal, be as if ($\log S_G - \log S_L$) equalled the mean deviation of that distribution, i.e. $\cdot778\sigma$.

If reaction times level off with very fine discriminations, the Confusion Function can account quite well for the results of Birren and Botwinick (1955) and of Botwinick *et al.* (1958). The data of Fig. 2.12 replotted against Eq. 2.22 are shown in Fig. 2.17 to fall into a pattern similar to that of Vickers' results in Fig. 2.15. If this is accepted, all the available data are well fitted by the Confusion Function except Henmon's (1906) and those of Green *et al.* (1957), Swets *et al.* (1959)

and Schouten and Bekker (1967). Crossman (1955) claims that Henmon's results are reasonably fitted by Eq. 2.22 and Vickers has pointed out that Henmon's lines could hardly have been drawn accurately enough to merit precise treatment. The results of Green *et al.* are probably involved with threshold effects so that they are hardly relevant to our present discussion, and those of Swets *et al.* are really for a different

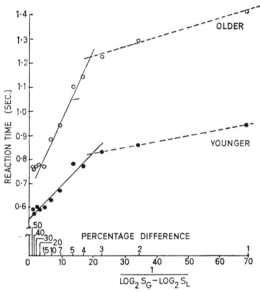

Figure 2.17. The data shown in Fig. 2.13 plotted against Eq. 2.22.

type of task: instead of giving a single exposure until decision is obtained, the subject is given a series of exposures on each of which he may be presumed to make a tentative judgment before arriving at a final decision. Schouten and Bekker's task is also of a different type since their subjects were making *choices* between clear signals rather than fine discriminations.

The Confusion Function as represented in Eq. 2.22 seems, therefore, to be able to account in a general way for all the relevant data available. It must be emphasised, however, that it can only provide an approximate, overall statement. There are likely to be several complicating factors in particular circumstances, especially at low absolute stimulus magnitudes. Other complications are implied in results obtained by Audley and Wallis (1964), Wallis and Audley (1964), who found that responses were quicker to the brighter of two relatively intense stimuli or the higher of two high tones, but slower to the brighter of two relatively weak stimuli or the higher of two low tones.

A great many studies have shown that reaction time shortens as the intensity or duration of the signal is increased (e.g. Piéron, 1920, 1936, Chocholle, 1940, 1943, Raab, 1962, Kaswan and Young, 1965a, b) and it seems reasonable to suppose that this is underlain by similar processes to those considered in this chapter. The problem of working out a coherent scheme of functional relationships between stimulus intensity and reaction time is, however, formidable. Some of the present data are not precisely quantifiable, many results are insufficient for treating in the present terms and many also seem likely to be complicated by the factors which operate at low absolute magnitudes. Added to all this, high intensities of ambient stimulation may have a facilitatory effect on response so that constant $\delta S/S$ may yield shorter reaction times when S is relatively intense (Raab and Grossberg, 1965). Again, short duration signals sometimes yield relatively short reaction times (e.g. Botwinick *et al.*, 1958), as if the subject decided that no further data were forthcoming and so that he might as well react at once. We shall, therefore, not attempt to consider this evidence here. It seems fair to suggest, however, that if what has been said here is true, reaction will normally occur when evidence favouring one decision rather than another has been built up enough to reach a critical level. The essential problem is thus to understand the several factors contributing to this evidence and its accumulation, and the course of their operation over time.

III

Identification and Choice

Why does it take time to react? What happens during a reaction time? The answers to these questions which have been given during the last 20 years are fundamental to much of our present understanding of the factors determining the speed and, as we shall see, the accuracy of performance. Broadly speaking, reaction time as usually measured includes, first, the time taken by the stimulus to activate the sense organ and for impulses to travel from it to the brain; second, the central processes concerned with identifying the signal and initiating a response to it; and third, the time required to energise the muscles and to produce an overt recorded response. The first and third components are in most cases relatively short although there are substantial differences of reaction time to stimuli applied to different sense organs – for example visual reactions commonly take some 50 msec longer than auditory. How far this is due to the sense organ and how far to the associated central mechanisms, however, is at present open to question. In any case, most studies which have attempted to establish laws about reaction time have been able to proceed as if the whole time is taken up by central processes, without running into anomalies. This is surprising and merits more thought than it has hitherto received. Are, for example, the three components truly successive in time, or do they overlap so that central processes begin before the signal has been fully received and motor processes are initiated before the programme for their fine control is complete?

During the time taken by the central processes the subject resolves uncertainty arising from two sources: firstly, he may not know exactly *when* the signal is coming and therefore when to respond; secondly, in choice-reaction tasks where different responses have to be made to each of several possible signals, he may not know *which* signal is coming and therefore which response to make. The fact that choice-reactions take longer than simple has been known since the pioneer experiments of Donders (1868) who distinguished what he called the a-reaction, with only one possible signal and response, from the b-reaction having more than one and thus involving identification and choice. It was also recognised that reaction-time rose progressively with the number of possible choices, but why and to what extent were not understood.

HICK'S INFORMATION-THEORY LAW

An important break into this last problem was made by Hick (1952a) who proposed, on the basis of his own data and also those of Merkel (1885), that in making choice-reactions the subject gains 'information', in the information-theory sense of the term, at a constant rate.

Merkel had presented his subjects with signals ranging, in different trials, from one to ten alternatives. The signals consisted of the arabic numerals 1–5 and roman numerals I–V, printed round the edge of a disc. The subject waited for each signal with his fingers pressed on 10 keys and, when a number was illuminated, released the corresponding key. The arabic numerals corresponded in order to the fingers of the right hand, and the roman to the left. When less than 10 choices were required some of the numerals were omitted.

Hick's own experiments used as a display 10 pea-lamps arranged in a 'somewhat irregular circle'. The subject reacted by pressing one of 10 morse keys on which his fingers rested. Choices of less than 10 were again obtained by omitting some of the lights. The frequencies of the various signals for any given degree of choice were carefully balanced and presented in an irregular order so as to ensure as far as possible that the subject should not be able to predict what signal was coming next. Each light appeared 5 sec after the completion of the previous response – an interval too long for the subject to judge accurately when the signal would appear.

Hick found that if the number of possible signals is taken as n and reaction time is plotted against $\log (n + 1)$, the observed reaction times for different numbers of signals lie on a straight line which also passes through the origin, as shown in Fig. 3.1. We can thus write

$$\text{Mean choice reaction time} = K \log (n + 1) \qquad (3.1)$$

where K is a constant. If we work in logarithms to the base 2, $\log (n + 1) = 1$ when $n = 1$, so that K is the simple reaction time – a convenient result. A table of these logarithms for whole numbers up to 100 is given in the Appendix. The $\log_2$ unit is known as the *bit*.

The obvious question arises, why $(n + 1)$ and not n? Hick pointed out that if the subject is uncertain when a signal will appear he is faced with the task, when it does appear, not only of deciding which it is, but also of deciding that a signal has occurred at all: failure to do so will result in his either reacting when there is no signal present or failing to react when there is one. The additional task of guarding against such errors can be conceived as adding one to the number of possible states of affairs that he has to distinguish – instead of states corresponding to signals 1, 2, 3, . . . n he has to deal with states corresponding to 0, 1, 2, 3,

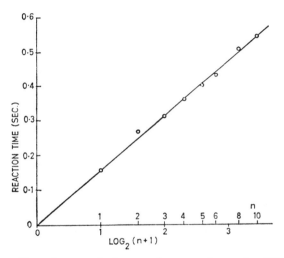

Figure 3.1. Data from a choice-reaction experiment by Hick (1952a) plotted in terms of Eq. 3.1. The total number of reactions represented is over 2,400 recorded after extensive practice.

. . . n. If the subject were in no doubt when a signal was coming, as, for example, if he were to determine the point of time himself at which the signal light came on, the $+1$ in Eq. 3.1 would not be required since there would be no temporal uncertainty to be resolved. We may denote the sum of the possibilities including 'no signal' as N, defining N as the *equivalent total* number of equally probable alternatives from which the subject has to choose, and may then rewrite Eq. 3.1 as

$$\text{Mean choice reaction time} = K \log N \qquad (3.2)$$

This formulation we may call *Hick's Law*. It should be understood that it is an 'ideal' formula and that time lags in the apparatus or in the making of a response may add a constant to the time: for example Costa *et al.* (1965) have shown that 40–70 msec may elapse between the first recordable electrical activity in the muscles and the making of a microswitch contact. Hick took elaborate care to avoid lags due to apparatus in his experiments. Since reaction-time can be a remarkably precise measure, such accuracy is well repaid in clarity of results.

Hick's approach was quickly extended by Crossman (1953) to another task demanding identification and choice, namely the sorting of playing

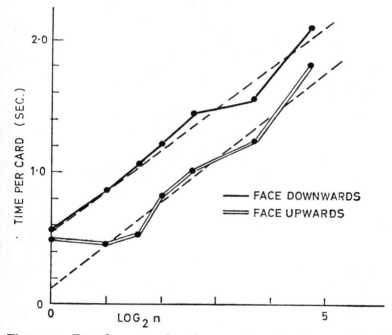

Figure 3.2. Data from a card-sorting experiment by Crossman (1953)
The points along each line represent, in order from left to right:
   Dealing cards in pre-arranged order
   Sorting into Red/Black.
           Pictures/Red plain/Black plain.
           Suits.
           Red pictures/Black pictures/Plain in 4 suits.
           Suits, dividing 6 and below from 7 and above.
           Numbers.
           Numbers, separating red and black.

cards. The subject held a well-shuffled pack face down in one hand: with the other he turned up the cards one by one and sorted them into various classes, working as quickly as possible without making errors. The number of classes was varied in different trials from 2 (Red/Black) up to 26 (the 13 numbers, dividing red from black). Additional trials were given in which the cards were in a pre-arranged order such as alternate red and black so as to provide a measure of the time taken to turn and place the cards when no identification or choice was required – in other words a measure of movement time. The results are shown by the upper line in Fig. 3.2. Roughly speaking

$$\text{Time per card} = \text{Movement time} + K \log n \qquad (3.3)$$

where n is the number of piles. The $+1$ of Eq. 3.1 is omitted in this case because, as the pack was always available, there was no uncertainty about when a fresh signal would appear. The point that falls farthest away from the line is that for the 13 numbers: these seem often to be easier to deal with than less familiar sets of signals. We shall return to this point later.

The question is sometimes raised of whether it is sufficient to estimate movement time by dealing on to only two piles: should dealing not be on to as many piles as there are classes to give a different estimate for each number of classes? An indication that this elaboration is unnecessary is contained in the results Crossman obtained with the pack held face up so that the subject could see each card immediately he had removed the previous one. The lower line of Fig. 3.2 shows that the time per card was either ·the movement time or roughly $K \log n$ *whichever was the longer*. It appears that identification and choice can overlap with movement, so that the two can develop together. Extra movement time required with large numbers of piles can thus be absorbed in the extra time needed for identification and choice.

Generalisation of Hick's Law

Hick's line óf approach is supported by three further findings:

(a) The amount of information transmitted in a choice reaction task is reduced if the signals are not all of equal frequency. The amount of information due to uncertainty about which signal will occur can be worked out by summing the amounts of information conveyed by each signal weighted according to the probability of its occurrence. We can therefore write in place of $\log n$ in Eq. 3.3

$$\sum_{i=1}^{n} p_i \log \frac{1}{p_i} \qquad (3.4)$$

and in place of $\log (n + 1)$ in Eq. 3.1

$$\sum_{i=1}^{n} p_i \log \left(\frac{1}{p_i} + 1 \right) \qquad (3.5)$$

where p_i is the probability of each signal in the set taken in turn. These expressions reduce to $\log n$ and $\log (n + 1)$ respectively when all the probabilities are equal. Hyman (1953) found reductions of about the expected amounts in average choice reaction times when signal frequencies were unequal, and Crossman (1953) found approximately the expected reductions in the times to sort packs of cards containing unequal frequencies of different classes. A table of $p \log_2 \dfrac{1}{p}$ and of $p \log_2 \left(\dfrac{1}{p} + 1\right)$ is given in the Appendix.

(b) Information transmitted is also reduced when signals tend to follow one another in recognisable sequences or when any signal is followed by any other more often than expected by chance, even though the overall signal frequencies are equal. This is really an extension of the foregoing case: the *probabilities* of different signals are functions of previous signals, and are thus unequal at any given point in the series although the inequalities even out over the series as a whole. Hyman (1953) found the expected shortening of average reaction times in these cases.

(c) The amount of information gained is reduced if the subject makes errors. A convenient method of calculating the amount gained when errors are present is to make a table with, say, a column for each signal and a row for each response, including 0 in each case where appropriate, and to enter the responses made to each signal in the corresponding cells. We can then write

Information gained

$$= \sum p_S \log \frac{1}{p_S} + \sum p_R \log \frac{1}{p_R} - \sum p_{SR} \log \frac{1}{p_{SR}} \qquad (3.6)$$

where p_S is the probability of signals in each column, p_R the probability of responses in each row and p_{SR} the proportion of signal-response pairs observed in each cell. The summation Σ is made over each column, row or individual cell respectively.[*] This equation is a fundamental one for calculating the information transmitted from signal to response.

[*] Hick has given the following formula which provides a convenient practical method of calculation:

$$\text{Information gained} = \log M + \frac{1}{M}\Sigma_{SR}\left(f_{SR} \log \frac{f_{SR}}{f_S \cdot f_R}\right)$$

where M is the number of readings, f_S is the total of the signals in each column taken in turn, f_R the total of the responses in each row taken in turn and f_{SR} the number of readings in each cell taken individually. Hick (1952a) sets out an example from his experiments.

When there are no errors so that each signal always leads to its own particular response, the equation reduces to Eq. 3.4, or when signal frequencies are all equal, to Eq. 3.2. It is also a means of providing an information measure of discrimination (Garner and Hake, 1951) by using, in the simple case, the four probabilities of 'Correct Yes', 'Correct No', 'Miss' and 'False Positive' mentioned on p. 33, or in the multiple case discussed on p. 40, the several categories of signal provided and response allowed.

Hick found that the shortening of reaction times when substantial numbers of errors were made was by approximately the amounts expected. By the same tokens we should expect the $+1$ in Eq. 3.1 to be reduced if premature responses occurred or responses were omitted. We have noted in the previous chapter that Schouten and Bekker (1967) also found a very clear increase of errors as reaction time shortened, and that Taylor *et al.* (1967) analysed this relationship in terms of a linear increase of d'^2 with time. They linked this with the linear gain of information with time implied in Hick's type of model through the fact that both can be treated in terms of signal-to-noise ratio. Evidence regarding the effects of both errors and sequential probability comes from experiments by Moray and Taylor (1958) and Triesman (1965) who showed that when a subject had to repeat words played to him by tape-recorder, the accuracy of performance increased as the words approximated more and more to connected English, to an extent which implied a constant rate of information-transfer. Howell and Kreidler (1963) and Fitts (1966), who compared groups of subjects performing choice reaction tasks with instructions for speed, for accuracy or for both, confirmed that overall rates of information gain were not significantly different for the three types of instruction although the balance between speed and accuracy was shifted as the instructions required, although Howell and Kreidler noted that instructions for speed produced a greater gain in errors than speed. Fitts observed that subjects who made very large numbers of errors seemed to gain information at lower rates than the rest. In part this may be due to Fitts having ignored the $+1$ in Eq. 3.1; in part it may be that Eq. 3.6 tends to underestimate performance. It does so because a subject may well have gained some information while still making an error, but unless he makes the same error several times he will get little credit for this information. Hick in a private communication has pointed out that Eq. 3.6 assumes that all errors are equally 'bad' and suggests that this may not in fact be correct: in other words the information gained is not a complete measure of performance.

In so far as the information measure is adequate, it provides a valuable means of combining speed and accuracy into a single score, and emphasises the important fact that times for different tasks are comparable only if errors are held constant, and conversely that error rates can be compared only if times are held constant.

Guarding against false reactions

The $+1$ in Hick's formulation has not always proved easy to understand and an alternative equation proposed by Hyman (1953) and also by Bricker (1955a) has often been preferred. They proposed in place of Eq. 3.1,

$$\text{Choice reaction time} = a + b \log n \qquad (3.7)$$

where a is the simple reaction time and $b \log n$ represents the increase over the simple reaction time due to the need for identification and choice. A few sets of results such as those of Suci *et al.* (1960) are about equally well fitted by both Hick's and Hyman's formulae, but in most cases Hick's fits better. This is true not only of Merkel's and Hick's data but also of Griew's (1958b, c), Brown's (1960), Hilgendorf's (1966) and Hyman's own, some of which are shown in Fig. 3.3.

As can be seen from Fig. 3.3, the reason why Hyman's formula fits less well than Hick's is that it underestimates simple reaction times: for degrees of choice above four the two formulae fit about equally well. It is conceivable that Hyman's approach is basically correct but that there is a minimum time required by some stage between reception of a signal and response to it, so that observed reaction time is either this minimum or the time required for identification and choice, whichever is greater.

The main difference between Hick's and Hyman's approaches seems to lie, however, in their treatment of the effects of preventing premature or false responses if there is uncertainty about when signals will appear. According to Hyman these effects should be dealt with separately from those of uncertainty about which signal has arrived. Hick's approach implies that temporal uncertainty affects the probability at any instant of 'signal' as opposed to 'no signal' and that the $+1$ is not necessarily a fixed quantity. We should, therefore, rewrite Eq. 3.1 as

$$\text{Choice reaction time} = K \log (n + n_0) \qquad (3.8)$$

where n_0 is the effect of temporal uncertainty expressed in terms of n. It might vary from zero if the subject could estimate exactly when the next signal will appear, to substantially more than $+1$ if he were deliberately misled as to the time of its arrival. Values between 0 and $+1$ ought to be found when the time of appearance is reasonably, but not completely, predictable.

Some evidence that this is so is contained in the results of another experiment by Crossman (1956). In this the subject sat facing a panel

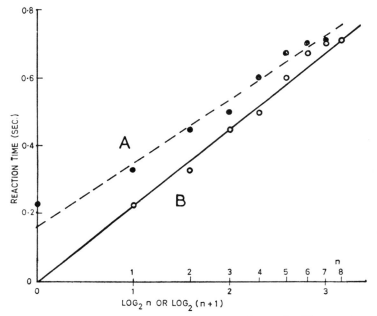

Figure 3.3. Data from a choice-reaction experiment by Hyman (1953) plotted against (A) Eq. 3.7, and (B) Eq. 3.1. The total number of reactions represented is about 20,000: 5,000 from each of four subjects. The signals were lights, two at each corner of a square, and the responses were the syllables BUN, BOO, BEE . . . BATE spoken by the subject and corresponding to the signals 1, 2, 3, . . . 8.

of signal lights numbered 1–8 beneath which was a row of eight push-buttons. As soon as he raised his hand from a key, one of the lights came on and he pressed the corresponding button. In different trials 1, 2, 4 or all 8 lights and buttons were used. For one condition ('symbolic') the lights were in scattered positions so that the subject had to use the number symbol to translate from signal to response. For the other ('non-symbolic') the signal lights were directly above the buttons so that no symbolic translation was required. The recorded time when only one light was used was really a movement time since it was not necessary to observe the display. Crossman had hoped to eliminate temporal uncertainty and the need to guard against false reactions by having the subject bring on the signal for himself, but the results suggest this was not wholly achieved. They are shown in Fig. 3.4 plotted against $\log (n + \cdot 45)$. It can be seen that the regression lines for both conditions converge on the movement-time point: if the results are plotted against $\log n$, the lines cut the axis at different points above the movement-time point. A possible reason for the failure to eliminate n_0 is that it is very difficult to make apparatus so reliable that the signal

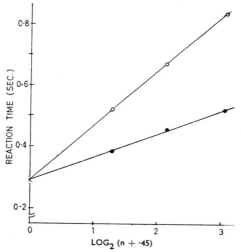

Figure 3.4. Data from an experiment by Crossman (1956) comparing performances with symbolic and non-symbolic displays. Each point is the mean of 160 readings – 40 from each of four subjects. Open circles = symbolic displays, filled circles = non-symbolic, X = movement time.

always appears as it should: even a very few occasions on which the subject raised his hand from the key without a light appearing would be enough to introduce appreciable uncertainty.

Several studies of simple reaction-time (e.g. Woodrow, 1914, Klemmer, 1956, Karlin, 1959, Botwinick and Brinley, 1962a, b, Aiken and Lichtenstein, 1964) have controlled temporal uncertainty by preceding each signal with a warning and varying the interval ('foreperiod') between them. All these studies are agreed that if the foreperiod remains constant over a series of trials, reaction time lengthens as the foreperiod is increased from somewhere between ·3 and 2 sec upwards. The increase has been shown to continue for foreperiods up to at least 320 sec (Bevan *et al.*, 1965). With foreperiods shorter than about ·5 sec other complications enter which we shall consider in the next chapter. If the foreperiod is randomly varied from trial to trial the reaction times with all foreperiods tend to approximate to that which would be obtained with the longest if they were given regularly. Klemmer (1957) has suggested that temporal uncertainty arises not only from variability in the length of the foreperiod but also from the subject's inability to estimate time consistently, and he has shown that these two sources can be treated together in a single information measure. This measure is, however, differently conceived from that of Hick's Law, dealing with accuracy of time estimation rather than guarding against false reactions, and it is not appropriate to try to tie them together. A more direct study of the effects of guarding against false reactions is that of Drazin (1961) who not only varied the foreperiod but also the probability with which a signal actually followed. He showed that reaction time increased as this probability fell.

These findings do not in themselves distinguish between Hick's and Hyman's formulae, but they suggest a way of doing so by comparing the effects of different foreperiods or probabilities of signal for various degrees of choice. According to Hyman, the only effect of these variables should be on a in Eq. 3.7 and this should be the same for all degrees of choice. According to Hick the effect should be on n_0 in Eq. 3.8 and should thus diminish as the degree of choice becomes larger. There are some indications from experiments by Boons and Bertelson (1961), Fowler (1964) and Broadbent and Gregory (1965) that the effect does diminish as the degree of choice increases, although only in Fowler's case was the result statistically significant and his observations were only on a single subject. Further indications in favour of Hick's formula are, however, forthcoming from an experiment by Bertelson and Barzeele (1965) who found that in a two-choice task with unequal frequencies of the two signals, the effect of lengthening the foreperiod was much greater upon the more than upon the less frequent responses.

CONCEPTUAL MODELS

Mathematical formulae such as Hick's Law are only a first step towards an understanding of performance. They provide a summary statement of a complex process of observation, identification, choice and reaction which must be analysed in detail if a clear picture is to be obtained. Several models to account for this process have been proposed, all essentially implying decision processes of the kinds we have considered in the previous chapter. Each has its advantages and difficulties, and it seems likely that there is no one model which applies in all circumstances. They fall into three main types which we shall consider in turn.

1. Serial classification models

Perhaps the most readily conceived model is one of those examined by Hick (1952a). The subject is thought of as making a series of sub-decisions each taking approximately the same time. With the first he identifies the signal and the response to it as lying within one half of the total possibilities; with the second as lying within one half of this half, and so on until the specific signal and response have been found. He is not able to make his divisions into exact halves unless N is an exact power of 2, but can do so approximately in other cases. In any case the model would still give approximately the correct result so long as the subject started by rejecting broad classes of possibility and then went on to reject finer classes within a broad class chosen.

If each sub-decision is conceived as an all-or-none affair this model is, however, unsatisfactory in three ways. Firstly, it must assume that errors are due to the process of elimination not being carried far enough, thereby saving one or more sub-decisions and the time these would take, but risking error because the final choice is made at random among the possibilities that remain: just how the final random selection is made remains unspecified. Secondly, the model does not adequately account for reduction of reaction time when frequencies of different signals and responses are unequal. So long as there are three or more possibilities, some reduction would result if the subject eliminated half the *probability* rather than half the set of signals in each sub-decision. For example, if there were five possible signals and one appeared four times as frequently as each of the others, time would be saved if the first sub-decision was between this one and the rest. Such a procedure would also account for expectancy effects by assuming that these represented a biasing of the subjective probabilities of the different signals. When, however, there are only two possibilities, as in some of Crossman's (1953) packs of cards, one sub-decision should be required in all cases whether or not signal frequencies are equal, and thus no reduction of reaction time would be predicted with unequal frequencies. Thirdly, the model does not account for the variances of the reaction times observed by Hick for different degrees of choice: if the total variance depends in part on the number of sub-decisions involved, it should be relatively low for degrees of choice which are exact powers of 2 so that all signals require the same number of sub-decisions, and higher for other degrees of choice where different choices will involve different numbers. Hick found that variance increased with degree of choice more evenly than would be expected on this model.

These difficulties are avoided in a modification of the model suggested by Fitts *et al.* (1963) and Fitts (1966) and implied also by Taylor *et al.* (1967). They regard the details of each sub-decision as roughly those of the sequential sampling model outlined in the previous chapter and illustrated in Fig. 2.12. If this is so, it is easy to envisage that with un-balanced frequencies or expectancies of two responses or classes of response the subject might begin his 'random-walk' nearer to the more frequent criterion, either by moving the criterion or by biasing the starting point. Either of these methods would also tend to smooth the increase of variance that occurs with rise in the number of choices. The gain of speed at the expense of accuracy noted by Hick and by Fitts is accounted for by moving the criteria closer together. Essentially the same would also apply if the sub-decisions followed Vickers' modified model illustrated in Fig. 2.16. This is an elegant and flexible approach: perhaps its main disadvantage is that it is *too* flexible and can account for almost any results provided appropriate assumptions are made about the shifting of criteria relative to the starting point.

A more rigorous treatment of the effects of unequal frequencies and expectancies is to assume that if during a sub-decision the subject finds the signal and corresponding response are *not* in the half he is examining, he checks that they *are* in the other half before proceeding. Each dichotomous sub-decision might thus require either one or two 'inspections' according to whether or not the first inspection was successful. Every inspection would represent a decision process of the type considered in Chapter 2. If we assume that each inspection takes an equal time, the average time required for a binary decision between equally probable random alternatives will be made up of 50% cases where one inspection-time was sufficient and 50% when two were needed. The mean time would thus be 1·5.

If signal frequencies were not equal, time could be saved even if there were only two alternatives, by trying the more likely signal first and so increasing the chance that the first inspection would be successful. If, for example, one alternative occurred three times as frequently as the other, trying the more frequent first would reduce the average number of inspections required from 1·50 to 1·25. The effect of frequency unbalance would be limited by the fact that the ratio of the times to respond to the more and the less frequent alternatives in a binary choice could never exceed 1 : 2. Two points follow from this, both of which are in line with Hyman's results. Firstly, the effects of extreme frequency unbalance will be less than those predicted on information analysis. Hyman found the reaction times for two-choice tasks with signals presented in the ratios 1 : 9 and 1 : 4 were almost identical. Secondly, the times will tend to be longer for more frequent responses and shorter for less frequent than expression 3.4 or 3.5 would predict. Hyman specifically notes the occurrence of this in his results.

This model has the surprising implication that binary decisions are not always the most efficient procedure: for choices between two and eight it is better to make a serial examination of each possibility in turn. This procedure requires one inspection for each possibility examined up to and including the correct one, so that a subject will, on average, arrive at the correct choice in $(N + 1)/2$ inspections. Beyond eight choices the method of serial examination is inferior to dichotomisation. Beyond six choices further economies can be achieved by dividing the possibilities into threes or fours and exploring these serially rather than dichotomising. The optimum strategy is thus serial exploration up to six with division into threes and fours for higher degrees of choice. The various strategies are compared in Table 3.1 and in Fig. 3.5. The optimum curve in Fig. 3.5 looks very much like an exaggeration of Hyman's slightly S-shaped curve in Fig. 3.3. The fact that this shape is not reflected in Merkel's or Hick's data is not a crucial argument

TABLE 3.1 *Average numbers of inspections required with different strategies to decide among* $n + 1 (= N)$ *alternatives*

n	$\log_2 (n+1)$ $= \log_2 N$	$1.5 \log_2 (n+1)$ $= 1.5 \log_2 N$	Strict dichoto- mising	Running along line i.e. $(N+1)/2$	'Optimum' strategy
1	1.00	1.50	1.50	1.5	1.5
2	1.58	2.38	2.44	2.0	2.0
3	2.00	3.00	3.00	2.5	2.5
4	2.32	3.48	3.55	3.0	3.0
5	2.58	3.89	3.94	3.5	3.5
6	2.81	4.22	4.25	4.0	3.7*
7	3.00	4.50	4.50	4.5	4.0†
8	3.17	4.75	4.80	5.0	4.0‡

* Divided into 4 + 3.
† Divided into 4 + 4.
‡ Divided into 3 + 3 + 3.

against the model. The attainment of maximum efficiency is likely to be rare as it involves the maintenance of a strategy in the face of many temptations to vary it. It may well take time to develop fully, for example Fitts *et al.* (1963) showed that when frequencies were unbalanced, the relative shortening of reaction times to the more frequent signals and relative lengthening of times to the less frequent gradually increased with practice.

Some kind of serial classification procedure seems evident in subjects

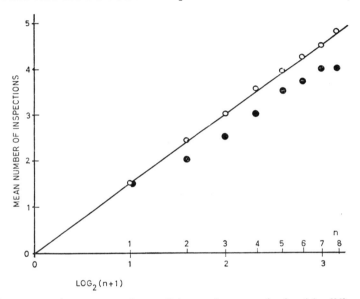

Figure 3.5. Average numbers of inspections required with different strategies in Table 3.1. The continuous line is $1.5 \log_2(n + 1)$, the open circles are for the strictest possible dichotomising strategy, and the filled circles are for the 'optimum' strategy.

sorting cards of different classes on to piles: they move each card to the appropriate part of the table and then make more detailed searches and finer movements until the correct pile is located. How far it occurs in conventional reaction-time tasks is more difficult to say since sub-decisions may not show in overt sub-responses. It is perhaps significant, however, that Leonard (1958) was able in a six-choice reaction to give two indications – in which of two groups of three the signal would occur, and which of these three was in fact the signal – about ·1 sec apart without lengthening the total reaction time beyond that for a straightforward six-choice task.

The precise strategy adopted is likely in any case to vary with the way in which signals and responses are arranged. If there are, say, very large numbers of lights in a display which are removed at some distance from their corresponding keys and the lights and keys are not split up into groups, counting from one end may be the only method of ensuring an accurate response; so that if all signals occur equally often in a random order, mean reaction time should be linearly related to $(N + 1)/2$ and thus to N. What seems to be an illustration of this is given by Morikiyo and Iida (1967) who compared reaction times for 2, 4 and 8 choices when the signals were either from lamps in a horizontal row or numbers on a 'Nixie' tube, and responses were made by different fingers. With the latter display Eq. 3.7 held well (temporal uncertainty was low), but with the straight-line display reaction time increased approximately linearly with N. The same was true with the linear display when responses were all made with one index finger, but with the 'Nixie' tube display and this method of response the increase was somewhat less with degree of choice than Eq. 3.7 would predict. Why this is so is not clear, but Crossman (1956) has pointed out, and Knight (1967) has confirmed, that when only a single finger is used the differences of reaction time for different positions exceed those for different degrees of choice. Average times for several positions may thus depend on precise details of layout and procedure. Knight found that in a serial task when each response brought on the next signal, reaction time was approximately $a + b \log D$ where D was the distance from the previous response key to the new one. When signals were presented at discrete intervals of time instead of serially, the same formula held with D representing the distance from the centre of the row of response keys.

Similar considerations may well apply in card-sorting tasks, so that sorting times would be affected by the layout of the piles on to which the different classes are placed. Suppose, for example, that 16 classes are arranged in a 4×4 square: an efficient strategy would be to search down the rows until the appropriate one was found and then along that row until the correct individual pile was reached. With such a strategy the average number of inspections would be $(4 + 1)/2$ for identifying the appropriate row and the same again for identifying the individual pile within the row. More generally we could write

$$\text{Mean choice reaction time} = K(\sqrt{n} + 1) \qquad (3.9)$$

This would apply exactly only when $\sqrt{n}$ was a whole number, but would hold approximately when it was not. The author has found Eq. 3.9 to give a good fit to some card-sorting results obtained in undergraduate practical classes although the conditions in these were not sufficiently controlled for the results to carry much weight. Of more interest is the fact that Eq. 3.9 gives a good fit to Hick's (1952a) results for two choices and above and a reasonable fit to data from other authors, although not quite as good as that provided by Eq. 3.2.

Taking a broad view of the evidence and theoretical considerations, we may think of Eq. 3.2, and thus of Hick's Law, as an 'ideal' statement of a serial choice model which is never likely to be attained precisely in practice, but is approximated in various different ways.

2. Simultaneous scanning models

The models discussed so far have attempted to break down the process of identification and choice into a series of subsidiary actions. The models now to be considered postulate a single continuous process. The earliest of them was proposed by Hick (1952b) who noted that Eq.3.1 could be rewritten

$$1/(n + 1) = e^{-T/K} \qquad (3.10)$$

where e is the base of the natural logarithms and T the reaction-time. He argued that we can imagine the total range of sensory input as divided into $(n + 1)$ phases and that the left-hand side of Eq. 3.10 can be regarded as the *a priori* probability of any one phase. The right-hand side of the equation is the probability of a phase lasting as long as time T when it has a fixed probability dT/K of vanishing at any instant dT. A decision to release the response is made as soon as the signal has lasted long enough for the probability of its having continued for that length of time to be less than the prior probability. Subsequent work in which several signals have been associated with each response has indicated, as we shall see later, that choice reaction time depends more upon the number of possible responses than possible signals, but Hick's model could cover this point by assuming that all signals leading to a given response are treated as one phase.

A different type of simultaneous scanning model is that of Christie and Luce (1956) discussed by Rapoport (1959) and Laming (1966). It postulates that the incoming signal is compared simultaneously with all possible identifications, and the decision to respond is taken when all the comparisons have been completed. Since the time taken by each comparison is subject to random variation, the larger the number to be made the greater the likelihood of one taking a long time and thus leading to a slow reaction. According to the version of this model set out by Laming

$$\text{Mean choice reaction time} = K \sum_{R=1}^{n} \frac{1}{R+C} \quad (C > -1) \quad (3.11)$$

where $R_1, R_2 \ldots R_n$ are the ordinal numbers of the various responses and K and C are constants. Eq. 3.11 can provide a good fit to Hick's data, with $C = 1$ and corresponding in a sense to n_0 in Eq. 3.8.

A mixed simultaneous and successive model has been proposed by Stone (1960) who suggested that the subject might accumulate data about all possible inputs for a given length of time, and then compare all possible pairs of inputs, to ascertain which was the largest, and decide for this. Such a model has clear affinities with the discrimination model of Fig. 2.9. It provides reasonably straight-line relationships between reaction time and log n, but requires at least one additional parameter. It must in fairness be said that Stone doubted whether his model was applicable to cases where the different signals were easily discriminable from one another, although in this his claim seems to have been over modest.

It is extremely difficult to draw clear distinctions between the various successive and simultaneous scanning models that have been proposed. They are so flexible and several fit at least portions of the available data so well that it is impossible to prefer one to another on mathematical grounds alone: distinction needs to be made in terms of their parsimony in accounting for a wide range of experimental results. The successive models at present have the advantage of being more thoroughly worked out in respect of unbalanced frequency and expectation effects and of detailed behaviour when carrying out choice tasks, but this is not to say that corresponding elaborations of the simultaneous models would not prove successful (see e.g. Laming, 1962). One possibly significant point is that the simultaneous models have been conceived as a means of handling *identification of signal*, whereas the successive models seem more applicable to *choice of response*: perhaps this is where their principal respective applications lie.

3. Neurological considerations

The processes postulated by the foregoing models must be underlain by events in the nervous system, and it seems therefore reasonable to ask whether any leads could be obtained by considering these events directly. The building of detailed neurological models is premature in the present state of knowledge, but it is reasonable to sketch one in broad outline.

Let us consider the making of responses in typical reaction-time tasks where the subject has from one to ten keys, each under a different finger. In the simple reaction condition when only one key is in use, his response can be relatively crude and undifferentiated: a gross movement of the whole hand, or even of the whole body, will suffice. For two-choice responses with one key operated by each hand, some differentiation is needed in that one hand has to move while the other does not. With four possible responses, two by each hand, still greater specificity is required but the movement can still be a rotation of the hand to put one *side* down rather than the other. With all 10 choices, there is no alternative to activating one finger to the exclusion of all the others.

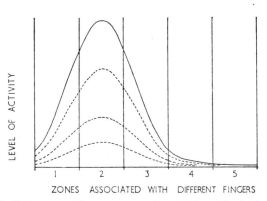

Figure 3.6. Diagrammatic representation of hypothetical build-up of neutral activity to control the fingers in a choice-reaction experiment such as Hick's.

It seems obvious that this increasing specificity of response corresponds to a more and more precise localisation of activity in the brain. Any response must be associated with activity in a restricted set of nerve cells, and for one response to be differentiated from another, the activity in these cells must exceed that in cells for other responses by a critical amount. We may envisage that a signal for a particular finger to move will have its maximum effect on the cells associated with that finger, but that there may be some spread of effect to surrounding areas associated with other fingers as suggested in Fig. 3.6. If the activity builds up progressively with time, it might be represented at successive moments by the series of curves in Fig. 3.6. If so it is clear that any critical difference between activity in one region and in others will be reached sooner if the specificity of the response is low – for example when it can be made with the whole hand – than if it is high as when it has to be made with one finger and not with adjacent fingers.

It is reasonable to suppose that a response would be triggered not by relative activity in different areas but by the absolute level in one. If so there must either, with the general build-up, go a 'backing off' which keeps activity in unwanted areas below the critical level, or the excitation of any one area must tend to inhibit other areas, somewhat as has been shown to occur between adjacent points in a sensory area (Hartline 1938, von Bekesy 1967). The postulation of inhibition as well as excitation is usually a weakness in a theory since, with suitable parameters attached, almost any behaviour can be accounted for. In this case, however, the objection is not serious since the excitation and inhibition are presumed always to occur together.

The model proposed here makes the subject's task in selecting a response essentially similar to that of discriminating between different signals as envisaged in Fig. 2.6. Its main limitation is that it is not, at its present stage of development, quantitative. Also it is perhaps a far cry from the spatial organisation of the motor cortex to processes of perceptual identification and the selection of non-manual responses such as nonsense syllables or names of letters or digits. The analogy is not, however, far fetched or unreasonable since perceptual identifications and verbal responses must be based on physical traces which have some kind of spatial location in the brain. Schouten and Bekker (1967) have suggested a somewhat similar approach to perceptual tasks in terms of 'perceptual focusing'.

This type of model appears able to account for a wide variety of evidence. It deals with the effects of unequal frequencies and of expectation by assuming that the subject can activate in advance the area corresponding to a given response, so that when a signal arrives the build-up required to produce a decision in favour of this response is less than that required for others. Evidence in favour of this view is contained in the results of Davis (1940) who found that muscle action-potentials in the responding limb built up during the foreperiod; although since the build-up it assumed to be central, such peripheral effects are not essential to the theory (Botwinick and Thompson, 1966). Ability to hold such a 'preparatory set' over an appreciable period of time seems to be poor, as evidenced by experiments already cited in which foreperiod was varied systematically (see also Karlin, 1966). Indeed the rise of reaction-time found with long or variable foreperiods seems inevitably to imply that such preparation cannot be maintained. We can only speculate upon the reason, but it seems possible that a build-up of activity would tend to spread to adjacent areas if it continued for a long time. The shortening of reaction-time when substantial numbers of errors are made could be accounted for by a lowering of critical values leading to a shorter build-up but greater chance of the wrong response being triggered.

Three more positive lines of evidence in favour of this type of model serve to distinguish it from the purely mathematical approaches. Firstly, it accounts well for the otherwise anomalous results obtained by Seibel (1963) who used a task in which all possible patterns of 10 signal lights and 10 response keys were used to yield 1,023 choices. He compared this task with one in which five lights and keys were used with one hand to give 31 choices. It is understandable in terms of the model that the reaction times in both conditions were very similar – the second was only about 25 msec faster than the first – since the discriminatory difficulties involved in selecting *patterns* of fingers to depress would differ little once it had become necessary to distinguish each finger from its immediate neighbours.

Secondly, it seems reasonable to suppose that any spread of effect in the motor cortex would affect other areas in proportion to their distance from the focal point, so that errors would be related to the 'neural distance' between correct and erroneous responses. There is some evidence from experiments by Blyth (1963, 1964) that this is so. He found that in a four-choice task in which responses were made by the two hands and two feet, the overwhelming majority of errors were due to the substitution of the wrong limb on the correct side. Occasional errors were made with the correct limb on the wrong side but never with the wrong limb on the wrong side. Further experiments by the same author made it clear that this result did not depend on the layout of the signals: it seemed clearly due to responses on the same side being more readily confused than those on opposite sides.

Thirdly, the build-up of activity we have postulated would probably take an appreciable time to die away. If so, the model provides an explanation for the results of experiments (Bertelson, 1961, 1963, Bertelson and Renkin, 1966, Leonard *et al.*, 1966, Hale 1967) which have found that, in a rapid series, responses which are the same as those immediately preceding are made more quickly than those which follow different responses. Bertelson found that the effect largely disappeared if the interval between the completion of one response and the appearance of the next signal was increased from ·05 to ·5 sec, and Hale found it much reduced when the interval was increased from ·1 to ·6 sec, giving time for any after-effects to die away. Further evidence of a different kind but in the same direction is contained in results obtained by Jeeves (see Welford, 1958, pp. 96–98, also Jeeves, 1961) who compared delays of 0, ·1 and ·2 sec between the end of one response and the onset of the next signal in a serial reaction task. He found that the delays shortened the reaction times, implying that some after-effect of the previous reaction which disappeared during the delay period could slow down a subsequent reaction – the after-effect of one response seems to have behaved as noise in relation to the next. Jeeves' results suggest that the average after-effect lasted about 30 msec for a group of subjects aged 18–33, and about 50 msec for a group aged 58–71.

Results which link Bertelson's and Jeeves' findings with Blyth's have been obtained by Rabbitt (1966b) who compared the times taken in a serial reaction task somewhat similar to Blyth's. He confirmed that a reaction was on average fastest when it was identical with the one previous, and slowest when preceded by a reaction with the other limb – hand or foot – on the same side: the after-effects which in Blyth's experiments caused errors, slowed down responses by Rabbitt's subjects.

It seems clear that similarity of response is more important than similarity of signal: Bertelson (1965) who compared situations in which each response was linked with either one or two signals, found that changing from one signal to the other leading to the same response had much less effect than changing from one response to the other. Williams (1966) in a two-choice reaction task in which somewhat longer periods elapsed between each response and the next signal, found that reactions were actually quicker to changed than to repeated signals. However in one of her experiments in which, instead of each response being associated with its corresponding signal, one response was made when a signal was the same as before and the other when it was different, she found reactions were quicker both with changed signals and also with repeated responses. The implication seems to be that change of signal and of response may in certain circumstances have opposite effects which tend in most cases partly to cancel one another. Confirmation that it is the actual limb moved rather than the control manipulated that causes the shortening of repeated responses is given by Rabbitt (1965) who used a multi-choice serial reaction task in which each hand was used for several keys, and these were placed too far apart for manipulation by individual fingers. He showed that responses were made significantly faster if the preceding response had been made by the same hand than if it had been made by the other. There is, perhaps, a perceptual equivalent to Williams' and Rabbitt's findings in the results of an experiment by Nickerson (1965a). He displayed pairs of consonants, one after the other, and required subjects to say as quickly as possible whether the second was the same as or different from the first. Responses of 'same' were substantially faster than those of 'different'.

Of the various successive, simultaneous and neurological models we have surveyed, some have, as we have already noted, been clearly aimed at explaining choice, while others have been conceived essentially in terms of identification. Their applicability may thus depend on the extent to which these two processes contribute to choice reaction-time. This is the question we consider next.

FACTORS AFFECTING THE EXTENT TO WHICH REACTION-TIME RISES WITH NUMBER OF ALTERNATIVES

The slope in Eq. 3.1 for many studies of subjects in their twenties using conventional light signals and key-pressing or spoken responses, is remarkably constant at about 5–7 bits per sec (e.g. Merkel, 1885, Hick, 1952a, Hyman, 1953, Brown, 1960). It rises a little with age in some studies (e.g. Griew, 1958b, c, 1964, Suci *et al.*, 1960) although not in all (Crossman and Szafran, 1956, Szafran, 1964), and it is possible that the increased slope with age is associated with cardiac deficiency rather than age as such (Szafran, 1966). Essentially the same rate was found by Pollack and Johnson (1963a) as the maximum for monitoring a series of binary digits (0 or 1) briefly flashed one at a time on a screen. However, several studies in which subjects have had to respond verbally have yielded much higher rates, ranging from 14 to 17 bits per sec for naming objects, colours or designs (Morin *et al.*, 1965, Oldfield and Wingfield, 1965, Oldfield, 1966), through about 16–90 bits for repeating digits shown singly (Brainerd *et al.*, 1962, Stone and Callaway, 1964) and about 40 bits for repeating words shown briefly from vocabularies ranging from 2 to 1,000 (Pollack, 1963b) up to about 100–160 bits per sec for repeating letters shown singly (Fitts and Switzer, 1962, Morin *et al.*, 1965).

It seems that the slope depends to a considerable extent on the relationship between signals and their corresponding responses. The earliest clear demonstration of this seems to have been Crossman's (1956) experiment already described in which he compared symbolic and nonsymbolic displays in a button-pressing task: the slope for the former was about five bits per sec and for the latter about 15. Confirmation is contained in results by Griew (1958b, c, 1964) for a task in which subjects moved a stylus from a central point to one of 2, 4 or 8 'targets' arranged in a semicircle around it. He compared conditions when each signal light was just beyond its corresponding target with those when it was just beyond the corresponding target on the opposite side of the semicircle, and found the slope in the latter case to be about twice that in the former. Further striking evidence is provided for a very different kind of task by Treisman (1965) who showed that the accuracy with which subjects could *repeat* English or French words fell off much less as speed of presentation was increased, than it did when they had to *translate* from the one language to the other. This was true even for bilingual subjects.

It has been claimed by Leonard (1959) that if the relationship between signal and response is made sufficiently direct – or 'compatible' as Fitts has termed it – the slope becomes zero. His subjects responded by pressing the armatures of relays on which their fingers were resting, and the signals consisted of vibrations in the same armatures. Leonard found a rise of reaction-time from simple to two-choice conditions, but none thereafter to four- or eight-choices. Some rise from simple to two-choice conditions is likely in that when only one response is required it can be prepared to an extent that is not possible when any of two or more may be called for – in the simple case the translation mechanism can be pre-set but in the choice condition it cannot. The equality of reaction time for choices above two is, however, surprising and certainly calls for an explanation.

It has been further claimed by Mowbray and Rhoades (1959) and Mowbray (1960) that with sufficient practice or familiarity, reaction-times for degrees of choice at least up to 10 can be brought to the same level as two-choice, even though the relationships between signal and response are not entirely direct. The degree of indirectness in the former case was slight – responses were made by keys under the subjects' fingers and the signal lights were laid out on a panel in the same pattern – and subjects were given extensive practice with two and four choices. Reaction-times rose appreciably with degree of choice early in practice but became equal after some 36,000 reactions had been made. In the latter case a familiar relationship was used – the signals were digits shown singly and the subject responded by speaking the number concerned. With different groups, 2, 4, 6, 8 or all 10 digits were used. Mean reaction times were very similar for all groups.

Unfortunately a doubt attaches to the interpretation of these results. In Leonard's and Mowbray and Rhoades' experiments each subject performed with every degree of choice. Hick in his experiment (1952a) found that, under these conditions, performance with one degree of choice tended to affect performance with another, unless substantial practice with the new degree was given immediately before testing. Hick provided this practice but Leonard and Mowbray and Rhoades did not. Mowbray's (1960) experiment avoided this difficulty by using different groups of subjects for different degrees of choice, but failed to equate the amount of practice given with the several degrees: each of the signals used in any condition was presented 60 times to each subject, so that those who were given two choices had a total of 120 trials, whereas those with 10 choices had 600. There were similar inequalities of practice in the other experiments. In Leonard's experiment subjects had 120 8-choice signals for every 80 4-choice and 48 2-choice. In Mowbray and Rhoades' experiment subjects had twice as many 4-choice signals as 2-choice. Leonard (1958), Mowbray and Rhoades' and others have shown that reaction times can shorten appreciably with practice, so that the additional practice given with higher degrees of choice would have tended to bring the reaction times for the different degrees closer together.

A further warning is contained in results obtained by Fitts and Switzer (1962). They found that mean times to repeat digits projected on a screen rose progressively with number of alternatives when familiar sub-sets were used such as 1, 2; 1, 2, 3, 4; or 1–8, but that results were less regular with unfamiliar sets such as 2, 7; 4, 7; or 4, 5, 6, 7. Similar results were obtained when the familiar sub-set A, B, C was compared with the unfamiliar E, B, P. The latter produced response times comparable with those when the whole alphabet was used, and suggests that when a subject has to deal with an *un*familiar sub-set drawn from a larger familiar set, he cannot rid his mind of the unwanted members of the larger set. In such cases the failure of reaction time to rise with size of sub-set does not imply a breakdown of Hick's Law in any fundamental sense – it merely implies that the size of set from the subject's point of view is larger than it is from the experimenter's.

In line with the results of these experiments are those obtained for maximum rates of reading. Pierce and Karlin (1957), using words drawn from the most frequent 500 in American use found that average reading time rose from about ·26 to ·31 sec per word as the vocabulary rose from 2 to 16 items – an incremental rate of about 60 bits per sec. There was a further rise to about ·40 sec when words were randomly drawn from a 5,000-word dictionary but, as the authors point out, these words were often longer. Average times were, however, closely similar for vocabularies of 16 to 256 common words and this fact has led the authors and others since to conclude that maximum reading rate is independent of the information contained in the items. It seems very possible, however, that it is difficult to abstract a restricted vocabulary from the totality of common words. Further evidence pointing in the same direction comes from two experiments by Conrad (1962a). In the first subjects read, as rapidly as possible, nonsense syllables drawn randomly from lists of 4, 8, 16 or 32. The times taken increased with the number of alternatives, but the increase was less for syllables having a high association-value than for those having a low one. In the second experiment subjects read lists of nonsense syllables drawn from either 4 or 32 alternatives on three successive days. The times required to read the lists decreased markedly and the difference of times for the two lists also decreased although it remained appreciable. By contrast over the same period, the times taken to read familiar three-letter words diminished little and the times for lists drawn from 4 and 32 alternatives were closely similar.

There is an additional difficulty in using maximum reading rates as a measure of capacity for processing information, in that the rates may well reach the level at which motor factors and the monitoring of speech limit performance. Admittedly reading of random words is, as Pierce and Karlin showed, slower than repeating a sentence over and over, but this latter is not an adequate control task since the repeated sentence will almost certainly not be monitored to the same extent as random words and may well not be so precisely pronounced.

Whatever reservations there may be about the view that compatibility and familiarity can *abolish* the rise of reaction time with degree of choice, there is clear evidence that they can markedly *reduce* it. Three sets of experiments may be especially mentioned:

Firstly, Davis *et al.* (1961a) played nonsense syllables recorded on tape to their subjects who responded by repeating each syllable as quickly as possible. The times taken to repeat back syllables drawn at random from sets of 2, 4 or 8 rose as predicted by Hick's Law. The slope flattened rapidly with practice from about 25 to 100 bits per sec: the two-choice time remained about the same while the times for four and eight choices became markedly shorter. The authors also argued that for very familiar sets the slope should be low without practice. Comparing digits with letters – a set of 10 with one of 26 – they found a difference of time which implied an incremental rate of about 70 bits per sec.

Secondly, Knight (1967) measured subjects' reaction times for all degrees of choice from 1 to 8 on two successive days: the subjects then practised the 8-choice task for 16 min per day for 20 days – five days per week for four weeks. After a further test similar to that on the first two days they again practised for a further eight weeks after which a final test was given. The simple and two-choice reaction times were little affected by the practice, but those for higher degrees of choice were all markedly reduced. The average slope from 2 to 8 choices on the first day was about 14 bits per sec. After both one month and three months of practice it had flattened to about 43 bits per sec but still remained appreciable.

Thirdly, the effects of compatibility on reaction time are shown by Brainerd *et al.* (1962) who gave their subjects two-, four- and eight-choice tasks with all possible combinations of two types of signal and two types of response. The four combinations, ranging from least to most compatible, and the results obtained are shown in Table 3.2. It

TABLE 3.2 *Signal-response combinations used and results obtained by Brainerd et. al. (1962). Figures are in bits per sec*

Signal	Response	Incremental rates of information transmission	
		Self-paced, presentation of signals in continuous series	Signals presented singly
Numbers projected on screen	Pressing keys corresponding to the numbers and placed conveniently under the subject's fingers	5·5	5·6
Lights arranged in same pattern as keys	Speaking numbers corresponding to lights	4·9	5·6
Lights as above	Keys as above	9·0	7·4
Numbers as above	Repeating the numbers	90·9	16·4

The results are based on a total of 240 subjects – 20 for each of three degrees of choice in each of the four conditions. Each subject had a run of 100 self-paced trials, and 50 trials with signals presented singly.

will be seen that the rates vary from values similar to those found by Hick and Hyman in the less compatible conditions to values similar to those obtained by Davis *et al.* with the most compatible.

Taking the evidence as a whole, two conclusions emerge clearly:

firstly, the flattening of the slope relating reaction-time to degree of choice is associated with increased familiarity or compatibility of the *relation between signal and response*. Thus in the experiment by Brainerd *et al.* the highest rate was attained when the familiar set of signals (numbers) was paired with its familiar, normal response (speaking). The next highest was when the unfamiliar set of signals (lights) was paired with a closely compatible but unfamiliar set of responses (key pressing). The numbers paired with key pressing or lights with spoken numbers both yielded relatively low rates. We can therefore identify the steepness of the slope as due largely to the involvement of the translation mechanism (Fig. 1.3, p. 19). We should perhaps add that the effect seems to be highly specific to particular conditions: for example Lamb and Kaufman (1965) and Kaufman and Levy (1966) using a highly compatible arrangement of lights and keys obtained nearly flat slopes relating times for different degrees of choice when all signals were of equal frequency, but in two choice tasks with unequally likely alternatives the less frequent response was substantially slower and the more frequent quicker than would be expected from the equal frequency results – the opposite of the result obtained by Hyman (1953) with his less compatible task.

Secondly, the flattening of slope represents a true raising of the rate of information transfer for higher degrees of choice: in other words, some of the 'work' that would otherwise have to be done by the translation mechanism has been saved. How this is achieved is not known, but one plausible suggestion is that the connections between various identifications and their corresponding responses become 'built-in' and thus ready for immediate use instead of having to be to some extent worked out afresh for each trial. Any residual rise of time with increase in the number of alternative responses might be due to the translation mechanism still requiring slightly longer time to deal with larger numbers of alternatives. This would follow, for example, if flattening of the slope implied a change from a selection procedure involving a series of sub-decisions to a single decision of the type envisaged in Fig. 2.9 (p. 45). Alternatively it might represent the time taken by the perceptual mechanism to identify the signal. For an answer to this question we turn to a further line of evidence.

SEPARATING IDENTIFICATION FROM CHOICE

Perhaps the most direct attempt to separate the times required for identification and choice is that of Hilgendorf (1966) using a task in which the signals were illuminated digits or other symbols shown on a small screen and the responses were made by pressing typewriter keys. Each trial started with the subject pressing on an additional 'home' key with the palm of the hand. He was instructed that as soon as the signal appeared he was to identify it and then press the appropriate key or keys on the typewriter. As soon as he raised his hand from the 'home' key the light illuminating the signal went out so that there was no chance of continuing to observe the signal once the responding movement had begun. Hilgendorf found that the total time to raise the hand from the 'home' key, press the necessary typewriter key or keys and return to the 'home' key was well fitted by Eq. 3.1 with a slope of about 5·5 bits per sec – a figure close to Hick's. The time between the appearance of the signal and raising the hand from the 'home' key was also well fitted by Eq. 3.1 but with a slope of about 27 bits per sec.

These results suggest strongly that identification and choice are separate processes with the former taking place much more rapidly than the latter. Further evidence leading to the same conclusion comes from two further types of experiment which we shall consider in turn:

Reaction to some only of the signals presented

Donders in his pioneer work (1868) studied not only simple- and choice- (a- and b-) reactions but a third arrangement which he termed the *c-reaction*, or as it has come to be called *selective response*. In this, two or more signals are presented, one at a time as in a b-reaction task, but response is made only to one. Donders found c-reaction times were intermediate between those for a- and b-reactions and argued that the difference between the b- and c-reaction times was the time required for choice of response, and the difference between the a- and c-reaction times was the time taken to identify the signal. Subsequent work has largely vindicated Donders' position, but has also shown that the situation is more complex than was originally supposed.

We may begin with an experiment by Broadbent and Gregory (1962) who compared two-choice b- and c-reactions for different levels of compatibility between signal and response. For the less compatible conditions c-reactions were quicker than b-reactions, as Donders found, but for the highly compatible conditions the times for b- and c-reactions were about equal – indeed the latter were slightly longer. The obvious implication is that in the highly compatible conditions identification of signal took no time at all. This equality cannot, however, be taken at face value. Forrin and Morin (1966) actually found c-reactions *sub-*

stantially longer than b-reactions, and suggested that the inhibition of response to the unwanted items affected the speed of reaction to the wanted ones. Mowbray (1960) found that c-reactions were quicker than b-reactions when response had to be made to one of two possible signals, but were substantially *slower* than b-reactions when response was to one of eight or ten signals, and suggested that this was because the average interval between responses was longer in the latter case: long intervals, like long foreperiods in simple reactions, should lead to long reaction times, and the c-reaction time may therefore be lengthened by temporal uncertainty effects. In confirmation, he noted (Mowbray 1964) that c-reactions are affected by the *distribution* of intervals between 'key' signals to which response has to be made.

Mowbray's suggestions can be tested by manipulating either the rate at which signals are presented or the relative frequencies of key and non-key signals so as to keep the mean times between key signals constant while varying the number of different non-key signals. Brebner and Gordon (1962, 1964) have shown that when this is done, there is still a rise of c-reaction time with number of different non-key signals, indicating that the time required to identify a key signal rises with the number of different non-key signals. It should be added also that Nickerson and Feehrer (1964) who exposed a series of letters one by one and required subjects to press a key in response to some but to ignore others, found that reaction time lengthened with increase in the number of letters to which response had to be made.

Perhaps the clearest confirmation of Donders' results is by Taylor (1966) who used a two-choice task in which one of two coloured lights was presented after a warning signal followed by a foreperiod ranging from ·8 to 1·5 sec. Taylor compared four conditions: (i) b-reactions in which responses were made to both lights, (ii) c-reactions in which responses were made to one light and the other was ignored, (iii) b-reactions in which only one light was used – one response was given to this and the other response was given when the warning signal appeared but no light followed – and (iv) c-reactions with response to the one light and no response to no light. Using only responses to the 'key' light, the difference between (ii) and (iv) provides a measure of the need to discriminate between signals and the difference between (iii) and (iv) a measure of the time taken for choice of response. The sum of these two differences should equal that between (i) and (iv). Taylor found that the first two differences were 25 and 22 msec respectively making a total of 47 as compared with 44 msec observed for the third – a very substantial agreement.

It should be noted that the c-reaction has obvious similarities to *scanning* tasks in which subjects search through lists for particular items – for example a particular letter or word among other letters or words. The concern of most of the experiments carried out so far is different from our present one, but Oostlander and de Swart (1966) have noted that the time required for searching increases with the size of the set from which the items have been drawn, in a manner consistent with Hick's Law. Time has also been shown to rise with the number of different items being sought in any one scan (Neisser, 1963, Kaplan and Carvellas, 1965, Kaplan *et al.*, 1966, Nickerson, 1966), and when the definition of a class of words or other signals sought is wide than when it is narrower (Foster, 1962, Neisser and Beller, 1965).

The broad indications from the evidence on c-reactions seem clear that, even when no choice of response is required, reaction-time rises with the size of the set from which the signals are drawn, so that it is difficult to avoid the conclusion that this time is taken in identifying the signal. The amount of the increase is usually much less than when responses have to be made to each signal and one must therefore suppose that perceptual identification proceeds much faster – between five and twenty times as fast – as the selection of response in situations where signals and responses are not highly compatible or familiar. If so, it is reasonable to regard the residual slopes found in such experiments as those of Davis *et al.* and Fitts and Switzer where signals and responses *are* highly compatible or familiar, as due to the time taken to identify the signals. It is perhaps fair to argue that there is a biological advantage in having the perceptual mechanism work substantially faster than the translation mechanism since it is much more at the mercy of external events which must be perceived as they occur. To do this a high peak capacity is needed even if on most occasions it is not fully used. Action, although it may have to keep approximately in step with events, usually permits some flexibility of timing and can thus be adequate with a lower maximum rate of information handling.

Fewer categories of response than of signal

Several experiments investigating the relative effects on reaction time of uncertainty regarding signal and response have used tasks in which more than one response has had to be given to any of two or more signals. The earliest is that of Crossman (1953) who found that the time taken to sort cards into two piles, one of Red Pictures plus Black Plain and the other of Black Pictures plus Red Plain, was similar to that for sorting into four suits and substantially greater than for sorting into two colours. This result was obtained from only one subject, but he had been well practised. It seems to favour the view that both the number of signal categories and response categories, or the number of *signal-response connections*, determines sorting time.

On the other hand, Morin *et al.* (1961), using a conventional choice-reaction task obtained indications that only the number of response categories was important, at least for well-practised subjects. They compared the five conditions set out in Fig. 3.7. Of these the first three are straightforward simple, two-choice and four-choice arrangements. Condition IV can also be regarded as a straightforward two-choice between circles and squares. The times for these four conditions

Signals:	●	■	●●	■■
Conditions:				
I	1			
II	1	2		
III	1	2	3	4
IV	1	2	1	2
V	1	2	2	1

Figure 3.7. Conditions used in a choice-reaction experiment by Morin *et al.* (1961).

The signals were projected from slides onto a small screen. The subject's responses were made by pressing microswitches on which his fingers were resting lightly. In each condition 10 subjects performed 7 blocks of 16 trials on each of 2 days.

The numbers 1, 2, 3 and 4 refer to the responses made to the signals under the various conditions.

rose as expected, although the increase from simple to two choice was somewhat larger than usual. Times for both two-choice conditions II and IV were closely similar. The crucial question concerned condition V, which was analogous to Crossman's task. The times for this condition were intermediate between those for the two- and four-choice tasks early in practice, but became virtually identical to those for two-choice after about 180 trials.

In order to pursue the apparent discrepancy of fact between the results of Crossman and of Morin *et al.*, Cameron (1964) used the latter's designs in a card-sorting task, reproducing conditions II, III, IV and V of Fig. 3.7. He found that the times for condition V were a little *longer* than for the four-choice condition III and much longer than for the two-choice conditions II and IV. Essentially similar results were reported by Fitts and Biederman (1965) who repeated conditions II–V of Fig. 3.7 in a task similar to that used by Morin *et al.* A possible explanation of the discrepancy between the results of the original and subsequent investigators lies in the fact that the subjects employed by Morin *et al.* were strikingly inaccurate, least so in the four-choice condition and most in condition V. The subjects in the other experiments made relatively few errors and their findings seem therefore to be the more worthy of acceptance.

The results surveyed so far, would be broadly consistent with the view that choice-reaction time is a function of the number of signal-response connections, so that in Crossman's task and condition V of Fig. 3.7 four rather than two connections were involved. To be precise it should be the probability of such connections rather than their number which influences reaction time, as is indicated in results obtained by La Berge and Tweedy (1964). Their subjects responded with one hand to a green signal and with the other to either a red or a blue. Reaction times to red and blue were influenced by altering their relative frequencies even though their combined frequencies, and thus the frequency of the response made to them, remained the same.

Results of experiments by Rabbitt (1959) suggest, however, that this view is too simple. His subjects sorted packs of cards on which letters or digits had been stencilled into 2, 4, 6 or 8 piles. With some packs only one letter or digit had to be sorted into each pile, with others 2, 3, 4 or 8. He found that the times taken rose sharply as the number of symbols per pile increased from one to two, but relatively little thereafter. Rabbitt repeated the experiment using a more conventional reaction-time apparatus with which subjects pressed keys in response to digits or letters projected on a screen, and found the same pattern of results, although only after fairly long practice. Very similar results have been obtained by Pollack (1963c) who timed subjects classifying lists of words into superordinate classes and varying in different lists the number of words belonging to each class. The times rose substantially with the number of superordinate classes. In most cases they also rose substantially with the number per class from one to two but relatively little thereafter. The same implication is perhaps contained in a further experiment by Rabbitt (1964) who found that when subjects sorted cards on which there was one relevant symbol and from 0 to 7 irrelevant, times rose substantially as between 0 and 1 irrelevant symbols, but little more with larger numbers.

These results suggest a two-stage process consisting of (i) the identification of a letter or digit or word as belonging to a particular *group* of symbols which the subject has been told to place together, and (ii) the selection of the correct response to it. These two stages seem unlikely to overlap because until the first has been completed the second can hardly begin. If so we can regard the times for one symbol per pile as a measure of the speed of (ii) and the differences between the times for one and two symbols per pile as a measure of the time taken by (i). The fact that in Rabbitt's (1959) experiment times continued to rise a little when six and eight piles were used with three or four symbols per pile could be accounted for by assuming that the subject has some difficulty in remembering the groups to which the 18–32 symbols concerned belong. This might imply a limit to the number of items which can be 'held ready' in some kind of short-term memory: if so, Rabbitt's results suggest the number is about 16. Such a two-stage process could equally apply to Crossman's and the other experiments using condition V of Fig. 3.7, if account is taken of inaccuracy in the case of Morin *et al.* The time taken to identify the group to which the signal belongs has been shown to vary with such conditions as the degree of familiarity of the grouping (E. Smith 1967), and presumably also varies according to the discriminability of the signals, so that it should not be expected, except fortuitously, to equal the difference between two- and four-choice reaction times. In an attempt to test the validity of this two-stage theory by comparing reaction times when the group to which a signal belonged was and was not indicated in advance, Forrin and Morin (1967) showed that the advance information did in fact save time, although not to the full extent predicted. If the theory is tenable there are evidently some complicating factors still to be worked out.

The question has been raised of whether the identification stage follows a serial classification¦ or a simultaneous one or, more specifically, whether particular *aspects* or 'dimensions' of a signal are identified separately in series or together in parallel. The problem has been lucidly discussed by Treisman (1966). We may consider it in terms of an experiment by Nickerson (1967a) who presented signals for brief intervals and required subjects to press one of two keys to indicate whether or not the signals satisfied certain criteria. The signals were of three shapes: circle, square or triangle; three colours: red, yellow or blue; and three sizes: large (2 in), medium (1 in) or small ($\frac{1}{2}$ in), in all possible combinations making 27 in all. In any run, half the signals satisfied the criterion or criteria and half did not. The criteria used are set out in Table 3.3 together with the predictions of the two different theories. Results were on the whole more consistent with series than with parallel analysis although Nickerson noted some anomalies requiring further investigation.

Indications that different features are processed independently are

TABLE 3.3 *Combinations of criteria used in a classificatory task by Nickerson (1967a), together with predicted results according to two theories of perceptual analysis*

Criteria designated as relevant	Predicted results if different features are analysed serially	Predicted results if different features are analysed simultaneously
Single Red ⎤ Other Circular ⎬ features Large ⎦ irrelevant	Quicker than both disjunctive and conjunctive.	Slower than disjunctive. Quicker than conjunctive according to Christie and Luce (1956) model.
Disjunctive Red *or* circular ⎤ Large *or* red ⎬ Large *or* circular ⎦	Slower than single. Quicker than or equal to conjunctive. Quicker if both criteria satisfied than if only one.	Quicker than both single and conjunctive. Quicker if both criteria satisfied than if only one.
Large *or* red *or* circular	Slower than other disjunctives.	Quicker than other disjunctives.
Conjunctive *Both* red *and* circular ⎤ *Both* large *and* red ⎬ *Both* large *and* circular ⎦	Slower than single. Equal to or slower than disjunctive.	Slower than single or disjunctive.
Large *and* red *and* circular	Slower than other conjunctives.	Slower than other conjunctives.

contained in the results of a series of experiments by Posner and Mitchell (1967). Subjects were presented with pairs of letters, which might be either capitals or lower case, and had to indicate as rapidly as possible whether the members of the pair were 'same' or 'different' according, in different runs, to criteria of either physical similarity (e.g. AA) or similarity of name (e.g. Aa) or according to whether both were vowels or both consonants (e.g. Ae or BC). The reaction times obtained were such as to imply that the processes involved in these three types of identification were independent, although it was not clear whether they occurred successively, or simultaneously with the subject reacting as soon as the longest required had been completed.

FURTHER STUDIES OF PERCEPTUAL SELECTION

The principles underlying the models we have outlined appear to apply also to the results of some other experiments on identification which are not concerned with reaction-times. For example, Fraisse and Blancheteau (1962), whose subjects identified nonsense-syllables drawn at random from sets known beforehand, found that the minimum time syllables had to be exposed to secure recognition rose approximately linearly with the logarithm of the number of syllables in the set from a mean of 12·9 msec with two alternatives to one of 15·4 msec with fifteen – a small but consistent and significant rise. As a further example, Miller *et al.* (1951) used monosyllables drawn at random from different size sets, again known to the subjects beforehand, and presented them through earphones in wide-band noise which made them difficult to hear. They found that the proportion of syllables heard correctly fell as the number of syllables in the set increased from 2 to 4, 8, 16, 32, 256 and 'all possible' syllables. Similar results were obtained by Miller (1957) who also showed that the fall became steeper as the signal-to-noise ratio became poorer. This kind of simultaneous relation to both set size and signal-to-noise ratio fits well with the simultaneous scanning models and with Fitts' approach to serial classification (p. 72) since in all these cases the subject's task is conceived as one which will be affected by both these variables.

Further evidence in the same direction has been provided by Reid *et al.* (1960) who found that words exposed briefly were more accurately perceived the greater the extent to which the category within which they fell was specified beforehand, and by Binder *et al.* (1966) who found that the accuracy with which parts of briefly exposed pictures of objects were recognised increased with the extent to which the pictures had been learnt beforehand. Such familiarity does not seem to affect the subject's ability actually to *see* the object, since it makes no difference to his ability to identify an object as the 'same' or 'different' from one exposed before: it is rather his ability to *identify* it that is improved (Robinson *et al.*, 1964). Long *et al.* (1960) have suggested that the reason for such easier identification is that the smaller the set the more the subject is able to identify and use 'key' distinguishing features between the different items. In other words, he can perceive accurately on the basis of a part only of the data. The same argument is used by Rabbitt (1967) to explain some of his results with choice-reaction tasks. Evidence in favour of this view is also contained in the fact that when irrelevant material remains the same throughout a trial or series of trials it has less effect than when it changes (Rabbitt, 1967a, Zeaman and Denegre, 1967).

Similar indications that the greater the information in the items presented, the stronger the signals required for adequate identification are given by experimenters using 'natural' sets of material. Postman and Bruner (1949) found that the exposure time required to recognise which of two words shown denoted a colour, was shorter than that required to decide which denoted either a colour or a food: the average times were 191 and 228 msec respectively. Again Miller *et al.* (1951) found that words were more accurately recognised when presented in sentences than alone. This result is to be expected from expression 3.4 since the context of a sentence severely restricts the number of words likely to occur at any point, so that if the subject can glean anything of the structure and content of the sentence as a whole, he is in effect recognising each word from a restricted range of possibilities.

Further effects of the sizes of 'natural' sets on identification are shown in experiments where subjects had to identify material without any previous indication of what the objects might be. For example, several investigators (see Spielberger and Denny, 1963) have shown that exposure times needed for recognition of common words are shorter than those needed for words in less frequent use. Turning to non-verbal material we may note particularly experiments by Verville and Cameron (1946) and by Wallace (1956). The former used incomplete pictures projected on to a screen until identified, or until 9 min had passed. The latter used geometric designs, silhouette figures and more complex pictures shown on a band moving behind a slit. The slit could be varied in width and with it the exposure time. Subjects were given exposures until recognition was achieved or until a fixed number (usually five) had been made. The authors in each case noted that subjects who tried an identification which they were told was wrong tended to choose others within the same general class before moving to other classes: for instance, if they had volunteered the name of an animal, they would try other animals before moving to, say, plants or inanimate objects. It looked, in short, as if their categories of identification were ordered in 'natural' sets of this kind and they tended to run through likely members of one set before moving to other sets. The relationships observed by Wallace between correct identification and exposure time are perhaps in line with this view. She found that the proportion of designs identified correctly rose approximately linearly with the logarithm of the exposure time totalled over all exposures. A sample of her results is given in Fig. 3.8. The slope varies with the complexity of the material, but seems to be strikingly linear in all cases.

The time relationships in these various experiments are what would be expected with a serial classification model operating 'in reverse'. When the total set of possible identifications is known in advance, the subject selects first a broad class, then finer sub-classes until one sufficiently precise is attained. When the total set is not known, he

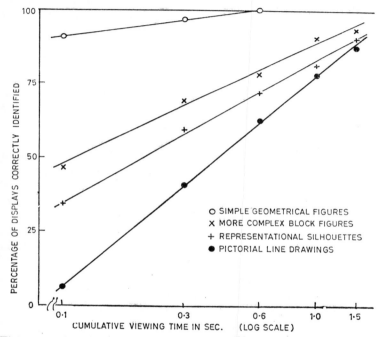

Figure 3.8. Results from an experiment by Wallace (1956) showing the increase in the percentage of displays identified correctly with increase in viewing-time.

Each of 16 subjects aged between 18 and 30 viewed 4 of each class of display.

selects a restricted class and runs through it, then if he is unsuccessful he tries progressively broader classes until identification is achieved. The perseverative tendencies shown by Verville and Cameron's and Wallace's subjects could be plausibly regarded as another manifestation of the after-effects already discussed in relation to the repetition of response. It is reasonable to suppose that any spread of effect from one member of a class will tend to affect other members of the class more than members of other classes: it would thus make identifications within the original class more readily available than those in other classes. Perhaps the most extreme form of this process is seen in senile states. Hurwitz and Alison (1965) note that a senile patient asked 'what is the capital of England' may correctly reply 'London'. If immediately after he is asked a different question such as 'what did you have for breakfast' he is likely again to reply 'London'. If, however, a few minutes' gap is left between the questions the answers to the second will also be correct – the after-effect of the first question and answer have died down so that the answer 'London' is no longer in the fore-front.

Selective perception

It has been recognised for a long time that a person reacts to only a small fraction of the total information that comes in through his sense organs. There appear to be two ways in which this selection occurs: firstly, if we conceive of identification as proceeding by a process of serial classification, one form of selectivity would be that classification is carried only so far as is necessary for the task in hand. Thus, for example, a subject sorting cards into suits observes the suit-symbols on the cards and ignores the numbers which on other occasions he might attend to. Many of the classical experiments on perception, showing that a broad design is observed while specific details are not, can be explained in this way.

A second method of selection appears to be that certain classes of incoming data are 'filtered off' at a relatively early stage of the perceptual process. This conclusion has resulted from a substantial number of experiments on selective listening. The subject is required to respond to one of two or more messages presented simultaneously, and to ignore the others. The task is in many ways analogous to Donders' c-reaction with more complex signals and, usually, more complex responses. Early evidence has been summarised by Broadbent (1958) to whom also much of it is due. We shall, therefore, outline only some of the main indications and more recent work.

When two conversations arrive simultaneously over a loudspeaker, subjects usually have difficulty in listening to one and ignoring the other (Broadbent 1952a). The effect has sometimes been thought to result from masking in the inner ear, but this is not so because on occasion the two voices can be distinguished reasonably well: the confusion is central. Selection is easier if the wanted and unwanted voices differ in physical characteristics, as when one is a man's and the other a woman's (Broadbent 1952b), or when one voice is used for both conversations but one conversation is louder than the other or has the lower frequencies removed (Egan *et al.*, 1954). Selection is also facilitated by spatial separation of the two voices in different loudspeakers, one on each side of the subject (Poulton, 1953). Similar improvements are obtained by using stereophonic recordings in which the two voices appear to come from different positions (Broadbent, 1954) or when the messages arrive with different relative intensities at the two ears (Treisman, 1964b). These results are in line with those of Hirsch (1950) who found that speech was easier to hear in noise if the loudspeakers conveying the speech and the noise were placed on opposite sides of the subject or when the speech was to one side and the noise directly in front. They are also in line with results obtained by Licklider (1948) who presented speech and noise in earphones and found that hearing was easier when the speech was in phase and the noise out of phase, or vice versa, between the two ears.

Taking these results together, they imply that selection can be made not only on grounds of straightforward physical characteristics such as pitch and intensity, but on more subtle phase differences between the two ears, and the various complex physical characteristics which differentiate one person's voice from another.

The clearest separation is obtained, however, if the wanted and unwanted messages are fed by earphones separately into the two ears, as in the now classical experiments by Cherry (1953). In these, subjects repeated ('shadowed') a message played into one ear while ignoring one played into the other. Practically nothing could be reported from the 'rejected' ear, and subjects were unaware of a change of language or the substitution of a record of speech played backwards.

Facts of this kind led Broadbent (1958) to postulate a 'filter' between the sense-organ and the central mechanisms responsible for identification, which can block off signals so as to pass only those with certain physical characteristics or from a particular sense organ. However, it soon became clear that the mechanism must be somewhat more complex. For example, Treisman (1964b) compared a condition similar to that of Cherry's experiments in which the two messages come one to each ear, with two other conditions: either one message came to one ear and the other to both, or there were three messages, one to each ear and one to both. She found, as expected, that rejection of the unwanted message was more difficult in both these alternative conditions than when one message had exclusive access to each ear. The separation of the messages to different ears did not, however seem to be the essential difference between the conditions, because in a control experiment in which the unwanted messages were rhythmic, repeated sounds, the separation of the wanted message from the unwanted was equally easy in all conditions. Again Moray (1959), repeating Cherry's experiments, found that the subject's own name would sometimes 'break through' to be heard if it was introduced into the unwanted message, and Peterson and Kroener (1964) found that some items from unshadowed messages could be recalled, although recall of the messages as wholes was poor.

Broadbent himself suggested (1958, p. 54) that the filter might act on *classes of words*, and cited evidence by Peters (1954a, b). Treisman (1964a) in a series of experiments in which two messages by the same voice were presented each to both ears and subjects repeated back one, found that more was correctly repeated when the wanted message was a passage from a novel and the unwanted a statement on biochemistry, than when both were from the novel. Still more was repeated accurately when the messages were in different languages or when one was nonsense or speech played in reverse. It is doubtful whether these are truly separations in terms of 'meaning' since even those subjects fluent in French did not reject a French translation of the passage from the novel any less successfully than an irrelevant passage of French. To some extent it may be in terms of rhythm or phonetic quality and is thus, perhaps, to be classed with selection based on difference of voice – Treisman in the same experiment noted that all these aids to rejection were much less effective than having the wanted message in a woman's voice and the unwanted in a man's. Whatever the exact basis of separation it is clear, however, that it could not have been by a purely peripheral filter – there must have been *some* analysis of the data before the rejection was made.

Treisman (1960) in an experiment in which subjects repeated the message to one ear and ignored that to the other, found that occasionally words from the unwanted message would break in if they were especially suitable in the context of the wanted message. The wanted message was connected narrative and the unwanted a statistical approximation to English. Half-way through a trial the messages were switched to opposite ears. Subjects were told always to repeat what came into one *ear*. At the changeover a few words from the wrong ear tended to break in without the subject realising they had done so. One example quoted by Treisman is given here, the words spoken by the subject are printed in capitals and the words rejected in lower case. The changeover point is indicated by the vertical line.

Wanted:	THE GROWL OF THE	GOAT*	swim	fast	DURING THE
Unwanted:	book is she went to	thunder INCREASED	STEADILY	and	the

* GOAT was a mishearing of GO TO.

Treisman suggested in explanation of these results and of Moray's finding that a subject's own name was sometimes heard from the unwanted channel, that the filter does not block unwanted messages completely but merely attenuates them. Several further experimental results support this view. Lawson (1966) combined the task of shadowing a passage played to one ear while ignoring a passage to the other, with responding to 'pips' played to either ear. The response consisted of pressing one of two keys according to the ear to which the pip had come. She found that all the pips were responded to although, in the case of the unwanted channel, responses tended to be slower and several were to sounds that should have been ignored. Treisman and Geffen (1967) in a somewhat similar experiment found that responses to certain words or classes of word designated beforehand could be made whether the words occurred in the wanted or the unwanted message, although very much more frequently with the former (86%) than with the latter (8%). The difference was greater than in Lawson's experiment, perhaps because her 'pips' were more readily discriminable than Treisman and Geffen's designated words. Looking at their results in signal-detection theory terms the latter authors found that, on the basis of correct detections and errors, β remained unchanged as between the two channels, but d' was substantially greater for the wanted than for the unwanted – in other words the criterion was the same for both, but the effective signal strength of the unwanted was lower. These results are similar in their implication to those of Broadbent and Gregory (1963a) who asked subjects to rate the confidence with which they judged a tone to be present in a burst of noise played into one ear while a string of digits was played into the other. They found that d' was substantially higher if the subject ignored the digits and reported only the tone, than if he had to report the digits as well. The general idea that attention to one signal attenuates data from other signals is also supported by the results of Webster and Haslerud (1964) who found that attention to either auditory signals or to signals in foveal vision raised thresholds and slowed reaction times for signals shown in peripheral vision, and of Yates (1965a) who showed that shadowing a message played into one ear was less disturbed by white noise in the other than by another message or by delayed feedback of the same message. It is also supported by recent evidence showing that electrical responses in the brain (evoked cortical potentials) produced by incoming stimuli are diminished when attention is directed away from them (Wilkinson 1967).

We may note in passing that Treisman and Geffen's results imply that the attenuation is in perceptual rather than response processes, since the response to the designated words was the same – tapping with a ruler – whichever channel the word was on.

The results we have surveyed seem clearly to imply that it is not enough to postulate a filter acting only on the input from the various sense organs and capable of discriminating against simple sensory categories such as pitch or intensity (Deutsch and Deutsch 1963). There must be some mechanism facilitating or inhibiting categories of identification. We are faced, therefore, with having to postulate at least two filtering processes or of explaining away the more peripheral in terms of the more central. It is, in general, reasonable to suppose that there may be two or more stages of filtering, but on the other hand explaining away the peripheral filter is perhaps not very difficult. Qualities such as loudness and pitch could be just as well filtered late as early if it is assumed that some representation of them remains, as it almost certainly must, after analysis in the perceptual mechanism. The chief reason for postulating a peripheral filter is the ease with which data from one ear can be excluded, but even this would be consistent with filtering after some analysis if it could be argued that the data enters the perceptual mechanism 'tagged' with the ear from which it has come. Some such tagging seems essential to account for the facts of auditory localisation – mere phase or intensity differences between the two ears without tagging would lead to identification of a signal as 'to the side rather than on the midline' but would give no indication of *which* side. If this argument is accepted, one filter system in the perceptual mechanism would be enough to cover not only the results of selective listening experiments, but Donders' c-reactions as well. How such a filter works and how many stages it entails, are matters for future research to decide. Meanwhile a first hypothesis would be that it operates in the manner of one of the models we have already discussed in relation to Hick's Law.

The experiments on selective listening, like those on selective response, can be conceived as having tried to hold the 'setting' of the filter constant and to study its limitations. They thus represent the opposite pole from choice-reaction experiments and perceptual identification tasks such as those of Miller *et al.* (1961) and of Fraisse and

Blancheteau (1962), which can be thought of as studies of the speed at which the filter can be reset from one item to another.

The mechanism of identification

To explain why it was mainly words which were appropriate in the context of the wanted message that got through from the unwanted, Treisman suggested that words are stored in some kind of 'cerebral dictionary' and that the occurrence of one word brings about some kind of partial activation of others which would normally tend to follow it. If one of these words is also partially activated by the attenuated unwanted message, the combined effects might be sufficient to cause it to be spoken. The same general principle seems to be illustrated in an experiment by Bruce (1958) who presented twelve-word sentences in noise and prefaced them by a word purporting to indicate their topic. He found that perception was more accurate when the prefatory word was appropriate than when it was not. Thus the sentence 'I tell you that our team will win the cup next year' was correctly heard when prefaced by 'sport', but when prefaced by 'food' became 'I tell you that our tea will be something to do with beer'. The effect is the verbal counterpart of the finding by Carmichael *et al.* (1932) that perception of designs seen briefly could be distorted in the direction of names given to them beforehand. Further support is given by experiments such as those of Pollack (1963) and Tulving and Gold (1963). The former showed that the hearing of words in noise was facilitated by giving one or more initial letters either before or after presentation. The latter obtained better recognition of words exposed briefly if a sentence leading up to them was shown beforehand.

The principle that the identification of an item can be influenced by spread of effect from other preceding, simultaneous or immediately succeeding items and that these effects may summate from different sources, is an extremely powerful one with very wide application. For example it accounts for the finding by Miller *et al.* (1951) that words are more readily identified in the context of a sentence. It accounts at the same time for the fact that perception may be easier if the signals concerned have been received before even though at such a low intensity that they could not be reported (for a review see Schiff, 1961), that signals can be detected at lower levels of intensity following a warning signal (Howarth and Treisman, 1961) and that familiar signals such as one's own name are detected at lower intensities than other signals (Howarth and Ellis, 1961). If similarity implies some kind of neural proximity, the same principle also provides an obvious framework of thought in which to account for the fact that errors and intrusions show similarities to correct responses, for example the phonetic similarities between errors and correct responses observed by Bruce (1958) for words in sentences and by Conrad (1964a) for individual letters heard in noise.

Looking at perceptual identification in broader perspective, we can think of each object seen or event which occurs as pre-activating potential identifications and responses for other likely objects and events which will, in consequence, when they arrive be reacted to more quickly than if they had occurred in isolation – in common parlance the subject knows what he is looking for and tends to ignore other things. Perception can thus be conceived as the continual formulation and checking of a kind of running hypothesis. In this process, regular and predictable chains of events may be dealt with so rapidly and readily that the subject is hardly aware of them: less well anticipated events which involve a revision of the hypothesis will engage his main attention. The span of such a running hypothesis involves matters of coding, checking and retaining data which we shall consider in more detail in later chapters.

IV

Single-channel Operation

We mentioned in Chapter 1 that Craik (1948) noted how the course pursued when tracking a moving target did not follow the target motion smoothly, but showed a series of oscillations, implying that correction of misalignment between target and follower was not made continuously but at discrete intervals of about half a second. In short, the human operator was performing as an *intermittent-correction servo*. Craik pointed out that this could not be due to the misalignment having to build up to some critical value before the subject could detect it, because the intermittency was not reduced by magnifying the display. Nor could it be due to any motor limitation, since hand movements of the extent and nature required could be made very much more rapidly than two per sec. The effect, he concluded, must be in the central mechanisms of the brain. We shall in the present chapter look more closely at the evidence on this point.

Searching for a cause of the intermittency Craik was led to consider the reasons for the reaction time between the presentation of a signal and the emergence of a response. He argued:

'We must . . . ask ourselves whether this delay is more likely to consist of the transmission-time of nerve impulses continuously travelling down an immensely long chain of nerve-fibres and synapses connecting sensory and motor nerves, or of a "condensed" time-lag occurring in one part of the chain. If the first hypothesis were correct, there would seem to be no reason why a continuous stream of incoming impulses should not evoke a continuous stream of motor ones. . . . If, on the other hand, the time-lag is caused by the building up of some single "computing" process which then discharges down the motor nerves, we might expect that new sensory impulses entering the brain while this central computing process was going on would either disturb it or be hindered from disturbing it by some "switching" system.

'These ideas can be tested to some extent by recording the human response to a series of discrete stimuli presented at various time intervals, to see whether there is a minimum interval within which successive stimuli cannot be responded to. Such an experiment is analogous to physiological investigations of the "refractory phase" of a nerve or synapse, as pointed out by Telford (1931). The results of Telford and of the writer suggest a refractory period of about ·5 sec, such that a stimulus presented within this interval after the preceding one is responded to later, or may be missed' (Craik, 1948, p. 147).

The use of the term 'refractory phase' was unfortunate because the analogy is not really at all close. Apart from the gross difference of time-scale, the refractory phase of nerves is clearly a recovery phenomenon whereas the 'psychological refractory period', as it has come to be called, is due to the time occupied by some central process of translating from stimulus to response. However, the idea of testing by experiments using discrete stimuli has been fruitful indeed, and to these we now turn.

THE EFFECT OF A SIGNAL DURING THE REACTION-TIME TO A PREVIOUS SIGNAL

The first experiments designed to test these ideas used a type of tracking task. The subject had to keep a pointer on a line drawn on a paper band which passed behind a narrow slit. From time to time the line abruptly changed position and the subject's reaction time (TR) to begin to follow it and movement time (TM) to reach the new position could be measured from the record of the pointer movements (Vince, 1948a, 1950). When a change of position was well separated in time from the previous change, TR averaged 250 to 300 msec. When, however, two changes (S_1 and S_2) occurred close together so that S_2 came during TR_1, TR_2 was longer than normal. With one class of exceptions which will be discussed later, the lengthening could be roughly accounted for by assuming that the central mechanisms took the same time to deal with the data from both S_1 and S_2, but did not begin to deal with those from S_2 until they had finished dealing with those from S_1. In other words, data from S_2 had to be held in some kind of store until the end of TR_1 when the central mechanisms became free. The events envisaged are shown in Fig. 4.1 and the result can be expressed in the equation

$$TR_2 = TR_1 + TD_2 - I \qquad (I < TR_1) \qquad (4.1)$$

where I is the interval between S_1 and S_2 and TD_2 is the time taken to 'process' the data from S_2: this was taken in Vince's case to equal TR

to a change of position well clear of others in time (Welford, 1952). Eq. 4.1 implies that if TR_2 were plotted against I and TR_1 had no variance, the result would be a line sloping at 45 degrees as shown by the solid line in Fig. 4.2. Since in any practical case TR_1 always does

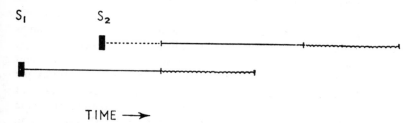

Figure 4.1. Lengthening of reaction time to a signal which arrives during the reaction-time to a previous signal.
■ = Signal —— = TD 〜〜〜 = TM . . . . . . = time held in store

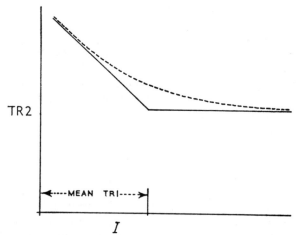

Figure 4.2. Ideal plots of TR_2 against I when S_2 comes during TR_1. The solid line shows the results expected if TR_1 is exactly the same in all trials: the dotted line shows those expected when TR_1 varies appreciably from trial to trial.

have substantial variance, the actual plot expected would be as shown by the dotted line in Fig. 4.2.

This result has been confirmed many times in subsequent experiments using lights or sounds as signals and key-pressing responses which make clearer cut measures of TR possible than Vince was able to attain.

Some of these experiments have followed Vince's in using a continuous stream of signals (Hick, 1948, Welford, 1959) but most have differed from hers in presenting discrete pairs of signals. The subject thus knew that in any one trial he would have only one signal in each of two classes. This procedure saves time but in some cases makes it difficult to estimate TD_2. If the subject does not know in advance which of the signals will come first, S_1 will require a two-choice reaction, but S_2 when it comes will require only a simple reaction (Elithorn and Lawrence, 1955, Marill, 1957, Halliday *et al.*, 1960, Kerr *et al.*, 1963, 1965, Elithorn and Barnett, 1967). The difficulty can be partly overcome by testing simple reaction time to each class of signals separately (e.g. Davis, 1956), but it is clear that conditions in this case are not always truly comparable with those when both signals of a pair are given (M. Smith, 1967b). The difficulty is reduced although not entirely eliminated when the subject is told in advance which signal will be S_1, so that this too leads to a simple reaction which can be used as an estimate of TD_2, or if both S_1 and S_2 are each drawn from different classes of two or more signals.

Despite their difficulties, these experiments show clearly that the delays which lengthen TR_2 are not eliminated by practice (Hick, 1948, Davis, 1956, Slater-Hammel, 1958), are central rather than sensory in origin because they still occur when one signal of a pair is visual and the other auditory (Davis, 1957, 1959), and are not caused by the actual *execution* of the movement (M_1) in response to S_1 because they occur when M_1 and M_2 are made by different hands (e.g. Davis, 1956), Welford, 1959). Indeed they sometimes occur when S_1 has merely to be observed and no response to it is required (Fraisse, 1957, Davis, 1959, Elithorn, 1961, Koster and Bekker, 1967), although they do not always do so (e.g. Borger, 1963). Davis suggested that delays occur in these latter cases when some established response to S_1 has to be inhibited or when there is difficulty in discriminating between S_1 and S_2. Some evidence for the latter view is provided by Rubinstein (1964) who found substantial delays when S_1 (to which no response had to be made) was a large-field stimulus to one eye and S_2 (which was responded to) was a similar stimulus to the other or when S_1 and S_2 were bursts of noise to different ears, but no delays when S_1 was visual and S_2 auditory or vice versa.

It seems reasonable to suppose that delays occur insofar as data from S_1 are processed immediately even though no overt response is made. Nickerson (1967c) has shown that delays when no response is required to S_1 are greater when it conveys information than when it can be ignored: for example when S_1 indicated to the subject which of two keys to press when S_2 arrived, delays were substantially greater than when S_1 was neutral and the indication of which key to press came only with S_2. The complementary finding was made by Davis (1965) that no delays occurred when, instead of S_1 being given, the subject himself pressed a 'trigger' key which led after a variable I to the appearance of S_2. This finding has, however, been both confirmed and challenged (Koster and Bekker, 1967, Kornblum and Koster, 1967). Some variability of result is perhaps to be expected since it may be difficult for the subject to ignore feedback from his triggering movement.

The evidence implies that although only one signal, or as we shall see later one *group* of signals, can be dealt with at a time, overlap is possible in the sense that data from one signal can be dealt with by the translation mechanism while that from a subsequent signal is being received and stored by the perceptual mechanism, and the response to a previous signal is being executed by the effector mechanism. It is the translation mechanism that seems to form the single channel which gives rise to the delays in responding to S_2.

If this is so, however, a difficulty arises with Eq. 4.1. Although it fits the facts well, it assumes that the time for which the single channel is occupied by data from S_1 is equal to the whole of TR_1, and takes no account of the fact that appreciable times are required for data to reach the cortex from sense organs and for efferent impulses and muscular contractions to make a response effective (Davis, 1957). A possible way of avoiding this difficulty is to assume that some minimum feedback from the responding action, indicating that it has begun, is necessary to clear the decision mechanism. If this were so, the time taken for efferent impulses to initiate a movement would automatically be included in the decision time, together with the time required for afferent impulses from the responding limb to return to the brain. This last time would approximately balance the time taken by external signals to reach the brain from a sense-organ, so that total reaction time would give a close estimate of the time required to make a decision and clear the mechanism in readiness for making another. The time relationships envisaged can be expressed in the equation:

$$TR_2 = TP_1 + TC_1 + TE_1 + TK_1 + TP_2 + TC_2 + TE_2$$
$$- (I + TP_2) \qquad (4.2)$$

where TP is the time taken in the sense organ and afferent pathways, TC is that taken by the central mechanisms, TE is that taken in the efferent pathways and TK is the time required for the kinaesthetic or other feedback from the responding limb to reach the brain. Since

$TP_1 + TC_1 + TE_1 = TR_1$, and $TP_2 + TC_2 + TE_2 = TD_2$, Eq. 4.2 reduces to Eq. 4.1 if $TK_1 = TP_2$.

Some feedback of the kind envisaged almost certainly plays an important part in checking whether errors have been made: in copying activities such as rapid typing, feedback data seem to be compared with some trace of the input and any discrepancy alerts the subject to stop and discover where the error has occurred. Support for the view that feedback is necessary to clear the central mechanisms to deal with further input data comes for the 'motor stuttering' observed with delayed visual feedback. A subject writing a word when he cannot see his hand directly but only via a television screen where its movements are shown after a delay of about ·5 sec will often repeat a letter, suggesting that the 'orders' to write it go on being effective until visual feedback confirming that it has been done are received (W. Smith *et al.*, 1960). Similar results occur with delayed auditory feedback: for example Chase *et al.* (1961a) found that subjects who had to repeat the sound 'b' or tap on a morse key in groups of three produced more sounds or taps than they should when feedback was delayed by about ·25 sec. Similarly Yates (1965b) showed that delayed auditory feedback impaired the accuracy of Morse code operators, usually by causing them to insert extra dots or dashes.

A more positive indication that such feedback time is included in decision time is perhaps contained in the finding by Fraisse (1957), Davis (1959) and M. Smith (1967c) that delays found when no response is required to S_1 are shorter than when a response is demanded – presumably in these cases the release signal for the decision mechanism comes from within the brain.

THE EFFECT OF A SIGNAL DURING THE MOVEMENT MADE IN
   RESPONSE TO A PREVIOUS SIGNAL

Several experiments have shown that some lengthening of TR_2 may also occur when S_2 comes shortly after the end of TR_1. Vince's (1948a, 1950) results suggested that if S_2 came during the initial 150 msec or thereabouts of M_1, dealing with the data from it was delayed until the end of this period (Welford, 1952). More recent results (Welford, 1959) where this point was examined in detail suggested that the delay was until the end of M_1. Probably the most plausible reason for the delay was given by Hick who suggested that 'the attention may be switched to that sensory field from which confirmation of the occurrence of the response is expected. Or alternatively, to avoid the teleological concept of "expecting confirmation", we may suppose that the attention is reflexly deflected by the inevitable stimulation of kinaesthetic or other receptors by the response' (Hick, 1948, p. 43). If this is so, and if the central mechanisms deal with data fed back from responses in the same way as that from signals coming from the outside, we should expect data from the beginning of the response to 'capture' the decision mechanism for a brief period (TFb) – in other words the response would be *monitored*. Any fresh signal from outside arriving after TFb had begun would be dealt with only after it had ended. TFb_1 might or might not coincide with TM_1: when it does so it may well be that M is 'tailored' to TFb rather than vice versa – we shall give other examples later of where this seems to be true (p. 127). The time taken by such monitoring presumably depends on the information conveyed by the feedback and will therefore, like reaction time, depend upon such variables as the frequency of the response as well as on its complexity.

The time relationships envisaged are expressed in the equation

$$TR_2 = TR_1 + TD_2 + TFb_1 - I$$

$$(TR_1 < I < (TR_1 + TFb_1)) \quad (4.3)$$

Delays in responding to S_2 have also been found when it comes shortly after the end of M_1, suggesting that the decision mechanism may become occupied for a further brief period at the termination of M_1 if no S_2 has by then arrived. The time of occupation cannot be measured with certainty but has been estimated for Vince's experiments at about 150 msec (Welford, 1952) and for the present writer's (Welford, 1959) at about 200 msec – in each case a time similar to TFb. It seems reasonable to suppose that *any* 'high point' of kinaesthetic, tactile or other stimulation arising during a response might capture the decision mechanism and that the end of a movement often provides such a 'high point'. Alternatively, there may be some monitoring of the completion of each response which enables the subject to set himself in readiness for the next. The time relationships involved are set out in the equation

$$TR_2 = TR_1 + TD_2 + TM_1 + TFe_1 - I$$

$$((TR_1 + TM_1) < I < (TR_1 + TM_1 + TFe_1)) \quad (4.4)$$

where TFe is the time for which the decision mechanism is occupied by data fed back from the end of a response.

If neither TR_1, TFb_1 nor TFe_1 varied from trial to trial the plot of TR_2 against I would, according to Eqs. 4.1, 4.3 and 4.4, assume a saw-tooth form, starting high when I was short, and falling at 45 degrees as in Fig. 2 until the end of TR_1; thereafter it would rise sharply to fall at 45 degrees until the end of TFb_1, and would rise again at the end of M_1 to fall once more at 45 degrees to the end of TFe_1. Variations in the times concerned will, however, always obscure this picture and tend to produce a gradual fall of TR_2 as I increases up to a point some time beyond the end of M_1.

Confirmation that monitoring of the kind envisaged in Eqs. 4.3 and 4.4 does in fact occur and that it takes time is contained in the results of an experiment by Leonard (1953). His task could be presented in two ways. In the first a lever had to be moved to the corner of a triangular guide corresponding to that of a signal light in a triangular display. On reaching this corner the light would go out and another one of the three come on, and so on. The task in the second condition was the same, except that with each light a second light came on which gave the subject foreknowledge of which light would be the next in the series. Performance in the second condition was faster than in the first, presumably because the advance signals enabled a decision to be made about the direction of each movement during the preceding movement. The important point in the present context is that the advance signals also seemed to prevent attention to feedback from the responding movements. Many subjects, to their surprise, found that with the second condition in contrast to the first, they had little awareness of what they were doing – the movements seemed 'automatic' and without conscious control.

Why the signals in the display should have taken precedence over the monitoring of responses is not easy to see, but Leonard's experiment is not alone in posing this problem. If Eq. 4.1 holds, it seems clear that whenever S_2 comes during TR_1 monitoring of M_1 must either be cut out or deferred, otherwise TR_2 would be lengthened by a delay to the end of TFb_1 or even TFe_1 instead of to the end of TR_1. This is a point which merits further investigation. Meanwhile we may note that performance in Leonard's experiment when advance signals were given seems in many ways comparable with that of expert semi-skilled industrial repetition workers who, over months and years at the same job, attain high speeds of working while at the same time losing awareness of their detailed actions.

Davis (1956) and Marill (1957) in paired signal experiments with simple key-pressing responses, found no lengthening of TR_2 if S_2 came after the end of TR_1 – it looked, in fact, as if the responses made by their subjects were not being monitored. This is plausible in that practice is likely to increase the accuracy of actions so that they do not need to be checked – in other words, the feedback will become redundant (Annett,

1966a). The amount of practice needed before this state is reached is likely to increase with the complexity of the response: for simple actions such as those used by Davis and Marill, the practice possible within a normal laboratory experiment could well be sufficient. With more elaborate, graded actions, however, the practice required to do without monitoring would probably be much longer, and attained only by musicians, typists, industrial repetition workers, professional games players and others who exercise a skill over a number of years.

SOME ANOMALOUS RESULTS

Although Eqs. 4.1, 4.3 and 4.4 seem to hold reasonably well for a very substantial range of experimental data, there are two important types of case in which TR_2 tends to be shorter than these equations predict.

Grouping of signals and responses

When I is very short, reaction to S_2 is sometimes delayed as Eq. 4.1 predicts, but is often hardly delayed at all. When this is so, however, there are signs that M_1 and M_2 are in some way co-ordinated: in some cases both are made simultaneously or M_2 begins before M_1 has finished; sometimes the responses are in the wrong order suggesting that the order of S_1 and S_2 has not been resolved: an interesting discussion of temporal factors in the perception of simultaneity is given by Norman (1967). More often temporal order seems to have been perceived correctly, but as a unitary pattern. In Vince's experiments, where S_2 in effect cancelled S_1, the total result with short I was sometimes that no response was made. In some cases the short TR_2 is coupled with a TR_1 which is longer than normal, suggesting that the subject has as his categories of response, not only M_1 and M_2 but also $(M_1 + M_2)$ which, because it is rare, takes longer to produce (Hick and Welford, 1956). In other cases both TR_2 and TR_1 seem unusually short suggesting that, when both signals have appeared, the subject makes an undifferentiated, and therefore rapid, response to both. The different types of grouping effect have been illustrated by Halliday *et al.* (1960), by Kerr *et al.* (1963, 1965) and by Elithorn and Barnett (1967) although their evidence has to be taken with caution because they used *only* short Is (of up to 100 msec) and the subjects' whole strategy of performance may therefore have been different from that in experiments where a wider range of Is were presented.

The evidence suggests that when I is very short – up to about

100 msec – S_1 and S_2 may in some way be treated together as a single *group*. Such grouping might arise if the subject deliberately waited a brief interval after S_1 to see if any further signal arrived before committing himself to a response. This seems to have been done by one group of Adams' (1962) subjects and by one of Borger's (1963) subjects, and was clearly done by Sanders' (1964) subjects when instructed 'to collect all perceptual data before any response is carried out' as opposed to completing TR_1 'without taking any notice of S_2'. Alternatively grouping might occur if both S_1 and S_2 arrived while the decision mechanism was occupied with a previous signal, so that data from both were waiting when the mechanism was cleared.

These explanations are, however, insufficient to account for all cases and it seems necessary to postulate in addition that the 'gate' which prevents data from subsequent signals entering the decision mechanism once it has started its computations, takes an appreciable time to close. The time appears to average about 80 msec: signs of grouping are very frequent when I is less than this, rare when it is greater. The time is probably, however, affected by a number of factors at present imperfectly understood: for example Kerr *et al.* (1963) found grouping to be less frequent when S_1 and M_1 were on the non-dominant side and S_2 and M_2 on the dominant than with the reverse order of sides, but that among grouped responses those where TR_2 was especially short tended to follow the presentation of S_1 to the dominant side. Meanwhile it is perhaps significant that the time during which grouping occurs is very similar to that over which perception of a pattern exposed briefly (say for ·1 sec) can be prevented by a subsequent bright flash of light (e.g. Cheatham, 1952).

The result of such grouping is that, if grouped and ungrouped responses are not separated, the average TR_2 is shortened (e.g. Slater-Hammel, 1958, Adams, 1962). In extreme cases it is actually *shorter* when I is very short than when I is a little longer instead of falling continuously with increase of I in accordance with Eq. 4.1 (Elithorn and Lawrence, 1955, Marill, 1957, Koster and Bekker, 1967).

It must be emphasised that grouping of this kind is not a process confined to the conditions we have been discussing, but seems to be a common – indeed essential – feature of many high-speed performances. Craik (1948) pointed out that if a musician dealt with each note, or a typist with each letter, separately they would perform very much more slowly than they in fact do. The rates actually attained imply that the decision mechanism takes in data from whole musical phrases or words or even groups of words as single units and issues 'orders' to the effector side in terms of correspondingly complex series of actions. Vince (1949) has demonstrated this point with experiments in which subjects had to tap a Morse key in response to dots on a paper band moving past a slit in a screen. She found the number of dots that could be reacted to accurately was very much higher if they appeared in groups of two, three or four than if they were presented singly.

Selective perception

A special question about grouping arises with regard to certain aspects of selective perception discussed in the previous chapter (pp. 98–103). In a general way the single-channel model covers the facts of selective perception in that when two or more streams of data each require different actions, only one is dealt with at a time unless the data and actions can be in some way co-ordinated. However if, as we have suggested, signals queue until the decision mechanism is free, we should expect rapid alternation between tasks according to the precise moments at which signals in the different streams arrive, so that it should not be possible to keep attention focused on one stream to the exclusion of others. This can nevertheless be done in experiments such as those of Cherry and Treisman surveyed in the previous chapter (pp. 99–101) in which subjects repeat ('shadow') a passage of prose played into one ear while ignoring a different passage played into the other, and the question arises of why there is not instead continual switching from one passage to the other? Admittedly, as we have seen, occasional words from the passage to the neglected ear are produced, but these seem to be determined by their appropriateness in the context of the shadowed passage or because of special familiarity – such as the subject's own name – and not by their precise timing.

Broadbent (1957b) has suggested that a continuous flow of data through one sensory channel might of itself be enough to maintain the attenuation of data from others, and certainly he has shown (1952b) that when the individual words of two messages are presented alternately, selective listening to one is difficult. Vince's and subsequent experiments suggest, however, that continuity would have to be such that no gap occurred which was longer than about 80 msec – that is the time taken for the 'gate' to close. Such a maximum seems impossibly short, so that some additional reason for the maintenance of selectivity is required. One possibility is to postulate a filter or switch prior to the decision mechanism which enables data from all channels except one to the excluded (Broadbent, 1958), but this has the disadvantage of making an *ad hoc* addition to the chain of mechanisms between input and output. The alternative seems to be to question whether the time taken by the gate to close is always as short as Vince's and subsequent experiments suggest. Is it, perhaps, that with more connected data, especially with verbal material in which coherent phrases last much longer than 80 msec, the 'grouping period' can be lengthened and with it the gap that can be left before attention is spontaneously switched elsewhere?

Modification of response

Several studies concerned with the single-channel hypothesis have examined the time taken to modify an action (Vince, 1948b, Hick, 1949, Poulton, 1950). The results appear to be consistent with Eqs. 4.1, 4.3 and 4.4, the equation applicable depending upon whether the modification depends on an amending signal given during TR_1, upon the beginning of M_1 or upon its results. In some tracking experiments, however, modifications are occasionally made in a very much shorter time than these equations would predict – in about 100 msec as opposed to 200–300. It is perhaps reasonable to regard these as cases where an error has been made by the central effector mechanism rather than by the decision mechanism – the 'orders' given by the latter have been correct, but have not been correctly carried out. Such modifications seem to imply a comparison of feedback from the moving member with the decision mechanism's 'orders', and correction without the issue of fresh 'orders'. If this is true, modifications should take place in these cases without visual observation of the error concerned.

Some evidence supporting this view is provided by Rabbitt (1966c) who found in a serial choice-reaction task that errors could be detected and corrected even when no indication that they had occurred was given by the display, and that corrections were in most cases substantially faster than the corresponding accurate responses. However, although corrections tend to be quicker than accurate responses (Rabbitt, 1966a, Rabbitt and Phillips, 1967) they are often not greatly so, suggesting that in these cases an error has occurred in the translation mechanism and that some of the work of selecting the response has therefore had to be done again. It is understandable that in these cases the correcting response should still be somewhat quicker: Rabbitt (1967b) cites an unpublished study by Burns who showed that errors in choice-response tasks were not entirely random but were in part correct. They might, for example, in a four-choice task be in the correct pair but the wrong member of the pair. This is not the whole explanation because Rabbitt

(1967b) has shown that responses to errors may be faster even if they are quite different from correct responses. He used a choice-reaction task in which responses were given by keys under the several fingers of one hand. Whenever an error was made the subject had to depress keys under both thumbs. Rabbitt regarded this as an 'anatomically awkward' response, but from what was said in the last chapter (p. 78) about the neurological control of the fingers, it might be regarded as relatively easy and thus understandably fast: while each finger would have to be depressed individually without moving the others, the thumbs could be depressed by a relatively gross rotation of the hands. It should be emphasised in passing that rapid correction of errors is by no means universal: in some cases it takes substantially longer than making a correct response (e.g. Adams and Chambers, 1962). We may surmise that in these cases there is not only recalculation of orders by the translation mechanism, but some review of the strategy of performance.

The corrections discussed by Rabbitt do not seem to involve any breach of the principle implied in Eqs. 4.1, 4.3 and 4.4. A clear breach does, however, seem to be shown by the results of an experiment by Vince on changing the *speed* of a response (Vince and Welford, 1967). These results suggest that an amending signal may sometimes get through the closed 'gate'. Subjects were presented with vertical lines rising 1·5 in from a baseline on a paper band revolving on a kymograph drum behind a screen in which was a vertical slit 10 mm wide. The lines were spaced so as to appear at irregular intervals of 2–3 sec. One group (A) was told that as soon as a blue line appeared they were to draw a line of the same length in the slit and then return to the baseline, making the whole movement smoothly and without hurrying. After some practice lines they were told that occasionally a red line would appear, in which case they should make the movement as rapidly as possible. A second group (B) made their normal responses to the blue lines as rapidly as possible and their occasional responses to the red lines at leisure. A third group (C) were given the same instructions as group A, except that when a red line occurred they were to stop their movement and pause before returning to baseline.

The results are set out in Fig. 4.3, in a way suggested by Bertelson (1967a). They consist of all cases in which S_2 arrived during the reaction time to S_1 and separate responses were made to both. Cases were excluded in which the response to the red line was wholly substituted for that to the blue – a kind of grouping effect which sometimes occurred when the interval between S_1 and S_2 was less than 100 msec. According to the hypothesis, the points for each group should lie on a straight line sloping at 45 degrees. Those for group B are in very fair agreement with prediction, and this was so for each of the subjects individually. The fact that the observed TR_2 were rather too long when S_2 came only a short

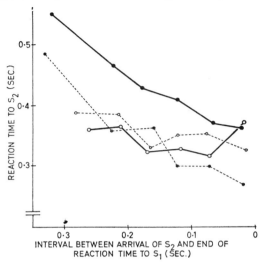

Figure 4.3. Times taken to modify the speed of a response. Results of an experiment by Vince (Vince and Welford, 1967).

    O——O, Group A (slow to fast): three subjects.

    ●——●, Group B (fast to slow): three subjects.

    O – – O, One subject in group C (slow to stop) whose performance resembled that of group A.

    ● – – ●, Two subjects in group C whose performances resembled that of group B.

Each point is the mean TR_2 for a range of intervals between the arrival of S_2 and the end TR_1. The ranges (from right to left) in msec were 0–49, 50–99, 100–149, 150–199, 200–249 and 250 and over. The numbers of readings contributing to each point for groups A and B vary from 7 to 38 (mean 20); those for the single subject in group C from 2 to 14 (mean 8·2) and for the two subjects in group C from 7 to 21 (mean 13·7).

time before the end of TR_1 may have been due to monitoring of M_1: feedback from the beginning of M_1 may have become grouped with S_2 and thus lengthened TR_2. The results for group A showed no systematic trend and this was again true for each subject individually. Two members of group C behaved like those of group B: their shorter mean reaction times are understandable in that the decision to stop a response is probably simpler than one to change its speed. The third subject in group C behaved like those in group A.

The results suggest an important refinement of the single-channel hypothesis. The central processes following S_1 were concerned with the initiation of a phased pattern of muscular action, which had to be modified in response to S_2. Clearly, the extent of this modification was very different for groups A and B. The latter, in order to slow a movement down, would have had to change the pattern of muscular innervation substantially, bringing antagonists into play in order to arrest the rapid motion. For group A, however, the speeding up seems likely to have involved merely an intensification of the pattern already in operation. Group C should at first sight all have behaved like group B, but it is possible that the subject whose performance was like that of group A managed simply to discontinue his movements instead of actively arresting them. If so, it seems reasonable to suggest that the decision process protected by the 'gate' is the *initiation of a fresh pattern of action*, or to put it another way, the *changing of relations between input and output*. Thus a signal to bring other muscles into play is excluded, while signals conveying instructions merely to increase or reduce the activity of those already in action can get through.

Indications that the gate does not block potentially interfering signals completely but merely attenuates them is in any case suggested by the results of several experiments in which TR_1 has varied with I, sometimes increasing and sometimes decreasing, although the amounts have been small. Further indications are contained in an experiment by Helson and Steger (1962) who found simple TR to be lengthened by the occurrence of a second signal to which the subject did not have to respond. S_2 was presented from 10 to 180 msec after S_1. The effect was maximum (13%, i.e. about 25 msec) when I was 40–120 msec. It was less with longer Is, perhaps because in many cases TR_1 was by then over. This additional evidence is, however, not strong for two reasons. Firstly Koplin *et al.* (1966) failed to duplicate Helson and Steger's results; secondly Gottsdanker *et.al.* (1963) found some lengthening of TR under these conditions even when S_2 came ·5 sec after S_1. In this case I was clearly too long for there to have been any interaction of S_2 with the decision relating to S_1, and the lengthening of TR_1 must imply a change of strategy on the subject's part. If so, a similar change might underlie the lengthening of TR_1 in other cases as well.

More generally, the results reported by Vince and Welford are perhaps consistent with the finding that an irrelevant stimulus given just before a signal can quicken response, and that the quickening is greater with strong than with weak stimuli (John, 1964).

ALTERNATIVE THEORIES

Anyone who has attempted to test the single-channel hypothesis will know that the experiments required are difficult to conduct and still more difficult to interpret and present clearly. It is therefore understandable that despite almost overwhelming evidence, a number of alternative explanations have been offered. These have been discussed by the present writer (1952, 1959), by Bertelson (1966) and by M. Smith (1967a) so they will be mentioned only briefly here, except for one about which evidence has recently accumulated. We may discuss them under four heads, showing in each case how far the theory accounts for the writer's (1959) data.

(*a*) An early suggestion was that there is a *refractory state*, independent of TR_1 and TM_1, following an event in some part of the chain of mechanisms leading from signal to response. Various periods ranging from ·1 to ·5 sec have been proposed. None of these gives a good fit to the data in that no one fixed interval will account for the observed delays both when S_1 comes during TR_1 and when it comes during TM_1 (see Table 4.1(a)).

(*b*) Several authors have proposed that perception may be quantised into samples about a third of a second long, and Broadbent (1958) suggested that a subject begins a new sample when S_1 arrives so that when I is less than a third of a second the data from S_2 have to wait until a new sample begins. This theory makes fairly close predictions of TR_2 in some cases but does not account for certain other features of the data. For example it implies that when S_2 comes during TR_1, TR_2 for any given I, or more generally $(TR_2 + I)$, will be independent of TR_1 whereas Eq. 4.1 implies they will be correlated. It also suggests that when S_2 comes during TM_1, TR_2 and TR_1 will be positively correlated since short TR_2 would be secured if TR_1 ended and S_2 arrived before the end of the first sample, but TR_2 would be much longer if S_2 missed the end of the first sample and had to wait to be dealt with until the end of the second. Substantial correlations were in fact found by both the present writer and by Borger (1963) when I was *less* than TR_1, becoming very low when I was *longer* (see Table 4.1 (b)). The theory also predicts that any factor affecting TR_1 will also affect TR_2 if S_2 comes during TR_1. This prediction was tested by Broadbent and Gregory (1967) who varied the degree of compatibility between S_1 and its corresponding response while holding the relationship between S_2 and its response constant. If intermittency is due to a division into fixed quanta, TR_2 should be unaffected by the compatibility of S_1 and its response: if the *given in msec. In all cases M_1 and M_2 were made with different hands. Reversed and grouped responses have been omitted. TD_2 has been taken as 282 msec. – i.e. the mean TR to a signal coming 1 sec or more after the end of the movement made to the preceding signal*

	S_2 arrives during TR_1		S_2 arrives during M_1		Total discrepancy regardless of sign	Correlation $(TR_2+I) \times TR_1$ for cases in which S_2 came during TR_1
	Mean	Predicted minus Observed	Mean	Predicted minus Observed		
Observed (± standard error of mean)	458 (±15)		393 (±14)			$\tau = +\cdot473$ ($p < \cdot001$)
Predicted						
(a) Refractory period of ·5 sec after beginning of M_1 before M_2 can begin	631	+155	409	+16	189	+
Ditto ·327 sec†	458	0	292	−101	101	+
Ditto ·1 sec	303	−155	282	−111	266	+
(b) Intake dealt with only at instant of S_1 and at intervals of ⅓ sec thereafter	434	−24	471	+78	102	0
(c) M_1 inhibits M_2 so that M_2 cannot begin until M_1 has finished: eq. (4)	312	−146	282	−111	257	+
(d) Temporal uncertainty	No quantitative predictions					0
(e) Single-channel hypothesis: Eqs. 4.1 and 4.3	413	−45	356	−37	82	+*

* More rigorous evidence for the single-channel hypothesis is a positive correlation between $(TR_1 - I)$ and TR_2. τ in this case was found to be $+\cdot466$ ($p < \cdot001$).

† The value of ·327 sec was chosen to give the result most favourable to the theory when S_2 came during TR_1.

121

single-channel hypothesis is correct the incompatibility which lengthens TR_1 should lengthen TR_2 by the same mean amount. They showed that the latter was true. Broadbent and Gregory also found that when one of the two possible signals which might constitute S_1 was given less frequently than the other so that the reaction time to it was longer than to the other, the delays to S_2 were also longer. Further confirmation is given by Smith (1967b) who lengthened TR_1 by reducing the intensity of S_1 and found that TR_2 was correspondingly lengthened.

(c) Elithorn and Lawrence (1955) seem to imply the suggestion that the results of experiments using pairs of responses made by different hands could be accounted for in terms of cortical or other central interaction. A somewhat similar suggestion appears to be made by Reynolds (1964, 1966). The fact that the cortical response to S_1 in some sense inhibits that to S_2 is not in doubt – it is indeed the foundation of the single-channel hypothesis. The question is whether the first response blocks the second at the output end of the decision mechanism or whether it blocks entry of data at the input end. At present the latter seems more likely on several grounds. If M_1 blocks the emergence of M_2, the lengthening of TR_2 should depend on TM_1 in such a way that in place of Eqs. 4.1 and 4.3 we could write

$$TR_2 = TR_1 + TM_1 - I \qquad (TD_2 < TR_1 + TM_1 - I) \quad (4.5)$$

This equation gives a very poor fit to the experimental data (see Table 4.1(c)). On an observational level, when grouping occurs one response seems often to facilitate rather than inhibit the other. If an argument on grounds of functional efficiency can be admitted, inhibition at the output end implies a wasteful manner of operation by the brain with two or more independent decision mechanisms each of which would presumably have less capacity than one which made use of the total resources available.

(d) The most persistently canvassed alternative to the single-channel hypothesis has been the suggestion that the delays in responding to S_2 can be accounted for in terms of temporal uncertainty effects. Many studies have shown that when a warning precedes a signal by an interval (foreperiod) which varies from one trial to the next, reaction to the signal is slower on those trials when the interval is very short – say 200 msec or less – than when it is somewhat longer: it is generally assumed, as we noted in the previous chapter, that the subject makes some kind of preparation during the foreperiod but that the state of preparedness cannot be held at optimum level for more than a fraction of a second, so that the subject prepares for the mean or modal foreperiod and is less than fully prepared if the signal comes earlier. We may note in passing that in signal-detection theory terms, the warning and preparation seem to lower β so that response becomes readier but less accurate. Bertelson (1967b) who demonstrated this showed that changes of reaction-time with foreperiod closely corresponded to changes in numbers of errors. He suggested that the warning signal may have a direct facilitatory effect by, in a sense, adding to the signal.

It has been held that lack of preparedness can account for the delays to TR_2 in the experiments we have been discussing, although it seems equally plausible, *prima facie*, that the temporal uncertainty effects are, at least in some cases, due to single-channel delays caused by the warning capturing the decision mechanism.

Attempts to distinguish between these views consist of separating temporal uncertainty and single-channel effects. The methods used so far fall into five classes:

(i) Klemmer (1956), Karlin (1959) and Drazin (1961) each controlled single-channel effects while varying temporal uncertainty by presenting a *range* of foreperiods which remained the same while the *minimum* foreperiod changed from one block of trials to another. Drazin, for example, compared ranges of 2·0–4·0 sec with 1·0–3·0, ·5–2·5, ·25–2·25 and ·125–2·125 sec. In all cases, reaction times were a little longer at the beginning of the range. The absolute lengthening – about 20 msec – differed little between the three higher ranges, all of which could be regarded as clear of single-channel effects. Klemmer's and Karlin's results were roughly similar. It looks, therefore, as if temporal uncertainty effects do exist apart from single-channel delays but that they are much smaller.

(ii) Nickerson (1965b) used a somewhat similar plan but required responses to both S_1 and S_2 while presenting different ranges of I: ·1–·5, ·3–·7, ·5–·9 and ·1–·9 sec. As I increased TR_2 became shorter over each of the ranges used, by about 60 msec in the ·1–·5 sec range to about 30 msec in the ·5–·9 range. Unfortunately little weight can be attached to his results as he took no account of possible effects of feedback from M_1.

(iii) Nickerson (1967b) secured the independence of temporal uncertainty and single-channel effects by arranging that I in a succession of trials varied in such a way that there was always at any instant an equal momentary probability of S_2 appearing. He varied this momentary probability in different blocks of trials, and found that TR_2 increased both with increase of I and with decrease in momentary probability, implying that both single channel and temporal uncertainty effects were occurring. Thomas (1967) has calculated from various sets of data by previous workers that expectancy in terms of the conditional probability that a signal will arrive, given that it has not arrived before, is insufficient to account for single-channel effects.

(iv) In some experiments temporal uncertainty has been minimised by keeping foreperiod length, or in double signal experiments I, the same over a block of trials. Subjective temporal uncertainty is not wholly excluded by this method since the subject's ability to judge time intervals is not perfect, but after a little practice temporal uncertainty effects seem clearly to be reduced (Reynolds, 1966).

(v) Several experiments have compared delays in double signal conditions when responses are required to both S_1 and S_2 with conditions when response is made only to S_2 and S_1 becomes in effect a second warning. Delays in the latter condition have almost always been substantially less than in the former.

Methods (iv) and (v) are both illustrated in an experiment by Kay and Weiss (1961) whose subjects made trials under several different conditions after considerable practice. In all cases a trial began by pressing a 'ready' key. There followed after a 1, 2, 3 or 4 sec foreperiod a click (S_1), and this was followed after an I of 25–1,000 msec by a second click (S_2). Their results are shown in Fig. 4.4. When both foreperiod and I were constant over a block of trials and no response was required to S_1 (condition cc), the subject could in effect begin to react to S_2 as soon as he pressed the 'ready' key although occasional catch trials in which S_2 was omitted would prevent him doing so completely before S_2 arrived. Both temporal uncertainty and single-channel effects were thus excluded and, as expected, TR differed little with I up to 250 msec. The slight fall of TR with longer I perhaps indicates that 500 msec or so were required to take full advantage of the warning given by S_1. With an irregular foreperiod (condition vc) S_1 would convey more information and it would be expected that its full benefits would take longer to realise. It is therefore not surprising that in condition vc TR became longer with short values of I. The extra delays with irregular I (conditions cv and vv) were clearly small and well within the range of temporal uncertainty effects found by Drazin (1961). The difference between TR_2 in conditions VC and VV in which a response had to be made to S_1 was also within this range. Delays in these latter conditions were much greater than when no response was made to S_1, and it is particularly important to note that delays were not abolished in condition VC when I was held constant: the delay here clearly cannot be accounted for in terms of temporal uncertainty. Similar evidence has

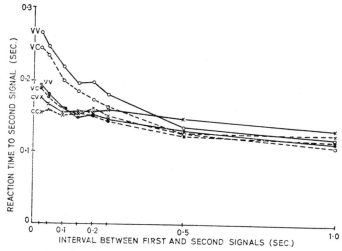

Figure 4.4. Results of an experiment by Kay and Weiss (1961). The results are plotted as follows:

	Foreperiod	I	Response to
cc	Constant	Constant	S_2 only
cv	Constant	Variable	S_2 only
vc	Variable	Constant	S_2 only
vv	Variable	Variable	S_2 only
VC	Variable	Constant	S_1 and S_2
VV	Variable	Variable	S_1 and S_2

The data are from a total of some 20,000 readings from five practised subjects.

been provided from experiments by Borger (1963), Creamer (1963) and Bertelson (1966, 1967a).

A further indication that the delays in responding to S_2 are not simply due to the effects of temporal uncertainty is the substantial correlation between $(TR_2 + I)$ and TR_1 shown in Table 4.1. Since temporal uncertainty should have nothing to do with TR_1, no correlation would be expected (Table 4.1(d)).

The predictions of the single-channel hypothesis shown in Table 4.1(e) give a better overall fit than any of the alternative theories although the times predicted are a little too short both when S_2 comes during TR_1 and when it comes during TM_1. The discrepancy is more than enough to cover the temporal uncertainty effects found by Kay and Weiss and by Drazin. Some at least of the extra time was probably due to grouping of Fb_1 with S_2 in a few cases when it came just before the end of TR_1

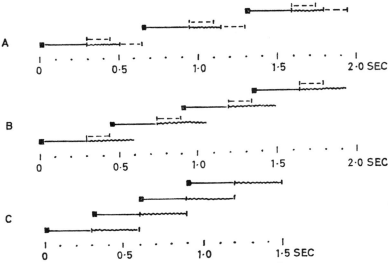

Figure 4.5. Successive responses in continuous performance.
A. When both *TFb* and *TFe* occur.
B. When *TFb* occurs but not *TFe*.
C. When all *TF* is cut out.

and produced very long TR_2s instead of the very short ones predicted by Eq. 4.1. Similar grouping may have occurred with TFe_1 when S_2 arrived close to the end of M_1. The instances were too few to treat separately, but had they been omitted from the calculations the mean TR_2s would certainly have been appreciably closer to those predicted.

THE SPEED OF CONTINUOUS PERFORMANCE

Craik (1948) assumed that the speed of a continuous performance such as tracking was limited by the times, firstly to observe and decide upon corrections for misalignments, and secondly to carry out the correcting actions – in short by the sum of the *TR*s and *TM*s involved. He observed, however, that correcting movements tended to run into one another as subjects became more practised and, as we have noted, subsequent work has shown that *TR* can overlap a previous *TM*. We should, therefore, rather say that, so long as *TM* is shorter than TR_1 the speed of a continuous performance will be limited by the decision times involved *plus* the times required to carry out any essential monitoring of responses – that is by the sum of *TR*s and essential *TF*s. This may be either greater or less than $(TR + TM)$ according to circumstances:

(*a*) When actions have to be carried out meticulously and the display is static, as for example when tracing carefully over a pattern, subjects may well monitor the ends of movements as well as any earlier significant points, as shown in Fig. 4.5(A), so that *TFe* will have to be added to (*TR* + *TM*).

(*b*) When action does not have to be so precise, or when the display is changing so that misalignments are continually building up, *TFe* is likely to be cut out, and the speed of performance limited by (*TR* + *TFb*) as shown in Fig. 4.5(B). For tracking, taking *TR* as 300 and *TFb* as 150 msec, as in Vince's (1948a) experiments, yields a correction rate of 1 per 450 msec which is close to the half second suggested by Craik, and in fact a better fit to Vince's data. This figure is also consistent with the breakdown of high-speed tracking performance found when the track changes direction more than about twice per sec (Welford, 1958, pp. 86–96).

(*c*) When the display changes very fast even *TFb* may fail to capture the decision mechanism. In tracking tasks this would follow from Eq. 4.1 if misalignment built up so fast that there was always a substantial correction waiting to be made before the end of the *TR* to the previous observation. Speed of performance in this case would depend on *TR* alone as shown in Fig. 4.5(C). Accuracy in these circumstances would, however, tend to be low unless responses were very simple and ungraded, since any error made in one movement could not be corrected in the next, but only in the next but one. This type of performance seems to have been attained in the writer's high-speed tracking experiments already mentioned: when the track was changing direction three times per sec, subjects maintained the correct *number* of changes, but accuracy was very poor compared with that attained with changes of two per sec or less.

Limitation of the speed of performance by decision processes rather than motor action is illustrated in several everyday activities, perhaps most notably in speaking (Goldman-Eisler, 1956, 1958, 1961, Henderson *et al.*, 1965). Although occasionally people think faster than they can speak, more often they are unable to formulate the content of a statement fast enough to maintain a constant rapid flow of significant words. They may in consequence speak slowly and so adjust the speed of action to that of central control. If not, they introduce redundant words or meaningless sounds (such as 'er'), make pauses or reduce the average information per word of their statement. Such effects tend to be more pronounced preceding high-information words and in sentences involving difficult constructions or other complex cognitive activity, as would be expected on the ground that these require relatively long times to retrieve data from memory or to order words in a sequence.

The fact that both data from outside and feedback from a subject's own voice have to be processed, and that doing so takes time, is illustrated in an experiment by Broadbent (1952a) in which subjects had to reply to a series of questions resembling military signals messages. Occasionally a question would be asked while the subject was answering a previous question. In these cases errors tended to occur either in the reply he was making or in replying to the message coming in at the time, indicating that the decision mechanism was being overloaded by the task of speaking and listening concurrently. Simultaneous translators seem to acquire the ability to do this after long practice, but they appear to operate under the conditions of Fig. 5(C), ignoring the feedback from their own voices. In consequence their speaking voices are often strange and they themselves report that they have little idea of what they are saying or confidence that it is correct.

MEASURING 'MENTAL LOAD'

Vince's (1948a, 1950) and the present writer's (1959) experiments presented examples of tasks which were *paced* in the sense that the times at which signals for action arrived were not under the subject's control. The load imposed on the operator varied from moment to moment and the times when two signals came close together can be regarded as brief periods of overload. In such a case the *average* rate of response is not an adequate measure of the demand made by the task: account must also be taken of the maximum instantaneous rate required – in other words of the way in which signals for action are from time to time 'bunched' together. A good example of the effects of bunching is given by Mackworth and Mackworth (1956) who used a task in which signals on a number of moving belts appeared for limited times in windows, and found that the number of signals missed was approximately linear with the extent to which the signals presented in different windows overlapped in time. Putting the matter another way, pacing reduces the extent to which a subject can compensate for slowness at one instant by extra speed at another, and thus increases the number of errors made at any given average rate of responding – as Bertelson *et al.* (1965) showed for operating a letter-sorting machine.

This type of task is analogous to many conveyor line and machine-minding jobs in industry. Often in these tasks the signals for action develop slowly and many decisions have to be made which do no issue in overt action. A detailed record of signals presented and of actions taken, even if it could be obtained, would therefore give an inadequate picture of the load imposed on an operator. The single-channel model suggests a way of measuring such loads: research is still in the exploratory stage, but two approaches appear promising. Both are based essentially on the simple assumption that dealing with the data from each signal requiring decision takes time, and that if this is more than the time available, responses will be delayed or omitted.

Attempts to measure loading directly

If the time t required to deal with each signal is an unvarying quantity and all signals arrive at identical intervals i, every signal can be responded to so long as t does not exceed i. If it does, every alternate signal can be responded to so long as t does not exceed twice i, and so on. The relationship between response rate and signal frequency will take the form shown in Fig. 4.6. Any variability in t or i will quickly lead to

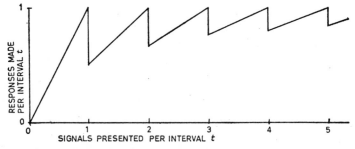

Figure 4.6. Theoretical relationship between response rate and signal frequency when each signal takes a time t to deal with and has to be responded to immediately it appears or be missed. Signals are assumed to arrive at equal intervals of time.

smoothing of the 'saw tooth' pattern and its replacement by a curve which is convex upward and asymptotic to a rate at which the subject's whole time is taken up in responding and there are no gaps during which he is waiting for a signal. The smoothing will be quicker still if he can not only respond to signals immediately they arrive but can also respond a little early or late. Such latitude can arise either from the arrangements of the display which enable responses to be made at any time during an appreciable period, or from the subject being able to predict items or hold them in running short-term memory, and for the present purpose all these are equivalent.

E

Conrad (1960b) has assumed that the number of responses made under paced conditions will be the same as the number made within the same time under unpaced conditions so that paced performance can be predicted from the distribution of unpaced performance times, but this is clearly not always so. Brown (1957) found that subjects in a plotting task made more plots under paced conditions than would have been predicted from their unpaced performances: detailed study of the results indicated, however, that their approach had become more hurried and the extra speed was attained at some cost in accuracy. Conrad himself (1956) in a study of telephone operators showed that the time taken per call decreased linearly with increase in the log frequency of calls coming in, although it is not clear how far this represented a true speeding up and how far a reduction of ancillary activities and is therefore an illustration of Parkinson's Law. Evidence on the precise effects of pacing on performance are surprisingly scanty.

The assumption that, even if t changes from unpaced to paced conditions, it is unaffected by *degree* of pacing yields reasonable results when applied to data obtained in a series of experiments by Conrad (1951, 1954a, b). The subject's task was to respond by pressing a key or turning a knob each time one of a number of rotating pointers coincided with one of several irregularly spaced marks on the edges of dials. The number of signal sources was varied by using 2, 3 or 4 dials in different trials and the signal frequency was independently varied by changing the speed at which the pointers rotated. An increase of either variable led to an increasing proportion of signals failing to secure a response. Conrad in a private communication has indicated that the rate of responding was not limited by motor factors – subjects could respond much faster when they made responses in a predetermined pattern without regard to the display, and although subjects were allowed to use both hands, the intervals between responses were such that they could easily have made them with one hand alone. The limitation seems clearly to have been in the speed at which the central mechanisms could deal with the data from the signals and, perhaps, monitor the responses.

Crossman in a private communication has shown that Conrad's results can be fairly well fitted by assuming that subjects dealt with data at 4 bits per sec and responded whenever there was a long enough gap between one signal and the next in the series he used. The present writer obtained close fits, shown in Figs. 4.7 and 4.8 to Conrad's data, assuming constant t for any given number of pointers, random i and a latitude of either one or two items. The treatment is the more plausible in that the values of t for 2, 3 and 4 dials (Fig. 4.7) give a good fit when

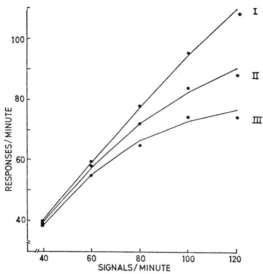

Figure 4.7. Conrad's (1951) data fitted assuming that signals arrive at random intervals and that dealing with each takes an equal time t. It is also assumed that if the subject cannot deal with the signal at the instant it arrives it can wait, but that data from not more than two signals at a time can wait in this way – in other words the latitude (λ) in responding is two signals.

I: 2 dials, $t = \cdot37$ sec.
II: 3 dials, $t = \cdot59$ sec.
III: 4 dials, $t = \cdot74$ sec.

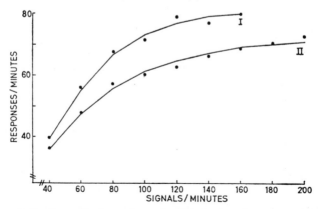

Figure 4.8. I: Conrad's (1954a) results fitted using the same assumptions as for Fig. 4.7. 4 dials, $t = \cdot74$ sec. II: Conrad's (1954b) results fitted using the same assumptions except that $\lambda = 1$. 4 dials, $t = \cdot83$ sec.

in the ratio $1 : 1 \cdot 58 : 2$ required by Hick's Law for 2, 3 and 4 choice responses. Also group B in Fig. 4.8, who show a latitude of one instead of two items, was a rather poorer group of subjects than the others. The method of calculation is described in the Appendix.

The model is obviously a gross over-simplification taking no account of possible grouping effects or of subtleties in the results such as the fact that at high signal frequencies many subjects neglected one dial, and missed all signals on it, for a minute or so at a time. Such a procedure could raise the rate of responding because the loss of potential responses to signals from the neglected dial would be more than offset by the shortening of t as a result of reducing the number of possible responses combined with the effective lengthening of i when signals on one of the dials are neglected. The assumption that t and i remained constant with signal speed would, however, then underestimate performance at high signal speeds.

The interaction of two simultaneous tasks

It has long been known that if the attempt is made to perform two tasks at the same time, the speed or accuracy of one or of the other or of both is likely to be lower than when the tasks are carried out separately. Early experiments in this field are those of Bornemann (1942) who paired mental arithmetic with a task in which the subject had to 'dot' with a stylus through holes in a paper band passing over a drum, and of Mowbray (1952, 1953, 1954) whose subjects were required to report on data such as letters, digits, or prose passages presented either visually or aurally. He found that subjects could not deal adequately with two different streams of information, one presented to the eyes and one to the ears, at the same time. The limitation could obviously not have been sensory and, since subjects did not have to report until afterwards, it was not on the motor side. The effects seemed clearly to be the result of an overloading of some central mechanism, and it is reasonable to suppose that the impairment was due to the single channel being captured by data from one task at a time, to the exclusion of data from the other. Some evidence in favour of this view is Mowbray's finding that when the two tasks were of unequal difficulty, it was the easier that tended to suffer more. This is understandable if the more difficult task tends to occupy the single channel for longer periods than the easy: capture of the single channel by the more difficult task would mean the omission of a relatively large block of data from the easier task, whereas capture by the easier task would cause a relatively brief interruption of the more difficult task. Alternatively the subject might try to maximise his overall performance by concentrating on the easier task and doing it well, in which case he would tend to do relatively better with the easy task. This may have been the reason why Brown *et al.* (1965) found that a tactile discrimination suffered more when paired with an easy visual discrimination than with a more difficult one – a result which is otherwise surprising in view of Mowbray's evidence.

From what has been said earlier in this chapter, it would be expected that the main interference between two tasks would result from their competing for the time of the translation mechanism. If so, interference will depend on the extent to which each task requires active choice of responses and on the compatibility between signals and responding actions. Results obtained by Noble *et al.* (1967) and by Trumbo *et al.* (1967) suggest this is the case. They paired tracking with a task in which the subject had either (*a*) to try to predict a series of numbers presented aurally at 3 sec intervals or (*b*) merely repeat them or (*c*) generate random numbers in response to clicks at 3 sec intervals. The first and third tasks clearly involved a more active choice of response than the second, and were shown to cause much more interference. Tracking while performing the second task seemed little if at all different from tracking with no extra task added.

A number of further studies indicate the range of usefulness of what is potentially an important means of assessing the load imposed by tasks for which direct measurement is not possible, and of showing up differences of loading which would otherwise be difficult to detect. Some of them have been briefly summarised in Table 4.2. These studies indicate clearly that increase in the load of either the primary or the secondary task beyond a critical point can greatly impair performance at one or both, and that adding a secondary task can show up differences in the loads imposed by different primary tasks which are unobservable when they are performed alone. The effects of a secondary task on short term memory found by Murdock (1965b) are at first surprising since during the period his subjects were taking in and retaining the material no overt action was required, and thus it might seem that there were no translation processes with which the secondary task could interfere. We shall, however, see in Chapter 7 that the translation mechanism is often involved in short-term memory especially for the early items of a list – in fact for just those items Murdock found to be most affected. Perhaps the simplest example of the interference envisaged in these dual tasks is the interruption of performance caused by sudden loud noises which momentarily capture the single channel to the exclusion of the task in progress at the time (e.g. Woodhead, 1959, 1964a, b, Sanders, 1961b).

The dual-task technique is as yet in its infancy and a number of problems still remain to be solved. We may mention four as especially important.

(a) *Methods of measurement.* The primary task when given alone can be conceived as not occupying the single-channel fully, but as leaving some 'spare capacity' into which the secondary task can, up to a point, be fitted. Performance is impaired when this spare capacity is insufficient. There is some question whether the primary task occupies the single-channel *continuously* but not completely at any one instant, or whether occupation is *complete* but intermittent so that spare capacity is in the form of 'gaps' during which the single-channel is free. The experiments we have surveyed earlier in this chapter seem to favour the latter view although it is only fair to point out that if a subject is told to react *as quickly as possible* he can be presumed to use the whole of his available capacity in doing so. Whether when he reacts more slowly he uses only a proportion of his total capacity at any instant is a difficult question which remains to be answered. It is, of course a variety of the old and still unsolved problem of whether attention can be truly divided between two tasks, or whether it alternates rapidly between one and the other (Woodworth and Schlosberg, 1954).

If the intermittency view is correct, as it clearly is in many cases, the loads imposed by the primary and secondary tasks separately and together can in principle be calculated by methods similar to those used to provide the basis of Figs. 4.7 and 4.8 – the problem becomes essentially one of queueing by signals from the two tasks for use of the translation mechanism.

An empirical index of loading in dual tasks had been proposed by Michon (1964b, 1966, Michon and Van Doorne, 1967) on the basis of experiments in which the secondary task has been the tapping of a foot pedal at intervals of ·5 to 1·0 sec which the subject attempts to keep as regular as possible. Michon noted that the interval between each tap and the next seemed to be a sensitive indicator of interference by the primary task, and suggested that tapping performance can be measured in terms of the average difference of each interval from the one preceding. Adapting his equation we may write:

$$\text{Tapping performance} = \sum_{1}^{N-1} \frac{(t_i \sim t_j)}{N-1} \times \frac{1}{\bar{t}} \qquad (4.6)$$

where t_i is each interval from the first to the $(N-1)$th taken in turn, and $\bar{t}$ is the mean interval. Michon proposes that

$$\text{Index of loading} = \frac{\text{Difference between tapping performances with and without primary task}}{\text{Tapping performance without primary task}} \quad (4.7)$$

(b) *The stability of capacity.* It has been tacitly assumed in most studies using dual tasks that the subject's basic capacity remains the same whether or not a secondary task is added to a primary, and however severe the demands of the secondary task may be. Brown's (1957) and Conrad's (1956) results on the effects of pacing do, however, raise the question of whether some genuine increase of capacity occurs under pressure for speed. Certainly Kalsbeek and Ettema (1964) and Kalsbeek and Sykes (1967) have shown that effort, as measured by the increased regularity of heart rate, increases with the load imposed by a secondary task and produces an apparent increase of channel capacity, but evidence is insufficient yet to decide whether this is a true increase or merely represents a shift of criterion in the subject's decision making – that is a shift of β in the signal-detection model. The problem has been discussed by Kalsbeek and Ettema who distinguish the capacity a subject is 'willing to spend' from the maximum he can use in an emergency. We shall consider the general problem of the effect of effort more fully in Chapter 8.

(c) *Co-ordination of primary and secondary tasks.* Support for the view that in performing dual tasks we normally alternate rapidly from one to the other rather than expend parts of our total capacity simultaneously on both comes from the fact that it seems impossible to carry out actions, by say the two hands, which are truly simultaneous without their being in some way co-ordinated and fitted into a common temporal framework. For example, in the well-known children's party trick of making tapping movements with one hand and circular motions with the other, the number of taps seems to be inevitably a multiple of the number of circles. Such co-ordination is a type of grouping and seems to enable a more elaborate performance to be carried out than would otherwise be possible. For example, Kalsbeek (1964) noted that the subjects in his double-task experiments tended to build up a rhythmic pattern of performance in which the two tasks were regularly inter-digitated, and that when this was achieved, the impairment produced by combining the two tasks was reduced, implying presumably that they were no longer separate but had been combined into one more complex task. Further evidence that when the signals in one or both tasks come at regular intervals or are otherwise predictable, responses in the two tasks tend to be co-ordinated and performance improves has been provided for tracking by Adams and Chambers (1962) and for serial reaction times by Dimond (1966). Results obtained by Kalsbeek and Sykes (1967) suggest that co-ordination is fostered by training, but that the scope for it is greatest when the total loading is moderate and that it may break down when the loading becomes very severe. Such co-ordination obviously complicates measurement of the load imposed by the primary task in terms of the impairment of performance at the secondary, although it remains possible to make such measurement in principle.

(d) *Simultaneous responses to single signals.* It must be emphasised that the dual-task technique has typically used two independent streams of signals and not merely the execution of double responses. It is obvious that simultaneous responses by the two hands can be made provided they are in some way co-ordinated. It is not so clear, however, whether the time taken to initiate and control such responses is longer than that required for the corresponding responses made singly. A lead has been given to understanding in this area by Sanders (1967) who found that when a subject had to respond to a single signal with two responses, one by each hand, and one bearing a direct and the other an indirect relationship to the signal, the time taken to initiate both responses together was no longer than that required to initiate the second alone. When, however, both responses involved an indirect relationship to the signal, the double response took longer to initiate than either alone. Sanders suggested on the basis of his evidence that the direct relationship has to be worked out as an intermediate step in arriving at the indirect, so that a directly related response takes no extra time. Each indirect relationship, however, has to be worked out separately so that the translation mechanism is employed longer for a double than for a single indirect response.

V

Movement

Enough has been said in preceding chapters to indicate that movements involve a complex co-ordination of various muscles brought into play in a phased sequence, and that the *execution* of movements is in important ways distinct from decisions to *initiate* them. Further evidence for such a distinction is provided by the fact that there is commonly little or no correlation between reaction-time and speed of movement (e.g. Henry, 1952, 1961, Henry and Rodgers, 1960, Pierson, 1961, L. Smith, 1965) and factors which affect the one may hardly at all affect the other (e.g. Singleton, 1954, 1955, Weiss, 1965, Brichcin, 1966, Kimotsuki, 1967).

The psychological study of movement has been somewhat of a cinderella, partly no doubt because it is less open to introspective examination than, for example, perception; but largely because it is amenable to much more clear-cut physiological study than are other processes traditionally treated by experimental psychology. We shall not attempt to outline physiological studies here as excellent summaries are available elsewhere, notably those by Ruch (1951) and Paillard (1960). Nor shall we be concerned with the anatomical factors which determine the maximum mechanical forces that can be exerted in various positions: these have again been reviewed elsewhere (e.g. Darcus, 1954, Morgan *et al.*, 1963, Murrell, 1965). Instead we shall consider the *sensori-motor control* of movement. Anatomical and physiological factors undoubtedly play a part in such control, setting limits to its operation and showing, for example, in the differences of speed and accuracy of movements made with different limbs or in various limb-positions or directions relative to the body (e.g. Searle and Taylor, 1948, Begbie, 1959, Hammerton and Tickner, 1966), but they seem to be of secondary importance to the subtle interplay that takes place between action and sensory feedback.

SENSORY CONTROL

The control of movement follows a typical servo pattern in which action is monitored and modified by sensory feedback of various kinds, the relative importance of which vary with the precise tasks concerned. The feedback may be visual via sight of the responding limb or of the object manipulated: accuracy obviously suffers when movements are made blind and is commonly affected if visual feedback is in any way distorted. Our present knowledge of the effects of such distortion is largely due to the work of K. U. and W. M. Smith and their associates using a technique in which the subject manipulates objects without being able to see his hand directly: instead an image of the hand is picked up by a television camera and shown to the subject on a closed-circuit television screen with various distortions or transpositions introduced into the link between camera and screen (e.g. Smith and Smith, 1962, K. Smith, 1966). Experiments by Gould (1965) and by Gould and Schaffer (1965), using a similar technique and manipulating the contrast to show up particular parts of the field, have suggested that sight of the object being manipulated or of the tool being used is more important than sight of the hand itself.

Evidence regarding the quantitative effects of visual feedback comes from an experiment by Chase *et al.* (1965) whose subjects attempted to hold a finger steady and were shown the finger-tremor magnified on an oscilloscope. The extent of the low frequency components of the tremor decreased markedly as the magnification increased from 1 to 10 times, and thereafter remained steady when magnification was increased from 10 to 40 times. The same authors found analogous results when visual indication was replaced by a tone the frequency of which varied with displacement of the finger. These findings are similar to those of a number of tracking studies summarised by Poulton (1966), in which increase in the ratio of change in display to extent of movement by the corresponding control improves performance up to a point but not thereafter. Seidenstein *et al.* (1960) have emphasised that the relevant variable in calculating this ratio is the retinal image of the tracking error, so that absolute magnitude and viewing distance are compensatory if angular displacement is held constant.

Other senses can play an important part in such feedback. For example, Chase *et al.* (1961b) who set their subjects to tap a key with constant amplitude and pressure at a steady rate of three movements per sec found that inability to *see* the finger produced no impairment of performance. Regularity of tapping decreased, however, if the *sound* of tapping was masked by noise played through earphones, or if *proprioceptive* signals were masked by vibrators placed on the wrist and forearm, or if *touch* was abolished by anaesthetising the finger. Provins (1957, 1958) had previously observed that accuracy in applying a pressure was impaired by anaesthetising the skin over the part of the hand used to apply the pressure, although the maximum rate of tapping was little affected. It is more difficult to remove *kinaesthetic* feedback, but Laszlo (1966), using an inflated cuff on the arm to produce nerve blocking has shown that accuracy of tapping diminishes during the period after cutaneous sensation has ceased and before muscular power has been lost, implying that accuracy is affected by loss of kinaesthetic feedback. It is, of course, well known that patients suffering from *tabes dorsalis*, which is marked by interruption of the kinaesthetic pathways, show exaggerated movements which make adjustments to the limbs inaccurate and slow.

The origin of many studies in this area has been the problem of whether, when power assisted controls are fitted to cars, aircraft or other machinery, there is any advantage to be gained by leaving some 'feel' in steering wheels and joysticks. Such feel will obviously increase proprioceptive signals, and it is therefore not surprising that the accuracy of positioning a lever is improved by spring loading so that the *force* required increases with the extent of movement (Howland and Noble, 1953, Bahrick *et al.*, 1955a). There are indications that moderate pressures yield optimum results: Jenkins (1947) obtained constant Weber Fractions ($\delta F/F$) for increases of force over pressures ranging from 10 to 50 lb but higher fractions below 10 lb while pressures above 50 lb would introduce complications owing to the amount of muscular effort required. Some improvement in the accuracy of simple movements has also been obtained by adding *inertia* to the control (Searle and Taylor, 1948, Howland and Noble, 1953), and accuracy of both simple and more complex movements has been improved by making the moving control lever pull a plunger through a bath of oil thus adding *viscous friction* (Howland and Noble, 1953, Bahrick *et al.*, 1955b).

The suggestion has been made on the basis of such studies that *pressure controls* in which a control lever does not move at all but has an effect according to how hard it is pushed, might be preferable to moving controls and the results of several experiments indicate that this is so (e.g. Gibbs, 1954, North and Lomnicki, 1961, Burke and Gibbs, 1965). Other investigators have, however, found position better than force as a basis of accurate control (e.g. Weiss, 1954): presumably which is better depends on the degree of force and the extent of movement or change of position. Optimum performance seems, indeed, to be obtained with a combination of appreciable movement with spring-loading, thus enabling kinaesthetic as well as other proprioceptive signals to play a part. Briggs *et al.* (1957) suggest that their results bearing on this point, and those of Jenkins (1947) are well fitted by an equation proposed by Bahrick *et al.* (1955a):

$$\text{Accuracy in terms of distance moved} = \frac{\delta F}{F(\delta D)} \times \text{a constant} \quad (5.1)$$

where F is the force required to produce a specified displacement of the control and δF is the change of force associated with a change of displacement δD.

TIME REQUIRED FOR FEEDBACK TO BE EFFECTIVE

Woodworth (1899) in a classical monograph on voluntary movement, divided the time taken by a movement into a period of 'initial impulse' and a subsequent period of 'current control'. The former is a conse-quence of the fact that it takes time for sense data fed back from a movement to become effective in modifying its course, partly because of an inevitable reaction time and partly because of the delays discussed in the previous chapter. Brief movements are thus ballistic in the sense that they are initiated as a whole and have to run their course without the possibility of modification. The most striking illustration of this known to the writer arose from a Siamese cat belonging to Mr K. F. H. Murrell. It had the habit of sitting on the shoulder of anyone eating a meal and of pawing at his hand as he raised a forkful of food to the mouth. The result was that the food was deflected into the cat's mouth, and the diner was quite incapable of preventing this happening unless he moved his arm very slowly and deliberately. Crossman and Goodeve (1963) have obtained the same type of result experimentally by having subjects make movements of a rotating knob to bring a pointer to a target and adding aiding or opposing forces during the course of the movement. The effects were to cause overshoots and undershoots re-spectively. After a little practice, subjects attempted to minimise these by tensing the muscles being used – they were presumably increasing the forces applied to both agonists and antagonists so that the disturb-ing forces would have proportionately smaller effects.

Woodworth found that the accuracy of right-hand movements lasting less than about ·4 sec, and of left-hand lasting less than about ·75 sec, differed little whether or not the subject closed his eyes while the hand was in motion, implying that there was no current visual control. Accuracy of movements lasting longer than these times improved as duration increased with the eyes open, but did not do so when they were closed. This finding was confirmed by Vince (1948b) whose results are shown in Fig. 5.1. Analogous results were obtained by Provins

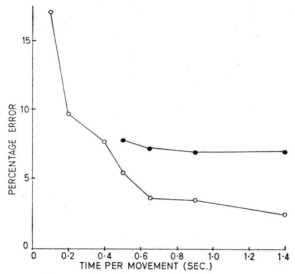

Figure 5.1. Relations between accuracy and duration of movements with eyes open and with eyes closed. Data from an experiment by Vince (1948b).

    ○ = Eyes open.
    ● = Eyes closed as soon as movement began.

Each point is the mean of a series of readings taken from each of ten subjects. The movements were made by pulling a cord attached to a pointer which moved downwards over the surface of a smoked drum to a target line 1 in away. The pointer was returned to its starting position by spring tension. Movements were made in time with a metronome.

(1957) who found that the accuracy of pressure with the side of the hand was greater when it was exerted at the subject's own preferred speed – usually over a period of 2–3 sec – than when it was exerted as fast as possible, but that the difference disappeared when the area of skin at the locus of the pressure was anaesthetised.

Both Woodworth and Vince showed that in the course of rapid movements there is a period of acceleration followed by an approximately similar period of deceleration, and that these normally shade into one another so as to produce a central zone of nearly uniform velocity. If distance travelled is plotted against time the curve seems to be roughly a normal ogive (Crossman and Goodeve, 1963). Peters and Wenborn (1936) found that such patterns were remarkably constant for different directions and extents of movements, and that when movements made as fast as possible were compared with those made at a moderate speed, all phases changed to about the same proportional extent. Woodworth's and Vince's slower movements showed the same

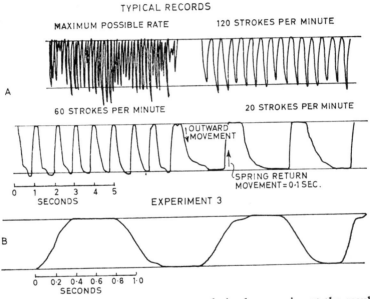

Figure 5.2. Examples of movements made in the experiment the results of which are shown in Fig. 5.1.

initial period of rapid acceleration, but this was followed by a much longer and less regular deceleration, suggesting that under conditions of 'current control' the movement was no longer a single entity but a series of movements which ran into one another. Some of Vince's results are shown in Fig. 5.2.

Looking at the matter from a slightly different standpoint, the S-shaped roughly symmetrical curve with approximately equal times taken over acceleration and deceleration, seems to be associated with movements intended to be of a given *extent*, whereas the type showing a prolonged final deceleration with one or more adjustments tends to occur when the movement is aimed precisely at a *target*: the final deceleration and adjustments represent a process of 'homing' on the target rather than merely bringing the movement to a halt. Most of the time taken by such accurate movements is thus spent over the last part of the travel (Annett *et al.*, 1958).

Fig. 5.2 illustrates the further point that within a series of rapid movements, each too fast to incorporate any secondary adjustments, there are nevertheless trends over groups, suggesting that adjustments are made between one movement or group of movements and the next. If so, it means that two servo-loops are operating. One is a short-term loop which has to do with the immediate phasing of each individual movement and, if one can judge from the fact that movements made at maximum rate averaged about five per sec, achieves about ten adjustments per sec – one to make each stroke and one to release it. Super-imposed on this is a slower-acting loop operating over periods of ·5 sec or so. The latter is presumably a visual loop, while the former is kinaesthetic or proprioceptive and local to the effector mechanism – in other words corrections made in terms of it do not require any new decision. Similar implications follow from the observation that when tracking a simple harmonic course at high speed subjects may make rapid harmonic motions which are, however, not 'time-locked' to the excursions of the target (Noble *et al.*, 1955). Further evidence for such a short-term loop comes from the rapid corrections for errors in some tracking tasks which we noted in the previous chapter (p. 116) and which are far too fast to be visually controlled. We may also note in this connection that Murrell and Entwisle (1960) and Crossman and Goodeve (1963) observed a periodicity of acceleration and deceleration of about ten per sec in detailed recordings of movements aimed at a target. It looks, in short, as if the translation mechanism feeds an 'order' into the effector mechanism, and that the latter carries out the order by means of a servo mechanism with a loop which takes about ·1 sec to traverse and which continues to act until sufficient accuracy has been achieved.

Further evidence for the importance of time factors in the control of movement comes from a consideration of how movements made at maximum speed differ according to their extent and loading. Increasing the amplitude of a movement while keeping its terminal accuracy the same makes relatively little difference to the time taken (Searle and Taylor, 1948), and if the ratio between amplitude and terminal accuracy is held constant, the times taken by movements of extents from about 2 to 20 in are almost identical (Fitts, 1954, Crossman, 1957, Fitts and

Peterson, 1964, Crossman and Goodeve, 1963). Similarly Fitts (1954) found that 'dotting' with a stylus back and forth between two targets took about the same time whether the stylus weighed 1 oz or 1 lb. Again El Temamy (1966), using a weight which slid back and forth on a rod, found that the time taken for any given degree of accuracy rose by only about 30% as the weight was increased from 1·25 to 12 lb. It can be argued that the rise is likely to be small because the arm itself is a large element in the total mass to be moved, but close examinations by Taylor and Birmingham (1948) of tracking performance and by El Temamy of his results made it clear that the force deployed rose considerably with heavier weights and larger amplitudes. Had the same forces been used with lighter weights or shorter amplitudes the movements would have been considerably faster. It seems, in effect, that with increased amplitude or load the subject increases the force applied while keeping the time roughly constant. This, of course, is what would be expected if the limiting factor was the time required to process the data on which control was based. Additional support for this general view comes from the well-recognised fact that complex movements involving a series of different directions or extents, and thus implying more elaborate control, take substantially longer than simple linear movements (Woodworth, 1899, Peters and Wenborn, 1936); also from the finding that speed of arm movement has little to do with the strength or effective mass of the arm (Pierson, 1961).

Time has an important bearing upon the optimum sensitivity of controls. Several studies have shown that when a pointer has to be moved to coincide with a target, performance varies with the extent of the pointer movement produced by a given control movement, being most rapid and accurate when the ratio between the two movements is at some intermediate value between very high and very low (Jenkins and Connor, 1949, Jenkins and Olson, 1952, Gibbs, 1954, North *et al.*, 1958, Hammerton, 1962). If small movements deflect the pointer a long way it is difficult to make fine adjustments because the pointer will move too far during the minimum time within which a movement can be executed and corrected. On the other hand, if large control movements have to be made in order to produce a relatively small deflection of the pointer, accuracy in terms of time and distance off target will suffer because of the time taken to execute the movements required. This latter is especially the case when the control is not a simple lever but, say, a handwheel as used for steering a car. If a steering wheel has to be turned a relatively long way to produce a given change in the car's direction, it may be difficult to corner at speed. If, on the other hand the steering is unduly sensitive, it is difficult to keep straight on an open road.

RELATIONSHIPS BETWEEN SPEED AND ACCURACY

The relation between amplitude, accuracy and the time taken to make hand movements had been a subject of discussion for some years before Fitts (1954) suggested a formulation in information-theory terms which connected all three together. Fitts proposed essentially that

$$\text{Movement time} = a + b \log (2A/W) \qquad (5.2)$$

where W is the *width* of the target within which the movement is required to end, measured parallel to the direction of the movement; A is the amplitude of the movement measured from its starting point to the centre of the target; and a and b are constants. The essential point of this formulation is that it makes movement time constant for any given ratio between amplitude and target width.

Fitts recognised that the multiplication of A by 2 was arbitrary although some such procedure appeared necessary in order to ensure that the logarithm was always a positive quantity: had the fraction A/W been used, W would have exceeded A in the case of movements made from just outside a target and this would have made log (A/W) negative. There was also some conceptual plausability in that the subject could be thought of as having to 'choose' a movement which had the possibility of either over- or under-shooting the target. Fitts also recognised that it would not always be accurate to take W as the measure of the scatter of the shots: the subject might, for example, concentrate his shots in a narrower width, in which case the movement time would be expected to be greater than that predicted by Eq. 5.2.

Fitts backed his formulation with four sets of experimental data. In one experiment the subject was required to 'dot' alternately on two metal strips 6 in long using a metal-tipped stylus weighing 1 oz and about the size of a pencil. The long axes of the strips were perpendicular to the line of movement between them. The strips were mounted on a board placed in such a position that the subject's movements were from side to side in front of him. Four widths of target strip were used: 2, 1, ·5 and ·25 in at each of four distances between centres: 2, 4, 8, and 16 in.

Average times per movement, plotted according to Eq. 5.2 with A taken at the distance between target centres, and W as the width of the target strips, are shown in Fig. 5.3. All the points, except those at the extreme lower end, lie close to a straight line and suggest that Fitts's formulation was right in principle. Fig. 5.3 does, however, have three unsatisfactory features which suggest that some modifications of detail are required:

(*a*) The straight line running through most of the points cuts the zero information line below the origin making *a* in Eq. 5.2 a negative

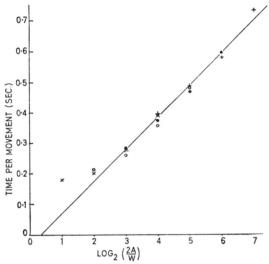

Figure 5.3. Times for reciprocal tapping with a 1 oz stylus plotted in terms of Eq. 5.2. Data from an experiment by Fitts (1954). The target widths (*W*) are indicated as follows × = 2 in, ○ = 1 in, ● = ½ in and + = ¼ in. The four amplitudes of (A) for each target width are, from left to right, 2, 4, 8 and 16 in. Each point is based on a total of 613–2,669 movements obtained from 16 subjects.

quantity. Crossman (1957) has suggested that this difficulty can be avoided by omitting to multiply *A* by 2 so that Eq. 5.2 becomes

$$\text{Movement time} = a + b \log(A/W) \qquad (5.3)$$

The constant *a* works out at about ·05 sec, a figure close to that found by Crossman himself in a similar experiment for the time spent on the targets as opposed to the time spent moving between them. It seems obvious at first sight that the time spent stationary on the targets ought not to be included in the measure of movement time. It has been found, however, in another similar experiment (Welford, 1958, pp. 99 and 103) that results are, on the whole, more uniform and plausible if the times on target and between targets are added together than if the latter measure only is taken. It seems as if there may be some compensatory tendency at work which makes it possible for time spent on the targets to be used to shorten time spent moving, at least to some extent. Such a compensatory effect would be consistent with the view that movement time is limited by the speed at which central processes can control and monitor movement. These processes must obviously to some extent precede and outlast the movements concerned, and the time thus required would be spent on the targets.

(*b*) Although the points in Fig. 53, except those at the extreme lower end, lie fairly close to a straight line, the best fitting line through them would curve gently upwards. The curve can be substantially lessened by making a further modification to the equations by writing

$$\text{Movement time} = K \log \left(\frac{A + \frac{1}{2}W}{W} \right) = K \log \left(\frac{A}{W} + \cdot 5 \right) \quad (5.4)$$

This formulation makes movement time dependent upon a kind of Weber Fraction in that the subject is called upon to distinguish between the distances to the far and the near edges of the target. To put it another way, he is called upon to choose a distance W out of a tota distance extending from his starting point to the far edge of the target. The formulation also preserves the advantage which Fitts claimed for the procedure of multiplying A by 2, in that the logarithm can never be negative, since in the extreme case when the movement begins at the edge of the target $A = \frac{1}{2}W$.

(*c*) The curve in Fig. 5.3 shows a distinct flattening at the lower end. This is probably due, as Crossman has suggested, to some limiting factor setting a minimum time per movement however short or unconstrained. Study by the present author of dotting between targets using a pencil as a stylus suggests that this limiting factor affects the amount of target used. When the targets are wide and the distance short, the subject uses very much less than the full target width. He is, in fact, transmitting more information than a calculation in terms of Eq. 5.4 would assume because the effective W is narrower. The narrowing of W is to some extent reflected in a reduction of errors and if due allowance is made for them Eq. 5.4 still holds reasonably well.

The method of correcting for errors has been described by Crossman (1957). It makes use of the fact that the information in a normal distribution is $\log_2 \sigma \sqrt{(2\pi e)}$, where σ is the standard deviation of the distribution. Now $\sqrt{(2\pi e)} = 4 \cdot 133$ and a range of $\pm$ half this, i.e. $2 \cdot 062\sigma$, includes about 96% of a normal distribution. We can therefore argue that if about 4% of shots fall outside the target, $\log_2 W$ is an accurate representation of the information contained in the distribution of shots. We can also argue that if the errors exceed 4% the *effective* target width is greater than W, and if the errors are less than 4% the effective target width is less than W. How much greater or less can be calculated from tables of the normal distribution (e.g. Fisher and Yates, 1938, Table 1). For example, suppose $W = 2$ in and the errors are 1%. Then the effective $W = 2 \times 4 \cdot 133/5 \cdot 152 = 1 \cdot 604$ in, since all but 1% of a normal distribution lie within a range of $\pm 2 \cdot 576$ (i.e. $\frac{1}{2} \times 5 \cdot 152$) of the mean.

It has been assumed so far that errors are distributed equally to both

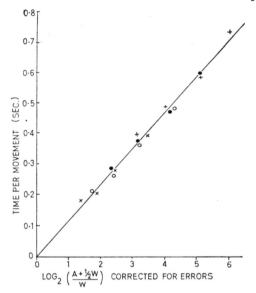

Figure 5.4. The same data as in Fig. 5.3 plotted in terms of Eq. 5.4 corrected for errors by Crossman's method. Target widths and amplitudes of movement are indicated as before.

sides of the target and that the mean is in the centre of the target so that the mean amplitude of movement is correct. If the mean falls to one side or the other of the centre, the effective A will be different from the distance A between target centres. Strictly speaking, the effective A should in any case be the geometric mean of the distances between each shot and the next, although it is usually approximately correct to take the distance between the means of the two distributions of shots. If the distributions can be assumed to be symmetrical it is not necessary to record the positions of all the shots in order to calculate the positions of the means: the mean of each distribution can be inferred from the proportions of shots falling on the near and far sides of the target concerned.

Fitts's data are plotted in Fig. 5.4 using Eq. 5.4 and making appropriate adjustments to W for errors. The data were unfortunately not given which would have made it possible to calculate the effective As, and these have been assumed to be correct. The results lie close to a straight line which passes through the origin.

Further data on movement times

Crossman (1957) has produced results which although obtained independently of Fitts's, are in striking agreement with them. He has also shown that the length of the target strip as well as its width affect movement time although to a smaller extent. The reason for this becomes clear when one studies records of dotting with a pencil between targets drawn on paper. The shots in each target fall roughly into an ellipse with its long axis parallel to the line of movement: the scatter perpendicular to the line of movement is very much smaller than that parallel to it.

Closely similar results to those of Figs. 5.3 and 5.4 were obtained by Fitts for a similar 'dotting' task but using a stylus weighing 1 lb instead of 1 oz, although the slope was slightly steeper with the heavier stylus. Knight and Dagnall (1967) using a task in which the subject aligned a pointer with each of two targets alternately, obtained results which closely followed Eq. 5.4 and were better fitted by this than by Eq. 5.2. The slopes were a little steeper than in Fig. 5.4, but were of the same order of magnitude. Adding inertia to the movement increased the slope significantly although, as in Fitts's case, the increase was not substantial.

Fitts and Peterson (1964) using amplitudes of 3, 6 and 12 in and target widths of 1, ·5, ·25 and ·125 in, found that Eq. 5.4 fitted well and slightly better than Eq. 5.2 for *single* movements each carried out following a separate signal to move. The slope was somewhat less steep than for continuous movements, perhaps because there were no turn-round times at end points to be included. The time saved was understandably less than the reaction-time between the appearance of the signal to move and the actual beginning of the movement, since this contained an element of temporal uncertainty absent from the continuous task. Fitts and Radford (1966) in a similar experiment showed that although accuracy improved as the time taken to execute a movement lengthened, it was little affected by extra time taken to prepare, and that rate of gain of information varied little whether instructions were for speed or for accuracy.

Some indication of the detailed actions lying behind the logarithmic relationship between speed, amplitude and accuracy is given by Crossman and Goodeve (1963) who plotted the course of movements made in continuous 'dotting' tasks like those of Fitts (1954), and with discrete settings of a pointer made by rotating the wrist. They found, as we have already noted, that the movements were not smooth but showed acceleration and deceleration with a periodicity of about ten cycles per sec. The pattern was such as to suggest that each movement consisted of a series of impulses which ran together to some extent but not completely. All took about the same time, but they differed in velocity so that the first covered approximately the first half of the distance to be covered, the second the next quarter, the third the next eighth and so on. When distance travelled was plotted against time taken, each impulse roughly resembled a normal ogive like that of a movement made to cover a given extent rather than aimed at a target. Crossman and Goodeve point out that this implies that movement is controlled by a servo-system which initiates impulses having a velocity proportional to the distance to be covered and which are corrected by feedback at intervals of approximately ·1 sec. They also prove that if the velocities are adjusted in terms of the distance to go to the centre of the target aimed at, and the subject institutes a stopping procedure at the near edge of the target, this system leads to Eq. 5.2. We may add that if instead velocities are adjusted in terms of the distance to the far edge of the target and stopping is again initiated at the near edge, the system leads to Eq. 5.4.

The authors suggest that this servo is within the motor system (effector mechanism) and largely independent of visual control since the same pattern of successive impulses was obtained with the rotating pointer task when a sector-shaped screen was arranged to hide the pointer from view as soon as it began to move, and the subject was required to rotate the knob so as to bring the pointer to rest as near as possible to the far edge of the screen. Some visual control might well have been involved, however, in checking whether or not the pointer had emerged from behind the screen and could perhaps have affected the adjustments made. In support of this suggestion we may note that Crossman and Goodeve in a further pilot experiment found the number of impulses to be fewer when the pointer disappeared from view half-way to the target than when it was hidden over the whole distance.

We have spoken of the subject 'choosing' a target width out of a longer extent, but this is obviously only a figurative description; some more detailed process needs to be specified. Fitts (1954) and Fitts and Peterson (1964) suggested that the subject could be conceived as trying to make a series of movements each of uniform extent but subject to random disturbances which may either add to or subtract from the extent aimed at. In criticism of this view it seems fair to reiterate two points we have already noted. Firstly, the subject's task was not, in the experiments we have been discussing, to make movements of a given *extent* but ones which ended within specified limits. Secondly, the actions when 'homing' upon a target are more complex than those involved in making a movement of a particular amplitude or duration. Taking these two points together, it is plausible to think of the subject as having to consider all movements of an extent short of the far edge of the target and to reject all those which are short of the near edge. He starts by rejecting a large class of those which are much too short and then rejects finer and finer classes as the target is approached. His behaviour would in a sense be analogous to that envisaged in the first of the models discussed in relation to choice reactions (p. 71), and i each sub-decision took an approximately equal time it is understandable that the first half, the next quarter and so on of the total distance would be traversed in approximately equal times as Crossman and Goodeve found.

Further evidence on 'dotting' times obtained by Welford *et al.* (1963) indicate that these views are somewhat too simple, and that Eqs. 5.2, 5.3 and 5.4, although on the right lines, need some elaboration. Before discussing this work, however, we need briefly to review experiments in which speed of movement has been studied in relation to accuracy, using a different type of task.

Inserting pins into sockets

Fitts (1954) reported two further experiments. In one the subject was required to transfer discs with holes in their centres from a vertical pin to another similar pin a given distance to the left. Four distances between pin centres were used with each of four sizes of hole. The 'target widths' were taken as the differences between the diameters of the pins and of the holes. The other task was the transfer of metal pins from one set of holes to another a given distance away. Four diameters of pins were used with each of five distances. The holes were in each case twice the diameter of the pins: the 'target width' was again taken as the tolerance between the pins and the holes.

The results of these last two experiments are, unfortunately, not suitable for detailed examination as the times taken to transport the discs or pins to their 'targets' were not measured separately from the return ('transport empty') movements of the hand to pick up the next disc or pin. We cannot assume these return movements to be of constant duration, or of a duration proportional only to distance. Evidence that they *may* be comes from results by Annett *et al.* (1958), but Crossman (1957) found that return movements tended to become slower as the accuracy of the outward movements rose. There is considerable support for the view that the speed of one movement in a cycle tends to affect those of others (de Montpellier, 1935, Wehrkamp and Smith, 1952, Welford, 1958, p. 105, Simon and Simon, 1959).

This difficulty does not attach, however, to the pin-transfer experiment by Annett *et al.* (1958). Their subjects, like Fitts's, were required to transfer pins from holders to sockets. The pins were $\frac{1}{8}$ in diameter and different sets of sockets ranged in diameter from $\frac{9}{64}$ through $\frac{12}{64}$ and $\frac{24}{64}$ to $\frac{72}{64}$ in, giving tolerances of $\frac{1}{64}$, $\frac{1}{16}$, $\frac{1}{4}$ and 1 in respectively. The distance between centres of holders and sockets was in all cases 8 in. The holders were $\frac{9}{64}$ in diameter. Movements were recorded by a film taken at 48 frames per second, and from this it was possible to determine the interval elapsing between the pin leaving the holder and its release after having been placed in the socket ('transport loaded' plus 'position'). 'Target width' was taken as the difference of diameter between pin and socket.

The average times taken by the three subjects plotted in accordance with Eq. 5.4 lay close to a straight line, but the times for the finer tolerances tended to be too short. The line would have been straight and have passed through the origin if the pins had been $\frac{7}{64}$ in diameter instead of $\frac{1}{8}$ in, and this fact led the present writer to consider whether there were any reasons why the *effective* pin diameter might have been a little less than $\frac{1}{8}$ in. Two factors appeared possible: firstly that the ends of the pins were slightly rounded, and secondly that the subjects were applying them to the holes at an angle so as to present a rounded edge which would 'find' the hole more easily than would the flat end of the pin. Enquiry from one of the authors revealed that both factors were present: the ends of the pins were slightly chamfered since if this was not done 'the subjects often fumbled when putting them into the smallest holes'; and the film clearly showed the pins being applied to the holes at an angle.

Further work by Schouten *et al.* (see Westhoff, 1964) on placing pins in sockets has shown that formulation in terms of tolerance is not quite adequate: some account must be taken of absolute pin, or socket, diameter. Their subjects moved pins as fast as possible over a distance of 25 mm into a hole of 1, 2, 4, 8 or 16 mm diameter. Different pins were used to provide, for each hole, percentage tolerances of 50, 25, 12·5 and so on for a total of between eight steps with the smallest hole and eleven

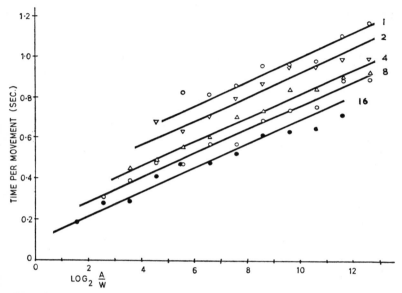

Figure 5.5. Times taken to place pins in holes. Data from experiments by Schouten *et al.* (see Westhoff, 1964).

A = 25 mm in all cases. W = the difference between the diameters of pin and hole. The diameters of hole used are indicated on the right in millimetres against the corresponding regression lines.

with the largest. Their results are shown in Fig. 5.5. If tolerance had been an adequate measure of W in Eqs. 5.2, 5.3 or 5.4 the regression lines for different diameters of hole should have been superimposed. We shall consider reasons why they are not in relation to the results obtained by Welford *et al.* (1963).

Detailed study of accuracy

The writer and his colleagues were concerned to overcome the difficulty in Fitts's original experiment and in others since, that times are scored for the task of landing within target limits rather than for recorded distributions of shots. Times were therefore taken for dotting from side to side with a pencil between two targets drawn on paper so that the point at which each shot landed was recorded. Continuous runs were made of 50 shots in each direction with all combinations of $(A + \frac{1}{2}W) = 50$, 142 and 402 mm and $W = 32$, 11 and 4 mm. The range of values was restricted to these because the task was part of a battery of tests being given to a large group of subjects and the time available was limited. The distributions of shots appeared to be rather too broad in the middle for normality: they seemed to fall between normal and rectangular. The width of the distribution for each subject on each target was therefore taken as the distance between the extreme shots, excluding occasional wild deviants. Group distributions as opposed to those of individual subjects would, of course, have been much nearer normal, so that this procedure is not in conflict with that adopted in correcting for errors in Fig. 5.4.

It was argued that, by analogy with Eq. 5.4, the present results ought to be fitted by the equation:

$$\text{Movement time} = K \log \left(\frac{A'}{W'} + \cdot5 \right) \qquad (5.5)$$

where W' is the mean width of the two distributions, one at each end, observed with any particular combination of A and W and A' is the distance between the centres of these distributions. The experiment was designed to study age differences: the results for the forties, the decade with the largest number of subjects, are shown plotted against Eq. 5.5 in Fig. 5.6. It can be seen at once that, while the times for each target width increased with amplitude at rates similar to those found by Fitts, the times for the narrower targets were too high, as they were with the results of Schouten *et al*. The results for each decade from the twenties to the eighties showed the same pattern.

Two possible partial reasons for the difference between these and Fitts's results are, firstly, that the metal targets he used may have tended to emphasise accuracy more than did ours drawn on paper: our subjects tended to scatter their shots well outside the narrow targets and not to use the full width of the wide ones, whereas Fitts's subjects seemed to have preserved accuracy relatively well on the narrow targets. Secondly, and as against this, the point of the stylus used by Fitts must have had an appreciable diameter and the electrical insulation between the targets and the surrounding metal plate must have had an appreciable thickness, so that all his targets might have been effectively wider by a small constant amount than he claimed them to be. This extra would be of little importance with the widest targets but would be a substantial proportion of the narrowest.

These reasons did not, however, appear to be sufficient to explain the poor fit of Eq. 5.5 to our results, and accordingly three other possible explanations were considered. The first of these was that movement times depend more on *aim* than on accuracy achieved, and thus more

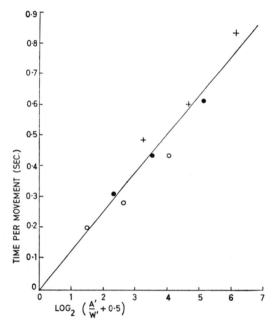

Figure 5.6. Times for reciprocal tapping between two targets plotted in terms of Eq. 5.4. Data from an experiment by Welford *et al.* (1963). $\bigcirc$ = 32 mm targets, $\bullet$ = 11 mm and $+$ = 4 mm. The distance from the centre of one target to the far edge of the other for each target width are, from left to right, 50, 142 and 402 mm.

Each point is based on 100 shots by each of 81 subjects. The subjects were all aged between 40 and 49.

on target presented than on scatter observed. If so, Eq. 5.5 is misconceived and should be replaced by Eq. 5.4. This view, apart from its intuitive improbability, appears to be untenable because it would assume no relationship between observed scatter and movement time for any given target and amplitude. There was, however, a clear tendency for time to rise as the distribution of shots became narrower, as shown in Fig. 5.7.

A second suggestion arose from the fact that the results could be made strikingly more linear by subtracting a small constant (*c*) of about

3 mm from the observed widths of the distributions of shots, thus replacing W' in Eq. 5.5. by $(W' - c)$. The constant might perhaps be attributed to tremor, the presence of which would broaden distributions slightly and mean that, in order to attain a given level of accuracy, the subject would have to aim at a slightly higher level. Such tremor might arise from the fact that the time taken to traverse the servo mechanisms controlling movement means that there is an inevitable period of about ·1 sec during which operation is open-loop. Alternatively it might arise from the fact that muscular action by a large member such as the arm is not very finely graded and that movements are likely to be slightly disturbed by factors such as the pulse. Some support for this general point of view comes from the fact that the constant required to make the present results plot approximately on a straight line is of the same order of magnitude as the scatter achieved when a series of shots all aimed at the same point are made at a moderate rate, also Fitts's results are appreciably better fitted than they are in Fig. 5.4 if the same constant is deducted from W. The slope of regressions such as that in Fig. 5.7, when plotted with 3 mm deducted from all the observed scatters is approximately that for joining equal targets at different distances in Fig. 5.6 – that is about 10 bits per sec. We may also note that when very accurate placing is required, subjects tend not to rely on arm movements but to support the wrist, thus minimising tremor.

On the other hand this view has serious disadvantages which seem to make it, like the first, untenable. The subtraction of a constant from W' of about 3 mm obviously makes nonsense of the data of Schouten *et al.* for pin sizes of 1 or 2 mm since in these cases the effective target size would be a negative quantity. Perhaps more important, we should expect tremor not to add a constant to W' but rather to add to the variance of the distribution of shots in such a way that one should write not $(W' - c)$ but $\sqrt{W'^2 - c^2}$. This, however, does not produce a good fit to the results shown in Fig. 5.6.

A third possibility, free from the objections to the previous two, arises from the fact that if in Fig. 5.6 we join the points for any one target width at different amplitudes of movement we obtain slopes of about 10 bits per sec as shown in Fig. 5.8(A), and if we join the points for any one amplitude at different target widths we obtain slopes of about 6 bits per sec as shown in Fig. 5.8(B). This suggests that two control processes or phases ought perhaps to be distinguished: a faster distance-covering phase and a slower phase of 'homing' on to the target. It seems reasonable to regard the former as similar in speed to that of a ballistic movement of a given amplitude and the latter as implying an additional process of visual control. If so, the appropriate equation would be of the type:

$$\text{Movement time} = a \log A' + b \log \frac{1}{W'} \qquad (5.6)$$

where a and b are the slope constants for amplitudes and targets respectively. Since ballistic movements show substantial accuracy without

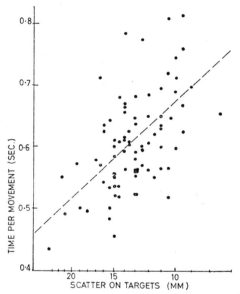

Figure 5.7. Relationship between the time taken per shot and the width of distributions of shots.

The results are those for targets 11 mm wide set with centres 397 mm apart. Each point represents the mean of 100 shots by one subject. The best fitting straight line is for an incremental rate of gain of 6·3 bits per sec.

current visual control we should probably write in place of Eq. 5.6:

$$\text{Movement time} = a \log \frac{A'}{W'_0} + b \log \frac{W'_0}{W'_i}$$
$$= a \log A' - b \log W'_i + (b - a) \log W'_0 \qquad (5.7)$$

when W'_0 is the scatter of shots for ballistic movements of amplitude A', and W'_i is the scatter observed with any particular target width under consideration.

The part played by $(b - a) \log W'_0$ depends on whether or not W'_0 increases with A'. This, as Woodworth (1899) has pointed out, is

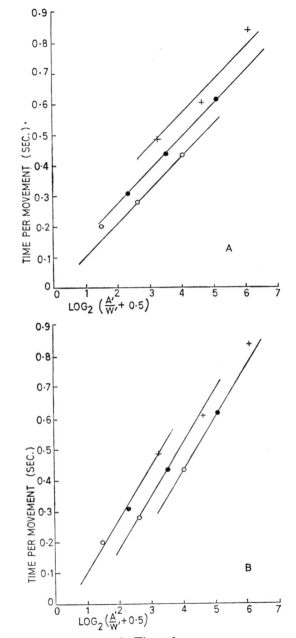

Figure 5.8. The same data as in Fig. 5.6.

A. Showing the relation of movement time to amplitude, keeping accuracy constant.

B. Showing the relation of movement time to accuracy, keeping amplitude constant.

difficult to measure directly as it involves controlling both movement time and also vision, but if Eq. 5.7 is valid we can infer an answer from the present data. Suppose, for example, that Weber's Law held and that W'_0 rose proportionately with A', it would then be possible to rewrite Eq. 5.7 thus:

$$\text{Movement time} = a \log \frac{A'}{CA'} + b \log \frac{CA'}{W'_i}$$

$$= b \log \frac{A'}{W'_i} + (b - a) \log C \qquad (5.8)$$

where $C = W'_0/A' = $ the Weber Fraction. It is obvious that Eq. 5.8

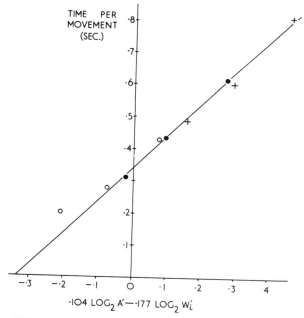

Figure 5.9. The same data as in Fig. 5.6 plotted in terms of Eq. 5.7. The regression line cuts the abscissa at $(b - a) \log W'_0$. The value of this, $-\cdot37$, corresponds to a W'_0 of 31 mm.

would imply that all the points in Fig. 5.6 should lie on the same straight line and that it therefore does not give a good fit to the observed data.

If alternatively we assume that W'_0 is constant at all values of A', the expression $(b - a) \log W'_0$ in Eq. 5.7 becomes a constant, and the data should fall on a straight line described by Eq. 5.7, provided suitable values for a and b are chosen. Values were accordingly calculated from the data of Fig. 5.6 omitting the leftmost point which was suspected of being somewhat too high because of the lower limit to movement time mentioned earlier. The resulting plot in Fig. 5.9 shows all the points falling close to a straight line with the exception of the leftmost. It thus indicates that Eq. 5.7 provides a good fit to the data provided the accuracy of ballistic movements (W'_0) is independent of their extent. Paillard (1968) has provided some evidence that this last point is true by showing that the accuracy with which one hand could be moved into alignment with the other did not depend on whether the distance moved was long or short. In other words it seems as if the accuracy of ballistic movements depends on some absolute appreciation of end position rather than of distance moved.

An estimate of W'_0 can be obtained from Fig. 5.9, since the distance from zero to where the regression line cuts the abscissa $= (b-a) \log W'_0$. In the example shown W'_0 worked out at 31 mm which is certainly of the right order of magnitude. The rates of gain of information implied by the slope constants a and b are respectively 9·6 bits per sec which is close to the figure for Fitts's results, and 5·6 bits per sec which is close to that found by Hick (1952a) and others for choice reaction times. It is tempting to suppose that the former represents the capacity of the effector mechanism and that the latter represents control involving the translation mechanism.

In concluding this chapter it must be emphasised that although we know a good deal about the mechanism responsible for the control of simple individual or repeated movements, we are still almost totally ignorant of the ways in which the more complex patterns of movement normally involved in everyday activities are phased, timed and co-ordinated. Perhaps the best guess that can be hazarded at present as a guide for future research, is that they follow the same principles as those which appear to govern the co-ordination of perceptual activities. These we consider in the next chapter.

VI

Economy of Decision

During the second decade of the present century the results were published of several independent researches all aimed at emphasising the fact that incoming sense data are grouped and ordered. Thus as regards vision, we do not normally perceive simply a mosaic of more and less stimulated points, but coherent objects which have form and structure. All these researches dealt essentially with visual perception but the principles they enunciated obviously had significance for other sensory modes, especially hearing. Most of the writers, and particularly those constituting the *Gestalt* school, were mainly concerned to relate conscious perception to the physical 'structure' or 'patterning' of the stimulus. Bartlett (1932), however, in his studies emphasised from the start that perception was in a very real sense an activity of the whole organism, shaped not only by the objective stimuli but by the attitudes, interests, hopes, fears and experiences an individual brought to the situation; there is, he urged, an *'effort after meaning'* which embraces far more than the dynamic interaction of various parts of a complex pattern of sensory stimulation. Bartlett's work was ahead of its time and anticipated in many important ways the modern treatment of perception in information-theory and similar terms. We shall not here examine these approaches, old and new, in detail, but shall instead try to outline some of the factors which seem to be important in shaping perception, and shall then look at some of their analogues and extensions in other areas of human performance. The issues involved are at first sight highly academic, yet they have important implications for the design of visual displays and of many types of machinery for practical use (see e.g. Easterby, 1967).

ECONOMY IN PERCEPTION

Hick, in a paper which has attracted less attention than it deserves, noted that

> 'a curious feature of mental representations, which has a bearing on certain coding problems, is the tendency towards economy . . . Professor Max Born, in his Waynflete Lectures, refers sceptically to the notion that elegant simplicity in a scientific theory tells in favour of its truth. In the literal sense of the proposition, he is obviously right to be sceptical. But we are not looking merely for truth, but for useful truth, by whatever standard we judge utility; and elegance, in this context, is apt to mean "fitness for function". A simple representation, if approximately true, is far more worth having than a complicated one; and a similar valuation appears to operate at the relatively primitive levels of perception. It has often been remarked how powerful is the compulsion to try to make sense of things, even when it is known to be impossible' (Hick, 1952b, p. 72).

The process of organising and grouping incoming data may be thought of as the *abstraction of constants* from the total mass of data presented in space and over time, together with the *selection* of some data as dominant and important while the rest are relegated to the background and more or less neglected. Neurological studies have shown that the cortex is constituted to analyse patterns into units such as lines, corners and their orientations, achieving economy by this elementary form of coding (Hubel and Wiesel, 1962, 1968). More complex perception may be thought of as involving the imposition of schemes or rules which reduce the effective amount of data to be handled.

Obvious examples are to be seen in concept formation and in the estimation of averages of, say, several positions of a pointer on a scale or spots on a diagram (Bartlett and Mackworth, 1950, Spencer, 1961, 1963, Edwards, 1963), and in both there is a link with topics covered in previous chapters. Concept formation can be regarded as a type of classification in which several differing objects are put into a single category (see p. 94) on the basis of some common feature, either an item or some relationship between items which is identical in them all. The estimation of averages can be thought of as an activity involving choice which may be handled in information-theory terms: the accuracy with which the average is judged can be expressed in terms of the distribution of the quantities which contribute to it, and thus can be expressed in informational terms (see p. 147).

Principles of abstraction and economy seem to apply on a more or less detailed scale in many types of perception. The fundamental approach of many modern studies on this subject is epitomised in a type of guessing game outlined by Attneave (1954). We may take as an illustration an experiment used for some years in the experimental psychology practical class at Cambridge. The experimenter has a grid in front of him containing a pattern as in Fig. 6.1. The subject cannot see the experimenter's grid but has his own blank grid and is required to guess for each square in turn whether it will be black or white. The experimenter tells him the correct answer immediately after each guess and the subject fills it in on his grid thus gradually building up a copy of

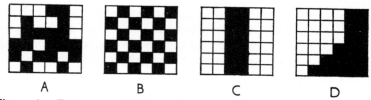

A B C D

Figure 6.1. Designs used in 'guessing game'. The subject is required to guess, without seeing the design, whether each square is black or white, beginning at the top left corner and proceeding along each row in turn.

the experimenter's grid. If the pattern is random as in Fig. 6.1(A), the subject will on average make 50% errors. If, however, the pattern is not random, as in Fig. 6.1(B) and (C), the subject will quickly detect the regularities and thereafter make no more errors. If the pattern changes as in Fig. 6.1(D), he will make a few errors around the point of change but none once its nature and direction have been recognised. The process is similar to that discussed in Chapter 3 (p. 104) whereby the subject sets up a running hypothesis which is at each step confirmed and extended or refuted and modified by the incoming data. It is not, of course, suggested that anyone does in fact scan a pattern like this in ordinary perception, but the game serves to emphasize that, once regularities are detected, much of the rest of the pattern can be inferred – in information-theory terms, it becomes, *redundant*. Information is concentrated at the points at which regularity changes, such as the beginning of the slope in Fig. 6.1(D). More generally one can say it is concentrated at *boundaries*, at *angles* and where curved lines change their *rate* of curvature.

The main principles by which such redundancy is attained can be roughly divided into seven types:

164 *Fundamentals of Skill*

Grouping

The Gestalt school, especially Wertheimer, emphasised that one of the fundamentals of perception was that discrete objects in close proximity tend to be grouped. This is obviously true of objects close together in space and is also true of successive events in time. Consider, for example, Fig. 6.2. Practically everyone sees the spots in pairs separated

●● ●● ●● ●● ●● ●●

Figure 6.2.

by spaces. If we put 1 for the spots and o for the spaces, the pattern could be presented as 110110110 . . . and the subject may be conceived as treating (coding) each 011 as a single unit. Such coding is economical in the sense that, if the regularity in the sequence is recognised, once o or 11 have occurred, the ensuing 11 or o can be inferred with certainty and are thus redundant in the sense that they convey no further information.

Attneave (1954) has pointed out that certain other kinds of spatial grouping can be economical in informational terms in the sense that the approximate locations of the individual objects becomes redundant. Consider the groups of points in Fig. 6.3(A). Their approximate locations can be specified in terms of the relatively coarse grid shown in

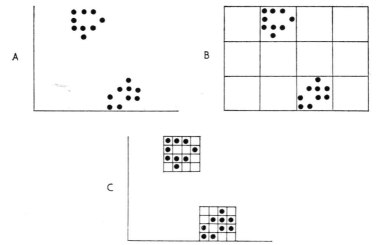

Figure 6.3. Economy in specifying position brought about by specifying the approximate positions of groups.

Fig. 6.2(B) and all shown to lie within two of the 16 squares. Precise locations can then be specified in terms of finer grids, shown in Fig. 6.3(C), which are confined to these two squares.

Continuity of line

We have already noted that information is concentrated at points in a pattern at which the directions of lines or contours change. The same is true at points where a line or contour is interrupted. It is thus understandable that a pattern such as that of Fig. 6.4 tends to be seen as —

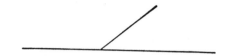

Figure 6.4.

plus /, rather than as __/ plus —: the former arrangement requires the specification of two lines only, whereas the latter requires the specification of three.

Continuity is not confined to straight lines but can also be perceived in curves, especially when the curvature has some easily specifiable characteristic such as a steady rate of change of direction as in an arc of a circle, or a steady acceleration as in a spiral. The same is true of several other types of constant change: for example few people observing the series

    o   oo   ooo   oooo   ooooo

would be in much doubt about how it would continue.

Regularity and symmetry

Hochberg and McAlister (1953) and Attneave (1954) have both emphasised that the Gestalt school's principles that regular and symmetrical patterns are easier to see than irregular, can be accounted for in terms of economy of specification. An irregular polygon, of which the number of sides is not known beforehand, requires for its specification either the lengths of all the sides plus all the angles except one, or all the angles and all the sides except one – in either case $(2n - 1)$ items if n is the number of sides. If, however, the figure is known to be symmetrical, only n items need be specified including the angle of one of the sides to the axis of symmetry. If the figure is completely regular, specification of only one side and one angle will suffice. Similar considerations apply to figures with curved sides although the process of specifying them is obviously more complex.

This kind of approach was extended by Hochberg and McAlister and by Hochberg and Brooks (1960) to the perception of ambiguous line drawings which can be seen as either two- or three-dimensional. For example, Hochberg and McAlister found that the percentage of

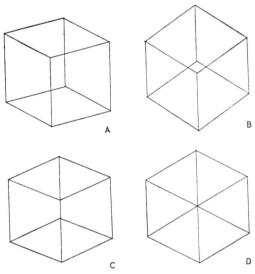

Figure 6.5. Various projections of a cube, together with the percentage of time each was seen as three-dimensional rather than two-dimensional, and certain stimulus characteristics. Adapted from Hochberg and McAlister (1953).

	Percent three-dimensional responses	Numbers of elements required to specify figures as two-dimensional	
		Line segments	Angles
A	98·7	16	26
B	99·3	16	26
C	51·0	13	20
D	40·0	12	18

time that cubes similar to those shown in Fig. 6.5 were seen as three-dimensional fell with the number of lines and angles required to specify them as two-dimensional – that is it fell from A and B to C and again to D in Fig. 6.5. If the patterns are seen as three-dimensional there are in all cases 12 lines and 24 angles, so that if the number of lines and angles is taken as the criterion, three-dimensions should be preferred for A and B, two-dimensions for D, and C should be equivocal, as was indeed the case.

Hochberg and McAlister recognised that scoring in terms of lines and angles is crude and that other possibilities need to be considered. Of these three may be mentioned which appear to have application far beyond the present case:

(*a*) The economy of three-dimensional perception is much greater than two-dimensional in A, B and C if the number of *different* angles is considered. In two-dimensions A consists of three pairs of overlapping parallelograms each with two different angles – a total of six – whereas when it is seen as a cube all angles are equal. In B and C two of the pairs of parallelograms are similar, but there are still four different angles. In D all angles are equal in both two and three dimensions.

(*b*) Although, if minor perspective effects are neglected, all four views are projections of a cube, they are not all equally probable. A real outline cube would only be seen as D by an observer who viewed it in one precise alignment with one eye from a fixed position. Viewing with one eye would also be necessary for C and movement would be permissible only along a vertical axis: lateral movement would turn the pattern into one of type A. Patterns of type B would be obtained from a real outline cube by fusing images from both eyes, so that monocular viewing would not be required, but movement could still only occur vertically without its becoming a pattern of type A. None of these limitations apply to patterns of type A: the size of the small parallelogram in the middle would differ according to precise orientation, but the same general pattern would remain with both vertical and horizontal movements and whether viewed with one eye or two.

(*c*) The fact that D is a completely regular pattern in two dimensions makes one wonder why it was seen in three-dimensions by Hochberg and McAlister's subjects for as much as 40% of the time. A likely reason is that all subjects were shown all patterns and were thus looking for three-dimensional appearance. In other words, their perception depended not only on the immediate stimulus, but on expectations brought from previous stages of the experiment.

Continuity of change

Considerations of probability mentioned in (*b*) emphasise that perception is concerned with stimuli which are not normally instantaneous but continue in, and may change with, time. A specification which is not economical in a static display may therefore become so if the display changes with time. A well-known illustration is Wertheimer's demonstration of grouping by 'common movement'. For example if the spots marked with arrows in Fig. 6.6 moved in unison they would be grouped together as distinct from those which remained stationary, even though in a static display they would be grouped in pairs.

The same principle can be conceived as underlying the perception of movement by objects: to specify a single object as moving from one location to another is often more economical than specifying a number of objects at different locations. This is shown in the so-called ϕ–phenomenon of apparent movement: a light at one point which goes out just as another comes on a little distance away produces a compelling

Figure 6.6. If the spots indicated by arrows move in unison they will tend to be grouped together as distinct from those that remain stationary, despite the fact that this is contrary to the grouping by proximity seen in Fig. 6.2.

perception of one light changing position, however much the subject knows that two lights are involved. It should be noted that the timing must resemble that of real movement: if the gap between the first light going out and the next coming on is too short the two lights appear distinct and simultaneous, and if it is too long they appear successive.

Continuity of movement can give coherence in cases where other sensory data would not. An illustration is contained in a class experiment conducted in Cambridge for some years past. Subjects view a coloured 'bar' which travels along a horizontal slit in a screen, passing behind three black bars as it moves. When the coloured bar remains the same throughout its journey, practically all subjects see a *single* bar moving the whole distance. If the coloured bar changes width or colour as it passes behind each black bar, most subjects still see only one bar moving. It is only when both colour and width change simultaneously at each black bar that a majority regard the moving bar as no longer one over the whole of its travel.

Perception of distance

We have already noted one example of economy resulting from perception in three dimensions with the projections of cubes shown in Fig. 6.5. The economy principle seems clearly to be involved also in other features of depth and distance perception:

(*a*) Perspective gradients, such as that in Fig. 6.7, enable objects of equal objective size but different retinal sizes at different distances, to be perceived as the same size once the gradient has been recognised (Gibson, 1950). The extraction of the gradient from the data in the observer's field of view thus increases the *invariance* of the objects in the field. For example, if Fig. 6.7 is specified in two dimensions it is necessary to assign different magnitudes to each row of bars and each distance between one bar and the next. If, however, a perspective gradient

Figure 6.7. Perspective gradient used in experiments by Vickers (1967).

is extracted so that the bars are seen as lying on a flat receding surface, all can be specified as equal in size and distance apart.

The gradient appears to be extracted at some cost. If, for example, the whole of Fig. 6.7 except the bottom two rows of bars is covered by a card, the uncovered portion is not likely to be perceived as three-dimensional. If now the card is slowly raised, to expose further rows, the three-dimensional effect will suddenly appear. The same is true of the example shown in Fig. 6.8 but the changeover from two to three dimensions comes later. This can be regarded as due to the fact that the amount of data per row rendered invariant in Fig. 6.7 is greater than in Fig. 6.8. In the former length, width and distances between bars are all made invariant, in the latter, only distance. Systematic studies of this phenomenon using the patterns of Figures 6.7 and 6.8 and others have been reported by Vickers (1967).

The gradients of Figs. 6.7 and 6.8 are for flat surfaces. Gibson emphasised that these are not the only ones that can be extracted: different gradients give impressions of curved surfaces, either concave or convex, and the rate of change affects the apparent angle of slope relative to the subject's line of regard.

Two corollaries to this principle are now well known. First, if a

Figure 6.8. A simplified perspective gradient used by Vickers (1967).

gradient is extracted, objects located along it are scaled for size accordingly, as is shown by some familiar visual illusions (e.g. Fig. 6.9). Second, when a wrong gradient is extracted the sizes of objects may appear to be anomalous. The clearest example of this is in the Ames room where the subject looks through a peephole into a room of irregular shape with one far corner much farther away than the other. The objects in the room are so shaped, however, that all the wall panels become similar in shape and all the floorboards the same width if the room is seen as rectangular – the invariance in the pattern seen is maximised by regarding the room as rectangular. When the whole room is seen in this way the sizes of isolated objects appear very different according to whether they are placed in the nearer or farther corner: for example, of two people of equal height the one in the farther corner appears shorter. We may note in passing that these phenomena have little if anything to do with the familiarity of rectangular rooms, but with maximising the invariance of the data received by the observer: it is, for example, possible to construct an objectively rectangular room which looks irregular in shape. The illusion of the irregular room which appears rectangular has been shown to break down after prolonged observation: this is likely because close scrutiny will reveal a number

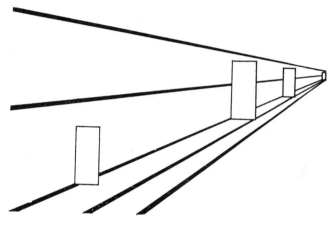

Figure 6.9. The two large rectangles are the same size.

of details, such as the fine textures of painted surfaces, which are not consistent with perception of the two corners as equidistant and thus reduce the extent to which the rectangular view achieves invariance. The inadequacy of familiarity as a basis for judging size in relation to distance has also been demonstrated in other contexts by Hochberg and McAlister (1955) and by Gruber and Dinnerstein (1965).

(b) Gibson was at pains to emphasise that the visual scene which is normally perceived is not the same as that observed in a single fixation of the eye, but represents the integration of many different glances. A good illustration of this is obtained by viewing Fig. 6.10 in a stereoscope. At first glance no depth effect will be seen: it comes only gradually as first one then another pair of circles are fixated and fused. It is, in short, achieved when the gradients of *retinal disparity* and *binocular convergence* have been extracted. Once this has been done, the depth effect is virtually immediate – if one looks away from the stereoscope and then back again, the depth effect is seen at once.

(*c*) Gibson also emphasised that the observer is not normally static but moves, and in doing so produces different changes in the relative positions of objects at different distances. Maximising invariance in these circumstances requires the integration of much more data than when the observer is stationary, and although the economy achieved is greater, the final complexity of what is seen is greater also. The same essential principles apply to the perception of solid objects: as the observer moves their shapes undergo a series of transformations which can be reduced to invariance by specifying the observer's movement.

Figure 6.10. If the right-hand circles are viewed by the right eye and the left-hand circles by the left eye in a stereoscope, the outer circles will appear nearer and the middle circles farther away than the centre circles.

(*d*) These several points jointly lead to the rather surprising conclusion that the visual scene as we perceive it has little to do with the actual data received by the eyes at any moment. It is rather a kind of *framework* in which the kaleidoscope of individual glances is reduced to relative invariance and stability, enabling each new datum to be fitted into a wider context, and providing the observer with a means of orientation and a continuity of space around him.

Constancies

The foregoing discussion of distance perception has obvious implications for size and shape constancies. Once a perceptual framework has been built up, perception of size as invariant with distance and of shape with orientation are economical. These constancies are destroyed only in cases in which the gradients indicating distance cannot be extracted. Thus Thouless (1931) found that a circular disc viewed tilted at an angle was seen as such except when it was placed against a black velvet background and viewed monocularly with the head held in a rest.

The fact that objects retain the same apparent degree of whiteness – or blackness – when seen in different illuminations can also be brought within the economy principle. In a manner somewhat analogous to that of grouping in Fig. 6.3 it is economical to specify the *brightness* of different parts of the field and to specify the *whiteness* of objects within these parts rather than specify all the different amounts of light reflected by the various objects in the whole field. Despite statements in some of the standard textbooks and the findings of classical workers such as Katz (1935), it is not generally recognised that the visual mechanism usually has fully adequate data for dividing the field up into areas of different brightness. The amount of light reflected by a white object in shadow is often far less than that reflected by a black object in good illumination within the same field of view – in other words, differences between black and white cover a relatively small part of the total range of light intensities present in any perceived scene.

Familiarity

The factors making for economy in perception that we have considered hitherto have been concerned with the physical characteristics of the incoming data and not with the subject's past experience. It must, however, be recognised that past experience can upon occasion play an important part in determining just how incoming data are coded. The categories of identification discussed in Chapters 2 and 3 are like *templates* which the subject tries to fit to incoming data. Normally he is successful and the process is so rapid that he is unaware of its happening, but when objects are uncommon, or seen from unusual angles or under adverse conditions, the process may take much longer and the search for a 'fit' may be much more conscious.

The imposition of a template from past experience has much the same effect as grouping, enabling a complex of data to be apprehended as a unitary whole. Typically the fit does not have to be precise but has to fall within acceptable limits of approximation, and the template itself seems constantly to be modified as the result of further experience. For example, the category 'modern car' will include a range of shapes, sizes and colours, and will change substantially during the lifetime of any individual. It was such facts that Bartlett (1932) expressed when he referred to the 'fitting' process as 'schematic' and the templates as '*schemata*'.

Bartlett noted that complex line drawings to which a match could be made in this way were regarded by his subjects as 'simpler' than less objectively complex drawings that could not be readily linked to common objects. Such observations would almost certainly be confirmed quantitatively by Attneave's type of guessing game, in the sense that fewer errors would be made if a familiar shape was recognised than if all the subject had to go on were simple continuities and regularities. One can perhaps see an analogy to Bartlett's results in Michotte's (1946, 1963) experiments on the perception of *causality* in sequences of events: the subject imposes a pattern, couched in terms of one event causing another, which gives coherence to several separate events and enables them to be treated as one. For example, if one object such as a ball moves up to another, which then immediately moves away, the first is seen as pushing the second. The successful application of such a pattern is likely to depend, as Michotte insisted, upon the objective sequence conforming to certain time limits: the causal sequence would not be seen if there was a substantial time interval between the movements of the two balls.

Bartlett was clear that the schemata actually imposed showed some effects of social conventions and of the subjects' individual interests, presumably implying that the likelihood of any one schema being applied depended to some extent on its availability at the time of the experiment. The possibility of deliberately shaping perception by inducing bias towards particular schemata was illustrated in the classical experiment of Carmichael *et al.* (1932) who showed, for example, that the reproduction of two circles joined horizontally by a short line and exposed briefly differed substantially according to whether the subject was told beforehand that he was going to see a pair of eyeglasses or a dumbell.

Two results run through Bartlett's and much preceding and subsequent work, whether concerned with effects of familiarity or of the objective structure of the stimulus.

(*a*) Much of the detail which is apparently perceived is in fact inferred. It seems as if a schema which is imposed on incoming data brings a considerable amount of detail with it and this detail is incorporated into the resulting perception.

(*b*) Details which cannot be fitted into the schema are either ignored or become what Bartlett described as 'dominant details' which are specially noticed. Woodworth (see Woodworth and Schlosberg, 1954) made some play of the same idea under the title of 'schema with correction', suggesting that a subject makes an approximate fit to the data with some familiar category which, if reasonably adequate, suppresses the perception of deviant details. If, however, the lack of fit is substantial in one or two respects, the deviant features are specified separately. Attneave has argued that such a procedure could still be much more economical than no categorisation. We might add that it could often be more economical to accept a fit with a *quickly found* schema and to specify deviant details than to make an extensive search of the material stored in memory for a more precise category.

Turning this second result the other way round, several studies have shown that the difficulty of detecting a given deviation from a standard pattern rises as the deviation becomes smaller in relation to the size or complexity of the pattern (e.g. Hillix, 1960, van de Geer and Levelt, 1963, Sengstake, 1965). Many other studies have shown that once a familiar schema has been applied it may be difficult to change: for example it is often very difficult to reorder the letters in a word to produce an anagram. The difficulty of such reordering rises substantially as the transitions from one letter or pair of letters to another in the words presented become more familiar (Beilin and Horn, 1962) or as those in the solution words become less familiar (Tresselt and Mayzner, 1965).

Problems of formulation

Economy in perception is a concept which runs through a number of somewhat different conceptual models of the processes involved. We have spoken here of economy of specification. In its crudest statement this may refer to the number of lines, angles or other features required to define a pattern. More fundamentally it means that several details of a pattern can be subsumed under some more embracing rule or schema which makes it possible to infer or predict one part of the whole pattern from another. In these terms there are obvious links with information-theory, although the precise manner of linking is open to a good deal of discussion (see Attneave, 1959, Garner, 1962, Staniland, 1966, Evans, 1967). Broadly speaking it can be claimed, on the one hand, that imposition of a rule or schema makes much of the detailed data redundant and that perception maximises redundancy or invariance. At the same time we can say that the number of separately variable items in the data is reduced, so that information is minimised. In other words, the co-variation between different items has been recognised and used to determine the way in which the data are ordered.

In either case the overall mathematical formulation describes a complex process within the subject which needs to be spelt out in detail if a full understanding is to be obtained. From this point of view we may tentatively suggest that economy can usefully be considered in terms of *the amount of data that has to be specified in order to arrive at*

a sufficient definition of the pattern. We can regard the process of definition as one of classification or choice analogous to those discussed in
Chapter 3, involving one or more decisions of the types discussed in
Chapter 2. What is 'sufficient' will depend as emphasised in Chapter 3
on the degree of precision with which the classification must be made.

This method of stating the process covers a number of results not
easy to account for in terms of other formulations:

(*a*) Consider the pattern shown in Fig. 6.11(A). Subjects tend not to
group by proximity as they do with Fig. 6.2, which would yield alternate groups X/ and /X, but by similarity so as to produce alternating

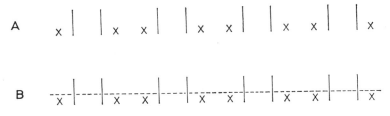

Figure 6.11.

groups of // and XX. There is no advantage of one arrangement over
the other in the simple information-theory terms used for Fig. 6.2,
but there is some advantage for alternate groups of lines and crosses in

RANDOM   CONSTRAINED

Figure 6.12. Examples of bar-diagrams used by Fitts *et al.* (1956).

that they can be defined in terms of whether or not they come above
the line in Fig. 6.11(B). In other words, the subject can group simply
in terms of the tops of the lines, and virtually neglect the rest of the
pattern.

(*b*) Fitts *et al.* (1956) required their subjects to identify bar figures
of the type shown in Fig. 6.12 from among sets of eight similar figures.
The bars could be of eight different heights and in different trials the
figures were constructed either with random bar-heights or with the
constraint that all eight heights were represented once but in random

order. It was expected that because there were 8^8 possible random figures but only 8! constrained, that the latter would be identified more quickly. The reverse, however, was found to be true, and this result has been confirmed by Anderson and Leonard (1958). Fitts *et al.* noted that the constrained figures appeared more similar to one another than did the random, and if one considers the subject's task in detail one can see that this is likely to be so. If he compares only the first bars of the standard figure and of one to be distinguished as similar or different he can, on average, decide that it is different seven times out of eight. On the eighth occasion, when the first bars are the same he will have to compare the second bars, and again he will be able to decide seven times out of eight. The same will be true if he has to go to a third or subsequent bar. With constrained figures he will again be able to decide seven times out of eight by inspecting the first bars only, but if he has to go to further bars he will only be able to decide six times out of seven for the second, five times out of six for the third and so on. Alternatively if he inspects the figure row by row from the top downwards he will in many cases be able to identify a random figure from its having two bars of the same height longer than any others, but he will never have this cue with the constrained figures. In short, whichever method he adopts he will, with the constrained figures, have on average to inspect more of the pattern than is necessary with the random figures.

(*c*) Attneave (1957) required subjects to learn to associate boys' names with sets of eight irregular polygons. Each set was constructed by making minor variations in a basic design. He found that learning was better when all the variations were in the same corners than when any of the corners might be altered. It is perhaps obvious that one design is likely to be distinguished from another more easily if all the variations are concentrated at a few points since the remainder of the figure can then be neglected.

(*d*) However, even if it is strictly possible to ignore some parts of a pattern, subjects may find it difficult to do so. For instance Bricker (1955b), whose subjects responded as quickly as possible with a different nonsense syllable to each of the eight patterns shown in Fig. 6.13, found that reaction was quicker when only the rightmost three items in each row were exposed than when all five were shown. The patterns could be unambiguously identified by means of either the first three or the last three items, so that there was no need to observe them all. Nevertheless subjects seemed to have done so, at least to some extent. The main advantage in having all five items exposed is that if one is unreliable, the correct response can still be inferred from the others so that accuracy does not suffer. This beneficial effect of redundancy was shown by Bricker to occur, as it has been by many others in other contexts.

Perception in everyday life is, of course, much more complex than it is with the single objects or groups of objects used in laboratory experiments. This is so not only in the sense that many and varied objects are dealt with more or less simultaneously but, more important, that the co-ordination and integration of data seems to take place on several different scales at the same time. A clear example is that when reading we simultaneously integrate letters (or graphemes) into words, words into sentences, sentences into paragraphs and perhaps also become aware of even broader features such as the style of writing. Similarly in looking at a painting we may be aware not only of the various objects depicted, but of details such as brush-work, and of broader aspects such as the overall composition of the picture. The upper limit to the integrative process at any one moment seems to be set by the extent to which there has been time and opportunity to observe enough detail to produce a larger framework within which it can be ordered.

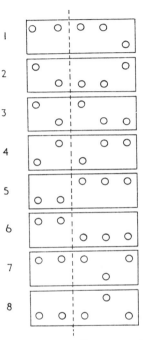

Figure 6.13. Patterns of lights used by Bricker (1955b).

The lower limit seems to depend on how far the action to which the perception is directed demands attention to detail. It is well known, for example, that when a book is being read rapidly, misprints may pass unnoticed that would almost certainly have been recognised when reading more slowly. Attneave (1954) gives the illustration that when looking at a furry animal we do not normally observe each separate hair, but see all the hairs together as a 'furry texture', or again that looking at a mottled surface we specify merely the overall texture and not each individual variation. This, he points out, is equivalent to adopting a relatively coarse grid in the 'guessing game' and so treating together coherent areas which contain given proportions and distributions of black and white (or whatever colours are involved), as having a particular texture as opposed to other areas with different proportions or distributions. The setting of this lower limit takes us beyond perception in the immediate sense to the interplay of perception and action to which we now turn.

RECODING AND TRANSLATION

The coding of input data in the manner we have been discussing is typically succeeded by one or more central stages of what may be broadly termed *recoding* – that is to say the coding initially imposed on the data is translated into a different code. These processes are obvious in translating from one language to another, or in putting into words material presented visually, and they clearly underlie tests of mental function such as digit-symbol substitution.

Recoding may result in substantial further economies in dealing with incoming data. Oldfield (1954) gives the following example:

100100011011100011100100001110010001

The series can be broken up into units of 100 or 011, and if we recode 100 as A and 011 as B it can be translated into the very much shorter series

AABBABAABAAB

This could be further shortened by recoding AAB as X and BAB as Y to produce

XYXX

The economy resulting from each recoding is achieved at the cost of having the 'key' to it stored in memory and available for decoding the message when it is required to put it back into its original form: if this key is not retained most of the original information is lost.

Recoding can make material easier to handle in several ways. For example, Miller (1956) notes that whereas a subject can repeat back only about nine random binary digits if he deals with them as such, he can reproduce many more if he groups them in threes and converts into decimal digits by taking 000 = 0, 001 = 1, 010 = 2 and so on up to 111 = 7. In this way the series

101000100111001110

becomes

504716

In this case the total information in the message is unchanged by the recoding, but the number of items ('chunks' as Miller terms them) is greatly reduced. An alternative, although less efficient, method of reducing the number of items is to retain the first and then the lengths of run of each type afterwards. Miller's sequence would in these terms become

1,113123231

Miller found that the method he described required considerable practice before its full effect was obtained: in other words the benefits of recoding again depended on the establishment of a 'key' in memory and having it readily available for use. Such recoding also implies grouping and can be hindered when conditions make this difficult. For instance Klemmer (1964) found that practice in transforming binary digits to octal did not substantially improve the span of perception for binary digits exposed for very brief intervals. Again several experiments have shown that patterns are less accurately perceived if different portions are shown successively in time than if they are shown all at once (e.g. Harcum and Friedman, 1963, Weene, 1965), and that words are less easily read if shown letter by letter instead of in larger units (Newman, 1966). Recoding also takes an appreciable time and may therefore not be achieved when material is presented at fast rates (Pollack and Johnson, 1965).

Introspectively such recoding seems to be a kind of *response* to the material and may therefore be only a special case of the recoding that takes place in the translation from perception to action – the difference being simply whether or not the response is overt. To consider the transition from perception to action as a process of recoding may at first sight seem surprising, yet a moment's reflection must make it clear that there is a difference between the neural activity involved in the identification of an object and that required to initiate action in response to it: in subjective terms there is a profound difference between knowing what has happened and deciding what to do about it.

Problems of recoding between perception and action have in recent years assumed considerable practical significance in the design of controls for vehicles and machine tools and of consoles for the monitoring and control of automatic plant, and it is research aimed at clarifying the principles involved in these that probably provides our most systematic present knowledge of recoding operations.

Compatibility' – the relationships between displays and controls

Many experiments have shown that performance of a task is affected not only by perceptual requirements and actions involved but by the relationships between them, and have attempted to relate performance to the nature of the intervening steps needed to bridge the gap between perception and action. Such steps are at a minimum in the situation used by Leonard (1959) for the choice-reaction experiment mentioned in Chapter 3 (p. 83) in which the subject held his fingers lightly on the armatures of a set of relays: the signals were vibrations by one or other of the armatures, and the subject responded by pressing the same armature. Relationships between perception and action are similarly straightforward when moving an object by hand from one position to another, in that the direction and extent of the movements of the hand are directly related to the perceived positions and changes in position of the object. Baker (1960), for example, found that tracking was much better with a stylus that could be used to trace the target directly on a cathode-ray tube than with a joystick which moved a spot on the tube.

One of the clearest examples of complicating these relationships is given by Garvey and Knowles (1954) who used the displays and control panels shown in Fig. 6.14. In system A each signal was the lighting of one of the 100 bulbs, and subjects responded by pressing the button immediately below the light concerned. The same was true of system B except that each signal consisted of two lights, one in each column, and responses were made by pressing the corresponding two buttons, thus again giving 100 possibilities. The completion of each response brought on the next signal so that the subject set his own pace of work: he was told to work as fast as possible without making errors. Systems C and D were similar to A and B respectively except that the lights and buttons were on separate panels. Performance with C and D took about twice as long as with A and B, presumably because with C and D the subject had first to identify the position of the light or lights on the display panel and then search for the corresponding positions on the control panels, whereas with A and B one search sufficed for both. We can perhaps assume that the same economy accounted for the flattening of the slope relating reaction-time to degree of choice with highly compatible arrangements which were found by Crossman (1956) and Griew (1958b) and mentioned in Chapter 3 (p. 82).

With system E the row and column of the display panel in which the light appeared had to be indicated by pressing the appropriate buttons in the left- and right-hand columns of the control panel: there was thus a recoding required between display and control. A recoding in the opposite direction was involved in F. These systems yielded considerably slower performance than any of the others, and this seems to have been due essentially to the need for recoding and not to any feature of the display or control as such. This is not to say that display and control features had no effects: systems B, D and E in which two

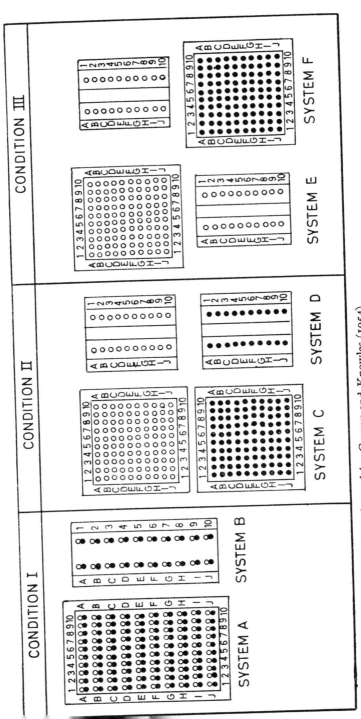

Figure 6.14. Display and control panels used by Garvey and Knowles (1954).

buttons had to be pressed for each response were all a little slower than the corresponding systems A, C and F which required only one, and the difference might well have been greater if it had not been partly offset by the difficulty of discriminating one light from another in the 10 × 10 displays used in systems A, C and E. Evidence of such difficulty has been provided by Garvey and Mitnick (1955) who found that performance with system C could be speeded up by marking the display and control panels with lines dividing the 10 × 10 matrices into

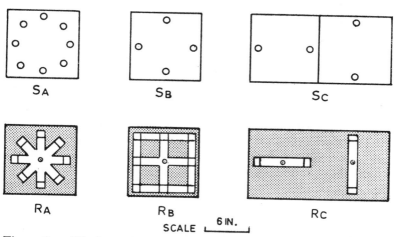

Figure 6.15. Display and control panels used by Fitts and Seeger (1953). With the display panel SA the signal was one of the 8 lights. With SB each signal consisted of either one light or two adjacent lights. With SC each signal consisted of either one light alone or one in each pair. All display panels thus provided 8 possible signals. With control panels RA and RB the subject responded by moving a stylus from the centre to one of the 8 indicated positions. With RC he had two styli, one on each bar, and moved one or both as indicated by the signal.

smaller groups. The differences between the several systems appeared to be resistant to at least moderate amounts of practice: although performance improved markedly over 1,500 reactions, the differences between the systems remained substantial. Whether they would have disappeared after much longer practice is, of course, another matter.

Similar effects of recoding have been shown by Fitts and Seeger (1953) who compared all possible combinations of the display and control panels shown in Fig. 6.15. They found that reactions were fastest and most accurate for each display when it was paired with its corresponding control panel – that is when the recoding between display and control was at a minimum. It was these authors who coined the term 'compatibility' to denote the degree of directness between display and control.

Looking at these experiments in the perspective of others, the recodings normally required between perception and action can be seen to fall into two main classes: *spatial transpositions* and *symbolic translations*. Included in the former are mirror reversals and the effects of various other arrangements of display and control which require some mental reorientation of the one in order to relate it to the other. An example, amongst the many that could be cited, is a serial reaction-time experiment by Kay (1955) who presented his subjects with a box containing a row of 12 lights and a second box with a corresponding row of 12 Morse keys under three conditions: (*a*) with each key immediately below its corresponding light, (*b*) the same but with the box of lights 3 ft away across a table and (*c*) the same as (*b*) but with the box of lights reversed end to end so that the leftmost light corresponded to the rightmost key and so on. The signal lights appeared in random order, each being brought on by correct response to the one before. The mean times to complete 30 responses under the three conditions were (*a*) 24·5 sec, (*b*) 40·8 and (*c*) 97·4 and the errors made were 0, 4·0 and 9·0.

Increases of time, errors, or both have been found also when horizontal movements have to be made to match distances indicated on a vertical as opposed to a horizontal display (Szafran, see Welford, 1958, pp. 142–146) and where view of a target is distorted by viewing through prisms (Kalil and Freedman, 1966a, b). The most extensive series of studies in this area has been made, as mentioned in the previous chapter, by K. U. and W. M. Smith and their colleagues. They observed writing and other activities by subjects whose hands were obscured from direct view but could be seen via a television screen on which the image was rotated by varying amounts (e.g. Smith *et al.*, 1956, Smith and Smith, 1962, Gould and Smith, 1963). Performance at these tasks improves rapidly with practice, and the adjustment once achieved seems to be general in the sense that when it has been acquired for actions by one limb, it transfers to other limbs (e.g. Bray, 1928).

The general concept of spatial transposition as a type of recoding which takes time and central capacity to achieve is of obvious application to certain spatial tests of intelligence which demand that shapes should be rotated 'in the head' to make them fit into other shapes. It also applies to the difficulty experienced when writing letters and numbers in reverse: for example Brown (see Welford, 1951, p. 66) found that the average time taken by subjects to write the ten figures 1–0 in a normal manner was 9·4 sec but rose to 33·0 sec when they were written with each digit reversed. The difference of time required by the same subjects to *trace* over normal and reversed figures was very small. The reason for the difference was presumably that when writing reversed figures subjects had to transpose the orders that would normally be given to guide the hand, whereas when tracing they had merely to

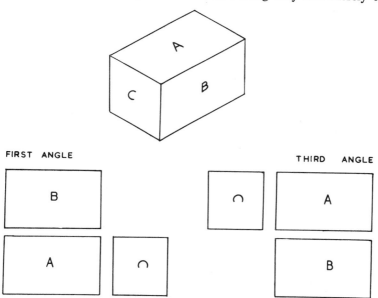

Figure 6.16. Illustration of first and third angle orthographic projections for machine drawings as studied by Spencer (1965).

follow straightforwardly the pattern presented to them. The reversed writing showed a substantial practice effect – the mean time for a second attempt at the figures 1–0 was only 22·2 sec – indicating that once the transposition had been made it remained to some extent available for use and did not have to be rebuilt from scratch.

A further problem in the field of spatial transposition has been studied by Spencer (1965) who compared the comprehension of two standard forms of engineering drawings shown in Fig. 6.16. Untrained subjects read the 'third angle' drawing more quickly and accurately than the 'first angle': it is obvious that the 'third angle' is the more straight-forward in that sides adjacent between A and C and between A and B in the actual article remain adjacent in the drawing. Again the difficulty can be reduced with practice – experienced draughtsmen performed equally well with both types of drawing. The cost of the recoding required is, however, indicated by the fact that all subjects found per-spective or isometric drawings easier than either first or third angle projections.

Comparisons of relationships involving *symbolic translations* between display and control with more compatible arrangements have been made by Knowles *et al.* (1953) and by Fitts and Deininger (1954). The former compared systems C and E of Fig. 6.14 with systems in which the display was replaced either by a window showing a letter and number (e.g. A-1 or E-7), or by a letter and number spoken over a loudspeaker, to indicate the response required. Their results are given in Table 6.1

TABLE 6.1 *Effects of symbolic translation between display and control. Results obtained by Knowles* et al. *(1963). Each figure is the mean time per response in sec based on 100 readings from each of nine subjects.*

Type of control panel	Type 10 × 10 matrix as C in Fig. 6.14	of Letter and number shown in window	display Letter and number heard from loud-speaker
10 × 10 matrix as C in Fig. 6.14	2·079	2·234	1·668
Double column as E in Fig. 6.14	2·700	2·179	1·550

which shows that although, as Garvey and Knowles (1964) found, the matrix response panel (C) was better than the double column panel (E) with the matrix display, the double column panel was relatively better with the window and loudspeaker displays: the double column panel is the more compatible with 'figure-letter' presentation. The superiority of presentation by loudspeaker over other methods was presumably due to its having enabled the subjects to look directly at the control panel all the time instead of transferring their gaze to it only after the signal had appeared.

Fitts and Deininger (1954) compared the display and control shown in Fig. 6.17 with an arrangement in which the same control was used but the display was replaced by a window in which figures could be shown indicating clock positions – for example 12.00, 4.30, 9.00 *p* correspond-ing to the different directions on the control panel. The average times taken to move from the centre of the control panel to the end of the appropriate 'spoke' and the errors made are shown in the first two rows of Table 6.2, from which it is evident that the symbolic translation impaired both speed and accuracy: taking both into account, it about halved the rate of gain of information. The remaining four rows of Table 6.2 show the effects of increasing the complexity of the spatial

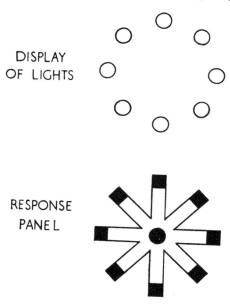

Figure 6.17. Display and control panels used by Fitts and Deininger (1965). Each signal was one of the 8 lights. The subject responded by moving a stylus from the centre of the control panel to the end of one of the arms.

rule relating display to control by either mirror-image reversal so that if the display signals 3.00 the subject moves to what would normally be the 9.00 position, or by complete randomisation. It can be seen that the effect of these changes is much greater for the normally compatible, spatial display than for the symbolic, so that when relationships are completely random the symbolic display yields better performance.

Kay (1954, see also Welford, 1958, 1962c, d) has shown that adding one recoding to another may impair performance to a greater extent than would be accounted for by assuming that the effects of the two recodings were simply additive. The apparatus already described (p. 184) was used but with the additional complication of an index card bearing

TABLE 6.2 *Effects of symbolic translation between display and control. Results obtained by Fitts and Deininger (1954). Each figure is the mean time per response in sec or percentage of errors based on 128 readings from each of ten subjects.*

Correspondence between display and control positions		Type of display		Difference
		Circular as in Fig. 6.17	Clock times shown in window	
Straightforward	Times	·387	·675	+·288
	Errors	1·9	5·0	+3·1
Mirror reversal	Times	·541	·777	+·136
	Errors	4·4	7·2	+2·8
Random	Times	1·111	·885	−·226
	Errors	15·1	10·0	−5·1

the numbers 1–12 (one for each light) in random order. The layouts for two of the three conditions used are shown in Fig. 6.18. Subjects were told to think of the lights as being numbered 1–12 in order from left to right, and when any one came on to find the corresponding number on

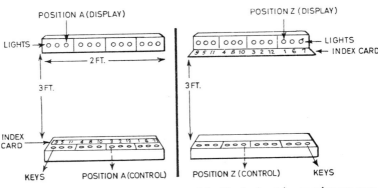

Figure 6.18. Layout of apparatus used in Kay's (1954) experiment combining spatial transposition with symbolic translation.

the card and press the key in line with this number. The task was performed with the index card in three different positions: (1) immediately above the keys as on the left of Fig. 6.18, (2) halfway between the lights and keys and (3) immediately under the lights as on the right of Fig. 6.18.

The instructions applied equally to all three conditions yet they differed widely in difficulty. The average times for a run of 20 responses by the same subjects as in Kay's (1955) experiment were (1) 65·9, (2) 108·3 and (3) 197·1 sec with average errors of 2·4, 6·9 and 21·9 respectively. Comparing these tasks with the purely spatial transpositions involved in Kay's other experiment, we can regard condition (1) as replacing the alignment required across the 3 ft gap in condition (b) by a symbolic translation using the numbered card. Condition (3) required the same symbolic translation and also alignment across the gap, and thus combined the difficulties involved in both conditions (1) and (b). If these difficulties were simply additive, we should expect the differences between the times and errors for conditions (a) and (3) to be the sums of the differences between (a) and (b) and between (a) and (1). In fact the differences between (a) and (3) far exceed these sums: allowing for the fact that 30 instead of 20 responses were made in conditions (a) and (b), simple addition would predict a time for condition (3) of 69·6 sec instead of the 197·1 sec observed, and 5·1 errors instead of the 21·9 observed. The combined difficulties of conditions (1) and (b) seem to have had a quite disproportionate effect on the speed and accuracy of performance.

Relationships between controls and their effects

The principles of compatibility between display and control also apply to relationships between controls and their effects, and both are obviously facets of the same problem. In the former the subject is conceived as translating from what he perceives on the display to an appropriate responding action, in the latter he has to relate action to its observed or expected effects on a display. The evidence in this area has been reviewed by Mitchell and Vince (1951), Murrell (1957, 1965) and Loveless (1962) so that only the general principles involved will be outlined here. They fall broadly into three classes:

1. *Arbitrary rules.* Conventions such as that electrical switches move down (or up) for 'on' lead to an obvious economy of decision and freedom from uncertainty and possible confusion in so far as they apply generally over a wide range of situations. Several studies have shown that many such conventions, or 'population stereotypes', become deeply ingrained, such as that a knob needs to be turned clockwise to increase the intensity of a sound or light (Bradley, 1959). The conventions are, however, arbitrary and differ from one country to another – for example the on and off positions of electric switches; or from one context to another – for instance a water-tap is turned *anti*-clockwise to increase flow. Difficulties have been noted in practical situations where

different conventions are inevitably mixed, such as in the engine-rooms of turbo-electric ships where both steam and electrical controls are present.

2. *Seemingly 'natural' linkages.* Many expectations about the effects of controls appear to assume a simple linkage between perception and action similar to that of the ordinary co-ordination between hand and

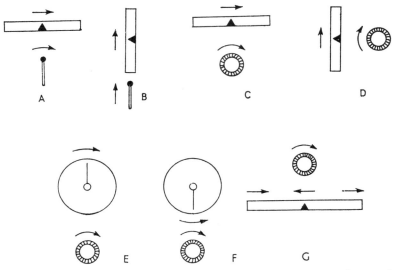

Figure 6.19. Expected relationships between the movements of controls and displays. Movements of the levers and knobs are expected to produce corresponding movements of the pointers in the directions indicated by the arrows.

eye, and several arrangements of display and control seem to be easier to operate if they are deliberately conceived by the subject in these terms (Abbey, 1964). Examples of such simple linkages are that moving a lever in a given direction is expected to move the pointer on a linear scale in the same direction, as shown in Fig. 6.19 (A and B). Other expectations seem to assume a simple mechanism connecting control and display. Thus where the pointer on a linear scale is controlled by a knob, the tendency is to assume that the pointer moves in the same direction as the part of the knob nearest the scale, as if the two were geared together by a rack and pinion (Fig. 6.19 C and D). Various expectations are not always consistent with one another. A conflict leading to confusion may occur, for example, with pointers moving on circular dials. If the clockwise movement of a controlling knob situated below the dial moves the pointer clockwise, the top of the knob and the pointer will move in the same direction while the pointer is near the top of the scale, but in opposite directions when the pointer is near the bottom (Fig. 6.19 E and F). The seriousness of such conflicts seems to be affected by a number of factors as yet imperfectly understood. For example, Thylen (1966) has noted that clockwise rotation of a knob placed above a linear scale as in Fig. 6.19 (G), is expected to move the pointer to the right from a starting position at either end of the scale but to the left from a starting position in the middle: presumably the expectation that the pointer will move as if geared to the knob does not extend to the ends of the scale.

Expectations of these kinds almost certainly contribute to the difficulties of operating velocity-controls where a movement of the control lever or handwheel produces a proportional change not in the *position* of the pointer, but in its *rate of change* of position. To move the pointer from one position to another it is necessary first to move the control in one direction to start the pointer and then in the other direction to stop it. There is still a seemingly natural linkage if the initial movement of the control is compatible with the direction in which the pointer moves, but it is not as direct as with a straightforward positional control.

Mitchell and Vince (1951) noted that more intelligent subjects were less affected by 'unnatural' linkages. The effects of these can also be reduced by training and tend to be less with tracking tasks where the subject is constantly making movements, so that each can be made with reference to the last, than when only occasional adjustments are required. They do not, however, entirely disappear as is shown by the fact that confusion from unexpected relationships may occasionally occur even with well practised subjects, especially under conditions of stress (Taylor and Garvey, 1959).

3. *'Mental models.'* The linkages between single displays and controls shade into more elaborate conceptual models, akin to the spatial frameworks of everyday perception (p. 172), which enable the various parts of a machine or industrial plant to be related together and conceived as a unified whole. Like the perceptual frameworks already discussed, the models need not be strictly accurate in order to be useful. The model conceived by the operator of an industrial plant is often crude and grossly inaccurate, but it enables him to co-ordinate the individual items of his task so that they appear less arbitrary than they otherwise would. It seems clear that these models represent a recoding of the data

provided by the plant and by observation of the effects of controls which is more economical than a set of rules-of-thumb in that fewer separate instructions have to be carried in the operator's memory. In some industrial plants deliberate attempts are made to show the essential relationships between different parts by means of 'mimic diagrams' such as circuit diagrams connecting meters and switches on an electrical control panel (for other examples see Welford, 1960a, pp. 7, 9 and 25).

The precise ways in which these 'mental models' are built, used and maintained is not at present well understood, and the pioneering studies in this area of Crossman (1960) and of Beishon and Crawley (1965) deserve to be extended.

HIGHER UNITS OF PERFORMANCE

The grouping and co-ordination of data in perception has its analogy on the motor side in the building up of sequences of actions which tend to become coherent 'higher units' of performance. The classical studies are those of Bryan and Harter (1899) who found that as Morse operators became more skilled, they tended to pass from dealing with single letters as units to syllables, words or even phrases. They suggested that these units constituted a 'hierarchy of habits' the levels in which could be conceived in terms of size of unit. Much the same ideas were put forward regarding typewriting in the classical monograph by Book (1908). Questions of how the higher units are related to the lower and how they come to be formed out of them were not pursued in detail, and the application the authors made of the hierarchy principle was limited to the tasks they were studying. The concept does, however, seem to be of very much wider application and, indeed, to denote an important general principle of performance.

Even a seemingly very simple response to a signal usually requires a complex interplay between perception and action. For example, we noted that the superiority of Garvey and Knowles's systems A and B (Fig. 6.14) in which signal lights and their corresponding response buttons were immediately adjacent was due to the fact that only one visual inspection was required to find both light and button. In other arrangements where lights and buttons were on different panels, the subject had to search the display panel to find the signal and then to search the control panel for the appropriate button, and thus had a twofold visual task. In everyday life this compound nature of performance is clearly marked, and we may indeed argue that the simple signal-response unit is an abstraction seldom if ever found except in reflexes and some very simple laboratory tasks.

Let us consider by way of example looking up a telephone number and dialling it. Looking up the number will require a series of actions, turning over pages, running the finger down the columns, and so on. It will involve a constant interplay between receptor and effector functions, each turn of a page being made in response to information on the page open at the time in relation to the information sought. The various actions are all in one sense discrete signal-response units but are bound together by the aim of finding the number required. In this sense, they are all included in the receptor activity aimed at obtaining information for a larger unit of performance. When this information has been obtained it is translated into a series of turns of the telephone dial which are then made. These are again in one sense discrete signal-response units each requiring the observation of a number and turning the dial. Again, however, they are in another sense all included in the effector activity of a larger unit of performance. We can thus think of the whole operation as a single unit of performance incorporating many smaller units, in which both the larger and the smaller units are similar signal-response units in the sense that in each, whether larger or smaller, information is gathered and used to direct action to a specific end.

The hierarchical ordering of units of performance is perhaps better illustrated in some industrial skills. If, for example, we went into a workshop where a man was using a lathe and interrupted his activity at a particular instant of time, we should find a detailed muscular action in progress – say a twisting of the wrist to turn a handwheel on the tool carriage. The action would, however, be only one of a series required to move the tool over the surface of the work. This again would be only one part of the cycle of operations required to machine the article concerned, and the article might be only one of several needed for the job of construction on which the man was engaged. The action, the series of actions, the cycle of operations, and the job of construction are all in a sense units of performance of a task. The larger units at each level embrace the smaller, organising, co-ordinating, 'steering' and indeed 'driving' or motivating those which lie below. Were we to ask the man on the lathe what he was doing we should be asking an ambiguous question because an answer in terms of any of the units would be correct. The actual unit he chose to give as his answer might be expected to depend on the level at which the outcome of his actions was least certain. Units higher in the hierarchy would be 'taken for granted', those lower would have become more or less 'automatic'. If this view is correct, we should expect the level at which awareness is centred to rise as the operator becomes more expert and masters larger and larger units, but that it might fall again if conditions of work, fatigue or other factors made the performance of smaller units sufficiently difficult for their outcome to be in appreciable doubt.

Where conditions require or permit virtually exact repetition of a unit many times, performance tends to become stereotyped in the course of practice, and the whole cycle can be run off very much as a chain response with each member acting as the cue for the one that follows. Even in this case, however, the unit seems to behave as a whole rather than as a simple chain because it is often impossible, and almost always difficult, if a cycle is interrupted, to begin it again in the middle without some rehearsal of the parts already completed.

Where conditions are more fluid, and in early stages of practice, performance appears to be more variable. The precise sequence of sub-units may differ from one performance to another in much the same way as the precise form of an action varies with detailed circumstances. Often the results of each sub-unit indicate what should be done subsequently, as when in looking up a telephone number the names appearing on each page of the directory opened indicate which way the pages should next be turned. Sometimes, however, the subject will have no alternative but to *remember* at each stage what he has done and what still remains to be done to complete the task. Thus in dialling a telephone number it is necessary to remember as each figure is dialled what remains to be done because the dial itself gives no indication of what has been completed. This last point focuses attention upon an important factor implicit in the whole idea of higher units of performance and the integration of data over time, namely *short-term memory* retaining data early in a series until they can be combined with later, holding data while the decision mechanism is 'busy' and keeping a tally of what has been done in a complex task. To this we turn in the next chapter.

Experimental studies of the hierarchical organisation of performance since those of the early pioneers have been remarkably few. We may, however, mention three which are especially relevant and which link our present approach with previous discussions:

(*a*) Craik (1947) noted that when a subject is required to turn a hand-wheel at a constant rate to keep a pointer in line with a target, his intermittent corrections are superimposed on a steady rate of turning. In other words the subject has extracted the steady rate of turning as a constant in a manner analogous to the extraction of constants in perception: he turns at a rate which roughly matches the rate required, and makes periodical adjustments to this.

(*b*) Several studies have shown that the speed of one part of a cycle of actions affects that of other parts so that a uniform tempo is imposed on the whole (e.g. de Montpellier, 1945, Wehrkamp and Smith, 1952, Simon and Simon, 1959, Simon, 1960). Perhaps the clearest illustration of this is in an experiment by N. Welford (see Welford, 1958, pp. 103–105) whose subjects tapped continuously from side to side between two targets of either 1 or 2 in diameter set either 1 or 2 ft apart. As expected from the results surveyed in the previous chapter, performance was slower when the targets were 1 in diameter than when they were 2 in. The interesting result in the present context was that obtained when subjects tapped alternately between one 1 in and one 2 in target. It might have been expected that movements in the two directions would have taken different times, those from the smaller to the larger target taking substantially less time than those from the larger to the smaller. Instead, movements in both directions took about the same intermediate length of time.

(*c*) Control of details by broader aspects of performance is further illustrated in a series of experiments by Pew (1966) whose subjects attempted to keep the spot on a cathode-ray tube in a central position by operating two keys. If, say, the left-hand key was pressed, the spot accelerated to the left. Pressing the right-hand key would cause it to decelerate, reverse direction and accelerate to the right. Pressing the left-hand key again would cause the target to slow down, reverse and move off to the left once more, and so on. Accurate performance demanded a rapid alternation between the two keys. Pew noted that the strategies used in dealing with this task could be divided into three types. The simplest, but least effective, was to observe the effect of pressing each key before pressing the other: this resulted in a series of large overshoots. A second strategy was to press the keys alternately in rapid succession, making corrections by leaving a longer interval when the spot was seen to wander appreciably to one side or the other. This strategy is similar to that employed by Vince's (1948b) subjects making series of movements at rapid rates (p. 143). The third strategy again involved pressing the keys alternately in rapid succession but adjusting the intervals between pressings so that the spot remained approximately centred the whole time: the subject essentially imposed a pattern of timing upon his performance which ordered the individual actions so as to maintain a uniform overall result. It should be emphasised that both the second and third strategies required each key to be pressed before the full effects of pressing the previous key could be observed so that performance was essentially anticipatory and ballistic. In this respect it resembles a number of skilled industrial tasks studied by Crossman (1960) and by Beishon (1967, Beishon and Crawley, 1965) which involved substantial time lags before controlling actions had their full effects. In these cases the operator may have to take a series of actions before he can observe any overall effects. Whether one regards his performance as open- or closed-loop depends on the scale on which it is viewed. Each individual action may be closed-loop in the sense that its immediate course can be observed, but open-loop in the sense that its ultimate effects may not appear until long after it has been completed.

One further point about the units of performance we have been discussing needs to be stressed. We have spoken of them as signal-response units and this is correct in that both perceptual and effector functions are involved. In another sense, however, such a description is misleading. The functional unit of performance does not typically consist merely of perceptual processes leading to motor responses, but of attempts by the organism to bring about modifications in the situation in which it finds itself. To put this in signal-response terms, we should have to say that the unit of performance extends from a signal to a modified signal and that response or action is merely a link between these two. This way of looking at performance has two important consequences. First, it places the main emphasis on perception and decision and thus makes the essential matrix of behaviour cognitive. Secondly since actions merely bridge the gap between one perceptual situation and another, they can vary substantially without the *functional* unit of performance having to be regarded as different: the central mechanisms are capable of producing a range of actions the details of which are matched to the precise requirements of the occasion so that the same end may be achieved in several slightly different ways. Perhaps the most striking evidence of this is the way that compensation can be made for deficiencies resulting from fatigue, age or injury, by adjustments of the method or manner of performance so as to shift the load away from capacities which are impaired to those which remain intact (e.g. Welford, 1958).

VII

Short-term Retention

It is well known that after a severe blow on the head which has produced temporary unconsciousness, the patient's memory for events prior to the blow is disturbed. At first he may be unable to remember anything that happened during a substantial time before the accident, except perhaps in a fragmentary or disordered manner. This period gradually shrinks, the more distant memories usually returning before the more recent. There remains, however, a short period of a few seconds or minutes which is permanently lost. Similar *retrograde amnesia* effects have been found using other agents producing violent assaults on the brain, such as electro-convulsive therapy (ECT) (for a review see Glickman, 1961).

Facts such as these have led to the view that learning is a two-stage process. The material being learnt is conceived as held for a few seconds in a short-term 'store' consisting of some kind of brain *activity* – self-regenerating circuits of neurones analogous to the dynamic memory stores of some early computers have been suggested (Hebb, 1949). This short-term retention is regarded as providing an opportunity for a more enduring memory trace to be built up in the form of either a sub-microscopic change of structure, or a stable biochemical change, in particular brain cells. The more enduring trace is assumed to be weak at first and therefore liable to be distorted or rendered unavailable by neural noise resulting from cerebral assaults, but to become stronger with time. There has been considerable controversy as to whether short- and long-term retention are stages of a single process or whether they imply two separate memory stores in the brain. Some evidence favouring the latter view is given by clinical studies which show that the one may be severely impaired while the other is little affected (e.g. Symonds, 1966). Further evidence is provided by Baddeley (1966a, b) who showed that the types of error differ in the two cases: in short-term memory they tend to be due to confusion between acoustically similar words but not between words similar in meaning, whereas in long-term memory the opposite tendencies appear.

In practice, however, it is difficult to separate the two mechanisms since they commonly seem to work closely together. Many of the very substantial number of studies which have been made of short-term memory, especially during the last 10 years, suggest that long-term as well as short-term stores have been participating. At the same time short-term retention appears to play an important part in the process of learning for long-term retention. We shall nevertheless for convenience treat the two separately, dealing with short-term retention in this chapter and leaving questions of learning and long-term retention to Chapter 9.

BASIC FACTS OF IMMEDIATE MEMORY

Early work on short-term memory has been summarised by Blankenship (1938) and more recent studies by Posner (1963, 1967a) and Peterson (1966a). The basic facts are well established and can be broadly summarised under four heads:

(*a*) Perhaps the most striking fact about short-term memory is the limited amount of material that can be retained at any one time. The 'immediate memory span' varies according to the criteria adopted in measuring it, but Jacobs (1887) who reported the first results in this field, found that the *maximum* number of random digits heard once that could be repeated back with complete accuracy was, on average, 10 for a group of subjects in their late 'teens. Cardozo and Leopold (1963) found the maximum number of random digits repeated back correctly *every time* in a series of trials to be about 6. Averages for the number correct 50% of times or for more subtle measures are usually between 7 and 8. Corresponding figures for random letters of the alphabet are about one less in each case.

(*b*) The span is reduced if the subject shifts his attention to other material during the period between presentation and recall. The magnitude of the effect is well shown in the results of an experiment by Brown (1958). The subjects viewed pairs of consonants on a paper strip which passed behind a small window at a rate of 1 pair per ·8 sec. The number of pairs varied from 1 to 4 in different trials. In one condition the last pair was followed by 5 pairs of digits, all at the same time intervals: the subjects read out the letters and digits as they appeared and immediately afterwards wrote down as many of the *letters* as they could remember. A control condition was similar except that instead of the digits there was blank interval of the same length. It can be seen from Table 7.1 that the letter span in this control condi-

TABLE 7.1 *Interference with short-term memory by material presented during the period of retention. Data from Brown (1958). The figures are the mean numbers of letters recalled, based on 9 trials by each of 10 subjects*

Number of letters presented:	2	4	6	8
Experimental condition: letters presented, then 5 pairs of digits	1·95	2·72	2·45	2·01
Control condition: letters presented, then blank interval of 4·7 sec	Not tried	3·98	5·61	5·23

tion was between 5 and 6, while in the experimental condition it was between 2 and 3: presumably the digits had interfered in some way with the retention or recovery of the letters.

Such interference can be substantial from even a single item as, for example, when a subject is required to say 'o' before recalling a string of digits (Conrad, 1960c, Dallett, 1964) or to dial o before a telephone number (Conrad, 1958). The effect of such a single item is negligible upon a string of 4 digits but becomes appreciable with 6 or 8 (Mortenson and Loess, 1964).

Interference may arise not only from extra items during the period of retention but from the presentation of additional items to be recalled (Norman, 1966), and it tends to be greater when the original and interpolated items are closely similar than when they are very different. Thus interpolated letters which are phonetically similar to those being retained produce greater effects than letters which are phonetically dissimilar (Wickelgren, 1966a, c, Dale, 1964), and learning a list of letters interferes less with the retention of digits than does either learning further digits or even merely reciting digits (Sanders, 1961a).

Loss of retention may also result if the subject has to perform certain kinds of recoding operation upon the data being retained and increases as such recoding becomes more radical. For example, Posner and Rossman (1965) showed that errors increased from a condition when each pair of a string of 8 digits had to be repeated backwards, through conditions where members of each pair had to be added together, to a condition in which each pair had to be identified as 'high' or 'low' (above or below 50) and odd or even. Posner and Rossman argued that the loss of retention depended on the extent to which the information in the original pairs (about 6·6 bits each) had to be reduced in the final answer, that is from not at all in the first condition, to reductions to 3·8 bits for the sums and to 2 bits for the classification. Posner and Konick (1966) in further experiments have indicated that the effects of such recoding and of interfering items are independent.

Similar interfering effects to those observed for digits and letters have been shown for simple *movements* by Boswell and Bilodeau (1964). Their subjects moved a lever a few inches from left to right and 28 sec later attempted to reproduce the same movement. The average correlation between the two movements was reduced from ·84 to ·72 by requiring the subject to pick up a pencil from the floor between the first and the second, instead of waiting passively by the apparatus.

(c) Short-term retention can be greatly improved by rehearsing the material between presentation and recall. Brown (1958) in a further experiment using the same general technique as that already outlined, found that leaving an interval of 2–5 sec between the last of the letters and the first of the digits substantially improved recall of the letters after presentation of the digits. It was clear from his subjects' remarks that they were going over the letters in this interval and that doing so reduced the disruptive effect of the digits. Similarly Sanders (1961a) who told his subjects to rehearse during an interval after hearing 8 digits found that retention of the digits after learning or reciting further digits or letters was better if the rehearsal had lasted 40 sec than if it had only lasted 12 sec – the longer period of rehearsal had increased the resistance to interference.

The reasons for these rehearsal effects are not, however, entirely clear. To some extent rehearsal may serve to keep the memory traces from decaying, but this cannot account for the increased resistance to interference from intervening activity. Brown reported that many of his subjects made remarks which implied that they were somehow recoding the material during rehearsal or were applying mnemonic devices such as forming associations – he mentions one subject who associated the letters ND with the words 'National Debt'. Such recoding has been shown to improve retention (Schaub and Lindley, 1964). It seems possible, on the other hand, that the active response to the material implied in rehearsal tends to transfer the material to the long-term memory store where it would be much more resistant to interference effects. There is considerable evidence that learning and long-term retention are enhanced by active response to material (e.g. Gates, 1917, Belbin, 1958) and indeed it seems reasonable to suppose, as suggested in Fig. 1.3 (p. 19), that entrance to the long-term store is via a decision about the material by the translation mechanism which would also tend to result in action. We shall consider this point again later and deal with it more fully in Chapter 9. Meanwhile direct evidence about the role of active response in short-term memory comes from experiments by Murray (1965, 1966) who found that letters were retained better if subjects spoke them aloud, or even mouthed them silently, as they were presented instead of merely reading them silently. Such vocalisation also improved resistance to interference. The complementary finding has been made by Turvey (1967) that repeated *presentation* of the stimuli under conditions unfavourable to any kind of rehearsal produces little or no improvement of retention.

While rehearsal generally aids retention, it seems that it may occasionally impair it. Heron (1962) found that 8-digit numbers were dialled on a telephone dial less accurately after they had been rehearsed vocally or written down than if they were dialled immediately after presentation. To some extent this may merely indicate that reproduction is better when immediate than when delayed, even when rehearsal takes place, or that rehearsal, while it consolidates retention may introduce and also consolidate errors. To some extent it may have been due to the fact that Heron's subjects rehearsed and recalled by different methods: the spoken or written rehearsal may perhaps have coded the material in a form unsuitable for use subsequently when dialling. Somewhat similar indications are contained in the results of experiments by Wickelgren (1965) and Margrain (1967).

(*d*) The immediate memory span can be improved to some extent by practice. For example, Martin and Fernberger (1929) found that the span for digits presented at a rate of 1 per sec rose by about 36% during the course of practice involving two trials a day for 50 days. Pollack *et al.* (1959) found even larger rises – up to 100% – in digit span between the first and eighth blocks of 15 trials, but their task differed from the majority in testing a *running memory span*: subjects heard groups of digits up to 40 in length and wrote down 'as many of the last numbers in the group' as they could remember. Martin and Fernberger emphasise that such practice effects seem not to imply a true increase of capacity to hold data in short-term memory, but rather increased skill in putting it in a form easy to retain. They reported 'grouping and organising' of the digits – in other words a form of recoding. Pollack *et al.* found much less improvement when digits were presented at a rate of 4 per sec than at rates of 2 per sec or less, suggesting the fast rate did not give enough time for recoding to take place.

The problems of accounting for these several effects seem to pose three main questions: firstly, what sets the limit to the short-term memory span; secondly, in what units should the span be measured; and thirdly what is the nature of the short-term store and where is it located within the central mechanisms? We shall in the rest of this chapter consider these questions in turn, and having done so will look briefly at some of the ways in which short-term memory seems to play an important part in higher mental functions such as intelligence test performance, problem-solving, thinking and the ordering of complex skilled activity.

SOURCES OF LIMITATION

In studies of long-term memory it has become customary to think of forgetting as due in part to the decay of memory traces over time and in part to interference by other material either during the period of retention or at the time of recall. Much of the study of short-term memory has been concerned with the question of how far the limited span can be explained by the same principles. Four main types of theory have been proposed:

1. Decay with time

A theory in these terms was put forward by Broadbent (1957b) who suggested that a subject can hold data for a limited *time* but can extend retention beyond the critical period by means of rehearsal which recirculates the material through the central mechanisms and back to the input. The length of span was thus held to depend on the amount of material that could be recirculated before the traces had decayed beyond repair.

Evidence which appears at first sight to favour this view is contained in results obtained by Conrad (1957) whose subjects listened to 8-digit numbers at a rate of either 30 or 90 digits per min, and had to write them down immediately at the same rates as soon as the last digit had been presented. The speed of writing was paced by a series of clicks. Conrad found that the faster rate was superior, yielding 41% correct recall as opposed to 32% for the slower rate. Similar results were obtained by Posner (1946a) who compared rates of 30 with 96 per min. and also, but for older subjects only, by Fraser (1958). A parallel finding with non-verbal material is that of Eriksen and Johnson (1964) who found that the accuracy with which subjects reported whether a tone had been sounded while they were reading a novel declined with the length of time elapsing between presentation of the tone and the posing of the question about whether it had occurred. On the motor side Adams and Dijkstra (1966) found that the accuracy with which subjects reproduced the movement of a lever fell as the interval between the original movement and the attempt to reproduce it rose from 5 to 80 sec.

On reflection, however, this evidence is unconvincing. One would expect that, if time alone was important, halving the rate of presentation and reproduction would halve the span. This it clearly does not do. What is more, a number of studies have found that memory span falls rather than rises with increased rate of presentation. Bergstrom (1907) obtained fewer errors in word and digit spans when items were presented at half sec than at 1 sec intervals, and fewer still at 2 sec intervals. Similar findings were obtained by McReynolds and Acker (1959) for nonsense-syllables presented at rates of 2–12 per sec. In both these cases recall was an approximately linear function of the logarithm of the interval between items. Again Pollack *et al.* (1959) found that the running memory span improved as the rate of presentation fell from 4 through 2 and 1 to ·5 items per sec. Similar indications in a non-verbal context come from an experiment by Fraisse (1942) who found that errors made in tapping out rhythms which had been heard once rose both with the number of sounds in the pattern and with the speed at which it was presented. It is, of course, true that extremely rapid rates of presentation might give rise to problems of grouping and failure to distinguish number and order discussed in Chapter 4, but the rates in all these experiments were far too slow for this explanation to be valid.

Looking at the problems from a different angle, Murdock (1960) found the number of words learnt in a single trial to rise linearly with the product of the number of items and the time per item – that is with the total time taken to present the list. Again Murdock (1965a) found that retention of pairs of words from a list depended upon the length of time for which they were presented and not upon the total number presented or upon whether the time was concentrated in a single trial or distributed over a number of trials. Similar findings have been reported by Waugh (1967) who found that probability of recall was a linear function of the time for which material was presented. It is interesting to compare these results with those of Wallace (1956) who found that probability of correct identification was a function of the total time for which material was viewed, more or less regardless of whether the time was continuous or split up into several shorter periods (see p. 97).

One difference of Conrad's (1957) and Fraser's (1958) experiments from others is that they controlled the rate of recall whereas the others did not. We may perhaps suspect that the clicks which Conrad and Fraser used to pace recall may have acted as a source of interference which would have been more severe at slower speeds in that the longer the time between each click and the next, the less easy it would have been for the subject to acquire a rhythm which would have enabled him to ignore the clicks. Conrad and Hille (1957) have produced evidence in line with this view by showing that errors in the immediate reproduction of strings of 8 digits were less with unpaced than with paced recall, and less with a fast pace of recall (90 per min) than with a slow (30 per min). Rate of presentation had little effect, although what it had was in the direction of the faster rate being superior. More recently Waugh and Norman (1965) have shown clearly that recall of individual digits from lists of 16 read at rates of either 4 or 1 per sec was greatly affected by the number of digits intervening between presentation and recall, but very little by the time interval concerned. Similar indications appear in a study by Conrad and Hull (1966).

Evidence regarding the effects of time on short-term memory span are still not quite unequivocal, but it can be argued that it is virtually impossible to be sure that time is important *as such*: the longer the time between presentation and recall, the more chance there is of random disturbances and distractions interfering with retention. As against this, slower rates of presentation give greater opportunity for recoding and rehearsal which might more than offset any effects of interference. Some indication in favour of this view is given by Corballis (1966) who found that retention was better at slow speeds when the material was also exposed (visually) for long times, but that with short exposures faster speeds were better – the relatively long gaps between presentations with short exposures at slow speeds would have given the opportunity for distraction of the subject's attention. Time cannot on present evidence be wholly excluded as a cause of limitation of the short-term memory span, but it is clearly an *insufficient* cause, and may well prove also to be *unnecessary*.

2. Interference by retrieval

It is an obvious possibility that just as retention is impaired when another task has to be done between presentation and recall, so the actual recall of items may impair the retention of others waiting to be recalled. Evidence in favour of this view has been provided by Anderson (1960) whose subjects listened to three groups of four digits and then either immediately or at intervals ranging up to 30 sec were told which group or groups to write down. She found that recall was most accurate when only one group was called for and least when all three had to be reproduced. Similar results have been reported by Howe (1965, 1966) using three groups of three consonants all of which had to be repro-

TABLE 7.2 *Effect of having to retain one set of material on the recall of another set. Data from Brown (1954). The figures are the percentages of correct recall*

	A Series recalled alone	B Series recalled as first	C Effect of retaining second series on recall of first i.e. B–A	D Series recalled as second	E Effects of previous recall of first series on recall of second D–A	F D–B
Series of 4 two-digit numbers and 4 arrowheads presented simultaneously. Based on 32 trials by each of 6 subjects						
Numbers	51	36	–15	39	–12	+3
Arrowheads	19	19	0	20	+1	+1
Series of 2 pairs of digits and a single digit, and of 2 pairs of consonants and a single consonant presented simultaneously. Based on 24 trials by each of 12 subjects						
Digits recalled first	49	42	–7	39	–10	–3
Letters recalled first	74	64	–10	39	–35	–25

duced immediately following presentation of the last group: the groups were recalled in various orders and accuracy tended to increase the earlier the group came in order of recall.

The interpretation of these results is not entirely straightforward, however, because of earlier findings by Brown (1954) whose subjects were presented with a series of arrowheads together with two-digit numbers, and had to reproduce either the one or the other or both – *which* was indicated after they had been presented. Recall of the numbers was substantially poorer if the arrowheads were to be recalled subsequently than if only the numbers were required. Similar results were obtained using series of digits and letters. Both sets of results are shown in Table 7.2. These results seem clearly to imply that recall of some items may be impaired by the need to retain others. The magnitude of the effect of prior recall will therefore very much depend on whether or not this effect is taken into account – as can be seen by comparing columns E and F of Table 7.2. An analogous result has been reported by Crowder (1967) who found that performance at a four-choice serial-reaction task was impaired by the need to retain strings of 3 or 5 words during the period of the task.

We may remark in passing that this principle can also explain the fact that material presented before items to be retained may impair recall (Pillsbury and Sylvester, 1940, Murdock, 1961) although it does not always do so (Brown, 1958): its effect seems to depend on whether it can be ignored or can be dismissed before the material to be retained is presented. Thus Pollack *et al.* (1959) in experiments on running memory found that length of span fell as the number of items increased when the number to be presented before recall was demanded was not known beforehand, so that all had to be retained. When, however, the number to be presented was known in advance, it had no effect: subjects could ignore all except the last few items. Again Murdock (1963) and Conrad (1960) have both shown that although items become confused within lists, there is relatively little interference from previous lists – presumably the memory store is effectively cleared once retention is no longer required.

What appears at first sight to be clearer evidence that the recall of some items impairs the retention of others is given by Inglis and Caird (1963) who used Broadbent's (1954, 1957) technique of presenting simultaneous pairs of digits, one of each pair to each ear. When asked to recall, subjects tended spontaneously to reproduce all the digits from one ear before any from the other. The 'earful' reproduced first tended to be strikingly more accurate than those reproduced second, and the obvious implication seems to be that recall of the first had impaired retention of the second. However, further studies by Inglis and Ankus (1965) showed that this was only partly true. They compared the situation studied by Inglis and Caird in which subjects had been free to choose which ear's digits to reproduce first, with conditions in which they were told the order either before or after the digits had been presented. Their results were extensive, covering from 1 to 6 pairs of digits and each decade of age from the 'teens to the 'sixties. A sample is set out in Table 7.3, showing that the difference between the series reproduced

TABLE 7.3 *The effects of order of recall and of whether or not this order was known beforehand on the accuracy of reproducing two series of digits, one presented to each ear. Two samples of results obtained by Inglis and Ankus (1965). The figures are the mean numbers of digits recalled, based in each case on twenty subjects, ten men and ten women, who performed 4 trials in which they were free to choose which 'earful' to reproduce first, 8 in which they were told the order for reproduction beforehand and 8 more in which they were told after presentation*

	A Subject free to choose order of recall	B Order of recall given beforehand	C Order of recall given afterwards	D Effect of not knowing recall order beforehand i.e. C–B
Subjects aged 31–40 3 digits to each ear				
Series recalled first	1·79	2·61	2·06	− ·55
Series recalled second	·90	1·51	1·42	− ·12
Difference	− ·89	−1·07	− ·64	
Subjects aged 21–30 4 digits to each ear				
Series recalled first	2·26	3·37	2·47	− ·90
Series recalled second	1·04	1·20	1·10	− ·10
Difference	−1·22	−2·17	−1·37	

first and second was greatest when the order was known beforehand and least when it was signified afterwards. In other words, the disadvantage of not knowing the order of recall until after presentation was

greater for the first series than for the second. The implication seems
clear that part of the difference when order of recall is left to the subject
or dictated in advance is due to the first series being more thoroughly
learnt – the subject employs a different strategy in the process of acquisition. This point was made by Kay and Poulton (1951) in a pioneering
study and has emerged to varying degrees in subsequent work. The
results of three studies are summarised in Table 7.4. The essential
points to note are that the differences in column A are consistently more
negative than those in column B, and that the figure in column C for
the upper of each pair of rows is more negative than that for the lower.
Further evidence that dictating the order of recall before presentation
affects strategy is perhaps contained in the rather surprising result
shown in Table 7.3 that performance was poorest when the subject
was left free to choose his own order of recall.

Taken together, these results suggest that, although recall of some
items may sometimes impair the retention of others substantially, the
effect is often small and certainly not enough to explain the limitation
of the immediate memory span. Further evidence supporting the same
conclusion has been provided by Murdock (1963) and by Tulving and
Arbuckle (1966).

3. Interference during presentation

Both Anderson (1960) and Howe (1965, 1966) who, as already mentioned, presented three groups of items to their subjects and required
recall of one or more, found that groups presented last were recalled
best. If, as we have seen, time held in store is not important as such,
this must mean that the presentation of later items interfered with the
retention of earlier. Confirmatory evidence comes from Mackworth
(1964a) who showed that accuracy of recall fell linearly with length of
list, and from experiments in which a series of paired items has been
presented and then the subject has been given one member of one pair
and asked to recall the other: accuracy of recall falls with increase in
the number of pairs presented between the pair concerned and its
recall (Murdock 1963a, 1966a). Similar results have been obtained using
single items: at the end of a string of items one is re-presented and the
subject is asked to recall the one which followed it (Waugh and Norman 1965). This technique has been elegantly employed by Norman
(1966) who showed that *rate of forgetting* depended essentially upon the
number of items intervening between presentation and recall and was
little affected by speed of presentation, sense modality, type of item or

TABLE 7.4 *Further effects of order of recall and of whether or not this was known beforehand. The figures are in each case the percentage of items correct*

	A Order of recall given beforehand	B Order of recall given afterwards	C Effect of not knowing recall order beforehand i.e. B–A
Kay & Poulton (1951). Two series, each of 4 pairs of arrows given in each trial. Each of 32 subjects had 20 trials. First series			
Recalled before second	39	36	−3
Recalled after second		30	
Difference		−6	
Second series			
Recalled before first		30	
Recalled after first	32	31	−1
Difference		+1	
Brown (1954). Including some of same data as in Table 7.2. Numbers			
Recalled before arrowheads	62	36	−26
Recalled after arrowheads	45	39	−6
Difference	−17	+3	
Arrowheads			
Recalled before numbers	26	19	−7
Recalled after numbers	24	20	−4
Difference	−2	+1	
Rabbit (1962). Series of 5 cards each bearing coloured letter. Based on *100* trials in each condition by each of 18 subjects. Colours			
Recalled before letters	87	79	−8
Recalled after letters	72	76	+4
Difference	−15	−3	
Letters			
Recalled before colours	83	70	−13
Recalled after colours	49	62	+13
Difference	−34	−8	

length of list, although all the factors affected the starting level from which forgetting began and can thus be regarded as having influenced *acquisition* of the material.

Several attempts have been made to treat the results of this type of experiment in terms of signal-detection theory: subjects have been asked to recall or to recognise an item as having appeared or not appeared in a series, and to rate the confidence with which they made their judgments. The results thus obtained have been plotted to produce the typical ROC curves of the signal-detection theory model (Fig. 2.3, p. 35). If this can be done it implies that traces are not wholly destroyed but are in some way progressively impaired or rendered unavailable (Murdock, 1965c, 1966a, Norman and Wickelgren, 1965, Wickelgren, 1966d).

It is an obvious first guess that they are rendered 'noisy' as postulated by Brown (1959). Support for this view is contained in the fact that short-term memory may show 'reminiscence effects' in that recall may be better a few seconds after presentation than it is immediately: the noise has died down during the interval (Crawford *et al.*, 1966, Peterson, 1966b). One would also expect a fall of d' with forgetting. Wickelgren (1967a), who presented two items and asked whether the second had followed immediately on the first in the original list, indeed found that log d' fell approximately linearly with the number of items intervening between presentation and recall. Murdock (1966a) however, who presented one item from an original list and asked for recall of the item immediately before or after, found that although recall of early items was less frequent, it tended to be accurate, implying a change of β rather than of d'. The conflict of evidence is more apparent than real because the two authors were asking different questions. Wickelgren was asking what was the probability of obtaining the correct response at each serial position, whereas Murdock was concerned with the likelihood of each item being attributed to its correct serial position. The results can be reconciled if it is assumed that the serial order of the early items became uncertain so that more items were competing for recall or recognition at the early positions. In terms of Fig. 2.9 (p. 45) d' would fall if each item was viewed against the noise produced by all the competing items together, but could remain the same if the item was viewed against its own background noise only. In the latter case, however, a rise of β would be required for accuracy to be maintained (p. 47). In both cases, by analogy with experiments showing that reaction-time rises with degree of discrimination and of choice, it is understandable that speed of response should be slower for items earlier in the series (Murdock, 1966a, Morin *et al.*, 1967).

Interference effects are particularly severe when the acquisition of new items coincides with the recall of items already in store, as occurs in a certain type of running-memory task. The original experiment on this kind of task seems to have been that by Kay (1953, see also Welford, 1958, pp. 248–250). The subject sat facing a row of 12 light bulbs with a Morse key directly under each numbered 1–12 in order. For the first part of the task one of these lights was put on by the experimenter and, by pressing the key immediately under it the subject put it out and another on. Pressing the key under this second light made it go out and a third appear, and so on through the whole 12 in random order. This simple task caused no difficulty. The task was then changed so that the lights came on automatically in random order at 1·5 sec intervals, and the subject had to press the key under each light *which had just gone off*: in other words he had to work 'one back' in the series. The task was then changed again and the subject required to work two back, then three back, then four back. The 'one-back' task was found to be easy: subjects simply moved their hands to the key where the light was on, waited until it went out, pressed the key and then moved to the new position of the light. On the 'two-back' task subjects would sometimes mark the position of the intermediate light with a finger of the hand they were not using, thus making the task somewhat similar to the 'one-back', but beyond this they were compelled, if they were to make a perfect score, to carry the intermediate light positions in some form of running short-term memory. This they found extremely difficult to do: every time they 'took a number from store' in order to make a response they seemed to forget the other numbers still in store. It seemed impossible to take one item from store and leave others: taking one item appeared to clear the whole store. Many subjects attempted to avoid this difficulty by placing a finger on the key under the light which was on, watching several changes and then pressing the corresponding keys while ignoring the lights which appeared while they were doing so. This involved abandoning any attempt to deal with more than about half the signals, but seemed often to be the only alternative to complete inactivity. The results are shown in Table 7.5, which gives both the total correct responses made and also scores which take account of the simplification of the task we have just mentioned. These latter scores gave credit for a correct response only when the subject both pressed the correct key and subsequently made some response to the light which was on at the time. Only one subject made a near-perfect score on the 'four-back' task. His procedure was, whenever he made a response, to shout aloud the other numbers to

TABLE 7.5 *Results of an experiment on serial short-term retention by Kay (1953). The figures are the percentages of correct responses out of a total of 36 by each of 58 subjects*

| | 1·5 sec between signals | | | | 4 sec between signals 4-back |
	1-back	2-back	3-back	4-back	
All correct responses	95	67	47	35	62
Correct responses followed by response to light on at the time	95	57	23	13	35

be retained including the new one for the present position of the light. In this way he seemed to have recirculated the data and thus avoided losing it. Several other subjects seemed to be doing something of the same kind in a less striking manner, and most verbalised the positions of the lights as they appeared. It is relevant to note that after the main series the 'four-back' task was repeated but with the lights at 4 sec intervals, and in this condition scores were much higher: presumably the longer intervals made it easier to rehearse and recirculate the material.

Additional experiments with Kay's apparatus carried out by Kirchner (1958) have shown that this kind of running-memory task is especially difficult for older subjects. Further studies showing the beneficial effects of longer time per item have been made using more complex but analogous tasks (Mackworth, 1959, Mackworth and Mackworth, 1959). Similar experiments using a simple running memory task for digits have also confirmed the effect of presentation rate and the fact that spans measured in this way are substantially shorter than conventional digit spans (Pollack and Johnson, 1963b).

The tendency by Kay's subjects to try to reduce the more difficult tasks to simpler ones appeared also in tracking experiments by Griew (1958a) and Poulton (1963). In both cases subjects had to follow an irregular wavy ink line on a paper strip. The course could be seen some distance ahead of the tracking point, but the portion immediately ahead was hidden by a mask. The subject had thus to retain the pattern of the track for the time it was passing under the mask if he was to follow accurately. The amount of pattern to be retained was varied in different trials by varying either the width of the mask or the speed of the track.

In all cases subjects tended to track earlier than they should. The amount by which they did so was related to the time taken by the track to pass under the mask, being small when the time was short and increasing very rapidly as it lengthened. The effect was to reduce markedly the number of swings of the track that had to be retained – to a maximum of about 1 in Griew's case and 1·5 in Poulton's.

Vince (1949) and especially Poulton (1954) have reported several other serial reaction tasks in which manual responses were required to visual displays and subjects were either instructed to react to items one or more back in the series, or were forced to do so for brief periods because the items were presented too fast for each to be dealt with before the next arrived. Performance was usually adequate when the subject was responding to items only one back in the series, but tended to break down when reaction was required to items further back. Performance in these last experiments has obvious similarities to looking ahead when reading and to copying behind during dictation (e.g. Hogan, 1961). Poulton (1958a) has pointed out that studies of reading or dictation are difficult to link up with other work as the material used has usually been connected prose, but it seems clear that subjects, especially when well practised, deal with the material in relatively large units, listening and responding to phrases or sentences rather than to single words. The size of the group dealt with can perhaps in principle be regarded as providing some measure of short-term memory span.

4. Limited capacity of the store

Probably the most frequently assumed reason for the limited span of immediate memory is that the short-term store has a limited capacity and that interference from subsequently presented items arises because they push out those already in the store. If this is true, however, it is clear that they do not do so on a strictly rotational basis of each new item pushing out the oldest already in store. Several studies have shown that when the number of items presented exceeds the immediate memory span, the beginning and end of the series are recalled more accurately than the middle (Fraisse, 1944, Deese and Kaufman, 1957, Murdock, 1962). Had there been a strict rotation in the store, the last few items should have been retained and the early ones forgotten.

It may, however, be true that there is a limited capacity store operating as part of a more complex system. The writer was alerted to this possibility some years ago by noticing in a class experiment that when recall was allowed in any order subjects tended to produce the last few items first, and to do so correctly. After a short pause they usually produced the first item followed by some of the intervening ones, and these tended to show the distortions found by Bartlett (1932) to be typical of long-term memory.

This impression has been confirmed by the results of two experiments by Kassum (1967) in which he presented subjects with lists of 10 monosyllabic English words. In the first he compared the effects of

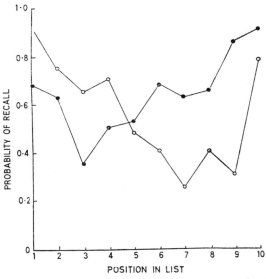

Figure 7.1. Relationships between position in which a word was presented in a list and the probability of its recall. Data from Kassum (1967).

○ = Recall required in order of presentation.
● = Recall permitted in any order.

Each point is based on 10 trials by each of 4 subjects.

requiring subjects to recall the items in order of presentation with those of leaving them free to recall in any order. The results are shown in Fig. 7.1. It is clear that with both types of recall the ends of the list are better reproduced than the middle. The fact that the terminal items are reproduced better when recall is in any order may either be a result of interference by recall which would place these items at a disadvantage in serial order reproduction, or may represent, as suggested earlier, a different strategy of performance under the two conditions. If so, however, it is relevant to ask why it should have been adopted: is there for example some advantage in recalling the terminal items first? There does seem to have been some advantage in freedom to recall in any order because the spans in this condition were on average about half an item longer than with serial recall – 6·30 as opposed to 5·67 items.

Kassum's second experiment was designed to study the recall of terminal items in greater detail. Again two conditions were compared: in one subjects were simply asked to recall in any order, in the other they were asked to recall the last few words first, before attempting to recall the others. With the second type of instruction, subjects tended to produce what Kassum termed a 'final block' of items which were correctly recalled with no omissions and no intrusions. Final blocks also occurred with the first type of instruction but less frequently as shown in Table 7.6. A substantial majority of these blocks, especially under the second type of instruction, were given either in order of presentation or

TABLE 7.6 *Results of an experiment by Kassum (1967) on the immediate recall of lists of 10 words*

	Experimental group 15 subjects		Control group 9 subjects	
	First 10 trials Recall in any order	Second 10 trials Last few items to be recalled first	First 10 trials	Second 10 trials
			Recall in any order	
Average number of words per trial recalled correctly	6·0	6·5	6·3	6·5
Average number of words in final block	3·5	4·6	3·7	
Number of subjects producing final blocks	12/15	15/15	8/9	
Percentage of trials in which final blocks appeared	42	83	34	
Percentage of final blocks recalled in				
Order of presentation	47	68	79	
Exact reverse order	24	13	6	
Other orders	29	19	15	

in exact reverse order. Concentration on reproducing the terminal items first seems again to have been beneficial, lengthening the span by an average of about half an item. There thus again seems to have been some special feature attaching to the last few items presented in each list. Additional evidence for this is provided by a scrutiny of words wrongly recalled which were intrusions from lists previously presented: three quarters of these words (36 out of 48) came from words recalled outside final blocks, although these were only about a third of the total words recalled. The intrusions thus came from words presented relatively near the beginnings of previous lists. Craik (1967) has noted the same tendency.

It seems fair to suggest with Waugh and Norman (1965) that the last few items of a list are held in a short-term store of limited capacity which works on a rotational basis so that later items tend to push out earlier, especially under running-memory conditions. Earlier items may, however, be preserved by getting through into the long-term store. This would be more true of the first than of subsequent items: if, as suggested in Fig. 1.3 (p. 19) the long-term store lies beyond the translation mechanism, the first item is likely to capture the translation mechanism and block the entry of subsequent items in the manner suggested in Chapter 4. The mechanism may be cleared at intervals, however, during a long list or one which is presented slowly, and this may be the reason why memory span lengthens slightly with the number of items presented (e.g. Binet and Henri, 1894, Seibel *et al.*, 1965), although the number of items that can be recalled from the extreme end of a list is independent of the length of the list (Waugh 1960).

Such a model seems to be consistent with a number of other results:

(*a*) When items are recalled in order of presentation the first items will have to be recovered from the long-term store and may tend to disrupt those being held in the short-term store: serial reproduction although understandably 'natural' (Corballis, 1967) since most everyday materials are sequential, is to this extent essentially inefficient. Evidence on this point is given by Shepard and Sheenan (1965) whose subjects reproduced strings of 8 digits of which either the first or the last 4 were a familiar sequence and could be regarded as a single item held in long-term memory, and the remainder were random and probably within the capacity of the short-term store. They found that performance was strikingly poorer when the familiar sequence came before the random digits than when it came after. In the latter case the short-term store could be cleared before the items were taken from the long-term store.

(*b*) The middle items of a list will obviously tend to be the least well remembered: they are liable to be expelled from the short-term store by later items, while they may be blocked by earlier items from entering the long-term store.

(*c*) The preservation of early items is likely to be favoured by rehearsal since this tends to transfer material to long-term store. The converse of this may be the reason why Gibson & Raffel (1936), who studied short-term retention of series of *designs*, found that initial items were not well remembered but that retention rose steadily from the beginning of the series to the end: designs are obviously less easy to rehearse than verbal material.

Looking back over the four theories we have discussed, the present position seems to be that time in store is of little importance as such although it may be very important in the opportunity it gives for, on the one hand rehearsal and recoding, and on the other for disrupting influences such as shifts of attention. Interference resulting from recall and from the presentation of new material to which attention has to be paid are both influential in limiting the immediate memory span, the latter probably more than the former. Theories of *limited capacity* are at present somewhat speculative but, especially in the form put forward here in which both short- and long-term stores are involved, seem able to account for a range of facts otherwise difficult to explain.

MEASURING THE CAPACITY OF THE STORE

The question was raised by Miller (1956) of whether the limitation of short-term memory was in terms of *information* in the information-theory sense: if the span for digits was between 7 and 8 this capacity would be between 7 and 8 times $\log_2 10$ – i.e. about 25 bits. The question and the answers given to it preceded most of the research outlined in the previous section and assumed a simple limited-capacity theory: they do therefore not at present link fully with other results. We shall discuss here what has been done and then suggest tentative links with the work we have already surveyed.

Miller concluded after studying the evidence then available that the capacity of the store should *not* be measured in terms of information, but that rather a maximum number of *items*, or as he termed them 'chunks', could be stored. His treatment was important because it called attention to the fact that short-term memory deals not only with single letters or digits but with coded items such as words or syllables as its units. We have noted in the previous chapter (p. 179) that the immediate memory span can often be substantially increased by recoding items such as binary digits into larger units such as decimal digits, so that the number of items to be stored is reduced. However, the evidence on which Miller based his conclusion was derived from studies in which items from different sizes of set drawn from larger sets were presented and these, as subsequent studies have shown, may be misleading. We have already seen in Chapter 3 that it seems to be no easier to deal with a selection of letters than with the whole alphabet, although performance is slightly better when the subset is a very familiar one such as ABC. The same is true of digits. In both cases the subject appears to behave as if he was all the time dealing with the whole alphabet or whole set of 10 digits.

Crossman (1961) attempted to overcome this difficulty by using familiar sets of different sizes as shown in the first column of Table 7.7. It can be argued that £.s.d. and N.S.E.W. constitute subsets of letters which are sufficiently familiar for them to be treated as separate from the whole alphabet. Items from each set were presented verbally in random order at a rate of about 1 per sec and recall was required in the order of presentation. If the immediate memory span depended straightforwardly on the information contained in the items concerned, the information per item multiplied by the number of items in the span should be constant. It can be seen from column 5 of Table 7.7 that

TABLE 7.7. *Item and order information in memory spans for different size sets according to Eq. 7.1. Data from Crossman (1961). Each figure is based on 5 trials by each of 6 subjects*

1 Set	2 Number of alternatives in set	3 Information per item (bits)	4 Average length of span	5 Item information (bits)	6 Order information (bits)	7 Total information (bits)
Black/White	2	1·00	9·1	9·1	18·8	27·9
£.s.d.	3	1·58	6·9	10·9	11·9	22·8
N.S.E.W.	4	2·00	6·8	13·6	11·8	25·4
Days	7	2·81	5·7	16·0	8·6	24·6
Digits	10	3·32	7·3	24·2	13·1	37·3
Months	12	3·58	5·4	19·4	7·7	27·1
Alphabet	26	4·70	6·8	31·9	11·8	43·7
States of USA	49	5·61	4·1	23·0	4·9	27·9
Playing cards	52	5·70	3·4	19·4	3·6	23·0
Dates of year	365	8·51	2·9	24·7	2·8	27·5

this is not so: the spans for the smaller sets are shorter than would be expected.

Casting around for a reason why there should be this discrepancy, Crossman was struck by the large number of cases in which errors occurred because the correct items were produced but in the wrong order, and suggested that in a typical short-term memory experiment the retention of items and of the order in which they were given are separate aspects of the information to be stored. He proposed that the order information for a span of m items can be expressed as the logarithm of the number of possible permutations of these items, that is $m(m - 1)(m - 2) \ldots 1$, expressed as $m!$, and that if n is the size of set from which the items are drawn, we can express the capacity of the store by the equation:

$$m \log n + \log m! = \text{constant} \qquad (7.1)$$

The final column of Table 7.7 indicates that this is roughly so for Crossman's data except with digits and letters where the figures are much too high. One possible reason is that these sets are more familiar than any of the others. There is a good deal of evidence to show that immediate memory is better with familiar than with relatively unfamiliar material. Thus Dale and Gregory (1966) obtained more accurate recall of lists of high-frequency than of lower-frequency words, and Postman *et al.* (1964) found that running-memory spans were longer for more familiar words, at least early in practice. Again Korn and Lindley (1963) found that the recall of consonants improved both with their frequency in written English, and with their frequency of presentation in the particular experiment, and Kassum (1967) found that with English speaking subjects the number out of 10 French monosyllabic words recalled accurately was only about $\frac{3}{4}$ of the number of English monosyllables similarly recalled. The more familiar items are perhaps more easily coded on presentation or may in some way be more readily 'available' at recall.

An alternative explanation of why digits and letters yielded longer spans than were expected in Crossman's experiment is that these particular items lent themselves to some recoding. For example, suppose subjects took the digits in pairs so that a span of 7 would consist of three *pairs* each drawn from a set of 100, plus a single digit drawn from a set of 10, instead of seven individual items each drawn from a set of 10. In this case Eq. 7.1 would yield

$$3 \log_2 100 + \log_2 10 + \log_2 4! = 27 \cdot 8$$

which is comparable with the figure for other sets. The recoding does not reduce the information in the items, but markedly reduces the order-information from $\log_2 7!$ to $\log_2 4!$. In the same way it might be argued that strings of random letters would be likely to throw up occasional pronounceable syllables which could be treated as single units and so reduce order-information.

Crossman's formulation has been attacked on two main grounds. One is that span is affected not only by the factors he considered but by the discriminability of the items from one another (Conrad, 1964a). For example, several experiments have shown that letters are less well retained when drawn from an acoustically similar set such as BCDGPTV than from a more readily distinguishable set such as FHLMQSX (Dale, 1964, Conrad and Hull, 1964, Conrad *et al.*, 1965). Similar difficulty with acoustically confusable words has also been demonstrated (Conrad, 1963, Baddeley, 1966a). This criticism is fair in the sense that information analysis, at least in the simple form of Eq. 7.1, assumes discriminability to be held constant. While, however, it calls attention to an additional complicating factor it does not invalidate Crossman's treatment as far as it goes. We may note that Wickelgren (1965b) found acoustic similarity to increase errors of order but not to result in wrong items being recalled: indeed Conrad (1965) suggested that acoustic similarity is capable of accounting for all the errors of order observed in letter spans, although McNicol (1967) has subsequently calculated that this is an exaggeration.

The second criticism of Eq. 7.1 is that it counts the order-information twice in the sense that order-information is already contained in $m \log n$. For example, the 10,000,000 possible different spans formed by 7 decimal digits will include all possible permutations of any 7, or in other words any 7-digit number can be specified as one out of 10^7 possibilites. For this criticism to be valid it is necessary to assume either that as each item arrives, its serial position is automatically preserved, as it would be if the store were conceived as analogous to a tube in which items were packed one after the other with no possibility of their exchanging positions afterwards, or else the subject must be able to observe the whole of the items simultaneously in order to code them with maximum efficiency. The many errors of order which occur seem to rule out the first possibility. The second might be true with visual presentation of the items all at once but with serial presentation it could not occur unless the items were already stored for inspection. In this case it would assume the storage we are seeking to explain. Similar arguments apply to the possible saving of order-information when two or more items in a span are the same: with serial presentation the subject cannot know in advance which these items will be and so cannot neglect to record their order. The fact that identical items could be interchanged might, however, save some errors during the process of recall.

Crossman proposed that order is not automatically preserved so that information has to be recorded not only about each item but also about the serial position in which it comes. He suggested that the short-term memory store is capable of holding only a limited total of such item and order information together, so that the two are in a sense interchangeable. This would tend to level up the spans for different size sets since, although the small sets would take less 'space' per item in the store and would thus produce longer spans, any lengthening would rapidly increase the space required for order-information.

Two other approaches to the storage of data about order deserve to be mentioned. First, Wickelgren (1964, 1967b) presented subjects with strings of digits at 1 sec intervals with instructions to rehearse silently in groups of 1, 2, 3, 4 or 5. Recall was found to be best after rehearsal in groups of 3, the superiority being more in the accuracy of order and position of items than in the recall of the items as such. The effectiveness of the grouping was shown by the fact that most errors of position were either within the correct group or between similar positions in different groups. Wickelgren suggested that items tended to be 'tagged' with labels indicating 'beginning', 'middle' or 'end' in a hierarchical fashion, so that for a list of, say, 9 items this tagging would be in two stages indicating first within which third of the total list the item lay, and then in which position of the third concerned. This approach can be brought within the broad informational scheme because it bears a striking resemblance to the second of the serial classification models proposed in connection with choice-reactions in Chapter 3 (p. 73). In this model the subject is assumed to divide the material into groups and to inspect the material in each group serially, so that on average he finds what he wants within a group in $(n + 1)/2$ inspections when n is the number of items in the group. His optimum strategy is to divide the material into thirds, find the required third and then divide this into thirds, and so on. Thus, suppose that to find an item for recall he had to search among a string of 9, he would take 2 inspections to decide whether it was in the first, middle or last group of 3 and then a further 2 inspections to decide which member it was of the group chosen, making a total of 4. If, however, he grouped in twos plus one single item, it would on average take approximately 3 inspections to decide to which of the resulting 5 groups the item belonged, and then a further 1·5 inspections with 4 of these groups – that is with 8/9 of the items – making an average total of 4·33. If alternatively he grouped into 4 + 5, it would take an average of approximately 1·5 inspections to identify the correct group, followed in 4/9 cases by 2·5 inspections and in 5/9 cases by 3 inspections to identify the precise member of the group, making an average total of 4·28.

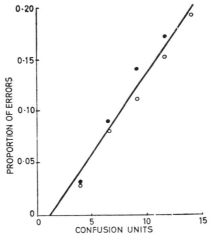

Figure 7.2. Relationship between probability of correct recall and the confusability of the serial position in which an item was presented, with other positions. Confusability is plotted in terms of Crossman's Confusion Function (Eq. 2.7). Data obtained by Ryan (1967) plotted by McNicol (1967).

    ○ = First 5 items in list of 9 with confusability calculated from beginning of list.

    ● = Last 4 items with confusability calculated from end of list.

Each point is based on 20 trials by each of 20 subjects.

The second alternative to Crossman's approach is that of McNicol (1967) who separated order- and item-information by presenting strings of digits aurally and then showing the digits visually in *cardinal* order, so that the subject was in no doubt about *which* items had been presented and had merely to recall their order. He noted that accuracy of positioning the first few items in the string could be accounted for by assuming that each item was tagged with a 'quantity' linearly related to its serial position, and that the subject discriminated between these quantities according to Crossman's Confusion Function Model (Eq. 2.7, p. 29). Thus the first item was better discriminated from the second than the second was from the third, and so on as one would expect if the subject was discriminating between 1 : 2, 2 : 3 and so on. The total errors of each position could be accounted for in terms of the total discriminability of that position from all the others. McNicol found that considering discrimination in this way did not account for the errors of position in the last few items of a string, but that these were well fitted if a similar process was envisaged as taking place with the end of the string as its base, discriminating the difference of each tag from the magnitude of the tag attached to the last item in the string. Data treated in this way are shown in Fig. 7.2, and support the idea that discrimination of order takes place from either end of the string, whichever is nearer to the item concerned.

Whether or not any of these models are found to be fully acceptable, Crossman's insistence that a more subtle measure of storage than discrete items is required, and the various indications that order of items has to be considered, are both important contributions to the theory of short-term memory. Their validity depends, in the first case, on whether size of set from which items are drawn does in fact affect immediate memory span, and on the other, whether various devices for saving order-information are effective. We shall consider the evidence about both these questions in turn.

Effect of size of set

Crossman's data provide good *prima facie* evidence that span does diminish as the size of set from which items are drawn increases, although some doubt might perhaps be cast on his results by arguing that playing cards and dates of the year represent two items each – number *and* suit or day *and* month. If so, the spans for these items should be regarded as twice those given in Table 7.7. The same would apply to some of the states in the USA such as New Hampshire and South Dakota. On this type of reckoning all the observed spans would lie between a little more than 5 and a little less than 7 items except for digits and for Black/White. The latter might perhaps be recoded more easily than other types of item by methods mentioned in the previous chapter (p. 179).

Further studies on the effects of size of set are not always easy to interpret. We have already noted that selections of letters or digits are unlikely to give very different results from the whole alphabet or set of 10 digits, and that studies using such selections do not constitute evidence against the view that span is related to set size (Pollack, 1953b, Pollack *et al.*, 1959, Pollack and Johnson, 1963b, Conrad and Hull, 1964, Baddeley *et al.*, 1965, Conrad *et al.*, 1965, Woodhead, 1966). In two cases *longer* spans have been obtained with larger sets. However, in one of these the effect was small (Crannell and Parrish, 1957), and in the other, where it was large, the task was of the running type (Woodhead, 1966): subjects had to report digits 3-back in a series drawn from either 2, 6 or all 10 digits. Accuracy of recall in this type of task tends, as we have seen, to be poor, and it is possible that the larger sets might have conferred an advantage by making the different members of the series more discriminable from one another.

Warrington *et al.* (1966) report that in an experiment in which the items were inclined and curved lines, memory span decreased markedly as the number of different types of line increased. All the lines in a given presentation were, however, shown together and the presentations with fewer types of line tended to be easier to group and to show more symmetry. The effect may therefore be one of perceptual coding rather than of memory span.

Probably the best authenticated difference of span associated with size of set is the longer span obtained with digits than with letters (e.g. Jacobs, 1887, Crannell and Parrish, 1957, Warrington *et al.*, 1966), although the evidence is not quite unequivocal: for example Cardozo and Leopold (1963) found that the span for digits was the same as that for letters when the items were presented visually all at once, although it was longer with auditory presentation: in the latter case the spans contained equal *item* information.

Further evidence indicating that memory span is affected by set size is given by Crannell and Parrish (1957) who found that the spans for random 3-letter words were shorter than for single letters, and by Lloyd *et al.* (1960) who found that errors tended to be greater when random words were drawn from large than from small sets.

A different method of varying set size was used by Harrison (1967) who presented strings of 4 items consisting of the words 'Black' or 'White' with each word varying in one or more of certain other ways: they might be presented to either the left or the right ear, in either a man's or a woman's voice, and with the voice either clear or distorted, so that each item contained either 2, 3 or 4 binary attributes giving a set of 4, 8 or 16 possibilities respectively. Recall became substantially poorer as the number of attributes per item rose. Harrison suggested that the different dimensions behaved as separate, additive items within a fixed overall capacity – a view which as far as it goes is consistent with Crossman's. We may note that adding dimensions did *not* extend capacity for retention as it does for discrimination (p. 43): the different dimensions appear all to use the same store.

Relationships between successive items

Several lines of study have shown clearly that memory span is related to the probability with which one item follows another. Thus Conrad *et al.* (1965) and Baddeley *et al.* (1965) have shown that accuracy in the recall of strings of letters rises as the transition between each letter and the next approximates to that found in normal printed English. Again, several experiments have found that the memory span for words increases as the sequence changes from strictly random and comes to approximate to that of normal English (Miller and Selfridge, 1950, Marks and Jack, 1952, Deese and Kaufman, 1957, Richardson and Voss, 1960). The span is still larger if connected passages of prose are used and reproduction of ideas is required rather than literal recall (Zangwill, 1956, Deese and Kaufman, 1957). In line with these results is Lawson's (1961) finding that subjects look further ahead in reading as the sequence of words becomes less random and more like normal prose.

Lachman and Tuttle (1965) have attempted to localise these sequential effects as between accuracy of *perception, storage* and *recall*. They found that the poorer recall of more random material and the better recall of that which approximated to normal English still occurred when subjects had to read the material aloud as it was presented, thus providing proof that it had been accurately *perceived*. In a second experiment they excluded the possibility that high approximations to English are easier to reconstruct at *recall*, by comparing recall with recognition of individual words presented one at a time amongst other words: the material which more closely approximated to English was both better recognised and better recalled. The authors therefore concluded that the effect lay in the storage processes. The distinction between the retention and recall phases is, however, extremely difficult to draw. Given that a trace has to be laid down, preserved and then recovered, the better the trace has been preserved, the easier it is likely to be to distinguish from other traces and thus the easier to recover accurately for recall: at the same time any difficulty inherent in the process of recovery will be accentuated by any deficiency in the traces to be recovered.

If so, we may appropriately consider effects of the probability with

H

which one item follows another in the light of the 'cerebral dictionary' concept put forward by Treisman and discussed in Chapter 3 (p. 103): if each item partially activates others which are similar to it or associated with it in some way, recall will be facilitated if these similarities and associations are in line with the material presented, and hindered if they are not. The same explanation can be advanced to account for the confusability of some items such as those which are acoustically similar. It can also account for a number of other results which are otherwise difficult to understand:

For example, Broadbent and Gregory (1964) noted that lists of alternate digits and letters were less easily recalled than lists consisting of all digits or all letters, but that the difference became less as the rate of presentation became slower. This finding resembles that of Bertelson (p. 80) who found that reaction times for repeated responses rose as the interval between signals increased: we may think of the item or response as facilitating for a brief period the production of those like it or in the same class and as acting as 'noise' to others in different classes. The effect of alternation between classes of item has been further shown by Warrington *et al.* (1966) who found that although sequences of letters were less well recalled than sequences of digits they were better recalled than mixed sequences of letters and digits. Recall in the latter case fell as the number of *transitions* from letters to digits or vice versa rose. In line with these results are those of Wickelgren (1966b) who found that pairs of digits presented once and followed by a task designed to interfere with retention of them, were recognised more accurately if they were both the same or in ascending or descending sequence (e.g. 56 or 43). Also in line are the findings of Cohen (1963)that when recall of a list of words is permitted in any order those which are in some way related tend to cluster together in recall: the production of one item tends to facilitate the production of others related to it. Further support for this last point is provided by Murdock and vom Saal (1967) who found that the items in lists of words were better retained if they all came from the same category, although the order in which they were recalled might be less accurate.

Looking over the evidence we have surveyed in this section it seems clear that both size of set from which items are drawn and the relation between one item and another affect memory span in the kind of ways that Crossman's approach requires. Qualitatively, therefore, the idea is well justified that information rather than items are stored and that item- and order-information need to be distinguished. It is also clear that Eq. 7.1 can be made to give a fair account of Crossman's data –

which is by far the most complete yet available for this purpose – but that the alternative formulation proposed by McNicol to account for order calls its precise terms into question. Difficulty also arises for Eq. 7.1 from the fact that the increase of span when recall is allowed in any order instead of being required in strict sequence seems to be far less than would be expected if no order-information was being retained. This last difficulty might, perhaps, be overcome by assuming that subjects inevitably record order to some extent, as Kassum's results suggest.

A possible synthesis with the ideas put forward at the end of the preceding section of this chapter is to postulate a short-term store dealing with the last few items presented and preserving order relatively efficiently, provided there is no interference by subsequently presented material or recall of earlier material. This, as suggested, might work in conjunction with a long-term store where order is less well preserved. Decision as to whether or not these ideas are correct must wait upon future work. Further progress seems to demand a much more detailed examination of items recalled and of the order of recall with different types of material and under different conditions of presentation and recall.

LOCATING THE STORE

Broadbent (e.g. 1954, 1957a) originated a series of experiments in which pairs of digits were played simultaneously, one to each ear, and found a marked tendency for subjects to recall all the digits from one ear then all from the other rather than in pairs as presented, thus digits presented:

Right ear	7	2	5
Left ear	1	8	3

would be recalled 725183 rather than 712853. On the basis of these experiments he postulated that short-term memory storage is located between the sense organs and the central data-processing mechanisms. He assumed that each ear is associated with a separate store and that when recalling, a subject takes all the material from one store before any from the other. He recognised, however, that part of the material, say from one ear, might not be held in such a peripheral store but could be passed direct to the central mechanisms which would thus participate in short-term memory.

The view that the short-term store holds unprocessed, 'raw' sensory data as opposed to the processed data retained in long-term memory has an obvious elegance and is at first sight supported by several lines of evidence. On close scrutiny, however, these appear less convincing. We shall consider three lines upon which discussion has centred:

(*a*) It is a matter of common experience that a remark may be heard in conversation but that at the time the listener is unable to understand what has been said. He does, nevertheless, retain the *sounds* of the words he has heard and may come to recognise their meaning later. The retention of the sounds in these circumstances may, however, imply merely that the data are retained in this form of coding only so long as a more efficient form cannot be achieved. Some support for this view is contained in Clark's (1965) finding that simple nonsense designs presented once were recognised equally well whether or not the subject named them, whereas complex designs were better retained when named – the capacity of the store is enough to cope with the raw data of simple designs but not of complex. The latter require a more efficient coding if they are to be retained.

(*b*) Murdock (1966b) showed that the retention of words presented visually follows a somewhat different pattern from that of words presented aurally, and argued that this implies different stores with different characteristics for eye and ear, since if both merely fed into one central store, retention should be the same in both cases. McGhie *et al.* (1965) in a somewhat similar experiment had found digits presented visually to be much less well retained than those presented aurally and suggested that subjects tend to recode visual material in auditory form by some kind of rehearsal because it is more difficult to retain in visual form. This indeed seems reasonable in the sense that visual patterns of digits, and certainly of words, could be regarded as more complex and so as requiring more storage 'space' than their auditory equivalents. If so, the difference between visually and aurally presented material may result from the recoding of the former. Murdock encouraged such recoding by requiring his subjects to repeat the material as it was presented and found that visual presentation produced better recall of early items in a list, as might be expected if the process of recoding had tended to transfer the material to long-term store. The importance of such recoding was confirmed by further experiments in which the material was not repeated as it arrived: in these visual presentation yielded poorer results than aural at all positions in the list except the last where recall in both cases was near perfect (Murdock, 1967).

(*c*) Several experiments in which a substantial amount of material is flashed on a screen all at once for a fraction of a second have shown that although the subject cannot reproduce it all, he can nevertheless produce any one part of it if this part is indicated to him within a half second or so *after* the presentation (Sperling, 1960, Averbach and Sperling, 1961, Klemmer, 1961, Mackworth, 1964a, Eriksen and Lappin, 1967). This obviously implies that the whole of the material has been stored briefly, probably in the form of some visual after-effect, but that the effect ceases before there is time to read off more than a part of the information it contains. Further evidence in favour of such a system is given by Michon (1964) who found that accuracy of reproduction was similar whether the material was presented as a whole or in groups, provided the total time over which presentation took place remained the same.

This very brief visual storage is far too ephemeral to account for the short-term retention we have been discussing hitherto. Sperling (1963) suggested, however, that the process of reading off recoded the material in auditory form and that this was more durable. Strong evidence that auditory recoding of visual material tends to occur automatically is contained in the finding that items which are acoustically similar – such as the letters B and V – are often confused even though they are presented visually (Conrad, 1962b, 1963), and that the frequency of such confusions increases if the letters are deliberately mouthed or spoken as they are presented (Murray, 1965, 1966). Items which sound alike are also more easily confused than those which merely look alike when written, such as the words THROUGH and COUGH (Baddeley, 1966b). These results do not necessarily imply, however, that the material is retained in a peripheral auditory store, but merely that auditory coding is preferred to visual, perhaps as we have already noted because it is more efficient, or perhaps because with material such as digits or letters the auditory form is more generic. For example, THREE, 3 and III are all pronounced 'three', and F, f and *f* are all pronounced 'eff'. Furthermore, *some* errors in short-term retention are due to confusion of items similar in meaning (Baddeley, 1964b, 1966b, Dale and Gregory, 1966), implying that storage is central rather than peripheral, although it is hard to say how far this indicates a central *short-term* store, and how far it results from material having got through to the long-term store: we mentioned at the beginning of this chapter that Baddeley (1966a) found similarity of meaning to be a greater cause of error than similarity of sound in long-term memory.

Arguments in favour of a central short-term store have also been based on the results of experiments using Broadbent's technique of presenting pairs of items simultaneously to the two ears. Moray (1960) noted that when subjects recalled ear by ear many errors were due to items from the wrong ear being substituted, and argued that such errors could not occur if there was a separate store attached to each ear and subjects reproduced all the material from one before any from the other. The alternative is either to assume that part of the material can be taken from one store then part from the other alternately, or more simply that the material from both ears is stored centrally and is distinguishable by being 'tagged' with the ear from which it has come: some such tagging would be necessary if the material presented simultaneously to the two ears was not to be fused into a single combined sound. Such experiments as Kay's (1963) (p. 211) which indicate that it is very difficult to take one item from store while leaving others tends to argue against the first view and, by implication, in favour of the second.

More direct evidence has been provided by Gray and Wedderburn (1960) who presented three pairs of items to the two ears thus:

Right ear	CYC-	7	STYLE
Left ear	1	LO-	3

and found that recall by class of material – that is 'CYCLOSTYLE 173' was as good as ear-by-ear recall. Broadbent and Gregory (1964) using the same method with digits and letters or digits and names of colours alternated between ears also found that recall by class was as good as ear-by-ear. Yntema and Trask (1963) using digits and words found recall *better* when made class-by-class than ear-by-ear, which seems an unlikely result if subjects had been switching rapidly between stores for the different ears. Again Emmerick *et al.* (1965) who presented three pairs of words, obtained more accurate recall in the pattern RLRLRL than RRRLLL when the former made a meaningful sentence even when the words to the two ears were spoken in different voices. These effects seem to depend upon the association between items in successive pairs and not to occur within individual pairs. Thus Bartz *et al.* (1967) who presented separate halves of words thus

Right ear	AB-	EI-	CON-
Left ear	LE	THER	STRAINT

or

Right ear	FOOT-	HAIR-	MOON-
Left ear	BALL	CUT	GLOW

found recall tended to occur ear-by-ear.

As regards vision, Sampson and Spong (1961a, b) and Sampson

(1964) have shown that when digits are presented simultaneously to the two eyes recall in pairs rather than eye-by-eye is the rule. It is perhaps understandable that this should be so and that the two eyes should be regarded as feeding into a common store since they work so closely together, yet the close integration of data from the two ears in achieving auditory localisation argues that vision and hearing are not very different as regards the combination of data from the two paired sense organs, and that principles of storage might reasonably be the same for both. As between vision and hearing, Broadbent and Gregory (1961) found that digits presented alternately to eye and ear were recalled better sense-by-sense than in actual order of arrival. We may suppose that they were inevitably tagged with the sense from which they had come so that this method of recall does not necessarily favour a theory of separate stores for eye and ear but can be accounted for in terms of recall being easier class-by-class as found by Yntema and Trask.

Sperling (1967) in a revision of his former (1963) theory has suggested that material is rapidly read from a peripheral store capable of holding it for up to about ·5 sec into a central store capable of holding it for a somewhat longer period – long enough for it to give rise to overt or covert motor acts of rehearsal. The transfer of material to this central store is assumed to be very rapid: Sperling suggests about 3 letters in 50 msec – say about 140 bits per sec. The fact that such transfer does not necessarily imply auditory recoding appears to follow from results obtained by Parks (1965), who exposed designs on a band which moved horizontally past a fixed narrow vertical slit at a rate such that the whole design was seen in ·25 to ·5 sec. Under these conditions the whole design was seen simultaneously in the vicinity of the slit. This result implies some short-term storage of the early parts of the design in visual form until the later parts have arrived. One obvious possible explanation was that the storage was on the retina and that the eye tracked in the direction of the movement of the band, so projecting the slit on to different retinal areas. Parks ruled this out, however, by showing that the same results could be obtained for two designs presented simultaneously on bands moving in opposite directions. He concluded that the storage must be central. The extent of transfer from the periphery to such a central store would depend on both peripheral and central factors: on the peripheral signals lasting long enough and not being destroyed by the masking effects of signals occurring immediately afterwards, and on the central store not being overloaded by too much data (Lawrence and La Berge, 1956, Eriksen and Steffy, 1964, Steffy and Eriksen, 1965).

This model bears a striking resemblance to that proposed to account for single-channel effects in Chapter 4, where it was suggested that there is a short-term store located between the perceptual and translation mechanisms, and that data from signals can be stored there until the translation mechanism is ready to use them as a basis for action (p. 109, see also Fig. 1.3, p. 19). We have already seen in Chapter 3 (p. 86) that the perceptual mechanism appears to operate at a rate which is of the right order to fit in with the rate of transfer from peripheral to central storage proposed by Sperling.

We may therefore sum up the evidence regarding the location of the short-term store by saying that it seems necessary, and probably sufficient, to postulate three processes:

(i) Very brief peripheral storage holding data over periods of less than about 1 sec.

(ii) Central short-term storage holding data over periods of several seconds. Data thus held have been processed in the sense that they have passed through the perceptual mechanism, but they have not passed through the translation mechanism – they have been perceived but not responded to. Data in this store are extremely vulnerable to interference from other material coming after or to any shift in the subject's attention. The results obtained by Kay (1953) and others (p. 212) suggest that this store tends to be emptied completely if any item is taken from it.

(iii) Recirculation of the data from the short-term store through the translation mechanism not only prolongs the period of retention by 'rewriting' the traces in the short-term store itself, but also tends to pass material to long-term storage. It is understandable that the digits, letters, syllables and words that have been commonly used in short-term memory experiments have tended to be recirculated and stored with an auditory coding, but other codings are also possible.

SHORT-TERM RETENTION AS A FACTOR IN COMPLEX PERFOR-
MANCE

Jacobs (1887), who measured digit and letter spans for the girls in a North London school, found that average spans increased from the lower to the higher forms in the school and tended to be higher among the abler pupils in each form. On the basis of these results, which are set out in Table 7.8, he suggested: ' "span of apprehension" should be an important factor in determining mental grasp, and its determination one of the tests of mental capacity'. Digit span has indeed been incorporated into a number of intelligence tests such as the Wechsler Adult Intelligence Scale. We may suspect, however, that it enters into many other intellectual tasks besides. We mentioned in the previous chapter

TABLE 7.8 *Digit and letter spans attained by London schoolgirls. Data from Jacobs (1887). Figures are the averages of the highest span attained by each individual in two sets of trials.*

Class	Digits		Letters		
	Top ½ of class	Bottom ½ of class	Top ½ of class	Bottom ½ of class	Mean of Means
VI.	10·5	9·1	9·0	8·1	9·2
Upper V.	9·8	9·1	8·8	8·2	9·0
V.	7·9	8·6	8·1	7·8	8·1
Lower V.R.	8·2	8·1	8·0	8·1	8·1
Lower V.	8·5	9·0	8·2	8·0	8·4
Upper IV. R.	8·4	8·0	8·4	7·5	8·1
Upper IV.	8·4	7·8	7·4	6·5	7·5
IV.R.	8·6	7·6	7·2	6·9	7·6
IV.	8·0	6·6	7·0	6·5	7·0
Lower IV.R.	8·0	6·7	7·1	7·5	7·3
Lower IV.	7·5	7·5	7·0	6·3	7·1
Upper III.	7·4	6·4	6·4	5·4	6·4
III.	7·8	8·5	6·7	6·4	7·4
II.	6·8	4·9	6·5	6·0	6·1
I.	7·4	7·1	6·8	7·0	7·1
Mean of means	8·2	7·7	7·3	7·1	

the example of skilled performance in which a complex sequence of actions is undertaken to achieve a given end and short-term memory is required to keep a tally on what has been done and what remains to be done. We may here outline briefly four types of situation in which different kinds of tally are required.

1. Keeping track of several variables

Yntema and Mueser (1960) presented subjects with a number of small doors behind each of which could be written a symbol, for example a *shape*, i.e. circle, square, triangle or heart; or a *number*, i.e. 1, 2, 3 or 4; or a letter denoting a *colour*, i.e. R(ed), Y(ellow), G(reen) or B(lue). Each set of symbols was associated with a particular door. The subject

heard a series of messages indicating the symbol to be written behind
each door: sometimes these were the same as the symbol already there
in which case the subject left things as they were, sometimes they were
different in which case the subject erased the existing symbol and substituted the new one. At intervals questions were asked as to what
symbol was present behind a particular door and the subject had to
answer without opening the door concerned to inspect. He had therefore
to retain the present states of the symbols behind all the doors at the
same time. Further similar experiments using a slightly modified apparatus were carried out by the same authors (1962). The task was found
to be relatively easy when only one in four messages informed the subject
that one of the series had changed and when the sets associated with the
various doors were all different. Accuracy fell, however, if every message
modified one of the sets or if all the sets were the same – for example if
all were numbers. Difficulty increased as the number of *sets* rose from
2 to 8 but did not do so to any significant extent as the number of
possible *symbols* in any one set rose from 2 to 21. These results are in
line with the results of more orthodox short-term memory experiments
in showing that retention becomes poorer as the number of items to be
retained increases and as they become less readily discriminated from
one another, but is often relatively little affected by increase in the size
of set from which the items are drawn.

A similar fall of accuracy with increase in the number of variables to
be monitored was found by Mackworth and Mackworth (1958, 1959)
when subjects had to keep track of a number of simultaneously developing situations. Their subjects, unlike those of Yntema and Mueser,
were able to observe the present states of all the variables continuously,
so that it is understandable that they were able to cope with a rather
large number. The interesting point is that errors were nevertheless
made: it seems that even when a whole display is on view at once, the
fact that only one part of it can be scrutinised at any one instant imposes
a substantial load on short-term memory if all parts of it are to be kept
under review. Several studies of similar type have shown that, as in
Kay's (1953) task, performance improves as the length of time between
messages increases, suggesting that the time for which data have to be
held in store is less important than the opportunities for rehearsal given
by a slower pace of presentation (Monty *et al.*, 1965, 1967a, b, Glucksberg *et al.*, 1967, Taub *et al.*, 1967).

Somewhat similar principles seem to apply to a concept-formation
task studied by Restle and Emmerick (1966) in which subjects were
shown a series of simple designs and required to discover the salient

features by which they should be classified. To do this, if they were not to proceed by blind trial and error, they had to retain data about examples presented previously and about the correctness of their responses to them. The authors found that this task was much more difficult if, instead of each example coming from a single set of classes, successive items came from 2 to 6 different sets in turn. These latter conditions clearly increased the memory load since with, say, two sets the subject would have had to retain twice as much data in total in order to retain as much data about any one set as he would if he were dealing with one set only.

2. Problem-solving

As mentioned in Chapter 1, short-term retention seems to play a crucial part in certain types of problem-solving in which subjects have to gather data and then hold it while gathering further data. It seems as if performance is often limited by their forgetting the earlier data while acquiring the later. Results have so far come from experiments designed to study differences between adults of different ages, and the decline of short-term memory with age has made them clearer than they would otherwise have been. We may briefly consider two examples. The first, an electrical problem experiment in which subjects had to relate terminals on small boxes to points on circuit diagrams by taking readings on a meter, has already been described in Chapter 1 (p. 22). The preferred method of tackling this problem seemed to be that of taking readings until one pair of terminals had been identified, then taking further readings to identify a third, and so on. At each stage the readings not immediately required were usually forgotten, so that they had to be taken again when required for the identification of another terminal later. This strategy, although seemingly wasteful, had the advantage of keeping the load on short-term memory to a minimum. Similar results were obtained in closely analogous tasks not couched in terms of electrical circuits by Clay (see Chapter 1 p. 22, also Welford, 1958, pp. 205–209) who also noted that accuracy improved when subjects wrote down the readings they took instead of trying to hold them in memory.

Clay (1954, 1957, see also Welford, 1958, pp. 211–219) also found much the same kind of difficulty due to short-term memory with a different kind of problem. In this subjects placed counters on chequerboards – 3 × 3, 4 × 4, 5 × 5 or 6 × 6 – so as to add simultaneously to marginal totals specified for both columns and rows. The 5 × 5 board, with counters in place, is shown in Fig. 7.3. The difficulty of this task seemed to lie mainly in the making of corrections for errors when all, or almost all, the counters had been placed upon the board. Subjects would make one or two rearrangements of the counters and then seemingly become confused. Such confusions seemed to arise from a failure to hold enough data in mind to effect the required correction. For example, to correct the error in Fig. 7.3 the subject would have had to note that the second column added to 12 instead of 13 and then find which of the other columns added to one too many. Having

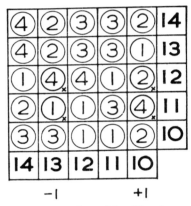

Figure 7.3. 5 × 5 chequer board used by Clay (1954, 1957). The numbers enclosed by circles represent counters placed by a subject in the attempt to make them add to the correct totals on both rows and columns simultaneously. The rows are correct, but the second column from the left adds to 12 instead of 13 and the rightmost column adds to 11 instead of 10. To correct this error two pairs of counters marked with small crosses need to be exhanged between the columns.

found this he would have to discover which counters to interchange between the columns in order to correct the error without introducing errors into the rows. Many subjects tended to lose essential data during this process: for example they would forget the column first discovered to be wrong while searching for the second. It was interesting to see, in confirmation of this, that many subjects indicated incorrect totals by devices such as moving a counter slightly out of place, for the acknowledged purpose of helping them to remember which totals needed correction. Closely analogous results have been obtained with a more complex problem by Jerome (1962) who again found that performance fell with age from young adulthood onwards.

It seemed fairly clear that, when solving problems such as these, subjects more or less gradually obtained some kind of grasp of the way in which the various pieces of data fitted together. What this means in precise terms is not yet possible to say confidently. It does not appear to depend wholly on building up a 'structure' in long-term retention because, at least in its earlier stages, the overall 'picture' is plastic and subject to modification by subsequent data. It seems rather to be akin to the conceptual frameworks discussed in the previous chapter in connection with the co-ordination of action and the maintenance of orientation, and we may note that the second of these tends to be lost in certain clinical disorders of memory.

3. Thinking

Perhaps the main interest of problem-solving is the lead it gives to the study of certain processes involved in thinking. Bartlett (1950, 1958) has described a number of experiments by himself and by Adiseshiah (1951) and Jeeves (1957) which treat thinking as a series of discrete *stages* which are either interpolated between a starting point to a known conclusion or extrapolated towards a conclusion as yet unknown. Anyone who has been required in his student days to undertake exercises in introspection will recognise the plausibility of such stages. Subjects set to think about a problem and to introspect while doing so commonly report a series of images. These do not seem to represent the true processes of thought: rather they are the stations between one process and the next. It is tempting to suggest that they are a kind of storage between *computations* which, as the so-called *Wurtzburg School* recognised in the early years of the present century, are outside the scope of introspection. Obviously little weight can be laid on such evidence, but it is attractive and provocative to conceive of thinking as akin to the operation of a computer going through a series of stages in each of which data are taken either from the sense organs or from a memory store to be combined with other data in some kind of computation, and the result is then stored temporarily to be used later with other data in a further computation, and so on.

If this is so, limitations in the range and capacity of thought could lie either as traditionally assumed in the computational process, or in the storage phase (Posner, 1965). Effects of storage could be due either to the limited amount of data that can be held at any one time or to particular conditions, such as distractions of attention, which are inimical to short-term retention. The former is suggested by Garner's (1962) finding that correlations between two dimensions or features of a stimulus can be readily perceived and used to simplify perception, whereas correlations between three dimensions are much less easily recognised and used. The possibility that thinking may be impaired by conditions which tend to disrupt short-term retention suggest that close scrutiny would be worth while of detailed procedures during experiments on tasks such as concept formation. Is it, for instance, that the requirement to make a judgment about each example from which a general principle has to be extracted tends to preclude the storage which is essential if one example is to be compared with another? Again we may well ask how far performance at certain tests, such as the pattern completions of Raven's Matrices Test, are limited by difficulties of observing one part of a pattern and then holding it in memory while looking away to another part to see if it fits?

The computations between each stage of storage and the next can perhaps be regarded as recodings comparable with those discussed in the previous chapter. Interpolation is analogous to the taking of action in a skilled performance in which the end to be achieved is determined in advance, but some flexibility of means is allowed. Extrapolation can be thought of as the application of a coding or schema to data which enables further data to be inferred in the same way as detail is often inferred in perception. The range of possible extrapolations from any given set of data will be constrained to a great extent by expectations based on familiarity. One facet of originality is, perhaps, to set aside the most probable extrapolation and to follow up a less familiar line.

4. Programming of action

The analogies between certain types of human performance and computer operation draws attention to the fact that short-term retention is required not only of *data* but also of *programmes* of action. Such programmes have been discussed under the term 'plans' by Miller *et al.* (1960) and the computer analogy has been well emphasised by Simon and Kotovsky (1963). Experimental studies are sparse but Broadbent and Heron (1962) have shown that speed and accuracy of cancelling digits in lists of random numbers tend to be poorer, especially for older subjects, when the digit to be cancelled changes frequently so that the subject has to keep revising his programme, than when it remains the same throughout a list. Simon and Kotovsky point out that relatively simple programmes couched in terms of computer operations can not only enable subjects to carry out routines but can be the basis of extrapolation from a series and of the inductive recognition of regularity. They show that the type and complexity of programme required for such tasks is related to the difficulty of the Thurstone Letter-Series Completion Problems in which subjects have to continue series ranging from simple sequences such as cdcdcd . . . through sequences such as abmcdmεfmghm . . . to more complex examples such as rscdstdetuef . . .

Short-term programmes raise a number of problems which are as yet largely unrecognised: what is the maximum length and complexity of programme – for example how elaborate a pattern can a woman knit without giving continuous attention to the task? In what units should the length of a programme be measured? Almost certainly the means of their retention are different from those of items in short-term memory spans: the short-term programme seems to be more robust than the memory span and much less liable to disruption by intervening activity and shifts of attention, although still vulnerable to some extent. It is tempting to draw analogies between, on the one hand the short-term retention of data and various clinical deficiencies of memory, and on the other hand between short-term programmes and certain types of aphasia, apraxia and distractability, and thus to link them to neurological mechanisms. Doing so would, however, take us beyond the scope of our present discussion. Suffice to say there seems to be a *prima facie* case for distinguishing between the retention of data and of programmes: just what the difference is remains to be seen.

VIII

Effects of Loading

We have already in Chapter 4 discussed some of the effects of brief overloading of the subject's capacity. In the present chapter we shall consider the effects of longer-continued overloading and also of under-loading, bringing together three areas of study which have been prominent in experimental psychology at different times, namely *fatigue*, *stress* and *vigilance*. It is impossible to separate these entirely from one another, but we shall for convenience deal with them in turn.

NEUROMUSCULAR FATIGUE

The study of fatigue stands at one of the traditional meeting-points between physiology and psychology. Until the early years of the present century research centred mainly round the decrements of performance that occur in the course of prolonged muscular work, and the division of labour between the two disciplines could be simply conceived: physiology studied the neuromuscular |mechanism itself, psychology the accompanying subjective feelings of discomfort and exhaustion. The shift of interest in the psychological field during the past fifty years from a predominant concern with conscious processes to an almost exclusive concentration on observable behaviour and measurable performance, served in its early stages to strengthen rather than diminish psychological interest in fatigue; here, it seemed, were striking changes of performance that could be related closely to definable conditions. Soon, however, it became apparent that neither in its physiological nor in its psychological aspect is fatigue a simple phenomenon. The neuro-muscular mechanism involved is complex, the changes that might be regarded as fatigue effects are manifold. Behavioural changes, though clear in outline, vary in important detail from one set of circumstances to another. The situation became even more confused when attempts were made to see analogies to neuromuscular fatigue in purely mental operations carried on for long periods.

240

These difficulties have led some to wish to abandon the term 'fatigue'. Yet there is need for a term to cover those changes of performance that take place over a period of time during which some part of the mechanism, whether sensory, central or muscular, becomes chronically overloaded. If fatigue is defined in this way, the task of the investigator ceases to be one of finding a single entity that can be labelled 'fatigue': instead he has, first, to study the detailed changes of performance brought about by such overloading and, secondly, to seek to explain them in terms of changes of function in any of the many bodily mechanisms concerned.

Summaries in English of work on fatigue have been provided by several authors (e.g. Viteles, 1932, Bartley and Chute, 1947, Floyd and Welford, 1953, Simonson, 1965) so that the subject will be discussed relatively briefly here, first re-examining the classical type of experiment on neuromuscular fatigue and then going on to the much more complex problem of so-called mental fatigue.

Classical experiments on neuromuscular fatigue have used an apparatus known as an ergograph. Typically an arm and hand are strapped in position in such a way that only one finger is free to move. With this finger the subject is required to depress a lever that can be loaded to different extents by means of a spring or weight. The lever is depressed and released in time with a metronome or other timing device giving regularly repeated signals.

If the loading is light or the rate slow or both, the task can be continued indefinitely, but if the load is substantial and the rate more frequent the depressions of the lever will, after a time, begin to diminish in amplitude and eventually fall to zero. A typical ergograph record is shown in Fig. 8.1. The decline of performance begins sooner and proceeds more rapidly as the load or the frequency increase. If, when performance has ceased, the subject is allowed to rest for a period and then tries again, recovery will have occurred: after a short rest it may be partial, in the sense that amplitude may not be reattained in full and will fall again to zero quickly. With longer rests, recovery will be complete.

The whole pattern of decrement and recovery may be envisaged as that of a system having a limited capacity for continuous operation and some reserve that can be used to deal with temporary overloads. If the overload is continued, as when the weight or spring tension is relatively heavy and the lifting frequent, the reserve becomes exhausted – slowly if the overload is slight, more rapidly as it becomes greater. Rest allows the reserve to be re-established. It must be emphasised, however, that such a conceptual model, though a convenient *aide mémoire*, is not necessarily true in a literal sense: the same pattern would hold if, for instance, exercise progressively built up inhibitory or toxic substances that were gradually dissipated and if work output depended on the

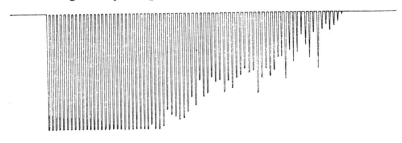

Figure 8.1. Section of ergograph record. Each vertical stroke was made by a flexion of the right forefinger against a lever weighted in such a way that the force required to move the point of contact with the finger was approximately 14 lb. The time marker below shows 1 sec intervals.

balance between accumulation and dispersion. Nor does such a model specify what part of the neuromuscular system is limiting performance: limitations at various points could produce the same pattern of overload and recovery effects.

A considerable volume of physiological research has aimed at finding the locus of fatigue under various conditions in, firstly the muscles themselves, secondly the myoneural junctions and thirdly the central mechanisms supplying the muscles.

Peripheral limitations

Experiments with nerve-muscle preparations have shown that, with repeated stimulation of the nerve, the muscle may after a time cease to contract. Although nerve cells can lose sensitivity and reactivity with long-repeated rapid stimulation and can thus show a fatigue effect, it is clear that the contraction ceases long before failure of the nerve. It also occurs before the muscle itself becomes incapable of contraction, as is shown by the fact that, when blocking has occurred, the muscle can be made to contract again if direct electrical stimulation is applied to it. The site of the blocking thus appears to be the myoneural junction.

Even direct electrical stimulation of the muscle may eventually fail to secure contraction. Although this is sometimes attributable to local conditions developing at the point of contact of the electrode, it is usually taken to imply that the muscle itself can show a fatigue effect. Convincing evidence that in the intact human subject the muscle can be the locus of fatigue has been given by Merton (1956), who showed conditions in which, when a muscle had been fatigued by repeated rapid contractions to the point of complete voluntary inactivity, it could not be made to contract again by direct electrical stimulation. Further evidence is given by Lippold *et al.* (1960), who showed that the electrical activity in muscles exerting a static force against a spring or weight rose with time and that the rise was steeper the heavier the load. This finding appears to mean that changes in the muscles rendered contraction less powerful for any given level of efferent stimulation, so that neural activity had to be increased to maintain the required output of muscular power. Both Merton and Lippold *et al.* found that cutting off the blood supply to the fatigued muscle or muscles prevented recovery during a period of relaxation. It therefore seems clear that the lowered performance of the muscles was either due to lack of oxygen or other supplies or to accumulation of 'fatigue products', which would have been corrected by blood flow. If so, it is understandable that fatigue effects are found to be greater with static contraction than with rhythmic, since blood flow is likely to be greater during the latter than the former. Direct evidence about the effects of sustained contraction on blood flow in muscles is equivocal (see Hemingway, 1953, p. 74), but we can perhaps expect that the force of the contraction would be critical in determining the extent to which blood flow is restricted, so that results would depend on the precise conditions of different experiments.

The fact that maintenance of blood-sugar level is important for athletic endurance (Edwards *et al.*, 1934; Douglas and Koch, 1951) is usually taken as further evidence that failing fuel supply to muscles is a direct cause of fatigue. The argument is not conclusive, however, since lowered blood-sugar can affect a wide range of bodily mechanisms, neural and central as well as muscular.

Central limitations

In his classical studies of the scratch reflex in dogs, Sherrington (1906) found that after a period of repeated elicitation the reflex ceased, though the same muscles would still respond to a different reflex. Clearly there could be no question of myoneural junctions or other effector parts of the mechanism constituting the limiting factor; the limitation was presumably sensory or central. The cessation came later when the reflex was elicited by stimulating various slightly different points on the skin rather than by repeated stimulation of the same point, but it came eventually nevertheless, indicating central rather than sensory origin. Sherrington's results have been directly confirmed by Lloyd (1942), who found that action potentials in the efferent nerve of the reflex diminished with repeated stimulation of the afferent nerve. We may note in passing that Sherrington found the fatigue effects to be highly specific: if a reflex had ceased after repeated˙elicitation by stimuli applied to one point on the skin, it could be restored immediately by shifting to a different point. There is no question here of regarding fatigue, as has sometimes been done, as due to the general circulation in the blood stream of 'fatigue products' resulting from exercise and of these affecting the central nervous system.

The importance of central factors in neuromuscular fatigue has been stressed by Reid (1928). Using an ergograph with human subjects he showed that, although voluntary contraction had ceased, the muscle could still be made to contract either by direct electrical stimulation or by electrical stimulation of the efferent nerve trunk. The essential locus of fatigue here seems clearly to have been central. Reid further showed, however, that recovery was much less after a period during which voluntary effort ceased but the muscle concerned was directly stimulated electrically and thus kept contracted, than after a period in which the muscle was rested. This result implies that, although the fatigue was central, local conditions in the muscle nevertheless influenced it, presumably by means of afferent impulses. If this conclusion is correct, the question is reopened in a new way of how physical or chemical changes in muscle resulting from exercise influence fatigue and of why continuous contraction causes fatigue effects more quickly than does rhythmic: although conditions in the muscles may not limit performance directly, they cause signals to the spinal cord and brain that affect conditions there. The subjective counterparts (if any) of these afferent impulses are not certainly known, though it seems reasonable to link them with the feelings of discomfort and pain that mount rapidly as severe muscular contraction continues. If so, it means that fatigue decrements in muscular performance will depend to some extent on a subject's sensitivity to and toleration of pain.

It must be emphasised that Reid's work did not imply that the limitation of performance due to fatigue was invariably central. His results showed that when a series of exceptionally rapid voluntary contractions had fallen to zero direct stimulation of the muscle or the nerve trunk did not restore contraction or did so only partly. It seems clear that with rapid or intense contractions a truly peripheral muscular fatigue can be produced, but that with conditions nearer to those of everyday life, central limitations are more likely.

Two further points about neuromuscular fatigue indicate the importance of central factors.

(*a*) *Motivation*. Figure 8.1 shows a number of minor variations typical of ergographic records; the rate of decline is not smooth, but is interrupted by temporary partial recoveries. To some extent such variation is to be expected from the random fluctuations of function to be found in almost any complex biological mechanism; but subjectively some, at least, correspond to periods of special effort, and it is easy to show that they can be produced by urging the subject to 'try harder'.

The effect of incentives upon fatigue effects has been vividly illustrated in an experiment by Schwab (1953), who required subjects to hang on a horizontal bar. He found that with instructions to hold on 'as long as possible' the average length of time before letting go was less than 1 min. With strong urging the time was raised to rather over 1 min. With the reward promised of a \$5 bill for bettering their previous records, subjects managed to hang on for an average of nearly 2 min.

What appears to be a different kind of motivational effect was shown by Ash (1914), who found that, after performance on an ergograph had ceased, it could be made to begin again not only by lightening the weight, but also merely by leading the subject to believe that the weight had been lightened. Again Jarrard (1960) showed that subjects who transferred from one weight to another which was in fact the same but because it was smaller in *size* appeared heavier, made fewer lifts before reaching 'exhaustion' than did subjects who had the same size weight throughout, while those who transferred to a larger size weight which appeared lighter made more lifts. He found that they adjusted their muscular tension according to what they believed the heaviness of the weight to be so that those who transferred to smaller weights were in a sense exerting themselves unduly. His results are complementary to the well-known fact that athletes pace their performance in races from the beginning according to the distance to be covered, thus adopting a strategy which prevents premature onset of fatigue due to over-exertion in the early stages (e.g. Ward, 1950).

These results are important, as showing that fatigue effects are to some extent under voluntary control in the sense, perhaps, that the subject sets levels of effort he is willing to make and of discomfort he is prepared to bear. Such variation is not strictly attributable to the system that fatigues, but must be taken into account when measuring fatigue effects.

(b) *Recruitment.* It is easy to observe in ergograph studies that when a load is placed upon a small group of muscles other muscles spontaneously become active and that, as fatigue proceeds, the activity in other muscles spreads until almost the whole body is involved: the subject may tense his legs and grit his teeth in the effort to depress one middle finger so strapped in position that these activities cannot possibly help. The classical demonstration of this phenomenon is by Ash (1914). A more recent demonstration of the same kind of effect has been given by Lundervold (1958), using electromyographic recordings in a typewriting task. In everyday life this recruitment would be adaptive in the sense that other muscles could take the load off the group that was becoming fatigued; the fact that the phenomenon occurs in ergograph experiments although it is not adaptive in them implies that it is largely involuntary. The extra muscles become active in a specific order (Seyffarth, 1940, Denny-Brown, 1949), presumably along lines of functional or neural proximity. One may perhaps assume the relatively simple neurological model that focal activity concerned with one muscle or group of muscles tends to spread to surrounding areas, the amount of spread becoming greater the longer the focal activity continues or the more intense it becomes. Lippold *et al.* (1960) showed that as other muscles become active, electrical activity in the fatigued muscle may diminish, presumably implying that activity in areas surrounding a focal area may continue after it has ceased in the focal area itself. It may be noted in this context that excessively exercised muscles tend to go into contraction more readily than rested ones, sometimes showing spasm, as in writer's or telegraphist's cramps. This appears to imply that a focal area, when it has recovered from acute fatigue, may be left hypersensitive – a condition found in some studies not concerned with fatigue to occur in nerve tissue subjected to prolonged stimulation.

It is in line with this general picture that any voluntary activity by an irrelevant muscle during a task will tend to increase the involuntary activity by the same muscle subsequently: for example Yensen (1965) found that when one arm was supporting a heavy weight, a single voluntary contraction by the other arm tended to increase the subsequent involuntary activity in it – the voluntary activity seemed to have facilitated the involuntary. The picture may, however, be complicated

247247247

by general activation effects produced by anxiety, and also by individual differences of approach to the task (Benson and Gedye, 1962): we shall return to these factors later in this chapter and again in Chapter 10.

To sum up the position reached in the study of neuromuscular fatigue, it appears that in the intact organism changes in the muscles brought about by prolonged or repeated contraction can, according to circumstances, have one of two limiting effects. Either the muscles themselves become temporarily incapable of further contraction or the condition of the muscles produces afferent stimuli and these in turn affect the central mechanisms and lead to the cessation of efferent impulses. Which effect occurs first depends on factors at present not entirely clear. It may, however, tentatively be suggested that peripheral limitations are likely to result from intense activity and central limitations from activity which is less intense but more prolonged.

MENTAL FATIGUE

If the term 'mental fatigue' is to have a meaning in line with that of neuromuscular fatigue, it must denote the impairment of some brain mechanism as a result of long-continued use. The impairment must be reversible in the sense that it disappears with rest, and may take the form of lowered sensitivity or responsiveness or capacity. The last of these may show as a reduction in either the amount of information that can be handled at any one instant, and thus in reduced 'mental power', or in the amount that can be handled in a given period and so in slowness of perception, choice and so on.

Such a definition enables a distinction to be made between mental fatigue and several other central changes, such as adaptation, habituation, satiation, inhibition and monotony or boredom, all of which lead to decrement of performance with time. Adaptation implies a loss of sensitivity or discriminating power over one part of a range of possible stimulus values, but simultaneous gains over another: there is not so much a lowering of sensitivity as a shift in the point of maximum sensitivity. Habituation denotes a learnt ignoring of stimuli. Satiation is a state in which action ceases because the need or appetite that gave rise to it has been satisfied. Inhibition, although often loosely used, strictly means the reduction of one process by the activity of some opposing process. Boredom or monotony refers to a state in which the organism is underloaded, not overloaded: it seems as if a certain throughput of information is necessary to maintain full efficiency, and typically boring situations seem to be those in which attention is required

but little information is conveyed; the classical bore compels his hearer
to listen to conversation that is insignificant in content.

The distinction between fatigue and these states is easy to make
formally, but is often difficult to draw in practice. For example, even
neuromuscular fatigue can in a sense be viewed as a central inhibitory
state brought about by afferent impulses from the muscles, although it
should be noted that Sherrington was able to distinguish between patterns of decrement in a reflex due to what he termed fatigue as opposed
to what he identified as inhibition. The greatest difficulty arises in
distinguishing fatigue from monotony or boredom: many tasks used in
studies of fatigue are repetitious and thus liable to become monotonous,
whereas some used for studying monotony require actions or decisions
to be repeated frequently enough for them to be a possible cause of
fatigue. It is indeed reasonable to suppose that some tasks are both
fatiguing and boring: some parts of the subjects' central mechanisms
may be overloaded even though the overall throughput of information
is low. Usually, however, it seems fairly clear which of the two effects
limits performance sooner.

We shall here survey work that has been regarded, probably correctly,
as studying fatigue, leaving till later studies of conditions producing
monotony and boredom.

Phenomena of mental fatigue

We may note at once two resemblances between mental and neuromuscular fatigue which, although peripheral to any discussion of the
nature of fatigue, have an important bearing on methods of measurement. Firstly, if given the opportunity, subjects tend to distribute their
efforts over a working spell so as to minimise fatigue effects, adjusting
their pace to the expected length of spell right from the beginning,
working fast if the spell is to be short, more slowly if it is to be long
(Bills and Brown, 1929, Krueger, 1937, Barmack, 1939, Katz, 1949,
Forrest, 1958, Saufley and Bilodeau, 1963). This means that fatigue
effects are likely to show more if the subject works under pressure for
speed for an unknown period than if he works at his own pace or for
a time known in advance. Secondly, fatigue effects tend to be specific to
the performances that produce them, leaving other performances little
if at all affected. As a consequence, tests in which a subject is taken off
his main task and put for a brief period on to another to assess his
state of fatigue are often unsuccessful: little change of performance at
the tests occurs until such extreme states of exhaustion have been

reached that no test is needed to supplement common observation. In consequence, the most sensitive indications of fatigue are usually obtained by a detailed study of the fatiguing performance itself. There have, however, been a number of researches reported in which fatigue tests have proved successful. We shall in discussing fatigue effects consider both types of evidence.

Bartlett's Ferrier Lecture to the Royal Society (1943) was a landmark in the development of ideas about fatigue and indeed about human performance generally. In particular it showed that the phenomena of fatigue are more varied and more complex than is often supposed. On the basis of this lecture and of work done since, we may recognise four main types of change that can come about in mental fatigue.

(*a*) *Sensory or perceptual changes.* The classical studies of visual fatigue have been summarised and discussed by Bartley and Chute (1947) and by Weston (1953). They have, for the most part, been concerned with the possible fatigue of eye muscles and its relation to feelings of eye strain under conditions of low illumination, glare or close attention to detail. It is doubtful if the effects are to be wholly, or even mainly, attributed to the eye muscles: some probably result from frowning and general muscular tension built up as a result of concentrated efforts to see under difficult conditions. Be this as it may, it seems clear that there are some more strictly sensory or perceptual effects. For instance, Berger and Mahneke (1954) found that visual acuity (cancelling Landolt rings) and critical flicker frequency (CFF) both fell when tests were made continuously for 55 min, but rose again after 5 min rest. Examples of their results are shown in Fig. 8.2. Haider and Dixon (1961) in experiments in which they made continuous recordings of the threshold for detecting the difference of intensity between two spots of light, found that thresholds rose substantially during the course of a 14 min session, mainly between the second and tenth minutes. Saldanha (1955, 1957) found that repeated settings made on the vernier scale of a calliper gauge for $\frac{1}{2}$ hr or more became less regular, and thus less accurate, with time, but that accuracy returned after $\frac{1}{2}$ hr or so of rest. We may note in passing that the return was greater after a period of rest than after a similar period spent cancelling Landolt Rings – the fatigue effect was such that a change of work was not as good as a rest. The motor components in all these tasks were trivial, and thus it is clear that there was some loss of fine differentiation either spatially, as with visual acuity or vernier settings, or temporally as with CFF.

It has also been widely reported that CFF is lowered by mental work such as calculating or reading. The evidence has been summarised by Simonson and Brozek (1952) and by Grandjean and Perret (1961). Falls of CFF have not always been found when they have been sought, but enough positive results have been obtained to suggest clearly that the effects are real. It is very plausible that they should be so if fatigue

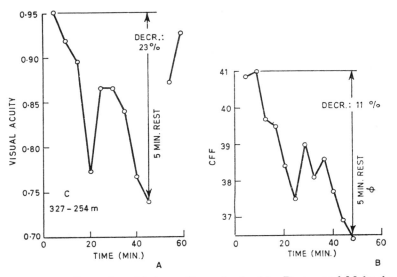

Figure 8.2. Examples of fatigue effects obtained by Berger and Mahneke (1954) with repeated measurements of visual functions.

A. *Visual acuity.* For each determination a Landolt ring was brought progressively closer to the subject until the direction of the gap could be recognised: 90 determinations were made continuously over a period of 55 min and 20 more after an interval of 5 min. Retinal illumination was held constant at 3·5 lux. Each point is the mean of 10 determinations by one subject.

B. *CFF.* Flicker was produced by a rotating disc illuminating a diffusing glass surface: 120 determinations were made continuously over a period of 55 min and further ones after an interval of 10 min. The flickering target subtended 1·15° at the subject's eye. Each point is the mean of 10 determinations by one subject.

implies some temporary central impairment since CFF has been found to decrease following brain injury and under the influence of depressant drugs, and to fall progressively with age during adulthood. The evidence suggests that CFF falls under conditions in which the signal-to-noise ratio in the brain is lowered so that there is a fall of d' in the signal-detection model when detecting the difference between 'on' and 'off'.

It is, however, possible that some at least of the effect might be due to a change in the criteria of judgment and thus of β.

As regards the site of the effect, Grandjean and Perret have shown that it is not due to a change of pupil size. They did, however, in line with Berger and Mahneke's results show that CFF fell as the time over which the test light was exposed increased from 10 to 28 sec. This fall tended to mask the effects of fatigue caused by having repeatedly to rearrange sets of seven random digits into their normal order. The observed fatigue effect thus depended to a considerable extent on the way in which CFF was measured, and this may explain some of the failures to find effects in the past. Evidence that the effect is not purely visual in origin is contained in work cited by Simonson and Brozek which found a substantial fall of CFF following calculations carried out while blindfolded. Further evidence is contained in the finding by Davis (1955) of a similar lowering of the critical rate at which an intermittent auditory signal ceases to 'flutter' and is heard as a continuous sound. Davis tested both CFF and critical flutter rate following 1 and 2 hr work at multiplying two-digit numbers mentally: the numbers were exposed visually and answers were written down. Both measures declined, with the flutter rate proving somewhat more sensitive than CFF.

(b) *Slowing of performance.* One of the most frequently observed fatigue effects is the slowing of sensory-motor performance. It is often suggested that this may be due to muscular fatigue, but there is no doubt that central factors are often, and probably mainly, involved. An indication of this is contained in the results of an experiment by Singleton (1953) who used a serial choice-reaction task. The apparatus is shown in Fig. 8.3. Subjects sat in a chair and pushed a joystick from a central position along slots in four directions in response to lights at the ends of the cross on the display shown in the top left corner of the Figure. Upon the subject's reaching the end of the correct slot the light went out, and on his return to the centre another came on, until 64 responses had been completed. He was told to work as fast as possible. Three variations of the task were presented; they were, in ascending order of difficulty, (i) 'Direct' with the joystick having to be pushed away when the top light came on, to the left for the left light, and so on; (ii) '180°' with the joystick pushed away in response to the bottom light, to the left for the right light, and so on; and (iii) '270°' with the joystick pushed away in response to the left light, to the left for the bottom light, and so on. The times per response gradually lengthened during each run, but, as can be seen from Fig. 8.4, the lengthening was much more in time spent at the centre, that is in deciding which way to move, than in the actual execution of movements. Moreover, this lengthening increased with the difficulty of the condition, implying that the fatigue effect became greater as the demands of the central task rose.

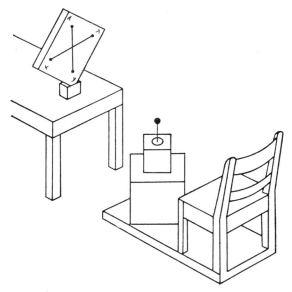

Figure 8.3. Four-choice serial reaction apparatus used by Singleton (1953).

Slowness may cause several complications when the subject cannot, as he could in Singleton's experiment, work at his own speed, but is externally paced. The classical example of such a task used in the study of fatigue is the Cambridge Cockpit, which was the basis of experiments by Craik, Drew and Davis (Davis, 1948). Subjects were tested for 2 hr spells in a simulated aircraft cockpit under blind flying conditions and had to deal with a series of manœuvres. Although in a general sense subjects could control the timing of these, the complications of the task were such that, once begun, many of the actions required in the manœuvre were in effect paced by the apparatus. Under such conditions subjects can react to slowing in one of two ways.

(i) Some of the actions required may be omitted. Drew, whose experiments are cited by Davis, found this tendency to be characteristic of some of his subjects during the latter part of their 2 hr spells. He also noted that most subjects tended to pay less and less attention to the more peripheral parts of the task as the spell continued, giving their

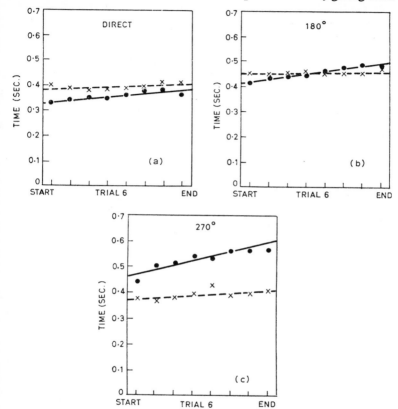

Figure 8.4. Results obtained by Singleton (1953) in three conditions of a serial reaction task.

The results shown are for the sixth trial of 64 reactions under each of the 3 conditions. Each point is the mean for 8 reactions by 10 subjects. The dots and solid lines are for times between the end of one movement and the beginning of the next, with the joystick in a central position, and are essentially reaction times. The crosses and broken lines are for the movement times from centre to end of slot and back.

main attention increasingly to the controls in constant use. For example, the fuel indicator had to be reset every 10 min, but came to be more and more often neglected, as shown in Fig. 8.5. We may note that Bursill (1958) found a similar tendency for peripheral items to be neglected under conditions of high temperature in a task in which subjects had to track a moving target and respond at the same time to signal lights at various distances from the target centre. Such omissions may perhaps be regarded as spontaneous attempts to simplify the task somewhat like those discussed in Chapter 7 (p. 211).

(ii) If, alternatively, the subject tries to complete all the actions required in the time available, he will have to hurry and may not have

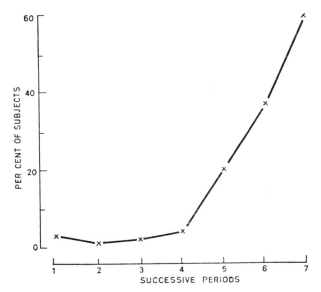

Figure 8.5. Percentage of subjects, in experiments with the Cambridge Cockpit, who omitted to reset the fuel indicator during successive periods of a 2 hr test. Based on results from 140 subjects. (After Davis, 1948.)

time to make his decisions and judgments accurately. In tasks like that of the Cambridge Cockpit, any slowing that results in a longer time being needed to observe the various instruments accurately may be felt as a 'stickiness of attention'. Performance under these conditions will tend to suffer a disruption that builds up in a vicious circle: the longer time taken to observe an instrument means that the resulting error tends to be larger before correcting action can be taken; when action is eventually taken it may, in order to make up time, be poorly controlled and require subsidiary corrections; these take further time and mean that subsequent correcting actions have to be larger again. The result, as Davis showed for many of his subjects, is that the onset of fatigue may lead to marked overactivity, often coupled with signs of anxiety. These in turn may direct attention from the task to worrying about whether it is being performed adequately and thus lead to still

Figure 8.6. Records of two different types of response in attempting to move a pointer on to a target by means of a velocity control. The records are plots against the time (from left to right) of the movements of the control. The upper record shows a normal skilful response with a movement of the control to get the pointer going and a second movement to stop it. The lower record shows a disorganised response made in the attempt to achieve the same result. Data from Davis (1949).

further slowing and disruption. An example of this kind of disruption is shown in Fig. 8.6, taken from the records of another experiment by Davis (1949), in which subjects had to bring a pointer from one position to another by means of a velocity control.

(c) *Irregularity of timing.* Long-continued performance tends to become not only slower but also less regular. Some of the most striking illustrations of these tendencies have been from industrial tasks in which, during a shift, there has been a moderate rise in the mean time required to perform each cycle of an operation, accompanied by a much greater rise in the standard deviation (for a review see Murrell, 1965). To some extent irregularity may be more apparent than real: the distributions of times for individual cycles of repetitive tasks tend to be skew, with a tail of long times and with a variance increasing with the mean; any overall slowing will therefore increase the variance and the number of what seem to be unusually long times. It has, however, been suggested by Bills (1931) that irregularity is due rather to occasional 'blocking'. That is to say, every now and then a short gap appears in an otherwise rapid performance, and the frequency of such gaps increases when the task is continued for a long time. On this view the greater part of the distribution might be only a little affected, but there should be a marked increase in the size of the tail.

One source of such blocking in paced tasks is easy to understand.

For example, Vince (1949) showed that subjects required to respond by pressing a key to signals at regular intervals kept pace up to a certain rate, but at higher rates gradually fell behind until eventually they stopped 'to make a fresh start'. Bills was, however, primarily considering unpaced tasks, such as alternate addition and subtraction of 3 from a list of digits, colour naming, substituting letters for digits according to a code or giving opposites of words. He found that the frequency of times for individual items exceeding twice the subject's average time tended to increase during 7 min of work. His results are not very convincing and could probably have been due to simple slowing, but much clearer evidence has been obtained by Bertelson and Joffe (1963) using a serial choice-reaction task. The subjects in this were required to press one of four keys in response to the figures 1 to 4 shown in random order on a 'Nixie' tube. Each response brought on the next figure, so that the task was continuous but unpaced. Samples of reaction times were scored at the second minute of work and at the end of 30 min. No change was found in the averages of the shortest or the median reaction times, but there was a marked increase in the average of the longest. The percentage of 'blocks' (defined as reaction times longer than twice the mean, excluding responses in which errors were made) rose rapidly during the first 5 min of work and slowly thereafter. More important, there was a clear tendency for reaction time and errors to rise during the responses immediately before a block and to fall immediately after, as shown in Fig. 8.7. The results are consistent with the view that some kind of fatigue effect builds up gradually over a series of responses and is dissipated by the block. It should be noted that on this view there are two fatigue effects involved: a short-term effect dissipated at each block and a longer-term effect causing a rise in the frequency of blocks. The longer-term effect could perhaps be regarded as due to recovery during a block being not quite complete, so that the time taken to build up to the next block is shorter than it would otherwise have been.

The cause of such blocking is not clear. Perhaps the most obvious suggestion is that some part of the sensory-motor mechanism becomes momentarily inoperative, although saying this does little more than restate the phenomenon. Broadbent (1958) has suggested that the mechanism which selects information relevant to the task in hand from the whole mass of data impinging on the organism, becomes temporarily ineffective and allows irrelevant signals to gain attention. This would neatly account for the increase of distractability often observed in fatigued subjects, although there is an alternative explanation available in the likelihood that stimuli arising from hard seats, awkward postures or tensed muscles would become more insistent with time. In other words, distraction could be due not to any failure of central mechanisms directly involved in performance, but to increased competition from ancillary stimuli which might capture the central mechanisms and so produce intermittency effects like those discussed in Chapter 4.

These irregularities of timing have all been observed in the actual

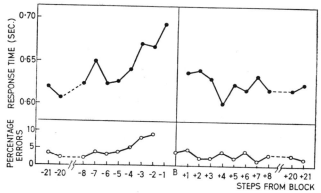

Figure 8.7. Response times and errors made before and after a 'block', in a serial reaction experiment by Bertelson and Joffe (1963). The graph was constructed by taking for each of 28 subjects the last 11 blocks observed (and not immediately associated with an error) during 30 min work and plotting the mean reaction times and errors for the first to eighth reactions before and after the block. The twentieth and twenty-first reactions before and after are also shown as an indication of reactions well clear of a block.

performance which has caused the fatigue. How far they are shown in other tasks undertaken immediately afterwards has not been fully explored although Rey and Rey (1963) found rate of tapping less regular after 45 min of work at a cancellation task, with reaction time becoming longer and CFF lower at the same time. Again Takakuwa (undated) found that the accuracy of aiming at a target over a period of one minute deteriorated after a number of tasks regarded as fatiguing, and that this seemed to be a better test of fatigue than CFF.

(d) *Disorganisation of performance*. Bartlett (1943), with the preliminary results of the Cambridge Cockpit experiments in mind, suggested that fatigued subjects may sometimes perform correct actions, but in the wrong order. In other words, the co-ordination of their performance, the ordering of individual actions into 'larger units', has broken down. This

I

line of thought has not been followed up to the extent it deserves, probably because it is far from easy to study the kinds of complex performance in which such breakdowns might show. It does, however, tally well with the mild confusion, inability for sustained thought and impairment of judgment often observed in states of fatigue. Three possible explanations seem likely to repay further research.

(i) *Failure to place items in context.* The tendency for a word or phrase repeated over and over many times to 'lose meaning' is well known and has been demonstrated also under experimental conditions (e.g. Bassett and Warne, 1919, Lambert and Jakobovits, 1960). The mechanism of this phenomenon is obscure but it seems to imply some loss of connection between the word or phrase concerned and its normal associations.

(ii) *Impairment of routine.* When a situation or task in encountered repeatedly we tend spontaneously, as discussed in Chapter 6, to build routines that enable us to treat several actions together as a single ordered 'unit', instead of having to make individual decisions about each one. The building of such units depends, however, upon the ability to carry out the individual actions accurately enough for one to follow another without the flow having to be interrupted in order to make corrections. Any change due to fatigue or any other factor that impairs accuracy will tend to break up these routines and make it necessary once more to deal with the task piecemeal.

(iii) *Disturbance of short-term retention.* We have noted in previous chapters that implicit in the concept of organised performance and the integration of actions or information is some form of short-term retention that holds earlier items to be combined with later ones and keeps a tally of what has been done and what remains to be done. Such short-term retention has been shown to be very liable to disruption by shifts of attention, especially after brain injury, in old age and in other conditions in which some organic impairment can be presumed. There is some evidence of a similar breakdown with fatigue from tests on civilian aircrews. In one experiment (Welford, Brown and Gabb, 1950) radio officers were tested with a type of electrical problem similar to that of Fig. 1.4 (p. 22) before and after flights from the United Kingdom to Africa, India, Australia or the Far East. For each problem subjects were given a box with six terminals on the top, a circuit diagram and a resistance meter and had to find out which terminal on the box corresponded to each on the diagram by taking readings on the meter. Subjects took many more readings if they were meeting the task for the first time after a flight than before, and it was clear that while taking one reading they were tending to forget others already obtained and so were having to take some readings several times. The results are shown on the left of Fig. 8.8 (the results on the right of this figure are discussed in Chapter 9). This experiment was on crews of unpressurised aircraft, and the results might have been partly due to chronic anoxia. This question does not arise, however, with an experiment by Kay (1953) on radio officers, stewards and stewardesses of pressurised aircraft on the Atlantic and Australian routes from the United Kingdom. This experi-

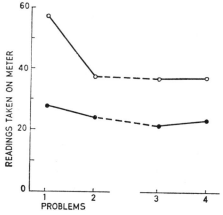

Figure 8.8. Numbers of readings taken on a meter by radio officers of civilian aircraft in solving electrical problems (Welford, Brown and Gabb, 1950).

The upper curve shows results of 12 subjects who solved their first two problems immediately on return from a flight and their last two after at least 8 days' stand-down. The lower curve shows results for 12 subjects whose first two problems were after stand-down and whose last two were after flights.

ment which involved a running short-term memory task has already been described in Chapter 7 (p. 211). Younger subjects were, on average, consistently poorer after flights. Surprisingly, the older were not so, but scored consistently less than the younger both before and after flights. It looks as if the effects of fatigue and age did not summate, perhaps because the lower achievement of the older subjects meant that they were exhausting themselves less. A rather similar pattern of results, with older subjects achieving less but showing less fatigue effect, was obtained by Botwinick and Shock (1952) with an adding task.

Two further points from experiments on fatigue may be mentioned more briefly:

(e) *Temporary improvement of performance.* Somewhat surprisingly, the first sign of oncoming fatigue is sometimes an improvement of performance, in the sense that it becomes more active and achievement rises: deterioration does not set in until later. For example, in another experiment by Welford, Brown and Gabb (1950) on the same radio officers as those who took part in the electrical problem experiment, performance at a plotting task was better after a trip with a relatively easy schedule than it was before going out. Performance was, however, poorer after a trip with a more arduous schedule than it was before flight, and the rise after an easy trip occurred only with the relatively easy plotting task: it did not occur with the more difficult electrical problems. Nor did it appear with the plotting task among stewards for whom physical demands during flight were rather more arduous than for radio officers and who were probably of less intellectual capacity. In short, the temporary improvement of performance seemed to be confined to narrow limits, which depended on the degree of fatigue, the difficulty of the task and the grade of the subjects. It was perhaps the analogy on a longer time scale of the 'warm-up' effect seen in many laboratory experiments: performance at a task such as tracking improves during the first few seconds or minutes of work even though it had been previously well learnt and well practised (e.g. Ammons, 1947, Irion, 1966).

(f) *Reduction of fatigue effects by familiarity.* Fig. 8.8 also shows that the differences between the performances of those tested before and after flight were much greater for the first than for the second problem. Similar results have appeared in several other experiments and imply that fatigue effects are greater for novel than for familiar tasks: some capacities called into play to deal with new material seem especially susceptible to fatigue. What these capacities are we cannot at present say.

Explanatory models of mental fatigue

The attempt to postulate more fundamental explanations of mental fatigue than those so far considered is made difficult by the fact that many other influences, such as local muscular fatigue or, as with the aircrews, anoxia or loss of sleep, may affect performance as well as any true mental fatigue. Taking the evidence as a whole, however, two main hypotheses about the nature of mental fatigue seem reasonable.

(a) *Local neural impairment.* The traditional assumption is that some group of nerve cells concerned with the performance that fatigues, or with some essential link in it, becomes insensitive or unresponsive through continued activity. Such a view explains well the similarity of some fatigue effects, such as fall of CFF, to those of brain injury. It can account for slowing of performance by assuming that some stage in the sensory-motor chain requires a stronger stimulus to operate it and that a given level of stimulation can be integrated over time. Blocking is accounted for by assuming that the breakdown may be of only short duration. Loss of short-term retention would result if the self-maintaining neuronal circuits, on which it must almost certainly depend, became insensitive, so allowing the memory traces to decay.

Rest, on this view, would have its effect by allowing for recovery of the nerve cells involved. Overactivity and improved performance in the early stages of fatigue could be accounted for either by analogy with the recruitment effect found in neuromuscular fatigue or by assuming that, faced with incipient failure, the subject makes compensatory increases of effort that may, for a time, more than offset losses due to fatigue. Such compensatory efforts are perhaps seen in the results obtained by Bills and Shapin (1936), who found that deterioration of performance could be postponed by pacing the task a little faster than the comfortable rate instead of allowing the subject to work at his own speed.

(b) Increase of 'neural noise'. An alternative view can be based on one put forward by Crawford (1961) as a possible explanation of fatigue in car drivers. He suggested that such fatigue might result from the accumulated after-effects of stresses and annoyances from other road users during prolonged spells of driving. If so, it could be regarded as due not to under-functioning of particular brain mechanisms but to overactivity in the brain or parts of it.

We shall discuss the mechanism of such neural overactivity in the next section of this chapter. Meanwhile we can argue that, on this view, fatigue results when neural activity, either general or local, rises beyond some optimum level. Such a theory would account for sensory fatigue directly in terms of the blurring effects of neural noise. It would account for slowing of performance by arguing that the effective strength of stimuli from one part of the sensory-motor mechanism to another should be measured in terms of signal-to-noise ratio and that a rise in the noise level thus implies a need for more powerful signals in order to maintain the ratio required. Any randomness from moment to moment in the level of neural activity would mean brief periods of specially intense noise, which might account for blocking or, at a lower level, brief periods of facilitation which might allow unwanted signals to cause distraction. Loss of short-term retention would be assumed to result from disturbance rather than decay of the memory traces. Rest would allow excess activity or sensitivity to die away. Overactivity and improved performance during the early stages of fatigue would be accounted for directly by facilitatory effects of mild rises in activity. This view could also account well for the irritability and difficulty of relaxing or sleeping often observed after a long period of taxing mental work.

Present data on fatigue seem to be equivocal in the sense that they are consistent, given plausible supplementary hypotheses, with either view. Distinction between the two models appears to need a substantial amount of new research carried out by a combination of physiological and psychological methods. The two models may well both operate in different circumstances, and it seems reasonable to suggest that new research should aim at establishing the conditions in which each applies rather than justifying one theory to the exclusion of the other.

STRESS, EFFORT AND AROUSAL

It has been recognised for at least three-quarters of a century that one of the important variables of human behaviour is the *intensity* with which action is carried out. A man may work either more or less hard at a job, he may be moved either more or less strongly by an emotion, his motives may be either more or less powerful. The methods of assessing intensity have, for the most part, been subjective using techniques such as rating scales. For the past 40 years or so, however, research especially in the field of emotion has attempted more objective measurement, linking intensity either to the activation of the skeletal muscles in terms of muscle-tone or to autonomic activity as indicated, for example, by skin conductance. Work along these lines favoured a concept of intensity in terms of *generalised activation* of the organism, with the *direction* of activity being determined by features of the immediate cognitive situation or of past experience. Such a view accorded well with ideas that had grown up in some other fields, for instance that hunger, thirst and other appetites lead essentially to a generalised activation of the organism which is given direction by knowledge and experience.

This broad line of approach received encouragement from findings that activity and mental effort increase the tone of muscles not directly involved in the task (e.g. Freeman, 1933, Eason and White, 1961,

Eason and Branks, 1963), and further that irrelevant muscular activity may improve performance. For example, Bills (1927) found that adding and reading were performed faster, and Andreassi (1965) obtained more accurate perception of figures exposed for 20 – 60 msec, if the subject at the same time squeezed a hand dynamometer. Again Boder (1935) found that the rate of tapping with one hand was increased when a bar was grasped with the other hand. It is interesting to note that the increase of speed was due more to a saving of time at the top and bottom of the movement than to the movements themselves becoming quicker. Early work in this field has been reviewed by Courts (1942). It is easy to see in terms of the evidence discussed in relation to the single-channel hypothesis in Chapter 4, how such unrelated activity might distract the subject's attention and lead to *poorer* performance, but difficult to see how it could lead to improvement unless the irrelevant activity produced some general facilitating spread of effect.

The main impetus of this approach has undoubtedly come, however, from two facts: firstly the increase in the dominant frequency of EEG rhythms from deep sleep, through relaxed waking states to states of concentrated attention; and secondly the neural mechanism provided by the pathways between sensory input, the brain stem and the cortex, by which the brain stem produces more or less general activation of the cortex in association with autonomic activity. The extent to which effort, muscular tension, EEG rhythms and autonomic activity tie up together varies in different studies but seems clear enough to indicate a real connection (e.g. Pinneo, 1961).

It was originally assumed that because the reticular formation in the brain stem, which is intimately concerned with arousal, receives fibres from the main sensory input channels, activation or arousal (the words tend to be used as synonyms) was directly due to raw sensory input, so that level of arousal was a direct function of the level of stimulation impinging on the organism. It is, however, clear from subsequent studies and from common observation that such an assumption is untenable. If it were true, we should be unable to sleep in a room overlooking a noisy street, and many people who are used to such noise sleep well. The stimulation that causes arousal may reasonably be identified as that to which the organism has not habituated, that is to say, stimuli conveying information of significance to the organism. This is not quite the same thing as saying that arousal is a function of presented information in the information theory sense, because information thus defined deals with objective signals without taking the state of the organism into account. Admittedly such a view, if it is not to be circular, requires us to specify what is 'of significance' to the subject using criteria other than arousal effects, but it seems to be possible in principle to do this by taking account of the relationships between present events and the subject's previous experience and future aims. In these terms, stimuli which cause arousal will be those which are novel, very intense or signals of danger because it is to these that habituation least easily occurs (e.g. Berlyne, 1960, Berlyne *et al.*, 1963, Grim and White, 1965). More generally one can suggest that arousal level is raised by any task which is in some way challenging or demands an effort, and by anything which acts as an incentive.

There has been some discussion as to how far arousal effects are general or are confined at different times to different brain mechanisms. It seems now clear that both very general and more restricted effects occur. We must also remember that the effects we are considering do not only arise from the arousal system: any spread of effect from activity in the brain and any continuing after-discharges from previous activity will have something of the same effect. For our present purpose the important point to note is that all such activation, whether widespread in the brain or not, is more general and diffuse in both space and time than the detailed signals involved in the perception of specific objects and in the taking of particular actions. We are thus essentially discussing tonic background activity to the more precise signals which carry information in the brain.

Activation and performance

One of the main difficulties in interpreting the nature and function of arousal has been that its effects on performance are varied. In particular, several studies in which performance and physiological indications of activation such as muscle-tone or skin-resistance have been measured together have shown that the relation between them is not linear: performance improves with activation from a low level up to an optimum and then, as activation increases further, performance deteriorates (e.g. Freeman, 1933, Hebb, 1955, Duffy, 1957, Stennett, 1957, Malmo, 1959). Studies in which only a rise or only a fall of performance has been shown with increasing activation may perhaps be regarded as having explored only one part of the whole range.

The mechanism linking rise of activation to improved performance seems to be fairly generally agreed. Freeman (1931) suggested that activation increasing from a low level might produce nerve impulses which would subliminally stimulate cells in the cortex and thus render them more readily fired by weak signals than they would otherwise be: in this way the organism would become at once more sensitive and more responsive. The same suggestion has been repeated by subsequent writers, especially by Hebb (1955). The fall in performance at high levels of activation is recognised as being more difficult to explain. It has been variously attributed to competition between incompatible habits called forth by unduly high levels of facilitation, to fatigue due to over-stimulation, to some kind of hormonal exhaustion following excessive cell activity or to the activity of inhibitory centres which are presumed to have a higher threshold than centres which produce positive action so that they come into play only when high activation levels are reached. None of these theories appears to have been much more than an *ad hoc* speculation and the last has the disadvantage of being unduly flexible: if both facilitation and inhibition are postulated with different thresholds almost any behaviour can be explained.

The simplest way of accounting for the fall in performance at high activation levels is probably to assume that, if the stream of impulses impinging on the cortex becomes very intense, the cells there are not only rendered more sensitive but are actually fired. When this happens the cortex becomes 'noisy' so that signals coming from outside or passing from one part of the brain to another tend to be blurred. Furthermore cells which would otherwise be ready to carry signals are unavailable because they are refractory from having just fired, so that the channel-capacity of the brain is reduced. Once this point has been reached, any further increase of activation tends to impair performance rather than improve it. The essential feature of this model is that it accounts for both the rise and the subsequent fall of performance accompanying progressive rise of activation, without postulating more than one type of process: both follow straightforwardly from the increase of activity in the system (Welford, 1962a).

The effects of activation on performance would, in terms of this model, depend on the balance between facilitation on the one hand and neural noise and loss of channel-capacity on the other. At the extremes of both activation and inactivation performance will be poor, but the type of inadequacy will differ in the two cases. When activation is unduly low the system will be inert and signals are likely to be lost either in the perceptual system or at some later point in the chain leading to response. With very high levels of activation the system will be over-reactive, action will be confused and capacity will be insufficient for high-level judgments or precisely graded responses which will tend instead to be undifferentiated, massive and tense. The measurement of such effects obviously cannot be made by merely taking single scores of overall achievement and relating them to measures of skin resistance, galvanic skin response, muscle tone, heart rate, suppression of sinus arrythmia or other indicators of activation. Enough data must be recorded from a performance to see not only what was achieved but also the detailed manner in which this achievement was attained.

It may be remarked in passing that if the breakdown of high-grade judgment under stress can be attributed to a lowering of channel-capacity, an important new approach is opened up to the problem of defining 'levels' of mental activity. It is often suggested that in states of fatigue and under stress the 'highest levels' are impaired first: what is meant by 'highest' has not, however, been clear. Attempts have sometimes been made to define it in terms of the newest acquired ability in the development of either the individual or the race. On the present view the 'highest' tasks would be those demanding the handling of most data, or the making of the finest discriminations or which relied the most heavily on short-term retention and through this on abstraction and thinking. 'Levels' would in this way be defined quantitatively rather than qualitatively, and we should be freed from any difficulty of trying to identify different levels with different parts of the brain.

The great majority of evidence so far gathered is not detailed enough to favour one theory of activation effects rather than another, but the model proposed here does not seem to be contradicted, and in a number of cases it either accounts for facts not otherwise covered satisfactorily or provides a more precise lead than others for further research:

(*a*) *Speed and accuracy.* The most direct evidence in favour of the present model is probably that of Freeman (1933). Electric shocks of various measured strengths were delivered to the subject's right middle finger, and both the latency and the extent of the reflex movements were recorded. The shocks were given in pairs and the subject had to respond with the left hand to indicate whether the second member of the pair was equal to or stronger than the first: the reaction-time and accuracy of this discrimination were recorded. The experiment was performed under three conditions: (i) 'normal' with the subject sitting in a chair, (ii) with the subject 'relaxed' by methods advocated by Jacobson (1929) and (iii) with 'tension' induced by a somewhat complex arrangement which made it necessary to tense the trunk muscles in order to maintain balance. The results are shown in Table 8.1 from which it can be seen that with increase of tension from the 'relaxed' through the 'normal' to the 'tension' condition the latency of the reaction to shock and the

TABLE 8.1 *Effects of relaxation and of induced muscular tension on reactions. Data from Freeman (1933). Each entry is the mean of 20 readings from each of 9 subjects*

	Relaxed	Normal	With induced muscle tension
Muscle-tonus in quadriceps (arbitrary units)	−29·1	+18·2	+64·9
Reaction time to shocks delivered to right middle finger (msec)	401	259	247
Extent of finger withdrawal to these shocks (mm)	10·3	28·0	27·5
Time taken to discriminate whether second shock of pair was equal to or stronger than first (msec)	634	442	355
Accuracy of this discrimination (%)	65	97	69

discrimination reaction-time shortened and the finger movements became greater, all of which would be expected from the facilitation due to increased activation. The accuracy of discrimination rose from the 'relaxed' to the 'normal' condition but fell again to the 'tension' condition: in short, the increased tension made performance faster but at the expense of accuracy. This is what would be expected if it produced both facilitation of action and noise in the systems involved in discriminating signals and selecting which responses to make. If alternatively accuracy was maintained, reaction time would lengthen. This result occurred in a later experiment by Freeman (1940) in which reaction time was found first to become shorter and then longer again with progressive fall in skin resistance. The shortening of reaction time was confirmed by Andreassi (1966) but not the lengthening, possibly because his subjects did not attain as high levels of tension as did Freeman's.

(b) Sensory thresholds. Increases of arousal from very low levels obviously improve sensory discrimination, but the effects of smaller changes on sensory and perceptual functions seem to have been very little studied and the results of studies that have been made are conflicting. It would be reasonable to expect that thresholds would be lowered as arousal rose, and Symons and Mackay (1962) have produced what is perhaps evidence in favour of this by finding that auditory thresholds

were lower when subjects were doing mental arithmetic than when they were relaxed. Yet Cohen and Lindley (1936) found that the threshold for detecting vibration on the skin was *raised* by increased muscletonus. Taking the model we have outlined in conjunction with the signal-detection model outlined in Chapter 2 (p. 31) we can see why results are likely to be conflicting. Any mild increase of sensitivity brought about by arousal would probably increase both noise and signal

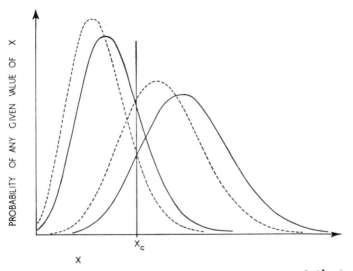

Figure 8.9. Hypothetical effect of arousal on the curves of the signal-detection model shown in Fig. 2.4 (p. 38). Increased arousal is assumed to expand both the 'Noise Alone' and the 'Signal plus Noise' curves in such a way that d' remains relatively little affected.

in roughly the same proportion, since the increased likelihood of cells being fired would raise the rate of random firing as well as of response to signals from outside. Any external noise would similarly be increased in strict proportion to the signal. The result would be to expand the curves in Fig. 2.4 (p. 38) as shown in Fig. 8.9. Such expansion since it affects both the means and the variances proportionally would leave d' relatively little affected. If, however, the cutoff point remained in the same position there would be a substantial fall in β leading to a higher rate of signal detection but also to a larger proportion of false-positives. In short, increased arousal would not greatly affect capacity for discrimination but would lower the criterion of judgment. It seems reasonable to suppose that, since the criterion represents the threshold of some later stage in the chain of central processes, it should remain the same and might even be lowered by increased arousal, if so it would accentuate the process we have described. If, on the other hand, the subject took steps to keep his false positive rate steady by raising his criterion-level his threshold would be little affected by mildly increased arousal.

Very high degrees of arousal seem likely to raise the level of neural noise more than that of the signal, thus leading to a fall of d' in addition to the change of β already discussed.

(*c*) *Results of stress*. From what has been said we should expect that stressing agents such as dangers, annoyances and incentives which increase arousal would all in mild degrees improve performance and in more severe degrees impair it. We cannot here attempt a full discussion of stress effects but will mention a few points briefly. The revival of interest in activation and arousal seems to have come largely from the suggestion by Lindsley (1951) that the excited emotions of fear and anger can be thought of as states of heightened arousal. Such a view provides, in terms of the model proposed here, a solution of the long-standing controversy about whether emotions 'organise' or 'disorganise' performance. Mild degrees of emotion, producing moderate degrees of arousal, are likely to be beneficial and therefore 'organising': more severe degrees will lead to disruption of performance and thus be 'disorganising'. This view tallies well with the observations made by Mira (1944) of fear reactions to civilian bombing during the Spanish Civil War. Mild degrees of fear, he suggested, led to prudence and self-restraint, concentration and caution, and tended to improve achievement. More severe degrees led to anxiety and alarm accompanied by breakdown of high-grade skills, disorganised activity and tremors. Very severe degrees resulted in panic marked by uncontrolled activity and loss of memory afterwards of what had happened, or in extreme cases led to collapse into a kind of tense stupor. The more severe states of fear and anger resemble those of animals from which the cerebral-cortex has been removed and led Darrow (1935) to describe these emotions as states of 'relative functional decortication'. This is effectively what the model proposed here postulates.

It should be emphasised, however, that the concept of arousal and activation applies also on a much more subtle scale. We have already noted that smaller but significant changes of skin resistance, heart rate and other indices of arousal can be observed with tasks such as mental arithmetic. Perhaps the most elegant example of such changes is in car driving, studies of which have shown the level to fluctuate continu-ally: every minor event such as passing or being passed, the approach to traffic lights or sight of a car turning in from a side road lowers the driver's skin resistance, which rises again during clear runs (Hulbert, 1957, Michaels, 1960, Taylor, 1964).

(*d*) *Interacting factors.* Relating stress effects to objective conditions is not always easy. For example loud noise might reasonably be expected to be arousing and has, indeed, been shown to be capable of counteract-ing some of the lowering of arousal which results from lack of sleep (Wilkinson, 1965). Yet it often fails to have an effect, seemingly because of the ease with which habituation can occur to at least some noises. The beneficial effects on performance that might be expected to follow from moderate noise levels are also liable to be offset by the raising of β that may occur with noise (see p. 47) and by the distracting effects of noise discussed in Chapter 4 (p. 133).

A different type of complication is illustrated by the finding that tension and arousal levels are often higher before an exacting task is begun than they are once it has started, or that they decline as perfor-mance proceeds (Freeman, 1933, Deane, 1961, Zimny, 1965, Pugh *et al.*, 1966) or the task is learnt (Freedman *et al.*, 1966): preparation for the task and the initial stages of performance may be more exacting than later stages when initial uncertainties have been resolved and some learning has taken place. A further anticipatory effect has been shown by Forrest (1958) who found that muscular tension increased with the length of task to be completed.

(*e*) *Effects of difficulty of task.* Freeman (1938) suggested that the opti-mal degree of muscle-tension, marking the transition between an im-provement and an impairment of performance, becomes lower as the difficulty of the task increases. This view, although not very convincingly supported by Freeman's own data, provides a plausible explanation of the classical work by Yerkes and Dodson (1908) on the learning by dancing mice to discriminate between different brightnesses. The mice had to learn to go to the brighter of two boxes and received an electric shock for entering the wrong box. The number of trials taken to learn when the two brightnesses were very different and the task therefore easy, fell progressively as the strength of shock was increased. For more difficult discriminations the trials fell as the strength of shock increased up to a point, but thereafter rose. The optimum shock was weaker for a very difficult discrimination than for one of moderate difficulty. These results have been repeated subsequently with both animals (e.g. Broadhurst, 1957, Denenberg and Karas, 1960) and, using rather different tasks and incentives, with human subjects (e.g. Castaneda and Lipsitt, 1959, Tecce and Testa, 1965, Elliott, 1965). Similar implications follow from the work of Ray (1965) who has shown that increasing pressure for speed leads to progressively poorer performance at solving relatively difficult problems. Again Stabler and Dyal (1963) found that reaction time was longer among highly anxious, than among less anxious subjects early in practice, but that the positions were reversed later when the task can be presumed to have become easier.

These results are susceptible of two explanations in the terms we have been using and both may be correct. The first explanation assumes that level of arousal rises with strength of incentive: a high level of incentive which resulted in the brain becoming somewhat noisy would have little effect on the performance of an easy task requiring relatively little channel capacity, but would have a much greater effect as the required capacity increased. Secondly it might be argued that the tasks themselves induce a degree of arousal which rises with their difficulty and that this is added to the arousal produced by the incentive. If the optimum arousal level was the same for all degrees of difficulty, the addition due to incentive that would produce this optimum would fall as the task became more difficult.

(*f*) *Relationship with fatigue.* If activation and arousal outlast the circumstances giving rise to them, they will be liable to build up progressively during performance unless time is allowed for them to die away. If so, they can be reasonably equated with the activity postulated in the second of the two theories proposed to account for mental fatigue. The main activation in fatigue would presumably result from effects spreading from the fatiguing activities themselves, but arousal due to annoyances or to discomforts resulting from prolonged sitting or standing in awkward postures might well add to it. Such activation and arousal would, in the Yerkes–Dodson principle, account for greater fatigue effects with more difficult tasks requiring greater channel-capacity (cf. Singleton, 1953) and for the fact that fatigue may attack the higher co-ordination of performance while leaving more elementary details unimpaired (Bartlett, 1943).

Effects of long-continued stress

Animals that have been used in studies of 'experimental neurosis' have tended to show fear and other stress symptoms for long periods, sometimes for years, after trials have ceased: in short, the stress in the experimental episodes has had a lasting effect (for a review see Liddell, 1944). Long-lasting effects can perhaps also be observed in some human beings engaged in hazardous or over-exacting work who seem· to 'lose their nerve' after a time. For example, some of the airline pilots who about 20 years ago were being compulsorily retired at the age of 45 would guardedly admit that they did not resist retirement because, over the years, they had been losing the will to fly. The possible dangers outlined in briefings before flight seemed to loom larger and larger, and the responsibility of the plane with its load of passengers began to weigh heavily upon them. Again Hauty *et al.* (1965) have shown that symptoms of stress among air-traffic controllers increase with age and length of time on the job, especially the latter.

The traditional explanation of these states is that stress reactions have become *conditioned*: that is to say, they have become firmly associated with certain situations, and occur in these whether they are really justified or not. Clinical studies of the effects of prolonged stress on human beings suggest a chronic state of heightened autonomic activity to which the subject's other bodily mechanisms adapt to some extent but not completely (e.g. Selye, 1950). The same appears to be true of laboratory animals kept under stressful conditions (e.g. Thiessen and Rodgers, 1961, Thiessen *et al.*, 1962).

To some extent at least, these effects can be attributed to over-development of the adrenals in stressful conditions and thus to a raising of the subject's level of adrenaline, but it seems likely that some neural mechanism must also be involved. We may perhaps argue that trains of impulses passing synaptic junctions make these more readily passed on subsequent occasions and that, although resistance may be restored with disuse, it is more readily lowered again on a subsequent occasion (see Eccles, 1953). This principle has been of the greatest importance in the development of some modern theories of learning (e.g. Hebb, 1949). It is held that the material to be learnt produces a pattern of neural activity and this in turn gives rise to a pattern of lowered synaptic resistances which constitute an enduring memory trace. It follows from this principle that the prolonged use of particular pathways, such as those involved in general activation and arousal, will tend to facilitate their activity. It also follows that continued *unpatterned* neural activity, such as might occur with chronic over-activation due to stress, would tend to produce widespread random lowering of synaptic resistances in the brain. If this occurred to a moderate degree it might merely render more sensitive and responsive a brain that would otherwise have been relatively inert. If it occurred to a more substantial degree as a result of prolonged severe stress, it could blur patterns of activity in the brain by, in a sense, breaking down the normal 'insulation' of one cell from another. In either case the effects on behaviour would resemble those of chronic heightened arousal which in severe cases would reach the level at which it impaired performance.

VIGILANCE

The extensive experimental work on the maintenance of vigilance that has been done since the Second World War arose from the fact that when radar and other watchkeepers look for infrequent signals they tend to miss them when they come if they have been on watch for an hour or so. Research in this area has gained attention not only because of its interest to the armed services, but for its obvious implications for inspection and monitoring work in industry and because it raises important theoretical issues.

The initial experiments on synthetic radar displays and other laboratory tasks made it clear that the proportion of signals detected fell sharply over a period of $\frac{1}{2}$ hr or so when the signals were faint, brief and infrequent. With synthetic radar displays showing signals at unpredictable intervals, it could be argued that the subject, in order to be sure of seeing them when they occurred, would have to make a rapid and continuous series of checks. These could be fatiguing, and the fall in performance might therefore be a fatigue effect. Other laboratory tasks have, however, presented the subject with clearly observable signals at discrete intervals and required him to detect occasional signals that are slightly different from the majority. The intervals have then been too long (1 to 5 sec) to make a fatigue theory tenable: some other factor is clearly involved. The problem appears to be one of *underload* rather than *overload*.

Of the 'pure' laboratory tasks probably the best known is the original Clock Test used by Mackworth (1950). The subject sat facing a circular dial on which a 6-in pointer moved in steps of 12' of arc once per sec. Occasionally the pointer made a jump of 24', and the subject's task was to report these by pressing a key. The double movements occurred twelve times in 20 min (1 in 200 movements on average) at irregular intervals. Other tasks have involved the use of a wide variety of signals, such as faint spots of light (e.g. Wilkinson, 1961) or small changes of sound (e.g. Mackworth, 1950), or occasional features of a regularly presented series of signals, such as the detection of 'odd, even, odd' in a series of digits (e.g. Bakan, 1952). The decrements seem to occur with both visual and auditory signals and may be shown not only by signals being missed altogether, but by slower responses to those detected (Wallis and Samuel, 1961, McCormack, 1962, Surwillo and Quilter, 1964, Buck, 1966). Failures are not the result of any peripheral factor such as omitting to look at the source of signals, since Mackworth *et al.* (1964) have shown that visual signals are often not reported even though they are being fixated at the time: some central failure appears to be involved. The fall of performance seems to follow a different pattern from that of simple, monotonously repetitive tasks such as adding, simple assembly or bean-sorting (Baker and Ware, 1966). It is not, however, due simply to lack of activity on the subject's part; thus, Whittenburg *et al.* (1956), when they repeated the Clock Test requiring the subject to respond to every jump, making different responses to small and large, found that the number of occasional large jumps detected still fell with time on watch. Nor is it due to lack of readiness for the signals, as Wilkinson (1961) showed that decrements still occurred when warnings of signals were given or even when the subject, himself determined the times at which they appeared: the subject, needless to say, did not know whether or not any particular signal would require a response, but he had every opportunity to be ready if it did.

Mackworth showed that performance could be temporarily restored by a telephone message during the 'watch' and later research has confirmed that periodical changes of activity (Bevan *et al.*, 1967), brief rest pauses (Bergum and Lehr, 1962) or the presence of others in the room (Fraser, 1953, Bergum and Lehr, 1963a, Williams *et al.*, 1965) which may be presumed to introduce momentary distractions, serve to maintain performance. Mackworth further showed that decline in performance could be prevented by telling the subject, each time after a signal had appeared, whether or not he had detected it correctly – in other words by giving him 'knowledge of results' of his performance. Subsequent work has shown that detection is improved even if knowledge of results is incomplete (McCormack *et al.*, 1963, McCormack and McElheran, 1963, Wilkinson, 1964) or false (Loeb and Schmidt, 1963), and that detection rate in a primary vigilance task rises if knowledge of results is given about a secondary task performed at the same time – the effect of the knowledge of results seems to spread to both tasks (Baker, 1961).

Detection tends to be better when signals are relatively strong (Mackworth, 1950) or of long duration (see Broadbent, 1958) or when, in a series of signals some of which are 'wanted' and some not, the proportion of wanted signals is raised (Colquhoun, 1961, 1966) and these factors appear to interact in the sense that signals can be detected at a lower physical intensity when they are more frequent (Martz, 1966, 1967). If the rate is raised very high performance may, of course, fall again due to the subject not being able to deal with all the signals presented in the time available: there is thus an optimum rate of presentation which avoids both overload and underload (Poulton, 1960). Several experiments have explored the possibility of raising detection rate by combining the vigilance task with another – in other words raising the wanted signal rate by giving signals from two different tasks. The results, however, are equivocal (Wallis and Samuel, 1961, Antrobus and Singer, 1964), probably because any improvement due to the extra signals from the second task may be offset by the subject having to divide his attention between the two tasks.

Theories of vigilance

Theories to account for the declines observed in vigilance have been critically discussed by Broadbent (1958) and by Broadbent and Gregory (1963b), and we shall not attempt to go over the ground again here. Broadly speaking the most plausible view seems to be that originally proposed by Deese (1955) that decline of vigilance represents a fall in the level of arousal or activation. Several other theories have, however, been advanced and we shall consider four of them briefly before returning to the arousal theory:

(a) *Motivation.* Mackworth compared the vigilance situation with that of a conditioning experiment in which the 'reinforcing agent' or 'reward' has been discontinued so that the response is inhibited or 'extinguished'. He argued that most of the watch for signals was unrewarded so that the decline of performance should be attributed to inhibition which could be disinhibited by brief interruptions and dissipated by longer rests. This theory in its simple form is little more than an *ad hoc* guess: it does, however, gain some support if the extinction situation is spelled out a little by saying that lack of reinforcement leads to decrease of motivation. The decline of vigilance with time has been reduced or abolished with better grade subjects who might be regarded as more highly motivated (Kappauf and Powe, 1959), or when army trainees performed their task in the presence of an officer (Bergum and Lehr, 1963a), or when subjects received money rewards for good detection (Sipowicz *et al.*, 1962), although this last effect may be short-lived (Bergum and Lehr, 1964). We have already noted that it can be prevented by knowledge of results – a factor known on other grounds to act as an incentive (Helmstadter and Ellis, 1952, Gibbs and Brown, 1956, Spielberger *et al.*, 1966).

An explanation in terms of motivation poses the further question, however, of how motives affect behaviour. We have already seen that one of their effects appears to be an increase of activation, so that a motivation theory of vigilance might be regarded as a sub-class of an activation or arousal theory – anything which increases motivation will tend to offset any fall of activation during a prolonged watch.

(*b*) *Expectancy*. Several experiments have shown that the level of performance at vigilance tasks and the extent of the decline with time are to some extent a function of the rate of signals expected by the subject on the basis of instructions or previous experience (Broadbent, 1958, Colquhoun and Baddeley, 1964, 1967). The same idea has been applied to individual signals by postulating that the likelihood of their being missed depends on the predictability of the moment at which they will arrive (Kappauf and Powe, 1959, Baker, 1959), although this latter result is controversial (Boulter and Adams, 1963). Further evidence for expectancy effects is the 'end spurt' of improved detection when a watch is known to be nearing its finish (Bergum and Lehr, 1963b). Expectancy has also been proposed as a reason for some of the errors made in industry and in the driving of transport, for example a train driver who is not used to being stopped at a particular signal may not notice when, exceptionally, it is against him (Davis, 1958, 1966, Buck, 1963). Expectancy might perhaps also explain the finding by Hardesty *et al.* (1963) that the improved performance in a monitoring task produced by knowledge of results persisted for a substantial time after knowledge had been withdrawn.

This theory again, however, leads to the further question of how expectancy exerts is effects, and from what has already been said earlier in this chapter it seems reasonable to regard it as raising or lowering activation level – the rises or falls of activation may anticipate the onset of the task to which they refer. If so the expectancy theory becomes, as Deese (1955) recognised, another special case of the activation theory.

(c) *Blocking.* The fact that signals are missed less frequently when they are of relatively long duration led Broadbent (1958) to suggest that they are missed because they come and go again during brief lapses of attention which increase in frequency as a watch proceeds. Such lapses have considerable intuitive support and some further evidence of their occurrence has been put forward by Johnston *et al.* (1966). From our present point of view the crucial question is why such lapses occur. We shall consider four possibilities:

(i) The mechanism responsible for perceptual selectivity fatigues if attention is concentrated for a long time upon one class of stimuli, so that it temporarily breaks down allowing other stimuli to gain admission.

(ii) Discomforts due, for example, to sitting for a long time in one position build up to a point at which they are strong enough to overcome the bias against them produced by the selection mechanism. When they gain attention they capture the central mechanisms in the manner outlined in Chapter 4 so that there are brief periods during which attention to other incoming signals is delayed, and during these delays they may be lost.

The weaknesses of both these hypotheses is that they give no reason why the decline of vigilance should be reduced or prevented by factors such as increase in signal frequency or knowledge of results.

(iii) It has been suggested by Hebb (1955) that arousal level tends to be self-adjusting with the organism tending to seek an optimum. Since novel stimuli tend to be more arousing than long continued ones (see Berlyne, 1960), a fall of arousal during a prolonged watch would increase the tendency to seek a change of stimulation. Such a view is questionable, however, following work by Johnston *et al.* (1967) who found that in a vigilance task in which some stimuli were repetitions of a signal that had appeared before and others were new, it was only the latter that were detected less well as the watch proceeded.

(iv) Activation level shows not only broad changes over relatively long periods, but also moment-to-moment fluctuations during which it might well fall occasionally to a level at which the system became so insensitive that incoming signals were temporarily blocked. These blocks would obviously become more frequent as the general level of activation declined. This seems to be the most plausible of the views we have outlined. It does, of course, once more make the blocking theory a particular case of the activation theory.

(d) *Changes of cutoff in signal-detection.* Several examinations have been made of vigilance decrements in terms of the signal-detection mode described in Chapter 2 (Broadbent and Gregory, 1963b, Loeb and Binford, 1963, Taylor, 1965, Binford and Loeb, 1966, Colquhoun, 1967). All these found that as a watch proceeded the number of both detections and false positives fell in such a way as to indicate a rise of β but little if any change of d' – in short the vigilance decrement was due to fewer signals passing the criterion and not to any true change of ability to detect them. This result is clearly consistent with a fall of activation level as indicated by Fig. 8.9: the distributions of both 'noise alone' and 'signal plus noise' are moved to the left in such a way as to leave the signal-to-noise ratio nearly the same but the cutoff point apparently raised.

This model can also account for a further result obtained by Broadbent and Gregory, who found that when the subject had to rate the certainty with which he detected a signal on a five-point scale from 'Sure', through 'Uncertain' to 'Sure not' the change of β for the most stringent criterion was greater than for the least, which was little affected. The curves of Fig. 8.9 are redrawn with two criteria instead of one in Fig. 8.10. It can be seen that when the curves change from one position to the other, β changes more for the upper criterion than for the lower.

The picture is not always as clear cut, however, as Fig. 8.10 would suggest. For example Chinn and Alluisi (1964) who studied effects of different types of knowledge of results on vigilance, obtained evidence which suggests that the cutoff point may be moved and that d' may also be affected. Informing subjects of the occasions when they responded in the absence of a signal reduced the number of false positives and increased the number of signals missed as would be expected from a change of cutoff brought about by 'punishing' false positives. On the other hand, information about correct responses or missed signals reduced both the number of signals missed and the number of false positives implying an improvement of detectability – that is an increase of d'. It seems fair to regard these results as complications due in the first case to factors affecting the setting of the cutoff as discussed in Chapter 2, and in the second to the improvement of performance brought about by detailed knowledge of results which we shall consider in Chapter 9.

What appears at first sight to be evidence clean contrary to the model proposed in Fig. 8.10 is provided by a series of studies which have shown substantial falls of d' with time during a watch (Mackworth and Taylor, 1963, Mackworth, 1964b, 1965). The task used in these experiments, however, was that of detecting momentary interruptions of the movement of a hand revolving round a dial and there was thus a risk of missing signals if the watch was not completely continuous. It was thus likely to have been fatiguing and in this respect differed from the tasks of the experiments mentioned in the previous paragraph: in these the points of time at which the signals might come were restricted so that the watch could be intermittent. Mackworth (1964c) compared her results with those of a number of other experiments on fatigue including the visual acuity data of Berger and Mahneke shown in

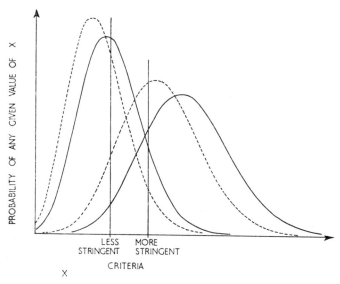

Figure 8.10. The same curves as in Fig. 8.9 but with two different criteria. As the curves move to the left from the positions indicated by solid lines, β for the more stringent criterion changes from about 1·2 to about 3·3 – a difference of 2·1. β for the less stringent criterion changes from about ·2 to ·4 – a difference of only ·2. d' changes from 1·4 to 1·3.

Fig. 8.2, and data from a tracking task, and found that in all of them log d' declined linearly with the square root of time on the task. These results of Mackworth's are especially interesting as pointing to one of the very few means at present known of distinguishing fatigue decrements from those due to loss of vigilance: fatigue appears to result mainly in a fall of d' implying a true impairment of function, while loss of vigilance leads mainly to a rise of β indicating a condition in which there is little change of basic discriminatory power but fewer signals pass the criterion of judgment.

(*e*) *Activation and arousal.* We now return to the activation theory itself and look at the evidence which bears directly on it. Suggestions in favour of such a theory are given by some of the results already noted, such as the prevention of a fall with time in detection rate by either stronger signals or the presence of others in the room or an occasional telephone message or knowledge of results, all of which involve some increase in the amount of stimulation from outside impinging on the subject. Again Adams *et al.* (1961) found that reaction times to changes in a display lengthened during a 3 hr watch when the changes had simply to be reported, but did not lengthen when subjects had to report more detail about the nature of the change which had taken place. Increased sensory input does not, however, always abolish decrements of performance, presumably because habituation can occur to input which is steady, regular or otherwise capable of being excluded. For example Kirk and Hecht (1963) found that the proportion of visual signals detected was higher when subjects were listening to a noise of randomly varying intensity than with a steady noise of the same average intensity. Complications may also occur when the conditions are extremely unarousing as in so-called sensory deprivation experiments. For example Smith *et al.* (1967) noted that their subjects who were given a vigilance test, in which faint irregular signals had to be detected, after 72 hr of living under dark, quiet conditions, performed *better* than did controls who were tested after living under more normal conditions. Why this was so is not clear: it may have been an indication that underarousal is itself arousing so that the organism tends to maintain an optimum state as suggested by Hebb (1955). Perhaps more simply, it may have been that the subjects had become adapted to the uneventful nature of their environment so that any event became more noticeable. If so we must postulate an adaptation which takes longer than the 2–3 hr which is the usual duration of a vigilance test.

More positive evidence for an activation theory is contained in the fall of skin conductance during the course of a watch noted by Nishioka *et al.* (1960), Dardano (1962) and Eason *et al.* (1965) although correspondence is not always as close as one might wish and some other measures of activation show little change: for example Eason *et al.* found heart-rate to be unchanged. Possibly, as Nishioka *et al.* suggest, these rather fickle measures are sometimes disturbed by other irrelevant factors or by compensatory efforts to restore a performance recognised as failing. Such compensation seems to be the reason why loss of sleep, which in some circumstances markedly increases vigilance decrements, does not always do so – the subject's efforts to keep awake prevent the lowering of arousal level (Wilkinson, 1965, Williams *et al.*, 1965). Compensatory tendencies may also be the reason why Micko's (1966) subjects tended to pay more attention as time passed to jokes projected on to a screen during an auditory vigilance task. The same explanation may also resolve the conflict of evidence about the effects of increased body temperature on vigilance: Bell *et al.* (1964) found that vigilance deteriorated as body temperature rose, Fox *et al.* (1963) found it did not but noted that their subjects tended to become restless and irritable with increased body temperature. Some vigilance tasks may also be fatiguing: if so, and if fatigue tends to increase activation, we should have the rather curious case of one potential source of poorer performance tending to compensate for another.

Perhaps the most striking direct evidence in favour of the activation theory is Mackworth's (1950) finding that no appreciable decrement of performance occurred during a 2 hr watch in subjects who had been given 10 mg of benzedrine shortly before the experimental session began: the drug, which has a known stimulating effect on the arousal mechanism, seems to have prevented any fall of vigilance. Complementary evidence is contained in the greater decrement found after taking 1 mg of hyoscine hydrobromide (Colquhoun, 1962). The effects of benzedrine further serve to distinguish vigilance decrements from impairments due to fatigue since Davis (1948), whose experiments with the Cambridge Cockpit have already been mentioned (p. 252) found that the drug had no consistent effect on the deterioration of performance in his task over a 2 hr period.

The most difficult data for an activation theory to accommodate are from experiments in which a decline of vigilance has occurred even though the task has been such as to keep the subject more or less continuously active (e.g. Whittenburg *et al.*, 1956, Adams and Boulter, 1962, Alluisi and Hall, 1963, Wiener *et al.*, 1964). These tasks obviously produced a stream of kinaesthetic and other signals which might reasonably have been expected to maintain arousal if sensory input alone was sufficient to do this. As we have seen, it is not: habituation seems often to occur readily and we may suppose there can be habituation to the feedback from repeated activity just as there is to repeated external stimulation. If so, however, and activation falls with time, how is the activity required by the task maintained? It seems fair to suggest from evidence of fatigue effects that relatively simple, repetitive, actions can be well maintained at a lower level of neural function, and thus at a lower level of arousal or activation, than higher grade and more complex judgments requiring greater channel capacity.

'FATIGUE' AT WORK

Much of the original interest in fatigue was directed at the elimination of accidents and poor productivity in industry, and a number of distinguished field studies have been done in the pursuit of this interest. From the theoretical point of view industrial tasks have the advantage of enabling performance to be studied over much longer periods than are normally possible in the laboratory. It is clear, however, that what is commonly regarded as industrial fatigue contains many diverse elements and that, just as in the laboratory, closely similar phenomena of slowing, blocking and disorganisation of performance can have widely different causes. We shall in concluding this chapter look briefly at work in this area in order to illustrate the subtle interplay of fatigue, vigilance and other factors which make their study at once challenging and rewarding.

Output measures at different times during a shift

Presumptive evidence of some kind of fatigue effect during an industrial shift is contained in the classical reports of the Industrial Fatigue Research Board (later renamed Industrial Health Research Board). These reports showed not only that shorter working shifts led to higher hourly output (Osborne, 1919, Vernon, 1919), but also that a net reduction in working hours could sometimes lead to a net rise in total output (Vernon, 1920a, b). It seems as if industrial workers tend to anticipate fatigue and to distribute their efforts over a working shift in much the same way as do long-distance runners and cyclists and subjects in some experimental tasks: they work faster throughout if the shift is short.

It was also found in many operations that the rate of production rose a little at the beginning of the shift, presumably owing to some 'warm-up' effect, fell towards the end of the morning, recovered somewhat during the lunch break and fell again during the afternoon. The falls could be largely prevented by introducing brief rest-pauses of 2 to 15 min shortly before the fall would otherwise have begun (Vernon and Bedford, 1924, Wyatt and Fraser, 1925, Wyatt, 1927). The early work has been summarised by Chambers (1961) and other writers on industrial psychology.

The interpretation of these findings is far from easy. When work involves heavy muscular effort, or is carried out in hot and humid conditions, heat stress may slow work down or make pauses necessary. This, however, cannot be the complete explanation of the changes found, because many of the jobs were light and done under reasonably easy environmental conditions. The fact that 'spurts' were sometimes found to occur during a shift, or even right at the end, need not weigh against a fatigue hypothesis in view of what has been found about motivation effects in laboratory studies of fatigue. Some effects may arise from physiological rhythms over the 24 hr and from physiological changes related to time from last meal; in this connection we may note that Wyatt and Fraser (1925) found breaks more effective if refreshments were taken. Again, however, such factors are not a sufficient explanation of the changes in production observed.

Apart from the suggestion of a true fatigue effect, two main alternative explanations have been offered.

(*a*) *Monotony*. Studies by Vernon (1924) and by Wyatt and Langdon (1932) showed that output per hour could be raised by switching from one job to another, and Wyatt and Fraser (1928, also Wyatt *et al.*, 1929) showed that switching also reduced irregularity in the speed of individual cycles in a repetitive operation. These findings have been taken to support the hypothesis that the falls of production towards the end of a shift are due to monotony, although in view of what is now known of the specificity of fatigue effects, they could still reasonably be attributed to fatigue. There is, indeed, some support for this view in the finding by Wyatt and Fraser (1928) that the benefits of switching were reduced if the jobs concerned were closely similar.

More telling evidence in favour of a monotony theory is that obtained by Wyatt and Langdon (1937), who compared output figures with answers to questionnaire items about the incidence of boredom and also showed that output could be raised by 'music while you work'. Wyatt and his co-workers have further shown that decrements of performance tend to be greater among workers of higher intelligence who, it might reasonably be presumed, are less 'absorbed' by their work.

It seems fair to say that present evidence does not enable us to distinguish clearly between fatigue and monotony as explanations of these findings; it would be necessary to do much more detailed studies based on the factors found to be significant in laboratory experiments.

(*b*) *Ancillary activities*. Dudley (1958) has suggested that the variations in output over a shift may not be due to fatigue or monotony but to the way in which the job is organised. In his studies of repetition work he found the usual output curves showing a rise at the beginning of the shift and a fall towards the end. However, when he made detailed studies of the work done, he found that the times for individual work cycles did not vary. In short, the initial rise and later fall were due to production work being interspersed at the beginning and end of the shift with other activities, such as getting out and putting away tools. These studies emphasise the importance of looking at jobs in detail, but they do not necessarily preclude an explanation in terms of fatigue. We have seen in the experiment by Singleton (1953) that there was little, if any, change in the speed of actual movements made during a working spell: fatigue effects showed in lengthening of the times between one movement and the next. Although the time scale in Singleton's study was much shorter than in Dudley's, it seems possible that fatigue effects did not affect cycle times in the operations Dudley studied, but tended to make the men turn briefly to other activities as a means of taking a rest. Such rests might not be taken consciously: the whole process was more likely to be unwitting. Certainly Dudley's explanation seems hardly adequate to account for the substantial effects of brief rest pauses found by Vernon, Wyatt and their colleagues.

Performance of long-distance lorry drivers

Several researches on long-distance lorry drivers in the United States have been summarised by McFarland and Moseley (1954) and discussed together with some other results by Crawford (1961). Lorry drivers tested with various sensory-motor tasks after long periods of driving have shown changes of performance similar to those found in laboratory experiments on fatigue. Comparable changes have also been found in studies of driving. Lauer and Suhr (1958) have shown that ill effects can be greatly reduced by frequent rests. On the other hand, accidents and near accidents have been found to be more frequent at the beginning of a trip, or after only a few hours of driving, than at the end of a long haul: in one study, McFarland and Moseley observed 22 out of 48 near accidents to occur during the first 2 hr of driving and only four in the last 2 hr of a 9 hr haul.

It is difficult to say how far the effects of prolonged driving are to be attributed to true fatigue effects and how far to monotony and loss of vigilance. We have already mentioned that Crawford (1961) suggested that fatigue may result from stress and annoyance caused by other road users. On the other hand, certain 'hypnotic' effects of long-distance driving which have been observed indicate that monotony may be important. It is perhaps reasonable to suggest that driving is both fatiguing and sometimes, especially on long American roads, monotonous, and that the observed effects are a balance between or combination of the two.

Long-term industrial fatigue

About the long-term tiredness, lassitude and lack of enthusiasm often termed 'chronic fatigue' there is little systematic knowledge. Subjectively, such states seem to arise from long-continued overload, leading to mild chronic overtenseness, which in severe forms can lead to inability to concentrate or make decisions, irritability and feelings of futility and seem to be effects of chronic stress. Perhaps these effects should be regarded as examples of the second type of mental fatigue effect we have outlined earlier. It may be that, just as in discussing the work of Bills (1931) and of Bertelson and Joffe (1963) it was necessary to postulate short-term and long-term effects operating over seconds and minutes respectively, so there may be still longer-term effects extending over, say, a week or a year and dissipated by rests at weekends and annual holidays.

On the other hand, some of these effects appear to be coupled with low morale and thus with various factors of social and industrial organisation, such as type of leadership, seeing 'results' for one's work and avoidance of hold-ups in the flow of production. Factors of this kind could reasonably link long-term morale to the same kind of mechanisms that we have considered in relation to monotony and boredom. Hold-ups in production, leading to waiting and idleness, are an obvious case in point. Seeing results of work has a clear affinity to the 'knowledge of results' which, as we have seen, tends to maintain vigilance. The same is perhaps true of leadership: it is often claimed that morale is better with a 'democratic' type of leadership, meaning that the worker, though taking orders from management, is also able to exert an effect on management. Looking at such leadership in cybernetic terms, we can say that the servo loop from management to worker and back is completed, just as it is by knowledge of the results of performance. We shall discuss this idea further in Chapter 10.

IX

Acquisition of Skill

It is not possible without artificiality to separate problems of acquiring skill from those of human learning in general and thus from a vast literature extending back to the turn of the century. No attempt will be made to survey the whole of this work here: the task would be altogether too great and has in any case been largely done in a number of text-books (e.g. McGeoch and Irion, 1952, Woodworth and Schlosberg, 1954, Bilodeau, 1966). Instead, some attention will be given to particular topics which are especially pertinent to the subjects discussed in previous chapters.

Experience, and therefore learning, are cumulative in the sense that each new situation is inevitably dealt with in terms of previous experience, and each new experience modifies what is carried to subsequent situations. The modification seems to take the form of selecting, qualifying and reordering the schematised material held in memory, and to affect all the main links in the chain of central processes shown in Fig. 1.3 (p. 19). As regards perception and translation, this means that material becomes more thoroughly coded or recoded as outlined in Chapter 6. On the effector side we seem to learn fine control and temporal ordering of action which can also be conceived as the achievement of a more thorough coding. The durability of what is learnt seems to vary somewhat between the different links. For reasons at present unknown, it appears to be much firmer and more resistant to interference from subsequent activity on the motor than on the perceptual side (e.g. Fleishman and Parker, 1962).

The kind of progress made as learning proceeds has been discussed in the case of tracking by Slack (1953) who showed that mastery began as a general acquaintance with the task and apparatus, and that this was followed by adjustment of the velocity of individual movements so that the longer were made at higher velocities than the shorter and later by recognition of the regularities of the track which enabled its course to be at least partly predicted. In the same way, the material brought from previous experience is at various levels of generality, including not only specific details of performance but broader strategies and techniques.

Past experience usually assists with the new situation, improving the speed or accuracy of dealing with it. Occasionally, however, the previous experience which is applied is irrelevant or bears only a superficial resemblance to what is required, so that it hinders rather than helps mastery of a new task – in short the 'transfer effect' from previous learning is negative rather than positive.

SOURCES OF LIMITATION IN LEARNING AND RECALL

For learning to take place and for the subject to furnish evidence that it has, a number of stages must be gone through:

(1) The material to be learnt must be perceived and comprehended and any responding actions selected.

(2) If the view outlined at the beginning of Chapter 7 is correct, the material must be held in some kind of temporary short-term storage, perhaps in the form of self-regenerating circuits of neural activity in the brain, until there has been time for more permanent registration to take place (Hebb, 1949).

(3) Some kind of durable trace must be established which is capable of remaining relatively unimpaired by subsequent activities of the organism and of standing up to gross assaults on the brain which may severely disrupt or temporarily suspend its activity. Such a trace seems to require either an alteration in the microstructure or a stable biochemical change in some cells of the brain.

(4) The traces have to endure until the time of recall. They may, however, undergo some changes during this period, either because of inherent instability or because they are overlaid or partly disrupted by subsequent learning.

(5) There must be recognition of a further situation which demands the re-use of the material as modified by any changes during stage 4.

(6) The material must be recovered from among other material stored in memory.

Stages 5 and 6 may at first sight appear to be the same, but should be distinguished from one another: we can often recognise what material is required without being able to recall it, as when we cannot remember a name although it is 'on the tip of the tongue'. This indicates a failure at stage 6. On the other hand, we show a failure at stage 5 if we can recall material without being able to see its relevance to a new situation.

(7) Finally the recalled material has to be used in such a way as to produce an overt, communicable response. Any one such response may incorporate many items of recalled material together with data from the situation present at the time.

It is important to bear in mind that although normally only the final result at stage 7 is observed, failures at this stage may be due to breakdown at any of the previous stages.

Let us consider the main stages in turn:

Understanding the task

Many apparent failures to learn are due to failure to comprehend what has to be learnt, rather than to any difficulty of registering or holding the material in memory (King, 1948, Seymour, 1954a). The practical importance of this has been strikingly illustrated in studies of the invisible mending of woollen cloth, traditionally regarded as a very difficult operation taking many months to learn (Belbin *et al.*, 1957). It was found that the main difficulty lay neither in the dexterity required to manipulate the needle, nor mainly in the visual acuity needed to see the weaves, but in understanding the way the weaves were constructed and thus the correct sequence of 'unders' and 'overs'. Trainees were accordingly set to construct waves out of elastic thread on frames and to mend specially produced large weave cloth before beginning work on cloth of standard size weave. This method of training drastically reduced the time required to learn as compared with the more usual method of watching a skilled worker, or with a method based on the principles of the 'Training Within Industry' scheme. The new method also enabled middle-aged women to learn a job traditionally regarded as possible only for school-leavers (Belbin, 1958).

The need to secure comprehension means that it is often beneficial to teach certain points about a task before practice begins. Most discussion has been about verbal formulation of the task, but other methods can also be effective: for example Chaney and Teel (1967) found diagrams of faults to be an effective aid to the training of industrial inspectors, and Posner (1967b) noted that the reproduction of movements which had been visually guided was much better than those which had originally been made blind and thus learnt by kinaesthetic cues only. Even if such 'pre-training' has little effect on performance of the task concerned, it may improve the extent to which the skill transfers to other tasks (Neumann, 1960). Two cautions about pre-training have, however, to be kept in mind. Firstly, although verbal or other formulation may help a trainee to understand a task, the formulation will inevitably be in terms of some 'conceptual model' or method of codifying the data and corresponding actions, and the efficiency of the pre-training will therefore very much depend on whether the 'model' is appropriate and easy to understand. For example, McAllister (1953) found when training subjects to position a lever that describing positions in angular degrees was less effective than description in terms of a clock face or directions related to the subject's own body. Secondly, the well practised subject will abandon the verbal or other intermediary and associate incoming data with action directly. For example, Fleishman and Rich (1963) noted how visual cues gave way to kinaesthetic with practice on a tracking task, and West (1967) observed that allowing typists to see what they were doing early in practice was helpful, but that vision later gave way to reliance on tactile and kinaesthetic cues. Pre-training methods need to take care not to make the subject dependent upon the extra cues provided in the early stages of training and thus to hinder the changeover to more direct relations between input and output at a later stage.

It is important to recognise that a trainee may use cues in his learning other than those which the instructor intended. For example, London post-office sorters are, or used to be, trained with packs of cards, each card bearing a name, street number and name of district, which had to be sorted into correct district numbers. Belbin (1964) found that trainees seemed, in some way, to use not only the district name but the whole of the data on the cards so that performance fell as soon as they began to sort different packs or actual mail. There is some conflict of evidence as to whether flexibility, in the sense of ability to tackle a range of similar although not identical tasks, is favoured by training with one example throughout or with several different examples (Adams, 1954, Callantine and Warren, 1955, Duncan, 1958). The conflict is perhaps due to the fact that although variation between one task and another prevents too close attachment to particular detailed methods, it also tends to impair the subject's grasp of essential principles. Optimum results may require a compromise: for instance Morrisett and Hovland (1959) found that subjects trained with 64 trials at each of three problems did better when transferred to a new problem than those trained with 192 trials at one problem or eight trials at each of 24 problems.

Several studies have considered the question of whether information given about a task should concentrate on general principles, or whether it should detail rules of procedure. Broadly speaking the findings suggest

K

that, with very complex tasks, instruction in principles yields better results than laying down a detailed drill, while with simpler tasks the drill is at least equally effective (for a summary see Clay, 1964). The reason is probably that a complex task commonly involves a number of alternative sequences of actions each appropriate to particular varieties of the circumstances under which the task is carried out. Any attempt to reduce this to a drill will mean that several different drills will have to be learnt, together with rules for applying them. In such a case, general principles, even if more difficult to master than any one detailed drill, may on balance effect a substantial saving.

A further implication of the need for comprehension is that the speed at which material is presented should be limited. If presentation proceeds too fast, a subject will be unable to deal with all the incoming material and will thus be left with gaps in his knowledge which, in the case of rote material, will lead directly to errors of omission and in the case of meaningful material will destroy the coherence of his understanding. Further, in lectures and demonstrations it is not easy for a trainee to go back and refer again to a point which may assume a new significance in the light of later information. For these reasons there are in some cases advantages in self-instruction methods rather than direct personal teaching. Much of the recent success of 'teaching machines' is probably due to the subject being free to take instruction from them at his own pace. Hulicka *et al.* (1967) have shown that time allowed for presentation is much more important than time allowed for recall.

These various requirements can only be met if there is precise information about what has to be learnt, and this in turn presupposes a careful and thorough analysis of the task to decide what should be perceived, what actions have to be taken and in which ways the latter are conditional upon the former. Such analysis is not always easy to make because a skilled performer seldom knows precisely how he achieves his results, and his actions may be so rapid that they are difficult to observe. We may presume that in the course of practice his actions have become accurate enough to be made ballistically without the monitoring of sensory feedback, and that in consequence he has lost awareness of his actions in the same manner as Leonard's (1953) subjects mentioned in Chapter 4 (p. 112).

Subtle variations of movement seem often to appear as qualitative differences to the subject who uses terms such as 'keeping the ball down' or 'follow-through'. These seem to be reflections of orders by the translation mechanism rather than observation of his own actions, and it seems clear that the main analysis of a task needs to be at the level of these orders rather than in terms of detailed movements.

The short-term link

If it is correct to assume that material has to be stored temporarily in short-term memory while long-term traces are being formed, the very small capacity of short-term memory we have seen in Chapter 7 implies a severe limitation upon the amount of material that can be handled at any one moment during learning. This view provides an approach to two questions each of which has been the subject of many experimental studies with somewhat conflicting results:

(a) *Should a trainee attempt to master a complex task as a whole, or should it be split up so that he can learn one part at a time?* Where the whole task is a closely co-ordinated activity such as aiming a rifle or simulated flying of an aircraft, the evidence suggests that it is better to tackle the task as a whole. Any attempt to divide it up tends to destroy the proper co-ordination of action and subordination of individual actions to the requirements of the whole (McGuigan and MacCaslin, 1955, Briggs and Waters, 1958, Crossman, 1959, Knapp, 1963, Naylor and Briggs, 1963), and this outweighs any advantage there might be in mastering different portions of the task separately.

Where, on the other hand, the task involves a series of component actions which have to be performed in the correct order but each is largely independent of the others, there seem to be advantages in practising the different components separately. An example is capstan-lathe operation studied by Seymour (1954b, 1955, 1956). The components of the cycle of operation – loading the collet, operating the cross-slide, operating the turret and unloading the collet – were practised separately, then in pairs, then in threes and finally all together. The advantages of this 'progressive-part' method of learning were small in the laboratory, but more substantial in the field (Seymour, 1959). The splitting-up of the task in this case enables each portion to be mastered quickly without overloading the learning mechanisms.

The same plan of learning separate portions of a whole task and combining them together was found successful by Singleton (1959) in training shoe-machinists. Belbin (1964) in her training of post-office sorters found them very slow to master the full range of destinations if all were given together at the beginning, but that if trainees learnt one group of destinations then switched to another, they tended to forget

the first group while learning the second. She accordingly used a modification of the 'progressive-part' method, which proved successful,
whereby sorters first used a restricted range of destinations then added
more, a few at a time, until all were included. In this way the amount of
new material to be learnt at any one time was kept small, while learning
already established was maintained.

A similar method to Belbin's has been shown by Postman and
Goggin (1966) to yield quicker learning of a list of nonsense syllables
than either learning the list as a whole or learning each part separately
before combining them. It seems possible in this case, and perhaps in
the others discussed here, that some of the advantage of the 'progressive-
part' method of learning lay, not in the avoidance of overload during
learning but in the fact that the early parts were learnt much more
thoroughly than the later. There is a good deal of evidence from other
work that the extent to which an item has been learnt can serve as a
distinguishing cue when it is being recalled, so that confusion between
items is less likely to occur when they have been learnt to different
extents (see McGeoch and Irion, pp. 415–417).

(*b*) *What is the optimum length of training session?* Is it easier to learn a
new task by practising it continuously until mastered, or is it better to
divide the time into short periods interspersed with rest or other
activity? At first sight, continuous practice ought to yield quicker
learning because it would ensure that traces were consolidated without
the chance of disruption by other activity which might interfere between
one practice session and the next. Yet many laboratory studies favour
the spacing of practice with frequent brief rest-pauses. The superiority
of continuous or spaced practice clearly depends upon a balance
between several factors.

Continuous practice seems to facilitate mastery of complex, meaningful material and the establishment of co-ordinated rhythmic activity.
Such comprehension or co-ordination means that individual items of
data or action are grouped together into larger units: in this way less
has to be recalled by rote because more is recovered by inference from
one item to another. Also, continuous practice seems to be preferred by
older trainees (Belbin, 1964) – a finding consistent with other experimental results which show that short-term memory is more liable to
interference from other activity during retention among older than
among younger adults (e.g. Kirchner, 1958, Inglis, 1965).

Two main types of reason has been advanced to account for the
cases in which spaced practice is superior. Firstly, if material is indeed

held in some kind of dynamic short-term store while more permanent traces are being established, 'consolidation' of the trace will outlast the actual presentation of the material to the subject and will continue during part of the gap between one practice session and the next. Spaced practice could thus be more efficient than continuous if only the actual duration of the sessions is counted and the time between sessions is ignored. This is what most studies of spaced practice have done: when the time between sessions is included, continuous practice is usually more efficient (Tsao, 1948).

The second type of advantage suggested for spaced practice is that the pauses allow certain after-effects of previous training trials to die away and thus reduce any adverse influences they might have on subsequent trials. One example is the very short-term mental fatigue discussed in Chapter 8 (pp. 225–227). Another possible adverse effect is interference caused by the cross-connections between items in the 'neural-dictionary' mentioned in Chapter 3 (p. 103). These would tend, unless time was allowed for their effects to subside, progressively to activate other erroneous responses and so blur the traces of the wanted items. Underwood (1961) has concluded that spacing of practice reduces confusion between responses rather than between signals. Such a finding is perhaps consistent with the evidence outlined in Chapter 3 (pp. 82–90) showing that choice of response is usually a very much slower process than identification of signal, and therefore likely to exert a longer after-effect.

Both factors imply two points about the effectiveness of spacing practice. Firstly it will depend very much on what is done during the times between practice periods. If they are spent in rehearsal of the material these times effectively form a part of the total practice time and learning will benefit accordingly, unless the task is fatiguing in which case the continued practice may depress subsequent performance (Adams, 1955, Knapp, 1963, Rosenquist, 1965). If on the other hand times between practice periods are spent on another task, learning or later recall of the first task may be impaired, the degree of impairment depending on the degree of similarity between the two tasks. For example, Sanders (1961a) found that learning a list of letters interfered less with the recall of a list of digits than did learning, or even merely reading over, another list of digits. Again it seems as if similarity of response is more important than similarity of signal (Postman *et al.*, 1965, Friedman and Reynolds, 1967).

The second implication is that very brief pauses between practice sessions should be as effective as longer ones since the kinds of perseverative or after-effects envisaged are likely to last only for a short time – a few seconds at most. Experimental studies have indeed confirmed that rest pauses of about one minute are almost as effective as those of a day (Lorge, 1930). The effectiveness of very brief pauses may in some cases be the reason why continuous practice appears to be as efficient as spaced: when a subject can perform a task at his own speed, he commonly takes many short breaks of a few seconds which are seldom recorded when his performance is studied, but may be very important in allowing learning to consolidate and in avoiding mental fatigue.

A further, as yet unanswered, question is raised by the problem of optimum length of training session. It is clear that there are severe limits to the rate at which material can be learnt when considered on a time scale of seconds and minutes, but are there any *additional* limitations operating over periods of hours, days or even longer times? Common experience suggests that there may be, but the question does not seem to have been posed in a scientific context. An indication that it might be worth asking is contained in the finding by Henshaw and Holman (1933) in an industrial study, that 80 min training per day at a chain assembly task yielded as rapid improvement as 160 min.

Passing material to long-term storage

Classical studies of memory by Bartlett (1932) showed very clearly that, in perceiving material to be remembered, subjects interpreted what they saw or heard, shortening, simplifying, re-arranging and sometimes elaborating it, and that it was this interpreted version of the material that was retained. His results imply that memory normally does not store the actual data provided by the subject's sense organs, but his *reactions to them*, and that if we want to represent the flow of data in the organism we need to put the memory store beyond the 'translation' stage as shown in Fig. 1.3.

It follows that anything which ensures that data are passed though the translation mechanism and not blocked at the previous stage will tend to improve learning. The classical work on this point is that of Gates (1917) who found that subjects learnt verbal material by rote much more thoroughly in a given time if they alternated reading with attempts to recite, than if they merely looked at the material for the whole time available.

It was at first thought that this effect was due to the sheer actions involved in recitation, but recent studies by Von Wright (1957b) and by Belbin (1958, 1964, Belbin and Downs, 1964) have shown that it depends on the subject making *active choices* instead of passively observing the data presented. We shall discuss Von Wright's work later. Belbin's experiments used a card-sorting task. In one of these which we may take as an example, subjects learned to 'post' numbered cards into coloured slots: 20–29 went into one slot, 30–39 into another and so on. Some subjects were given a list of associations between colours and numbers to memorise, others posted special cards each bearing a number *and* the appropriate colour until they felt confident they had learnt the required association. The latter tended to learn better. The extra cues can, however, in some cases impair mastery: a similar method used in the training of post-office sorters to place cards with different destinations into appropriate pigeon-holes did not prove superior to straightforward memorising: it appeared that the trainees relied on the colour code to the exclusion of active attempts to associate destinations with their corresponding holes.

A different method of securing that active choices are made is illustrated in an experiment by Chown *et al.* (1967) whose subjects learnt to associate 20 village names with their appropriate counties by a programmed-instruction method. The programme consisted of books with six 'frames' on each page, and subjects moved from frame to frame using a cardboard mask which exposed only one frame at a time. All subjects learnt five villages in one county (Buckinghamshire) first, then half the subjects were presented with 'discovery' frames listing five villages and headed by a statement such as 'TWO of the following villages are in SUSSEX, the others you know as they are in BUCKS.': the subjects had thus to infer the county to which the villages they had not seen before belonged. The other half were presented with further frames listing five villages all in one county to be learnt in the normal way. It was found that trainees aged 20–34 learnt about equally well by both methods, but the scores of those aged 35–49 were clearly higher with the 'discovery' method and about equal to those of younger trainees.

Further evidence that active choices rather than motor actions are an important factor in learning is provided by a number of experiments which have shown that 'mental practice' in which the subject performs a task in imagination, can often be substituted for a substantial amount of practice involving full performance with little if any loss of effectiveness (e.g. Hillix and Marx, 1960, Knapp, 1963, Ulich, 1967).

Two further points follow from the seeming fact that data are processed and coded before being placed in long-term memory:

(a) *The predominance of initial experience.* Zangwill (1937, 1939), who made a number of studies following Bartlett's work, found that when subjects were required to reproduce designs or passages of prose several times on different occasions and were then asked to recognise the original from among other similar versions, they tended to choose a version based on their own first reproduction rather than the original itself. The same tendency for initial experience to determine subsequent reaction has been found in several subsequent studies. For example Bilodeau *et al.* (1964) who required subjects to make movements against a stop and then to repeat them several times with the stop removed, found that the movements made on later trials tended to resemble the first ones made after the stop was removed. Again Welford, Brown and Gabb (1950) who, as already mentioned in Chapter 8 (p. 258), tested groups of aircrew with a series of problems both before and after flight, found that the style of performance adopted by the subjects when the problems were first encountered carried over to the later occasion. Thus, subjects tested first when they were tired after a flight adopted somewhat inefficient methods which they used again when they were tested a second time with similar problems after several days' stand-down. In the same way subjects tested first when they were fresh carried the more efficient methods they adopted over to a second test when they were tired after a flight. The effect can be seen in Fig. 8.8 (p. 259) where the numbers of readings required to solve the problem are less throughout for the group who started fresh than for the group who started tired. This type of result was obtained with four different sub-groups in two different experiments and seems, therefore, not to have been due to any accident of selection having produced groups of unequal ability.

Why the first experience should tend to have this predominant effect is not clear, but it is presumably bound up with the cumulative nature of learning. When a subject meets an entirely new problem he has to construct his solution of it from past experience dealing with *different* problems. Once he has done this, however, he has an outline method ready prepared for application to any similar problem on a subsequent occasion. Even if this method is not the best possible it will often be more efficient to use it than to work out a better method *de novo*.

(b) *Persistent errors and their prevention.* One of the less fortunate consequences of the predominant influence of initial performance is that errors in the early stages of learning tend to become ingrained. Indeed Kay (1951) could argue that one of the major problems of learning is concerned with getting rid of – unlearning – these initial errors. Kay's task was simple enough: learning to press a series of five Morse keys in the correct order by trying them again and again until all five could be gone through twice without error. Yet errors made in the first two or three trials tended to persist for many subsequent trials, in spite of the

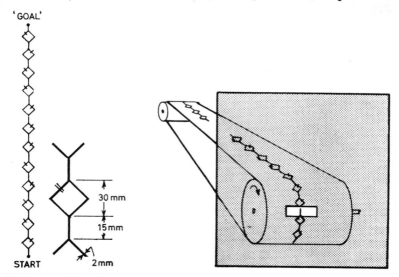

Figure 9.1. Von Wright's 'moving maze' (from Von Wright 1957a).

The pattern shown on the left was drawn on a white paper band and appeared, moving from above downwards, in the slit of the screen shown on the right. The subject had to hold a stylus in the slit and trace over the path of the maze, learning to move left or right as each diamond came into view so as not to cross the double lines drawn on one side or other of the upper half of the diamond. The double lines were sometimes on one side, sometimes on the other, as shown at the extreme left of the Figure. The subject could not see them at the moment when he had to decide which way to move. His only way of being sure not to make errors was, therefore, to remember the positions of the double lines from previous trials.

fact that the correct key at each point in the series had always to be found before passing on to the next. Even when subjects eventually avoided these persistent errors they were sometimes observed to move their hand towards a wrong key and stop just in time saying 'No *not* that one'.

Kay's work was followed up by Von Wright (1957a) whose subjects learnt a pencil maze of a type shown in Fig. 9.1. The first time through the maze they tended to adopt some kind of systematic procedure such as always going to one side or alternately right and left. The second time through they obviously tried to apply what they had learnt in the first trial, making some correct responses and some errors. The pattern of errors made on the second trial tended to persist, so that the positions of errors on subsequent trials correlated with those on the second trial. These findings of Kay and Von Wright will evoke echoes in the experience of those concerned with teaching athletics, games and skills such as typewriting: errors need to be corrected immediately or they tend to become ingrained.

Von Wright (1957b), following a number of earlier workers, argued

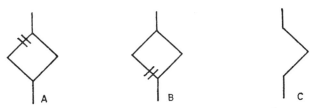

Figure 9.2. Three different versions of Von Wright's 'moving maze' used during the first four training trials. From the fifth trial onwards all subjects used version A. The mean results per subject with the three versions were:

	Total trials to learn to criterion	Errors made after fourth trial
A	23·25	76·30
B	10·45	15·80
C	18.80	52·15

The subjects were 60 undergraduates randomly divided into three groups of 20 – one group for each version of the maze.

that if errors could be prevented in the first few trials, mastery of the task should be very much quicker. He accordingly prepared three different versions of the same maze, as shown in Fig. 9.2. Of these A was the same as the original type of maze. B was the same as A except that the bars were moved down to a position which enabled the subject to see them just before he reached the choice-point and thus to make the correct choice every time. Type C omitted the incorrect paths altogether, so that the subject had merely to follow the correct path through the maze. Three groups of subjects were used: one (A) simply made trials with maze A until they went through twice running without error. Groups (B) and (C) had their first four trials with mazes B and C respectively and then transferred to maze A on which they made further trials until they too went through twice running without error. The results are shown with Fig. 9.2: groups (B) and (C) learnt much more quickly and made fewer errors than group (A). The superiority of group (B) to group (C) presumably reflects the fact that the former had to observe the bars and made an active decision at each choice point, whereas the latter could follow passively through.

Holding and Macrae (1964), who give a valuable list of references to early work in this field, obtained comparable results using the very simple task of sliding an aluminium sleeve a distance of 4 in along a steel rod by means of a knob. Each subject was given an initial test to determine the accuracy with which he made the required movement without training, and was then given one of several different kinds of training before a final test. Performance improved less between initial and final tests if the subject held the knob while it was passively moved over the required distance than if such guidance was alternated with unguided attempts or if, instead, the subject made free movements until he reached a stop set at the correct distance. Subsequent work by the same authors has shown that such guidance during training is especially beneficial when tracking movements have to be made with a relationship between display and control which is not fully compatible, presumably because it prevents the errors that would otherwise result from the incompatibility (Macrae and Holding, 1965, Holding and Macrae, 1966). They have also shown that although guidance in which the hand is passively moved is no better than normal practice when learning to track a simple repetitive course, it is superior for learning a more complex course, in this case probably not only because it prevents errors but because it forces the subject to move more actively than he otherwise would (Macrae and Holding, 1966).

An interesting analogue to the foregoing methods, especially Von Wright's, has been described by Annett (1966b) for training perceptual discrimination. Subjects were trained to discriminate whether small gaps in circles presented for brief periods were on the left or right by presenting the one type of circle on a green and the other on a red background. Complete circles with each of the two colours of background were also included so that the subject had to discriminate between 'left gap', 'right gap' and 'no gap'. The use of this aid greatly increased the accuracy with which rings on a neutral background were discriminated after the training had been completed. Presumably the colours served to concentrate the subject's attention on the appropriate parts of the rings while they were being exposed and thus helped him to observe what the gaps looked like.

Principles in this area are not yet fully understood and there is room for further research. For example Belbin (1964) in her study of post-office trainees found tendencies for sorting errors to become ingrained and attempted, seemingly successfully, to reduce them by requiring subjects, if they were doubtful where to place a card, to put it in a 'doubtful' box rather than hazard a guess. Yet Belbin *et al.* (1964) found that it made no difference to subjects required to associate lists of village names with corresponding counties, whether they guessed or not, and that they had no special difficulty in learning a fresh list of counties for the same villages on being told the original list was incorrect. The authors interpreted their findings as implying that the guess made with a low degree of confidence *faut de mieux* is less likely to become ingrained than the committed decision or choice.

Whatever the present unanswered questions and conflicts of evidence, it seems clear from the work reviewed here that relatively little learning occurs if the subject is a passive spectator or even a passive performer, but that he must be involved in active decisions and choices about what he is doing, and it is these that he will retain whether they are right or wrong. Indeed it is arguable that even in those cases where a subject appears to learn passively, he does so because he occasionally engages in active 'mental' practice.

Retrieval from memory store

The obvious confusions, omissions and substitutions that occur when remembering imply that memory traces are liable to be disrupted or overlaid by other traces established subsequently. There has in the past been some controversy as to whether subsequent learning destroys memory traces already laid down or merely makes their retrieval when required more difficult. Probably both processes occur (Melton and Irwin, 1940). Explanation of the gradual return of memories following retrograde amnesia poses a similar problem: how far is the return due to a piecing together of fragments of memory that remain, and how far is it due to the trauma not having destroyed the traces but having somehow rendered them unavailable? Again both processes probably operate. By the same tokens we can perhaps assume that re-use of memories as, for example, when a task is repeated, or a recall or recognition test is given, will tend both to strengthen the traces concerned and to make them more readily available. This will apply to errors as well as to correct responses, so that the effect of repetition may be beneficial or the reverse. For example a recognition test in which the original material is re-presented may facilitate later recall while a recall test in which errors are made may hamper later recognition (Belbin, 1950, Estes and Da Polito, 1967).

The main problem of retrieval can perhaps be conceived as the discriminability of traces from one another. It is thus obvious that confusion is likely to be greater between very similar than between widely different items. For example, Postman and Goggin (1964) found that learning a list of 10 consonant-vowel-consonant nonsense syllables in which each of four consonants appeared five times was slower than learning a list in which each of 20 consonants appeared once only. Again recall is easier when the possible items belong to a relatively small set, and the commonly found superiority of recognition to recall seems to be due essentially to this. For example, Davis *et al.* (1961b) presented subjects with lists of 15 two-digit numbers between 10 and 99 and then required either recall of the originals or their recognition from among a list of 30, 60 or all 90 numbers. They found that recognition was superior to recall only with the shorter lists in which, of course, range of choice was restricted. Recognition from among the whole 90 possible numbers was not superior to recall. Similar results have been obtained by others since (e.g. Dale, 1967, Slamecka, 1965).

Many of the facts about the availability of material in recall follow from the cross-connections between items in the 'cerebral dictionary' postulated by Treisman and discussed in Chapter 3 (p. 103). Availability is a function of the extent to which cross-connections converge on an item and thus on the likelihood of its being to some extent pre-activated. Thus nonsense syllables which evoke many associations are more readily recalled than those which evoke less (e.g. Postman and Goggin, 1964) and such 'association value' is more important than either 'meaningfulness' or pronounceability (Lindley, 1963). Again Murdock (1960b) noted that rate of learning a list of unconnected words was proportional to the logarithm of the frequency of usage of the words in normal English. Obvious illustrations of the same general principle are that rote learning of words is assisted by deliberate attempts to form associations (Eagle, 1967), and that when pairs of words are presented and the subject has to recall one member of the pair when given the other, recall is easier if the words of each pair are in some way related (Robinson and Loess, 1967). Less obvious, but clearly emphasising the role of association rather than familiarity is the finding by Baddeley (1964a) that trivial and meaningless associations between items in a list can improve rate of learning the list by rote: for example the pair of nonsense syllables QEM POG was more easily learnt than POG QEM, seemingly because the letters MP occur more frequently together than GQ in normal English.

KNOWLEDGE OF THE RESULTS OF ACTION

The basic fact that, as Sir Frederick Bartlett once put it, 'It is not practice but practice *the results of which are known* that makes perfect' has been shown for many tasks since the pioneer experiments of Thorndike (1931) on the increase of accuracy in drawing lines blindfold when the subject is told whether each attempt was too short or too long. Performance shows no improvement, without 'knowledge of results', but begins to do so as soon as it is introduced. If it is then removed, performance at once deteriorates. Dees and Grindley (1951) found the deterioration was due to subjects tending to overshoot – a finding which implies that they were acting as an over-sensitive or over-responsive mechanism held in check by the feedback provided by the knowledge of results. The same point is implied in a finding by Annett (1959) whose subjects regarded a bar which they had to press to a given extent as 'much stiffer' when knowledge of results was removed. Dyal (1966) also found a tendency to overshooting when knowledge of results was discontinued in a line-drawing task. It occurred, however, only with subjects who had shown an initial tendency to *under*shoot before knowledge of results was given: subjects with an initial tendency to overshoot tended to undershoot when knowledge of results was discontinued. It seems, perhaps, that knowledge of results produces a general tendency to overcorrect initial biases and that this in turn is modified and held in check by the detailed knowledge given trial by trial.

Baker and Young (1960) suggest that the improvement of performance with knowledge of results is in two stages: in the first the approximate limits of the action are learnt, and in the second finer adjustments are achieved. What is learnt in the first stage survives the removal of knowledge of results, but the fine adjustments of the second stage are quickly lost. The same implication follows from work by Bilodeau and Bilodeau (1958a) who studied the improvement of accuracy in moving a lever a required distance over a series of trials when knowledge of results was given either every trial, or one in three, or one in four, or one in ten. They found that accuracy improved according to the *absolute number* of trials given with knowledge of results. During intervening trials without knowledge of results performance tended to fall off, but the extent to which it did so diminished as the series of trials proceeded. In short, although there was no learning during trials without knowledge of results, something was carried over from the trials with knowledge of results to those without.

We have already seen (p. 278) from the work of Chinn and Alluisi (1964) using a vigilance task that, in terms of signal-detection theory, knowledge of results can raise d' and change β, implying that it can both improve discrimination and alter criteria of judgment. Further evidence of the latter is provided by Nakamura and Kaswan (1962) who found that giving subjects information about the speed of their responses in a reaction-time task shortened latencies but increased errors.

The timing of knowledge of results

In the typical experiment on knowledge of results, and in many training situations, the subject makes an attempt or 'trial' at the task and is then given information about the accuracy of his attempt before making a further trial. There is thus a gap between making each attempt and receiving knowledge of results during which the subject has to retain the 'orders' given to the effector mechanism – the aim and feel of the movement—for comparison with the results attained. There is a second gap, between receiving knowledge of results of one trial and making the next, during which he has to retain both the original orders and the comparison of these with the results so as to frame orders for the next movement. It has often been suggested that some loss of data carried over these memory links is likely to occur if knowledge of results is at all delayed or if there is an appreciable interval between trials. From what has been said of short-term retention in Chapter 7 we should expect lapse of time as such to have little or no effect, but that intervening activities and shifts of attention could be disruptive, and that time might be important as giving opportunity for these to occur.

The experimental evidence on the effect of time interval before knowledge of results is given comes from several experiments in which subjects had to make a movement and then after a time varying in most cases from 0 to 30 sec were given an indication of whether the movement had been of the correct length or too short or too long. The results divide into two sharply contrasting groups, one of which finds that delaying knowledge of results increases the number of trials required to attain a consistently correct response (Saltzman *et al.*, 1955, Greenspoon and Foreman, 1956, Denny *et al.*, 1960, Dyal, 1964), while the other finds no effect of delay up to 20 or 30 sec (Bilodeau and Bilodeau, 1958b, McGuigan, 1959, Bilodeau and Ryan, 1960) although some effects occur with delays of an hour or more (Bilodeau and Bilodeau, 1958b). The conflict between these two groups seems to be resolved by results from an experiment by Dyal *et al.* (1965) who found a substantial effect of delay if the score taken was the number of responses falling within a zone designated as correct, but no effect if the actual amounts of error were measured. All the studies in the first group used the first method of measurement, and all those in the second group the second method. This result presumably means that delaying knowledge of·results has little effect on the accuracy of most of the attempts but tends to result in rather more relatively large deviations, which is what one might indeed expect if the subject's attention was sometimes diverted during the period of delay. Results by Becker *et al.* (1963) run counter to this pattern in that they found no effect of delay although scoring 'number correct' rather than absolute error. Their procedure was more complex, however, including the administration of an electric shock at the time of the knowledge of results, and this makes their experiment hardly comparable with the others.

Clear evidence of the disruptive effect of activity intervening between a trial and knowledge of its results is the much slower learning found by Lorge and Thorndike (1935) and by Bilodeau (1956) when knowledge was delayed until one or more further trials had taken place. This result has been confirmed by Lavery and Suddon (1962) and by Lavery (1964).

The principle that information about the correctness of action should be available quickly has been used with success in teaching Morse code: correction letter by letter was found to lead to quicker learning than correction of several letters at a time (Keller, 1943). The same principle appears to apply to various types of equipment such as certain process plants in industry, where the operator has to take actions which do not have their full effects until several minutes or even an hour or so later. In such circumstances it is difficult for him to acquire and maintain adequate control, although astonishingly expert performances are sometimes attained. Experiments in which the subject has been given immediate indications, by means of a computing device, of what the eventual effects of his actions will be, have shown very substantial benefits to both training and performance (e.g. Taylor, 1957).

The effects of the gap between giving knowledge of results and making the next attempt have been less systematically studied, but evidence that learning becomes slower as the gap is lengthened has been obtained by Macpherson *et al.* (1949) and by Bilodeau and Bilodeau (1958b). The latter authors argue that the time between the giving of knowledge of results and the next trial has more effect than a delay of the same duration in giving knowledge of results. Why this should be so is not clear, but the memory load is presumably higher between one trial and the next than it is between the end of one attempt and the giving of knowledge of its results. Alternatively if the subject thinks of his task as a number of discrete trials each followed by knowledge of results, he might well be more likely to shift his attention between one trial and the next than between completing an action and receiving information about its effect. Such a shift of attention might have more effect than a relatively simple intervening activity, such as making another movement, which has been shown by Blick and Bilodeau (1963) to have a negligible effect.

The quality of data fed back

It is perhaps obvious that, other things being equal, the more precise the knowledge given of the results of action, the more accurate actions will become over a series of trials. Thus the lines drawn blindfold by McGuigan's (1959) subjects were more accurate if they were told their error to the nearest $\frac{1}{8}$ in than if they were told only to the nearest $\frac{5}{8}$ in or $1\frac{1}{4}$ in. Again Trowbridge and Cason (1932), using a similar task, showed that subjects learnt more quickly and attained greater accuracy if they were told the direction and extent of their errors than if they were merely told whether or not they were within $\frac{1}{8}$ in of the correct length.

It seems obvious also that the manner of conveying knowledge of results should be important. On general grounds one would expect effectiveness to be greatest when the information is clearly and simply related to the action concerned. Any distortion or equivocation in the information fed back to the subject will reduce its effectiveness (Morin, 1955, Shelly, 1961, Hunt, 1964). On the other hand, unduly full or complex information may be partly ignored (Crafts and Gilbert, 1935) or may confuse the subject (e.g. Katz, 1967): an example has been noted by Singleton (see 'Training Made Easier', 1960) who found that a scale at the side of an industrial sewing machine indicating how fast it was running, although of some help to a trainee, caused difficulties by taking her attention from the article she was sewing.

What is not so obvious is that the information given should indicate the *discrepancy* between what is required and what has been achieved rather than merely give a reminder of requirement or some broad measure of achievement. The former point is illustrated in an experiment by Lincoln (1956) who trained subjects to wind a handwheel at a given rate. He found it more effective to give his subjects knowledge of results by having them, between trials, hold the wheel while it was driven at a rate equal to the difference between the required rate and that at which they had been winding, than for them to hold it while it was driven at the required rate. The point that a broad measure of achievement is insufficient is illustrated by several studies of tracking a target which have shown that merely indicating when the subject has remained 'on target' for a given length of time make relatively little difference to his performance (Reynolds and Adams, 1953, Archer *et al.*, 1956, Archer and Namikas, 1958, Williams and Briggs, 1962, Bilodeau and Rosenquist, 1964, Karlin, 1965). The small improvement of performance that does occur may perhaps be attributed to the incentive effect of knowledge of results which we shall discuss later.

Effects of withdrawing knowledge of results

The purpose of the early experiments on knowledge of results was to study educational technique, and for this purpose the indications seem clear. More recent interest has been engendered by the question of whether some industrial and military training can be improved by giving detailed knowledge of results during the training period which will not be available afterwards on the actual job. Experimental studies are unanimous in finding that when knowledge of results is given during training and then removed, performance deteriorates in subsequent trials. The extent to which it does so differs in different cases, however, and the problem is to find whether some methods of giving knowledge of results during training lead to better maintained performance than do others when knowledge of results is removed.

Research on this problem is scanty but can be taken tentatively to indicate that performance is best maintained when the conditions are such as to emphasise the need for the subject to observe the feel of his actions in order to relate them to their results. Thus Annett (1959), using a task in which the subject had to learn to exert a particular pressure on a plunger, found that those who, as they pressed, observed the approach of a spot on a cathode-ray tube to a marked target, showed greater deterioration when the tube was removed than did those who had been told verbally how they had done or had seen an indication on the tube only after their movement had been completed. When the results of the pressure could be seen as it was actually being made, there was no need to remember the feel in order to link it to the indication of results, and it is therefore understandable that the subject retained little knowledge of how hard he had pressed.

Provided, however, the indication of results is not so direct as to remove the need to remember the feel of the task, performance seems to be better maintained if the knowledge of results has been direct and immediate. Thus Goldstein and Rittenhouse (1954) found that subjects in a tracking task who heard a buzzer sound all the time they were 'on target' retained their skill better than those who were merely told how they had done after a period of practice. Again Dyal *et al.* (1965) found that performance deteriorated less after immediate than after delayed knowledge of results. Presumably the clearer the association between action and result that has been learnt, the better it is retained. Probably consistent with this general view is the finding by Macpherson *et al.* (1949) that performance was better retained with somewhat longer rather than very short intervals between trials: a new trial following immediately might well interfere with the association of knowledge of results with the feel of a preceding action. These findings appear at first sight to conflict with the evidence of Lavery and Suddon (1962) and Lavery (1964) who found performance was better maintained when knowledge had been delayed until after one or more trials had been made than when it had been given after each trial. We may, however, suppose that in their case the relative uselessness of the knowledge of results had forced subjects to pay attention to other cues, and that these still remained available after knowledge of results had been withdrawn.

Several authors have made the complementary point that a subject must have *some* cues to the results of his actions if he is to perform accurately at all, and training procedures will be effective in so far as they help him to observe and use such cues as are inherent in the task for which he is being trained. They will fail in so far as they provide him with extra cues on which he comes to rely but which are not available when he changes from training to the actual job (Goldstein and Rittenhouse, 1954, Annett and Kay, 1957, Annett, 1959).

AIMS AND INCENTIVES

It is clear from studies of animals that speed of learning is substantially influenced by incentives. Motives in human beings are less straightforward but can probably affect several phases of learning and memory. We shall briefly mention three points, two of them directly linked with the concepts of arousal and activation mentioned in the last chapter, one of them less so but still within the general area of motivation.

The incentive effect of knowledge of results

Knowledge of results, as well as being a corrective, also acts as an incentive. Usually the two effects are inextricably mixed, but they can in a few cases be separated: for example Macpherson *et al.* (1949) found that when a subject was told that knowledge of results was to be discontinued, performance fell on the very next trial despite the fact that this ought to have benefited from knowledge of results of the previous trial. The two effects may be further separated in terms of the type of knowledge of results required. We have already seen that, for the corrective effect, an indication of error is needed and that an overall measure of achievement is of little value. For the incentive effect, however, a simple indication of achievement appears to suffice (Gibbs and Brown, 1956).

The way in which knowledge of results exerts its incentive effect is not yet fully clear. If the theory is valid that decline of vigilance during a watch is due to decrease of activation or arousal, knowledge of results, because it prevents this decline, must tend to increase arousal. Such a view is entirely consistent with the parallel view that knowledge of results affects the goal or aim the subject sets himself – an increase of arousal may be mediated by raising the goal. Helmstadter and Ellis (1952) found that a simple indication of achievement was as effective as setting a subject a goal or having him set himself a goal. Locke (1967, see also Locke and Bryan, 1967) found in an adding task that setting a goal which was 10% higher than comparable subjects had achieved with the instruction to 'do your best' substantially increased the speed of performance and made the task more interesting, but that telling subjects how many additions they had made every 10 or 15 min had no effect. He suggests, in consequence, that knowledge of results acts mainly by setting goals, although in his case, since subjects wrote their answers on sheets which they filled at approximately 1 min intervals, they had a fair knowledge of achievement in any case, without being told by the experimenter. Locke refers to a number of previous studies showing similar results extending back to one by Mace (1935).

Activation level and rate of learning

Bills (1927) in a classical study found that if the subject squeezed a hand dynamometer while learning, both the rate of learning and the level of subsequent recall were improved. Sidowski and Eason (1960) and Sidowski and Nuthmann (1961) failed to confi. n this result, finding instead that learning was slower when a dynamometer was squeezed. They, however, arranged for a signal light or buzzer to sound all the time the subject was maintaining the correct pressure and this signal may have distracted the subject's attention from the main task of learning. Other investigators have confirmed Bills' result but added the further finding that if the tension is increased beyond a certain point, performance falls again (Stauffacher, 1937, Courts, 1939). Whether this is due to overarousal, or whether the effort of squeezing a dynamometer very hard distracts the subject's attention, is not clear.

All these studies used the method of learning in which subjects were shown words or nonsense syllables in serial order and after the first trial had to try to anticipate which item was the next on the list. Learning was thus inextricably bound up with attempts at recall. Levin (1967) who separated the two processes by alternately showing, and requiring recall of, the whole list found that rate of learning rose progressively with level of induced tension during the learning phase, but that during the recall phase accuracy rose with increase of tension to an optimum and thereafter declined. A rise to an optimum and subsequent decline in both rate of learning and accuracy of recall has also been found with increasing skin conductance (Berry, 1962). Levin noted that increased tension during recall resulted not only in more correct responses but more errors due to intrusions from previous lists. If, as is reasonable, these can be regarded as a kind of 'false positive' in the process of recovering material from memory, the result is consistent with the change of β which accompanies a rise of activation as shown in Fig. 8.9 (p. 268) – the increased activation expands both the 'signal-plus-noise' and the 'noise-alone' curves so that more signals are detected but at the same time more false positives are made.

Measures of spontaneous muscle tension taken during learning appear to be broadly consistent with the foregoing results: Stauffacher and Courts both found that better learners tended to be more tense, and in an experiment on maze-learning Stroud (1931) found that rapid learners pushed the stylus somewhat harder than slow learners. It appears, in short, that part at least of the differences of learning between individuals can be accounted for in terms of their level of activation or arousal. Consistent with this view is the finding of Sherwood (1965) that subjects for whom a cube like that of Fig. 6.5A (p. 166) reversed frequently tended to be better learners. Again several studies have found that more anxious subjects learn better than less anxious, at least when the material is not such as to conflict with associations induced by previous material. Where such conflict occurs, more anxious subjects tend to be poorer learners (Spence *et al.*, 1956a, b, Lovaas, 1960a, b, Sarason and Palola, 1960, Lee, 1961, Gaudry and Champion, 1962). Since such conflict makes the task more difficult, this is perhaps another example of the Yerkes-Dodson effect discussed in the previous chapter (p. 270).

Stroud found in his maze learning task that pressure on the stylus tended to be higher at points of special difficulty and Sherwood noted that rate of learning tended to rise and fall with arousal level in the same individuals tested on different occasions. Measures of skin resistance taken during the learning by rote of a list of nonsense syllables have shown that resistance differed at different points in the list and that the resistance levels corresponded closely to the speed at which particular syllables were learnt – lower resistance indicating higher arousal was associated with more rapid learning (Brown, 1937). The ends of the list were, as is usually found, learnt more rapidly than the middle, and skin resistance was lower when the ends of the list were being presented. This finding provides an interesting line of evidence which is not usually taken into account when discussing reasons for the quicker learning of the ends of a list.

Several studies have shown that the beneficial effect of raising the level of activation during learning appears much more in long-term than in immediate recall. The former is markedly improved while the latter is either unaffected or actually impaired (Walker and Tarte, 1963, Kleinsmith and Kaplan, 1963, 1964, Berlyne *et al.*, 1966, Batten, 1967). The improvement of long-term recall is presumably due to activation facilitating long-term registration and thus reducing the rate of forgetting. Why it should do so is not clear, but a moderate level of activation would probably strengthen the signals entering the long-term memory store and perhaps strengthen those already there: Russell (1959) has put forward the interesting idea that random or rhythmic activity in the brain will tend to channel through established pathways and to confirm them, so that if memory traces can be conceived as pathways, they will be strengthened. The impairment of immediate recall is presumably due to the muscle-tension, noise or other activating agent used during learning tending to produce neural noise which takes some time to die away and, until it has done so, confuses recall.

The order of learning more and less difficult tasks

In the early 1950s several studies were published which addressed themselves to the problem of whether, when two tasks of unequal difficulty have to be learnt, it is more efficient to begin with the easier or the harder. These studies looked back to one by Cook (1937) who found that if the harder was tackled first the easier was learnt very quickly afterwards, but that if the easier was learnt first, little time was saved on the harder afterwards. Cook's results were open to the objection that his subjects spent longer learning the harder task and thus, if they learnt the easier subsequently, came to it at a later stage of practice. Most of the studies in the early 1950s endorsed Cook's finding while being free of this objection (Baker *et al.*, 1950, Szafran and Welford, 1950, Gibbs, 1951).

Let us consider Szafran and Welford's experiment by way of example. Subjects threw small loops of chain at a target on the floor under three conditions. In the easiest they threw directly; in a condition of intermediate difficulty they threw over a bar; and in the most difficult they threw over a screen the same height as the bar, which hid the target from direct view so that it could be seen only *via* a mirror placed behind it. Different groups of subjects performed the tasks in different orders. The results are set out in Table 9.1: the *total* error for all three condi-

TABLE 9.1 *Mean errors made when throwing at a target in inches per throw* (*from Szafran and Welford, 1950*). *Each mean in A is based on 150 and in B on 50 throws by each of 28 subjects*

A. Mean errors for all three conditions taken together

Direct condition first	5·93
Bar condition first	5·73
Screen condition first	5·35

B. Mean errors for the three conditions separately

	Presented first	Presented second	Presented third
Direct	5·59	4·50	4·49
Bar	5·29	4·95	4·96
Screen	6·99	7·16	7·13

tions taken together was *least* when the subjects began with the most difficult condition, and greatest when they began with the easiest. Moreover, while performance in the easiest condition was much more accurate if it came after one of the others than if it came first, performance in the most difficult condition was slightly *worse*. On the basis of their results Szafran and Welford suggested that when a more difficult task precedes an easier, the transfer effect is positive, but when an easier precedes a more difficult, the transfer effect tends to be negative.

Subsequent work (for a summary see Holding, 1962) has shown that this statement was a little too sweeping. In particular, several experiments in which subjects tracked a moving target have shown that practice with a slow moving, easy course benefits performance at a fast, difficult course more than vice versa. A possible reason for the conflict between these tracking results and those of other experiments is that, with a very fast-moving target, accurate tracking is impossible and is therefore not attempted. If so, a subject practising first on a fast-moving target will adopt less stringent standards of accuracy than will one whose first experience is with a slower-moving target. We might therefore reconcile these results with the others by saying that *if two or more tasks have to be learnt, it is most beneficial to begin with the one which elicits the greatest care and effort towards the attainment of a high standard of performance.* Some direct support for this view is given by a finding in Szafran and Welford's experiment not reported in their paper, that although subjects who began with the most difficult task were, on average, the most accurate, they also tended to be slightly slower: beginning with the most difficult task seemed to engender a more precise and deliberate performance.

Results published subsequently to Holding's review all conform to the same pattern. The tasks involved have included the discrimination of gaps in circles in the experiment by Annett (1966b) already mentioned, identification of patterns (Coules *et al.*, 1965), and various tracking tasks (Goldstein and Newton, 1962, Bilodeau, 1965, Dooley and Newton, 1965).

One further proviso needs to be mentioned regarding the relationships between difficult and easy tasks. The experiments we have mentioned have all carried practice at the more difficult task to the point at which reasonable mastery has been attained. If the subject were not allowed to continue to this point, he would be left with an inadequate comprehension of the task, so that his subsequent performance at an easier task might be confused and less satisfactory than it would have been if he had tackled the easier task first. Apart from this proviso, the rather surprising principle that has been outlined here seems to hold remarkably well.

CHANGES OF PERFORMANCE DURING LONG PRACTICE

It is well known that the initial attainment of reasonable competence at athletic, industrial, artistic and many other skills is followed by a long period of further improvement during continued exercise of the skill. What is the precise nature of this further improvement is by no means wholly clear, but several studies agree that if the time taken by a task is split up into movement times and times between movements, it is the latter which decrease more with practice: for example if a subject has to move his hand to grasp an object and then convey the object to a box where it is dropped, times taken in grasping and dropping improve most (Wehrkamp and Smith, 1952, Rubin *et al.*, 1952, von Trebra and Smith, 1952, Seymour, 1959). Presumably the central decision processes are modified with practice to a greater extent than the execution of movements.

De Jong (1957), following suggestions made by some previous workers, has proposed that the time taken to perform a repetitive task falls exponentially until it approaches some 'incompressible' minimum, so that if cycle time is plotted against cycle-number on log–log paper, time decreases approximately linearly until it approaches the incompressible minimum. He proposes that

$$T_n = T_\infty + \frac{T_1 - T_\infty}{n^k} \qquad (9.1)$$

where T_n is the nth cycle time, T_∞ is the incompressible minimum time – that is the time that would be taken if the task was continued for an infinite number of cycles – and T_1 is the time taken by the first cycle. The exponent k expresses the rate at which improvement takes place with practice.

De Jong found this formulation to fit reasonably well for a number of industrial operations. The approach was taken up by Crossman (1959) who found that this type of formula gave a reasonably good fit to the data from several laboratory studies and industrial operations. Examples are shown in Fig. 9.3. He suggested that the improvement is due to the operator starting with a range of slightly different methods of doing the task and gradually coming to select the quickest to the exclusion of others. He set out a statistical formula which assumed a progressive fall in the probability of using less efficient, and rise in the probability of using more efficient methods, with time. It differed from De Jong's formula mainly in predicting that the first few cycles will be a little quicker than they would be if a strict exponential formula held. The data in Fig. 9.3 give some support to this view.

Crossman pointed out a number of consquences of his model:

(i) It implies that successive performances of the same task will tend to become more uniform. Some evidence that this is so for tracking has been provided by Reynolds (1952) and for car-driving by Lewis (1954) who found that highly skilled drivers performed more consistently than less skilled.

(ii) Rate of improvement with practice will depend on the variety of methods from which selection has to be made, the variability of the

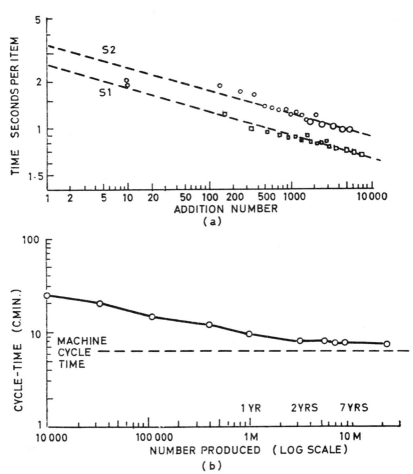

Figure 9.3. (a) Plot by Crossman (1959) of data by Blackburn (1936) showing improvements with practice in time taken to add digits. Data for two subjects, S1 and S2.

(b) Plot by Crossman (1959) showing improvements with practice in time taken at cigar making.

time taken by each method, and the pressure to select – that is upon the incentive to achieve a high rate of working.

(iii) The more sub-tasks there are in the overall task, and the more they interact with one another, the more opportunity there will be for improvement, and therefore the longer improvement will continue.

(iv) Transfer of skill from one task to another will depend not so much upon the extent to which methods *possible* for one are applied to the other, but the extent to which methods which *have been selected* for the one are applied to the other. This point provides a rational explanation of the finding by Singleton (1957) that, when learning a new method of work, there was little interference from an established skill among thoroughly experienced subjects, although there was among recent trainees: one can think of the former as having selected methods so precisely adapted to the old method that it contained nothing likely to interfere with the new.

Crossman posed the question of how such selection takes place, and suggested that it might do so in the short-term retention we have already noted as necessary to bridge the gap between the decision to act and the receipt of knowledge of results. He argued that if the short-term memory trace has any tendency to decay or be disrupted with time, quicker methods would automatically be favoured because they would provide more immediate knowledge of results.

In one respect Crossman's theory as stated is almost certainly too rigid. It assumes that a subject selects from a range of discrete, ready-made methods, whereas all we know of complex skilled performance suggests rather that we 'compute' a method unique to each occasion from the data present in the situation combined with various facets of perceptual knowledge, motor experience, aims, strategies and so on. This point does not invalidate the principle of Crossman's theory because these factors can be regarded as jointly defining the methods of which he speaks, and refinement of the computations made with them would be approximately equivalent to selecting among various discrete methods. If this point is granted, it makes Crossman's approach easy to link with a number of other observations about the progress of skill with long-continued practice:

(*a*) On the perceptual side, practice seems to enable the skilled performer to select from among the mass of data impinging on his sense-organs so that he neglects much of what is, to an unskilled person, striking, and reacts strongly to data that a normal observer would fail to notice. Practice may also enable him to make absolute judgments with much greater precision than would otherwise be possible. We have already seen in Chapter 2 that the number of categories of absolute judgment is normally very small but can, at least in the case of musical tones, be very greatly increased in those who possess 'absolute pitch'. The same seems to be true of other sensory judgments, for example the ability to make absolute judgments of colour seems to be much greater than normal among those engaged in some industrial tasks.

(*b*) On the motor side, action becomes more precisely adapted to the requirements of the task, so that reliance on detailed knowledge of the results of each individual action is reduced.

(*c*) In some cases, as we have discussed in Chapter 3 (p. 85), long practice greatly reduces the time required to make a choice of response once a signal has been identified.

(*d*) One of the most striking effects of repeated experience is that a subject recognises ways in which sequences of events hang together and establishes routines of action. In consequence he comes to deal with both incoming data and outgoing action in larger 'units' as we have outlined in Chapter 6 (p. 193).

All these four tendencies with practice are towards increased efficiency in dealing with incoming data and initiating action. It is thus understandable that the skilled man seems to have, as Bartlett (1947) noted, 'all the time in the world', because he has in a very real sense less to do than an unskilled man in order to achieve the same end. He is in consequence less likely to suffer from fatigue, and in many industrial tasks the speed of working will come to be limited by the machine he is using rather than by his own capacities.

At the same time these means of attaining efficiency may endanger 'flexibility' in the sense that methods should differ according to circumstances. All the four tendencies we have listed owe much of their effect to the attainment of uniformity and often to a judicious neglect of minor variations between one situation and another. At best this can result in a routine for a job which does not exactly fit the circumstances, but is good enough and very much quicker than one precisely tailored to the requirements of the situation. At worst it can lead to 'rigidity' in the sense that action is carried through in the face of clear evidence that it is inappropriate.

Our knowledge of the effects of long practice is less than could be desired because laboratory experiments can seldom be carried on long enough for the full effects of practice to be realised, and detailed studies in industry, where long-practised performances are available, are very difficult to make. The questions of how skill develops over the years, of what conditions favour the attainment of efficiency and the retention of flexibility, and of how all these matters are related to events early in training are clearly, however, of the greatest importance to all who are concerned with the design and conduct of training schemes, whether in industry, in athletics, or in any other branch of skilled performance.

X

Individuals and Social Groups

The research surveyed in the foregoing chapters has been within the traditions of experimental and physiological psychology. The study of human performance includes not only this but also work on individual differences, on abnormalities of mental function and on social behaviour. These branches of the subject have in the past developed different concepts and terminology from those of the main stream of experimental work. It seems obvious, however, that all represent different parts of what is fundamentally the same body of knowledge and that all must therefore eventually link up. Many of the ideas developed from the study of skill appear to have applications in these other areas of psychology and could play some part in bringing them together. No attempt will be made to cover the whole field systematically here: instead an approach will be outlined to three areas for which it seems especially appropriate and timely. They are certain facets of *personality*, *motivation* and *social relationships*.

PERSONALITY

When we speak of 'personality' we mean that certain uniformities can be detected running through an individual's behaviour, which typically seem to have no obvious connection with capacity but appear in a variety of circumstances and affect modes of dealing with other people and the environment generally. Research on personality has usually described syndromes of behaviour and devised measures of the extent to which they are displayed by different individuals (e.g. Cattell, 1946). Most of these syndromes or 'personality traits' have been arrived at by factor-analyses of correlations between ratings made by judges or statements of attitude obtained from subjects, and the labelling of traits with names such as 'Rigidity', 'Ascendancy', 'Emotionality', or 'Authoritarianism' has been largely intuitive. With a few striking exceptions, two of which will be discussed later, little attempt has been made to relate such syndromes to other aspects of behaviour and function except to note various correlations as, for example, between scores on personality inventories and certain occupational performances.

Principles outlined in previous chapters suggest a number of possible traits which, if they were proved to run through wide areas of an individual's performance, would provide much more precise behavioural measures of personality than those hitherto available. It would, for example, seem worth finding out how far traits could be defined in terms of individuals' characteristic settings of cutoff in the signal detection model (Price, 1966), or of the balance struck between speed and accuracy, or of the attention paid to feedback from performance, or of tendency to use existing codes to guide behaviour rather than work out new ones. Such traits would, however, almost certainly imply that personality was bound up with capacity and ability: to some extent all these characteristics reflect ability to cope with situations presented – for instance, a low criterion may compensate for poor discrimination if false positives are not serious. Some links between personality and ability have indeed been indicated already by factor-analytic methods: for example Chown (1960) identified three types of 'rigidity' of which one, implying an opinionated approach to life, correlated negatively with intelligence. The argument that the characteristic ways of acting which we call personality must, at least in part, reflect the extent to which capacities and skills developed in the course of experience make those ways possible, has been put forward by Wallace (1966).

Personality, physiological function and behaviour

There have been two notable attempts at explanation of personality in more basic biological terms. The first of these has been the relating of traits to *endocrine functions, localised brain activities and drug effects*. Many of these have been associated with characteristic styles of behaviour (e.g. Mottram, 1944, Uhr and Miller, 1960, Morgan, 1965). How a particular function leads to a corresponding pattern of behaviour has not always been clear, but important progress towards specifying the systems or mechanisms linking them has been made recently (e.g. Eayrs, 1964, Artunkal and Togrol, 1964).

The second example of a personality variable being linked to more fundamental human capacities is provided by the trait of *extraversion-introversion* as defined by Eysenck (1947, 1952) on the basis of studies correlating a wide variety of clinical ratings and test scores. There seem to be clear links between this trait and autonomic activity. Those who score high for extraversion tend to display lower normal levels of autonomic activity than do those with high introversion scores. Davies *et al.* (1963) who produced this finding suggested that a second personality variable, which we may tentatively term *stability-instability* was indicated by change of level when stress was applied. Autonomic activity is, as we have noted in Chapter 8, closely bound up with arousal, and it is now very widely assumed that introverts are more *chronically* aroused than extraverts and that 'unstable' people *become* aroused more easily than stable.

If so, we should expect extraverts to perform many tasks less well than introverts and stable extraverts less well than unstable. Furneaux (1962) found this to be strikingly so in a study of first-year examination results obtained by a group of engineering students. We should also expect unstable introverts to do well under easy conditions, but to be liable to breakdown under severe stress. The evidence in this whole area is complex and not always easy to interpret, but several recent experimental studies have indicated that extraverts perform less well than introverts under conditions in which arousal tends to be poor as, for example, after loss of normal sleep (Wilkinson, 1962, Corcoran, 1965), with tests done early in the day (Colquhoun, 1960, Colquhoun and Corcoran, 1964) and with vigilance tasks (Bakan, 1959, Hogan, 1966). Davies and Hockey (1966) have found the vigilance of extraverts but not of introverts to decline with time and the decline among extraverts was prevented by noise which may be regarded as arousing. Fine (1963) found extraverts to have higher rates of traffic accidents and offences, as would be expected if they were less alert. There is also physiological evidence in the larger amounts of narcotic drugs required to produce a given degree of sedation in more introverted individuals (Claridge and Herrington, 1960) and their tendency to have a stronger salivary reaction to acid in the mouth (Corcoran, 1964). Results are not, however, entirely straightforward. For example, although the performance of extraverts tends to be poorer than that of introverts in the morning, the positions are reversed in the evening. The most plausible reason for this appears to be that arousal level is associated with body temperature and that the diurnal rise and fall of this occurs earlier in introverts, so that their temperature tends to be higher than that of extraverts during the morning and lower during the evening (Blake, 1967).

The chain of evidence is not yet quite complete because it is not clear why the insensitivity resulting from under-arousal should produce the ebullient, outgoing personality associated with extraversion, whereas high sensitivity leads to the quietness and inhibition of introversion: at first sight the opposite is more likely. Probably the simplest explanation is, firstly, that those whose normal level of arousal is low can tolerate noisy environments and lively contacts with other people without being driven into a state of over-arousal – indeed it can be argued that they *need* such stimulation if they are to be optimally aroused to meet the exigencies of life. Secondly, they will tend not to perceive the effects of their own actions or other people's reactions to them, so that they will appear 'thick-skinned' and unheeding of others. In servo terms, their performance will be largely open-loop so that when they are stimulated, the resulting behaviour will tend to be unchecked. Those of them who react strongly to stress will be kept lively and well-adjusted by stimulation from the environment. Those who do not so react will tend to be inert.

People whose normal level of arousal is relatively high will be sensitive and need to keep their levels of external stimulation down if they are not to become over-aroused. They will be perceptive of their own behaviour and of the reactions of others to it, so that in servo terms they will possess closed-loop, negative feedback characteristics. They will thus tend to be quiet and controlled. Their quietness will, however, have a tense, dynamic quality as opposed to sheer inactivity. Provided such introverts do not react very strongly to stress they will be stable and tend to make the most of their intellectual and other capacities. If they do react strongly to stress, or if their normal level of arousal is unusually high, they will appear 'highly strung', and it has been suggested that extreme cases suffer from anxious or depressive neuroses (Davies *et al.*, 1963).

Work by Spence and Taylor (see Taylor, 1956) has suggested that there is an association between *anxiety* and general 'drive'. More recently it has come to be held that this is probably to be regarded as an association between anxiety and some kind of activation or arousal comparable to that between instability and arousal. It seems reasonable to suppose that anxiety, which implies the presence of mental activity resulting from unresolved fears, would tend to go with high levels of both autonomic and brain activity. Evidence that this is so is contained in findings such as those of higher palmar sweating, longer after-effects of viewing a rotating spiral, higher blink rate and, in some cases although not all, higher cardiac activity in more anxious subjects (Haywood and Spielberger, 1966, Levy and Lang, 1966, Harris *et al.*, 1966). The clearest effects of anxiety seem to be on intellectual activity where they seem to follow the Yerkes-Dodson principle (see p. 270):

performance by highly anxious subjects tends to be superior to that of less anxious on easy tasks but inferior on difficult ones which involve the recoding of data (e.g. Tecce, 1965). They seem prone to fall back on familiar codings and routines rather than attempting to form new ones more precisely fitted to the situation confronting them, and so tend to produce stereotyped responses (e.g. Weiss and Silverman, 1966), to be reluctant to seek change (Howard and Diesenhaus, 1965) and to have difficulty in making decisions (Riedel, 1965). We saw in the previous chapter that highly anxious subjects may have difficulty in learning material which conflicts with what has previously been learnt (Spence *et al.*, 1956a, b, Lovaas, 1960a, b, Lee, 1961). The picture is complicated, however, by the fact that the ease or difficulty of any given task depends on the subject's ability. More intelligent subjects are thus likely to be less affected by anxiety because the task itself will engender less arousal for them than it would for those less able. The level of activation produced by the sum of the effects of the task and of anxiety will thus be optimum with a more difficult task in the case of abler subjects than with those less gifted (Denny, 1966).

It must be emphasised that personality tests yielding scores for extraversion-introversion, anxiety and other traits are relatively crude instruments, and that measures of autonomic activity and other indices of activation and arousal are far from precise, so that any tie-up between the two types of measure can at present be made only in very broad terms. Further, the overall scores of personality tests cover many subtly different patterns of answers, and the autonomic reactions to any given stress vary in detail from one subject to another and from one stressful situation to another in the same subject (Lacey *et al.*, 1953, Lacey and Lacey, 1958, Kling and Schlosberg, 1961). If any unitary factor lies behind these varied patterns, it should perhaps be identified as a general *sensitivity* and *reactivity* which shows itself in different forms according to the operation of several other factors as yet not fully understood.

Capacity and environment

The analysis we have offered of these personality traits has essentially been in terms of fundamental capacities and characteristics of the organism, embodied in a dynamic *system* of which the individual is part together with his environment and other people in it. To 'explain' such traits we have therefore two fundamental tasks: firstly to identify the underlying capacities and characteristics, and secondly to specify the system in which their effects are displayed.

L

The operation of such systems to produce personality effects is further illustrated by some of the personality changes that come with advancing age. Let us consider three examples:

(*a*) While most of the personality characteristics seen in old age have probably been present throughout adult life (Reichard *et al.*, 1962), they tend to become exaggerated with advancing years. In many cases this seems to result from a change of capacity leading to lack of *control*. For example, it is well known that some of those who suffer from deafness develop mild paranoid symptoms, coming to believe that the people they can see but not hear talking are criticising or plotting against them. What appears to happen is that when sensory input is cut off the interpretative aspects of perception are left uncontrolled. The subject's beliefs then run along the lines of his underlying interpretative tendencies, and if these are in the direction of insecurity and suspicion, paranoid thinking results.

(*b*) Changing capacity with age may lead to *compensatory adjustments* in the method, manner or strategy of performance which tend to minimise adverse effects and optimise the use of capacities that remain (Griew and Tucker, 1958). Perhaps the clearest example is in certain types of sensory-motor performance where speed and accuracy are compensatory in the sense that one may be gained at the expense of the other (Brown, see Welford, 1958, pp. 67–68, Welford *et al.*, 1963). In these cases older people tend to choose accuracy, producing more deliberate and meticulous performances than those of younger. As a result they waste less time correcting errors, so that their overall achievement changes less than measures of speed alone would suggest: indeed in some industrial and other everyday situations where accuracy is vital, older people may, on balance, be at an advantage.

(*c*) Such compensatory changes imply attempts to keep one facet of performance *constant* while accepting changes in others. An older man may concentrate on a smaller range of activities and so become narrow in interests and restricted in outlook. Many of those in industry seem to maintain achievement in later middle age by stepping up the effort they make, working more continuously and with greater concentration, and in consequence come to show the over-arousal, impatience and intolerance that result from chronic stress. On the other hand, some older people appear to try to keep effort constant as well as achievement by recruiting the activities of others to supplement their own, and so become demanding and dependent.

One of the most interesting potential applications of the approach which has been outlined here is the analysis of *responsibility* and its personal counterparts *reliability* and *integrity*. Jaques (1956) suggested that responsibility could be measured by the length of time for which a man had to work without supervisory check. We might generalise such a time span to include not only supervisory checks but *any* knowledge of the results of his actions. On this view, two facets of capacity are likely to be involved within the overall servo system. Firstly, since a task is seldom fully dismissed from the mind until its successful completion has been recognised, a long span of responsibility will often imply that a man will not be able to concentrate on one task at a time but will have to deal with several incomplete tasks almost simultaneously, retaining enough data about each to be able to pick it up quickly when need be, while avoiding confusion between one task and another. Secondly he will, for the duration of the span, have to function openloop and, if he is to do this successfully, his performance will have to be accurate enough to be consistently effective without being checked by observation of results. Responsible performance in this sense must therefore be predictable within the limits of accuracy required. The need to take action with no immediate prospect of its being checked also involves special problems of motivation. We shall refer to these during the discussion of motives to which we now turn.

MOTIVES

It is obvious that, for any action to take place, the organism must have the necessary capacity and that there must be an occasion provided by environmental circumstances. It is commonly argued, however, that these are not enough and that there must, in addition, be some *drive* or *motive*. Thus, for example, the mere capacity to eat, coupled with the presence of food, is not enough to ensure that eating will take place: there must also be hunger or some social pressure to partake.

Several theories of motivation have attempted to trace all motives back to primary biological necessities, either for individual survival, such as food, water or air, or for the continuation of the race, such as sexual intercourse and care of the young. Normally, however, a person does not eat in order to preserve life or engage in sexual activity with a view to preserving the race. Motives may occasionally be of this kind at a highly sophisticated level, but are usually of a more sensual nature: a person eats because of sensations of hunger and enjoys food for its taste, smell and perhaps appearance. The biological necessity of eating is not in mind, and the sensory gratifications precede any satisfaction of bodily need: hunger is reduced long before food is digested and made available to the tissues of the body. In short, the mechanism of biological motivation is of a more immediate nature: conditions in various tissues and neural centres put the organism into a state in which it is restless until particular sensory stimuli or perceptual data have been received.

Many motives such as interests in work or hobbies, play activities and desires for social contacts seem, however, far removed from any biological mechanisms of this kind, or at least from the traditional biological appetites. Ways out of this difficulty which have been proposed, such as that activities which once served a direct biological purpose may become 'functionally autonomous' so that they are continued for their own sake (Allport, 1937), or that the achievement of sub-goals on the way to primary satisfactions may itself be satisfying (Hull, 1943), have an *ad hoc* quality which destroys their explanatory value. The problem is further complicated by the fact that the motives behind any action are usually mixed, and the ways of satisfying any one motive are many, so that an activity which starts for one reason may be continued for quite others: for example, a man may join a sports club because he enjoys exercise and may continue as a member for the sake of the friendships he has formed.

Perhaps the most radical solution is that proposed by Woodworth (1958) who suggested that the organism possesses an inherent and fundamental tendency to 'deal with its environment' and to develop its capacity for doing so. He indeed argued that this was the one fundamental motive and that biological appetites, such as those for food, water and sex 'use' this tendency, and are thus essentially subsidiary. This approach has been developed subsequently to some extent (e.g. McCall, 1963) but not as much as it appears to deserve. It has the important implication that motives will be linked to abilities in the sense that the most successful dealing with the environment will be through the skills at the subject's command (White, 1959). Hebron (1966) has amassed a wealth of data to show that, all through the span of human life, capacity, motivation and learning to go hand in hand, each depending for its development upon the progress of the others.

Whatever view is correct, the listing of motives and placing of them in orders of importance according to circumstances is an immensely laborious task, so that it is worth asking whether there are ways in which it could be by-passed – whether principles could be formulated which would transcend the several motives hitherto regarded as basic. In particular, it seems possible that if we knew *how* motives operate, knowledge of *what* they are would become of secondary importance.

Servo concepts of motivation

An obvious starting point is that whenever the organism seeks to satisfy a need, whether biological or social, primary or derived, alone or in co-operation with others, there is an example of the classical servo system in which action is initiated by signals arising from the need and is modified by the results of the organism's own activity. It is generally agreed that the initial signals give rise to general activity or arousal, together with some more specifically directed action. Both depend in part on the inherited structure of the nervous system but both, especially the latter, depend also on techniques and skills acquired in the course of experience.

Many features of motivation are straightforwardly accounted for by the simple servo model. To take only one example; if a subject is deprived of food, water or air his actions become more and more vigorous as the deprivation becomes more acute until physical exhaustion supervenes. Similarly, in a number of more complex human activities such as problem-solving and memory, the level of arousal, vigour of action and readiness of recall rise with increased incentive to the extent that in extreme cases achievement may be impaired by over-activation (e.g. Toppen, 1965, Weiner and Walker, 1966, Nakamura and Krudis, 1967).

Four elaborations to the simple servo model are, however, necessary.

(*a*) Several variables may combine to determine the effective signal strength. In particular, the effect of any discrepancy between present state and optimum seems to be inversely related to the effort, difficulty or other unpleasantness involved in correcting it; or to put the point in more traditional terms, the incentive effect of a reward is partly offset by the cost of achieving it. The effect is, however, complicated in some cases by the fact that effort seems to enhance the value of the reward eventually achieved (for a review see Lewis, 1965). Readiness to undertake an action may nevertheless be conceived as depending in part on some kind of *ratio*, or *difference*, between *result and effort or other cost*. Such a relationship, besides providing an obvious explanation for the common reluctance to undertake laborious or difficult tasks, suggests a reason for certain types of delinquent behaviour, such as *vandalism*, since the ratio of effect to effort is usually much greater with destructive than with constructive activities.

(*b*) A distinction needs to be drawn between cases in which each action taken contributes to the reduction of the conditions which initiated activity, and cases in which a whole chain of actions has to be completed before any reduction is achieved. To the first, the simple servo model applies well in the sense that motivation tends to diminish as activity proceeds: the reduction in the rate of eating towards the end of a large meal has its counterpart at the laboratory level in the lowering of arousal as learning proceeds (Freedman *et al.*, 1966).

In the second type of case, however, the speed and vigour of performance tend gradually to *increase* up to the point at which the goal is attained and action ceases. How this positive feedback effect arises is not at present clear, and any or all of several possible reasons for it may be true. It could, perhaps, be an additional effect of the inverse relationship between incentive and effort: at the beginning of a long chain of actions the effort to be expended before the final result is achieved will be large, but it will progressively diminish as the task proceeds.

The classical explanation is based on the finding from many experiments that the incentive effect of a reward diminishes if it is delayed after the completion of the achievement for which it is given (Hull, 1943). On this view the gap, in terms of time or intervening events, before obtaining the reward is relatively great at the beginning of the task and the incentive effect should therefore be low. As the task proceeds the gap shortens and the incentive effect should correspondingly rise.

Two other very different types of explanation are, perhaps, possible. One lies in the incentive effect of knowledge of results of action we have already discussed in Chapters 8 and 9 (pp. 276 and 308): knowledge that the goal was being approached should have a stimulating effect which would progressively enhance performance so long as the conditions originally giving rise to it remained in being. The other explanation lies in the finding that successful achievement of one task lowers, and failure raises, the level of tension with which a subsequent task is approached (Leshner, 1961): in these terms all action short of the goal would be a kind of temporary failure which would tend to raise the level of tension in the subject.

All these explanations, except perhaps the last, can account for the well-known difficulty of taking action before the need for it has become pressing and, in so far as this is a feature of responsible behaviour, emphasise that the corresponding facets of personality – reliability and integrity – depend on the responsiveness of the human servo system unaided by regenerative loops.

(*c*) It is implicit in the view of extraversion-introversion which we have outlined earlier that the human servo reacts not only to external stimuli but also to its *own state of activity*. Essentially the same point has been made, as we have already noted in Chapter 8, by Hebb (1955) and by Berlyne (1960) who regard the organism as trying to maintain an optimum state of arousal by seeking stimulation if under-aroused and quiet if over-aroused, although whether the optimum sought should be defined in terms of arousal-level or throughput of information or some other variable is a question meriting further thought. The result in any case seems to be that, when overloaded, the subject spontaneously sheds part of the load by neglecting certain aspects of his task (e.g. Davis, 1948) or by retiring from it altogether. When underloaded, however, he craves for stimulation, as in the conditions of extreme monotony produced by the now famous experiments on perceptual deprivation (for a review see Zubek, 1964, see also Petrie *et al.*, 1960, Jones *et al.*, 1961, Zuckerman and Haber, 1965, Smith and Myers, 1966). In everyday life, people seem clearly to prefer a moderate level of activity to either a very high level or complete idleness, and tend to fill their time with social contacts, games, puzzles and suchlike pursuits if there is nothing more pressing to do. Differences between individuals in the levels of activity and nature of pursuits required to avoid boredom suggests that the optimum level rises with intellectual capacity (Wyatt and Fraser, 1929), although this may not always be apparent because much of the activity of more able people is in the form of thinking unaccompanied by overt behaviour.

(*d*) In any real-life performance there are not one but *many servo loops operating simultaneously*. We have already in Chapter 6 (p. 193), mentioned the skilled turner who, moving the tool of his lathe over the face of a casting, is ordering and co-ordinating a series of actions which jointly accomplish the task of machining the face concerned: this in turn is only one of several involved in the larger task of machining the whole casting, and the casting may be only one of several required for a single job of construction. There are, in short, a whole hierarchy of tasks of different magnitudes and time scales all being performed simultaneously, the larger embracing the smaller and controlling the tempo, accuracy, order and manner in which they are carried out. It seems fair to argue that each larger task provides the immediate *motive* for its component smaller tasks.

The hierarchical principle does not stop at the individual unit of production. If we were to ask the turner why he was engaged on his job of construction, he might reply that it was part of his work at the factory, that this in turn was a means of earning a high wage, that his earnings would enable him to buy a car, and that this would enhance the opportunities enjoyed by his family. Each stage in this series can again be regarded as a task and as motivating those which lie below. It will be noted that the higher order tasks are of a social nature while the lower are more individual, but they shade into each other without any discontinuity of principle. In essentially the same way as a construction job co-ordinates skilled action, the higher, social tasks co-ordinate wider aspects of behaviour, determining priorities such as that money should be saved for a car instead of being spent on entertainment, deciding the choice of a job offering high wages and overtime rather than comfort or security, and so on.

Such a method of conceiving motivation may at first sight appear excessively complex, yet it is really very much simpler than many methods currently used. Instead of proceeding from a hypothetical list of basic needs downwards to their manifestations in detailed behaviour, we are free to give our main attention to the more immediate objectives of action and to the tracing of these in the service of larger units of performance. We still do not, of course, know *a priori* what it is that ultimately gives direction to a subject's dealing with his environment, but for many practical issues, we do not need to do so: it is enough to identify motives in immediate individual, family and social aims and to examine the precise ways in which they control behaviour. When a more fundamental identification is required, the tracing of reasons for action forward to larger tasks provides a promising method of getting at it. Such a procedure would probably reveal that the simple reflexes which must be regarded as 'ends in themselves' have their analogues in more highly organised behaviour: tracing forward might often carry us a very long way, but would eventually arrive at activities which seem to have no real aim beyond themselves. When such a point is reached we have a plausible candidate for recognition as a basic human motive.

In these terms the effects of any incentive are likely to be complex since they will occur at several different levels, but they will nevertheless be identifiable. Let us look, by way of example, at the possible nature and causes of *job satisfaction*. We should expect that an important factor in the satisfaction given by a job would be the extent to which its feedback loops were closed and revealed substantial results of actions taken: in plain language, one facet of job satisfaction is the extent to which a man's actions have a recognisable effect on his work or work situation. There will thus be an immediate satisfaction in operating large and powerful machines, and a more subtle, longer-term satisfaction in being able to influence the organisation within which one's work is done – it is, indeed, tempting to speculate that strikes and other industrial actions which bring powerful feedback effects arise when the feedback inherent in the job is deficient.

Satisfaction will, however, depend not only on the characteristics of the job itself, but also on the extent to which it ministers to broader personal aims – it is well known how a compelling long-term purpose can bring profound satisfaction from an otherwise tedious or distasteful routine; conversely, the fulfilment of such an aim can greatly affect the satisfaction given by everyday activities. Probably the most frequent example is the loss of a woman's interest in work when she marries or starts a family. Other examples occur when a man or woman reaches a coveted position to which their lives have long been oriented: the completion of such a 'lifetime' task can leave a person devoid of any strong motives until he discovers a fresh major objective. Perhaps it is not too fanciful to suggest that wider satisfaction in life lies in the pursuit of tasks which are sufficiently broad in scope to give coherence to the lesser aims and achievements of daily living, while having a reasonable chance of fulfilment and replacement each decade or so during the adult years.

SOCIAL RELATIONSHIPS AND BEHAVIOUR

Most of the studies surveyed in previous chapters have been of a subject confronting a piece of apparatus (taking 'apparatus' in a wide sense) which presented a task, and the total performance of subject and apparatus together has depended on the characteristics of both. Such interaction between man and machine is seldom discussed explicitly in relation to laboratory experiments although it has figured prominently in some recent treatments of industrial work (e.g. Singleton *et al.*, 1967).

It seems fair to argue that there is a close analogy between such man-machine systems and social groups in which individuals are in communication with one another, and that knowledge we already possess of the first could help in understanding the second. Let us take a straightforward, perhaps obvious, example by comparing the relations of, on the one hand, an operator with a semi-automatic process plant and, on the other, of a foreman with a skilled tradesman in a production shop. Just as a process plant and its operator form a closed-loop servo-system in which each action by one influences the other and the behaviour of the two in combination develops with time, so the same is true of any social situation in which there is two-way communication between the individuals concerned. All the well-known problems of information-transmission are present in such 'conversations', whether between man and machine or man and man. The limited capacity of both human and machine communication channels will set maximum rates at which messages can be accurately received and generated, the maximum depending on factors such as the range of possible messages that may be conveyed and the extent to which each is clearly discriminable from others and free from irrelevancies and random disturbance. Ease of communication will be profoundly affected by the receiver's understanding of the 'language' in which the information is coded and by the extent to which knowledge and familiarity enable decisions and instructions to be given in terms of broad sequences of events and routines of action, rather than about individual detailed items. Difficulties of short-term retention may arise when data are not presented all at once but spread over a period of time, and all the effects of continued performance such as learning, fatigue, loss of vigilance and boredom observed in machine operation have their close analogues in human interaction.

This approach has been implicit in a number of attempts to simulate the interaction between two or more individuals in terms of mathematical models (e.g. Restle and Davis, 1962, Richards, 1962) or by programming computers (e.g. Siegel and Wolf, 1962, Gullahorn and Gullahorn, 1963, Loehlin, 1965) working in each case only with characteristics of individuals and of tasks and without any additional characteristics attributable to groups as such. Probably the most direct example of the present approach has been in the work of Argyle and his colleagues on *social skills*. They have attempted not only to identify the principles common to social and sensory-motor performances, but also to study in detail the behaviour of subjects in social situations to see how skill is shown in the strategies used during conversation (Argyle, 1967, Kendon, 1967).

The same methods of analysis seem to be potentially powerful tools for the study of larger scale social organisations such as in factories or offices (Welford, 1960b, 1962b, 1966, Stager, 1966). For example, the study of *communications* in an organisation would involve asking a range of detailed questions about each individual in the chain. What is the variety of decisions as well as the number he has to make? How many sources of data does he have to co-ordinate? How directly do the data he receives indicate the appropriate action to take? Are all the data for a given decision present at one time, or do some have to be carried in memory until other data arrive? Are the data clear and precise, or may they be unreliable or vacillating? Even if the average rate at which decisions have to be made is well within a man's capacity, are there periods of overload? How far can he differentiate the results of his actions from those of actions by others? How long does he have to wait for feedback to arrive? Does he receive several feedbacks at different times? If so, do the indications of those which come quickly differ from those which are slower – for example, does action have to be taken which is immediately unpopular in order to bring long-term benefits?

Such communication can, to some extent, be measured in terms of information in a manner similar to that of Eq. 3.6 (p. 65). To calculate the information transmitted by a particular person in the chain we can make a table with, say, a column for each type of incoming message and a row for each type of action taken. We calculate $\Sigma p_S \log \dfrac{1}{p_S}$ the different columns, then $\Sigma p_R \log \dfrac{1}{p_R}$ for the different row, and finally $\Sigma p_{SR} \log \dfrac{1}{p_{SR}}$ individual cell. The information transmitted is then calculated in exactly the same way as the information gained in Eq. 3.6 by adding the first two sums and subtracting the third. To assess the load on the person concerned we need to consider the average and distribution of information transmitted per message in relation to the rate and intervals at which the messages arrive. More elaborate analyses can be made in the manner outlined by writers on multi-dimensional information transmission (e.g. Attneave, 1959, Garner, 1962). An interesting application of this type of analysis to reports of faults and actions taken to deal with them has been outlined by Leuba (1967).

Some further applications

To illustrate the possibilities of this approach further we shall apply it briefly to four other areas either of well recognised concern to industry or of traditional interest to social psychology. It cannot be claimed that any radically new conclusions are reached in any of these cases, but the treatment suggests ways of looking at some present problems which open up new methods of tackling them.

(a) *Flexibility of an organisation.* If a working group is to be adaptable to changing conditions, or is even to maintain a high standard in stable conditions, it must not only have clear instructions, but *feedback of information* about the quality of performance attained. This can be achieved to a limited extent by observation, on the part of a foreman or manager, of the end product of the group he controls, but much fuller information will obviously be obtained when there is rapid and easy two-way communication between manager and managed which gives detailed insight into difficulties encountered and ideas about how they might be overcome. In stable conditions, once the methods for a job have been established, it is possible to run on satisfactorily for an appreciable time without such feedback, and there may indeed be a temptation to avoid it as an unwelcome addition to the information load imposed by the job. When, however, conditions are rapidly changing, or in the early stages of developing an operation, such feedback will give a flexibility and rapidity of adjustment not otherwise possible.

(*b*) *Behaviour of crowds.* One of the traditionally difficult problems of social psychology is to account for the uniformity of the behaviour of crowds. Accounts in terms such as 'social facilitation' are not truly explanatory, since they are essentially *ad hoc*, and thus little more than descriptive. The present terms, however, provide the simple hypothesis that, when the members of a crowd are all acting alike, the sight and sound of others provides each individual with a kind of augmented feedback of his own behaviour. This would be especially so if the crowd were, say, shouting slogans in unison. It has its analogue on a smaller scale in the feeling of 'unusual power' reported by crews of rowing eights when their boats are going well: when all are pulling precisely together each man is said to get the feeling that the whole result is due to his own effort. The seeming ratio of effect to effort is thus greatly enhanced, and it is reasonable to suppose that the satisfaction gained from the activity is correspondingly increased.

How far other aspects of crowd behaviour could be accounted for in the same terms is not at present clear, but seems to be worth serious study. For example, how far is the effect of size of crowd to be explained in terms of signal-to-noise ratio, in the sense that, as the crowd becomes larger, augmented feedback increases in strength, and individual differences of behaviour tending to blur the unison are smoothed out?

(*c*) *Social norms.* The broad principles of coding outlined in Chapter 6 seem especially applicable to social norms and customs. These essentially represent the codifying of insights and building of routines which avoid complex *ad hoc* decisions by providing ready-made solutions to recurrent problems, and enable individuals to predict the behaviour of others. The learning of such norms and customs is an important process in the structuring of individual perception and behaviour. Modifications to norms and customs take place in the course of time, presumably as a response to changing circumstances or fresh insights into methods of dealing with the problems of living. There is, however, usually a substantial time-lag before adjustments become effective, so that they are often out of phase with the current needs of society and oscillation may occur with swings of over-adjustment and readjustment taking place over a period of years.

We have already noted that the building-up of routines in individuals as the result of experience makes for greater efficiency in stable conditions but greater rigidity in the face of change. The gradual accumulation of norms and customs in a society seems likely to have similar effects, making a mature society more stable, since fewer decisions of policy are open to question, but less capable of absorbing new ideas quickly than societies in which rules of conduct are less developed and entrenched.

(*d*) *Leadership and size of group.* Harcourt (1959) has suggested that the number of people one man can lead will depend on the amount of information they jointly generate: if they produce too much, the leader will be overloaded and will be liable to take hasty, ill-considered decisions. The amount of information individual members produce will depend on the nature of the job, the conditions under which it is done and their personal characteristics. If they are performing a routine job under stable conditions and are of even temperament, one man will be able to lead a large number. If, however, the work is not of a routine nature so that it requires constant detailed attention, or if various members are doing different jobs, or if working conditions are unpredictable or there are unstable personalities among the team, the maximum size of group that one man can lead effectively will be reduced.

Consideration of the capacities of both leader and group members together suggests possible reasons for relationships which have been claimed to exist between morale and size of working group. It has been urged that a small group is more 'democratic', while a large group tends to generate an 'authoritarian' leadership which is less acceptable. Evidence about which type of organisation leads to better results and greater job-satisfaction is, however, conflicting. A possible reconciliation is provided by the results likely to follow if a group generates more information than a single leader can deal with. In the terms we have been using, a 'democratic' system means that there is a possibility of effective feedback from group members to leader, whereas an 'authoritarian' system means that members of the group are unable to influence the leader's decisions. As we have seen in Chapter 8, a common reaction to overload in laboratory tasks is that the subject sheds part of the load by ignoring some of the signals he should observe and omitting some of the actions he should take. Usually these are the less frequent ones, so that the subject concentrates on the main features of his task and ignores side-issues. In this way he often manages to put up a reasonable, although not, of course, wholly adequate performance. One way in which an overloaded leader could readily 'shed load' would be to rely on routines established in his group to keep it functioning while ignoring feedback from members. This would in effect mean that leadership would become 'authoritarian'. It would doubtless have little adverse effect for a time, so at first it would seem to be working well, but an important means of recognising the need for modification or change would have been lost, and the group's performance would thus tend to become progressively less effective.

On the other hand, the alternative procedures available when a group becomes too large for one person to lead are not without difficulties of their own. There seem to be two main possibilities: firstly members of the group can be required to refer particular problems to one of a range of specialists added to the group as deputy leaders. The disadvantage of this system is that individual members may have to make difficult decisions about which specialist to go to, and may find themselves going a tedious round from one specialist to another until the right one to deal with their particular problem is found. They may well feel that a reasonably benevolent authoritarianism is preferable.

Alternatively, the group can be split into smaller sub-groups, each with a leader who can call on specialists and is responsible in turn to a leader higher in a hierarchy. In this way the members are still able to refer all their problems to one person, and although the difficulty of getting the right specialist service may merely be transferred to him, the morale and effectiveness of the group as a whole is likely to be higher than if such decisions have to be made by individual members. The superiority of the second system is likely to increase with the frequency of problems requiring decisions for individual members. Thus, with a routine operation under stable conditions, there may be little to choose between the effectiveness of the two methods of organisation, but if technical and management functions are highly complex the second could be expected to yield better results.

Towards unification of the human sciences

Over and above particular applications, perhaps the main importance of the approach which has been outlined here is that it links the study of human performance, and of the physiological mechanisms underlying it, to studies of social behaviour. Psychology occupies a position intermediate between the social sciences on the one hand and the older human biological disciplines on the other. In his studies of individual human behaviour the psychologist has been forced from time to time to recognise that certain social factors may exert important effects. On the other hand, he knows that he is studying a biological organism whose behaviour is based on a nervous system reacting via sense organs and muscles with the environment, so that he must sooner or later look to physiology for his explanations. Both physiologist and psychologist recognise that these explanations cannot at present be supplied, and indeed that the goal is not fully attainable because the detailed breakdown of behaviour into physiological terms would be impossibly complex.

The need to maintain contact nevertheless remains. The division between the two disciplines is in a sense arbitrary, in terms of the size of unit studied – between, for psychology, the whole organism and, for physiology, individual cells and structures. In many ways this division is both convenient and necessary, nevertheless there are occasions upon which consideration by the psychologist of the detailed mechanism of the human brain and body can tie together many facts at first sight disconnected or even discordant. At the same time, the physiologist considering the action of large masses of nerve cells has often to resort to the study of behaviour at the level normally within the realm of psychology. There is thus a two-way traffic between the disciplines in which psychology seeks theory and explanation downwards, and physiology seeks the testing of hypotheses upwards in the scale of functional units.

It is reasonable to suggest that psychology can and should play the same role in relation to social studies as physiology does in relation to psychology, providing the means of conceptualising the detailed mechanisms of the behaviour of groups and organised social units. For psychology to play this role, however, the principle must be recognised that social units are composed of individuals, and that it is their interaction with their environment and each other that produces social phenomena. Such recognition implies that accounts of social phenomena need to be broken down from steady states or slow changes into *processes* in which, ideally, chains of detailed individual actions can be described. It is often impossible to make this kind of breakdown, just as it is impossible to analyse individual behaviour into detailed physiological processes, but the attempt needs to be made, and even if it fails for a time, the ultimate aim must be acknowledged. The psychologist must in turn remember that, just as psychological findings have sometimes pointed to matters requiring physiological research, so social studies are likely to direct his attention to problems in his own field that might otherwise pass unnoticed.

The opportunities for co-operation appear to be very substantial. A sustained attempt to exploit them by the disciplines concerned would be very much to their mutual advantage, lending to social studies an often needed precision and to psychology a desirable perspective.

References

ABBEY, D. S. (1964) 'Control-display-subject interaction and performance on a complex perceptual-motor task', *Ergonomics*, **7**, 151–164.

ADAMS, J. A. (1954) 'Multiple versus single problem training in human problem solving', *J. exp. Psychol.*, **48**, 15–18.

ADAMS, J. A. (1955) 'A source of decrement in psychomotor performance', *J. exp. Psychol.*, **49**, 390–394.

ADAMS, J. A. (1962) 'Test of the hypothesis of psychological refractory period', *J. exp. Psychol.*, **64**, 280–287.

ADAMS, J. A., and BOULTER, L. R. (1962) 'An evaluation of the activationist hypothesis of human vigilance', *J. exp. Psychol.*, **64**, 495–504.

ADAMS, J. A., and CHAMBERS, R. W. (1962) 'Response to simultaneous stimulation of two sense modalities', *J. exp. Psychol.*, **63**, 198–206.

ADAMS, J. A., and DIJKSTRA, SANNE (1966) 'Short-term memory for motor responses', *J. exp. Psychol.*, **71**, 314–318.

ADAMS, J. A., STENSON, H. H., and HUMES, J. M. (1961) 'Monitoring of complex visual displays: 2. Effects of visual load and response complexity on human vigilance', *Human Factors*, **3**, 213–221.

ADISESHIAH, W. (1951) Unpublished Ph.D. Thesis, University of Cambridge.

ADRIAN, E. D. (1947) *The Physical Background of Perception*. Oxford University Press.

AIKEN, L. R., and LICHTENSTEIN, M. (1964) 'Reaction times to regularly recurring visual stimuli', *Percep. mot. Skills*, **18**, 713–720.

ALLPORT, G. W. (1937) *Personality: a Psychological Interpretation*. New York: Henry Holt & Co.

ALLUISI, E. A., and HALL, T. J. (1963) 'Declines in auditory vigilance during periods of high multiple-task activity', *Percep. mot. Skills*, **16**, 739–740.

AMMONS, R. B. (1947) 'Acquisition of motor skill: 1. Quantitative analysis and theoretical formulation', *Psychol. Rev.* **54**, 263–281.

ANDERSON, NANCY S. (1960) 'Poststimulus cuing in immediate memory', *J. exp. Psychol.*, **60**, 216–221.

ANDERSON, NANCY S., and LEONARD, J. A. (1958) 'The recognition, naming and reconstruction of visual figures as a function of contour redundancy', *J. exp. Psychol.*, **56**, 262–270.

ANDREASSI, J. L. (1965) 'Effects of induced muscle tension and auditory stimulation on tachistoscopic perception', *Percep. mot. Skills*, **20**, 829–841.

ANDREASSI, J. L. (1966) 'Skin-conductance and reaction-time in a continuous auditory monitoring task', *Amer. J. Psychol.*, **79**, 470–474.

ANNETT, J. (1959) 'Learning a pressure under conditions of immediate and delayed knowledge of results', *Quart. J. exp. Psychol.*, **11**, 3–15.

ANNETT, J. (1966a) 'A note on Davis's refutation of the expectancy hypothesis', *Quart. J. exp. Psychol.*, **18**, 179–180.

ANNETT, J. (1966b) 'Training for perceptual skills', *Ergonomics*, **9**, 459–468.

ANNETT, J., GOLBY, C. W., and KAY, H. (1958) 'The measurement of elements in an assembly task – the information output of the human motor system', *Quart. J. exp. Psychol.*, **10**, 1–11.

ANNETT, J., and KAY, H. (1957) 'Knowledge of results and "skilled performance" ', *Occupational Psychol.*, **31**, 69–79.

ANTROBUS, J. S., and SINGER, J. L. (1964) 'Visual signal detection as a function of sequential variability of simultaneous speech, *J. exp. Psychol.*, **68**, 603–610.

ARCHER, E. J., KENT, G. W., and MOTE, F. A. (1956) 'Effect of long-term practice and time-on-target information feedback on a complex tracking task', *J. exp. Psychol.* **51**, 103–112.

ARCHER, E. J., and NAMIKAS, G. A. (1958) 'Pursuit rotor performance as a function of delay of information feedback', *J. exp. Psychol.*, **56**, 325–327.

ARGYLE, M. (1967) *The Psychology of Interpersonal Behaviour*. Harmondsworth: Penguin Books.

ARTUNKAL, S., and TOGROL, B. (1964) 'Psychological studies in hyperthyroidism', in *Brain-Thyroid Relationships* (ed. Margaret P. Cameron and Maere O'Connor). Ciba Foundation Study Group No. 18. London: J. & A. Churchill, pp. 92–102.

ASH, I. E. (1914) 'Fatigue and its effects upon control', *Arch. Psychol.*, **4**, No. 31.

ATKINSON, R. C. (1963) 'A variable sensitivity theory of signal detection', *Psychol. Rev.*, **70**, 91–106.

ATTNEAVE, F. (1950) 'Dimensions of similarity', *Amer. J. Psychol.*, **63**, 516–556.

ATTNEAVE, F. (1954) 'Some informational aspects of visual perception', *Psychol. Rev.*, **61**, 183–193.

ATTNEAVE, F. (1957) 'Transfer of experience with a class-schema to identification-learning of patterns and shapes', *J. exp. Psychol.*, **54**, 81–88.

ATTNEAVE, F. (1959) *Applications of Information Theory to Psychology*. New York: Henry Holt & Co.

AUDLEY, R. J., and WALLIS, C. P. (1964) 'Response instructions and the speed of relative judgments. 1. Some experiments on brightness discrimination', *Brit. J. Psychol.*, **55**, 59–73.

AVERBACH, E., and SPERLING, G. (1961) 'Short term storage of information in vision', in *Information Theory* (ed. C. Cherry). London: Butterworth.

BADDELEY, A. D. (1964a) 'Language-habits, S-R compatibility and verbal learning', *Amer. J. Psychol.*, **77**, 463–468.

BADDELEY, A. D. (1964b) 'Semantic and acoustic similarity in short-term memory', *Nature*, **204**, 1116–1117.

BADDELEY, A. D. (1966a) 'The influence of acoustic and semantic similarity on long-term memory for word sequences', *Quart. J. exp. Psychol.*, **18**, 302–309.

BADDELEY, A. D. (1966b) 'Short-term memory for word sequences as a function of acoustic, semantic and formal similarity', *Quart. J. exp. Psychol.*, **18**, 362–365.

BADDELEY, A. D., CONRAD, R., and HULL, A. J. (1965) 'Predictability and immediate memory for consonant sequences', *Quart. J. exp. Psychol.*, **17**, 175–177.

BAHRICK, H. P., BENNETT, W. F., and FITTS, P. M. (1955a) 'Accuracy of positioning responses as a function of spring loading in a control', *J. exp. Psychol.*, **49**, 437–444.

BAHRICK, H. P., FITTS, P. M., and SCHNEIDER, R. (1955b) 'Reproduction of simple movements as a function of factors influencing proprioceptive feedback', *J. exp. Psychol.*, **49**, 445–454.

BAHRICK, H. P., NOBLE, M., and FITTS, P. M. (1954) 'Extra-task performance as a measure of learning a primary task', *J. exp. Psychol.*, **48**, 298–302.

BAHRICK, H. P., and SHELLY, CAROLYN (1958) 'Time sharing as an index of automatization', *J. exp. Psychol.*, **56**, 288–293.

BAKAN, P. (1952) 'Preliminary tests of vigilance for verbal material', *U.S.A.F. Human Resources Research Centre*, Research Note 52–7, Lakeland Air Base.

BAKAN, P. (1959) 'Extroversion-introversion and improvement in an auditory vigilance task', *Brit. J. Psychol.*, **50**, 325–332.

BAKER, C. H. (1959) 'Attention to visual displays during a vigilance task: 2. Maintaining the level of vigilance', *Brit. J. Psychol.*, **50**, 30–36.

BAKER, C. H. (1960) 'Factors affecting radar operator efficiency', *J. Inst. Navig.*, **13**, 148–163.

BAKER, C. H. (1961) 'Maintaining the level of vigilance by means of knowledge of results about a secondary vigilance task', *Ergonomics*, **4**, 311–316.

BAKER, C. H., and YOUNG, P. (1960) 'Feedback during training and retention of motor skills', *Canad. J. Psychol.*, **14**, 257–264.

BAKER, KATHERINE E., WYLIE, RUTH C., and GAGNE, R. M. (1950) 'Transfer of training to a motor skill as a function of variation in rate of response', *J. exp. Psychol.*, **40**, 721–732.

BAKER, R. A., and WARE, J. R. (1966) 'The relationship between vigilance and monotonous work', *Ergonomics*, **9**, 109–114.

BARMACK, J. E. (1939) 'The length of the work period and the work curve', *J. exp. Psychol.*, **25**, 109–115.

BARRY, E. (1964) 'Effects of prolonged deliberation on psychophysical judgment', *Amer. J. Psychol.*, **77**, 270–275.

BARTLETT, F. C. (1932) *Remembering*. Cambridge Univ. Press.

BARTLETT, F. C. (1943) 'Fatigue following highly skilled work', *Proc. Roy. Soc. B.*, **131**, 247–257.

BARTLETT, F. C. (1947) 'The measurement of human skill', *Brit. med. J.*, i, 835 and 877. Reprinted (1948) *Occupational Psychol.*, **22**, 31–38 and 83–91.

BARTLETT, F. C. (1950) 'Programme for experiments on thinking', *Quart J. exp. Psychol.*, **2**, 145–152.

BARTLETT, F. C. (1958) *Thinking, an Experimental and Social Study*. London: Allen & Unwin.

BARTLETT, F. C., and MACKWORTH, N. H. (1950) *Planned Seeing*. London: H.M.S.O. Air Publication 3139B.

BARTLEY, S. H., and CHUTE, ELOISE (1947) *Fatigue and Impairment in Man*. New York and London: McGraw-Hill.

BARTZ, W. H., SATZ, P., FENNELL, EILEEN, and LALLY, J. R. (1967) 'Meaningfulness and laterality in dichotic listening'. *J. exp. Psychol.*, **73**, 204–210.

BASSETT, M. F. and WARNE, C. J. (1919) 'On the lapse of verbal meaning with repetition', *Amer. J. Psychol.*, **30**, 415–418.

BATTEN, D. E. (1967) 'Recall of paired associates as a function of arousal and recall interval', *Percept. mot. Skills*, **24**, 1055–1058.

BECKER, P. W., MUSSINA, CAROLYN M., and PERSONS, R. W. (1963) 'Intertrial interval, delay of knowledge of results and motor performance', *Percep. mot. Skills*, **17**, 559–563.

BEGBIE, G. H. (1959) 'Accuracy of aiming in linear hand-movements', *Quart. J. exp. Psychol.*, **11**, 65–75.

BEILIN, H., and HORN, RHEBA (1962) 'Transition probability effects in anagram problem solving', *J. exp. Psychol.*, **63**, 514–518.

BEISHON, R. J. (1967) 'Problems of task description in process control', *Ergonomics*, **10**, 177–186.

BEISHON, R. J., and CRAWLEY, J. E. (1965) 'The control of a continuous baking oven, an analysis of a complex skill', *Ergonomics*, **8**, 375.

BEKESY, G. VON (1967) *Sensory Inhibition*. Princeton University Press.

BELBIN, EUNICE (1950) 'The influence of interpolated recall upon recognition', *Quart. J. exp. Psychol.*, **2**, 163–169.

BELBIN, EUNICE (1958) 'Methods of training older workers', *Ergonomics*, **1**, 207–221.

BELBIN, EUNICE (1964) *Training the Adult Worker*. D.S.I.R. Problems of Progress in Industry No. 15. London: H.M.S.O.

BELBIN, EUNICE, BELBIN, R. M., and HILL, F. (1957) 'A comparison between the results of three different methods of operator training', *Ergonomics*, **1**, 39–50.

BELBIN, E., and DOWNS, S. M. (1964) 'Activity learning and the older worker', *Ergonomics*, **7**, 429–437.

BELBIN, E., DOWNS, S., and MOORE, B. (1964) ' "Unlearning" and its relationship to age', *Ergonomics*, **7**, 419–427.

BELL, C. R., PROVINS, K. A., and HIORNS, R. W. (1964) 'Visual and auditory vigilance during exposure to hot and humid conditions', *Ergonomics*, **7**, 279–288.

BENSON, A. J., and GEDYE, J. L. (1962) 'Some supraspinal factors influencing generalised muscle activity', in *Symposium on Skeletal Muscle Spasm* (ed. P. C. Turnbull). Leicester: Franklyn, Ward and Wheeler.

BERGER, C., and MAHNEKE, A. (1954) 'Fatigue in two simple visual tasks', *Amer. J. Psychol.*, **67**, 509–512.

BERGSTROM, J. A. (1907) 'Effects of changes in time variables in memorizing, together with some discussion of the technique of memory experimentation', *Amer. J. Psychol.*, **18**, 206–238.

BERGUM, B. O., and LEHR, D. J. (1962) 'Vigilance performance as a function of interpolated rest', *J. appl. Psychol.*, **46**, 425–427.

BERGUM, B. O., and LEHR, D. J. (1963a) 'Effects of authoritarianism on vigilance performance', *J. appl. Psychol.*, **47**, 75–77.

BERGUM, B. O., and LEHR, D. J. (1963b) 'End-spurt in vigilance', *J. exp. Psychol.*, **66**, 383–385.

BERGUM, B. O., and LEHR, D. J. (1964) 'Monetary incentives and vigilance', *J. exp. Psychol.*, **67**, 197–198.

BERLYNE, D. E. (1960) *Conflict, Arousal and Curiosity*. New York: McGraw-Hill.

BERLYNE, D. E., BORSA, DONNA M., HAMACHER, JANE H., and KOENIG, ISOLDE D. V. (1966) 'Paired-associate learning and the timing of arousal', *J. exp. Psychol.*, **72**, 1–6.

BERLYNE, D. E., CRAW, MARGARET A., SALAPATEK, P. H., and LEWIS, JUDITH L. (1963) 'Novelty, complexity, incongruity, extrinsic motivation and the GSR', *J. exp. Psychol.*, **66**, 560–567.

BERRY, R. N. (1962) 'Skin conductance levels and verbal recall', *J. exp. Psychol.*, **63**, 275–277.

BERTELSON, P. (1961) 'Sequential redundancy and speed in a serial two-choice responding task', *Quart. J. exp. Psychol.*, **13**, 90–102.

BERTELSON, P. (1963) 'S-R relationships and reaction times to new versus repeated signals in a serial task', *J. exp. Psychol.*, **65**, 478–484.

BERTELSON, P. (1965) 'Serial choice reaction-time as a function of response versus signal-and-response repetition', *Nature*, **206**, 217–218.

BERTELSON, P. (1966) 'Central intermittency twenty years later', *Quart. J. exp. Psychol.*, **18**, 153–163.

BERTELSON, P. (1967a) 'The refractory period of choice reactions with regular and irregular interstimuli intervals', In *Attention and Performance* (ed. A. F. Sanders). Amsterdam: North-Holland Publishing Co.

BERTELSON, P. (1967b) 'The time course of preparation', *Quart. J. exp. Psychol.*, **19**, 272–279.

BERTELSON, P., and BARZEELE, J. (1965) 'Interaction of time-uncertainty and relative signal frequency in determining choice reaction time', *J. exp. Psychol.*, **70**, 448–451.

BERTELSON, P., BOONS, J-P., and RENKIN, A. (1965) 'Vitesse libre et vitesse imposée dans une tache simulant le tri mécanique de la correspondance', *Ergonomics*, **8**, 3–22.

BERTELSON, P., and JOFFE, RACHEL (1963) 'Blockings in prolonged serial responding', *Ergonomics*, **6**, 109–116.

BERTELSON, P., and RENKIN, A. (1966) 'Reaction times to new versus repeated signals in a serial task as a function of response-signal time interval', *Acta Psychol.*, **25**, 132–136.

BEVAN, W., AVANT, L. L., and LANKFORD, H. G. (1967) 'Influence of interpolated periods of activity and inactivity upon the vigilance decrement', *J. appl. Psychol.*, **51**, 352–356.

BEVAN, W., HARDESTY, D. L., and AVANT, L. L. (1965) 'Response latency with constant and variable interval schedules', *Percep. mot. Skills*, **20**, 969–972.

BILLS, A. G. (1927) 'The influence of muscular tension on the efficiency of mental work', *Amer. J. Psychol.*, **38**, 227–251.

BILLS, A. G. (1931) 'Blocking: a new principle in mental fatigue', *Amer. J. Psychol.*, **43**, 230–245.

BILLS, A. G., and BROWN, C. (1929) 'The quantitative set', *J. exp. Psychol.*, **12**, 301–323.

BILLS, A. G., and SHAPIN, M. J. (1936) 'Mental fatigue under automatically controlled rates of work', *J. gen. Psychol.*, **15**, 335–347.

BILODEAU, E. A. (1966) *Acquisition of Skill*. New York: Academic Press.

BILODEAU, E. A., and BILODEAU, INA MCD. (1958a) 'Variable frequency of knowledge of results and the learning of a simple skill', *J. exp. Psychol.*, **55**, 379–383.

BILODEAU, E. A., and BILODEAU, INA MCD. (1958b) 'Variation of temporal intervals among critical events in five studies of knowledge of results', *J. exp. Psychol.*, **55**, 603–612.

BILODEAU, E. A., JONES, M. B., and LEVY, C. M. (1964) 'Long-term memory as a function of retention time and repeated recalling', *J. exp. Psychol.*, **67**, 303–309.

BILODEAU, E. A., and RYAN, F. J. (1960) 'A test for interaction of delay of knowledge of results and two types of interpolated activity', *J. exp. Psychol.*, **59**, 414–419.

BILODEAU, INA MCD. (1956) 'Accuracy of a simple positioning response with variation in the number of trials by which knowledge of results is delayed', *Amer. J. Psychol.*, **69**, 434–437.

BILODEAU, INA MCD. (1965) 'Transfer of training across target sizes', *J. exp. Psychol.*, **70**, 135–140.

BILODEAU, INA MCD., and ROSENQUIST, H. S. (1964) 'Supplementary feedback in rotary-pursuit tracking', *J. exp. Psychol.*, **68**, 53–57.

BINDER, A., WOLIN, B. R., WEICHEL, ROSEMARIE, and TEREBINSKI, S. J. (1966) 'Uncertainty and stage of decision', *Amer. J. Psychol.*, **79**, 89–96.

BINET, A., and HENRI, V. (1894) 'La mémoire des mots', *Année Psychol.*, **1**, 1–23.

BINFORD, J. R., and LOEB, M. (1966) 'Changes within and over repeated sessions in criterion and effective sensitivity in an auditory vigilance task', *J. exp. Psychol.*, **72**, 339–345.

BIRREN, J. E., and BOTWINICK, J. (1955) 'Speed of response as a function of perceptual difficulty and age', *J. Gerontol.*, **10**, 433–436.

BLACKBURN, J. M. (1936) 'Acquisition of skills: an analysis of learning curves', *Indust. Hlth. Res. Bd. Rep.*, No. 73. London: H.M.S.O.

BLAKE, M. J. F. (1967) 'Relationship between Circadian Rhythm of body temperature and introversion-extraversion', *Nature*, **215**, 896–897.

BLANKENSHIP, A. B. (1938) 'Memory span: a review of the literature' *Psychol. Bull.*, **35**, 1–25.

BLICK, K. A., and BILODEAU, E. A. (1963) 'Interpolated activity and the learning of a simple skill', *J. exp. Psychol.*, **65**, 515–519.

BLYTH, K. W. (1963) 'Ipsilateral confusion in 2-choice and 4-choice responses with the hands and feet', *Nature*, **199**, 1312.

BLYTH, K. W. (1964) 'Errors in a further four-choice reaction task with the hands and feet', *Nature*, **201**, 641–642.

BODER, D. P. (1935) 'The influence of concomitant activity and fatigue upon certain forms of reciprocal hand movement and its fundamental components', *Comp. Psychol. Monogr.*, **11**, No. 4.

BOOK, W. F. (1908) *The Psychology of Skill*. Univ. Montana Studies in Psychol., Vol. I. Republished 1925. New York: Gregg.

BOONS, J. P., and BERTELSON, P. (1961) 'L'influence de l'incertitude temporelle sur le temps de réaction de choix', *Année Psychol.*, **61**, 361–376.

BORGER, R. (1963) 'The refractory period and serial choice-reactions', *Quart. J. exp. Psychol.*, **15**, 1–12.

BORNEMANN, E. (1942) 'Untersuchungen uber der grad der geistigen beanspruchung', *Arbeitsphysiologie*, **12**, 142–191.

BOSWELL, J. J., and BILODEAU, E. A. (1964) 'Short-term retention of a

simple motor task as a function of interpolated activity', *Percep. mot. Skills*, **18**, 227–230.

BOTWINICK, J., and BRINLEY, J. F. (1962a) 'Aspects of RT set during brief intervals in relation to age and sex', *J. Gerontol.*, **17**, 295–301.

BOTWINICK, J., and BRINLEY, J. F. (1962b) 'An analysis of set in relation to reaction time', *J. exp. Psychol.*, **63**, 568–574.

BOTWINICK, J., BRINLEY, J. F., and ROBBIN, J. S. (1958) 'The interaction effects of perceptual difficulty and stimulus exposure time on age differences in speed and accuracy of response', *Gerontologia*, **2**, 1–10.

BOTWINICK, J., and SHOCK, N. W. (1952) 'Age differences in performance decrement with continuous work', *J. Gerontol.*, **7**, 41–46.

BOTWINICK, J., and THOMPSON, L. W. (1966) 'Premotor and motor components of reaction time', *J. exp. Psychol.*, **71**, 9–15.

BOULTER, L. R., and ADAMS, J. A. (1963) 'Vigilance decrement, the expectancy hypothesis and intersignal interval', *Canad. J. Psychol.*, **17**, 201–209.

BRADLEY, J. V. (1959) 'Direction-of-knob-turn stereotypes', *J. appl. Psychol.*, **43**, 21–24.

BRAINARD, R. W., IRBY, T. S., FITTS, P. M., and ALLUISI, E. A. (1962) 'Some variables influencing the rate of gain of information', *J. exp. Psychol.*, **63**, 105–110.

BRAY, C. W. (1928) 'Transfer of learning', *J. exp. Psychol.*, **11**, 443–467.

BREBNER, J., and GORDON, I. (1962) 'Ensemble size and selective response times with a constant signal rate', *Quart. J. exp. Psychol.*, **14**, 113–116.

BREBNER, J., and GORDON, I. (1964) 'The influence of signal probability and the number of non-signal categories on selective response times', *Quart. J. exp. Psychol.*, **16**, 56–60.

BRICHCIN, M. (1966) 'Teoreticke a metodologicke problemy vyzkumu prubehu volnich pohybu', *Acta Univ. Carolinae, Philos. List. Monogr. No. 12*. Prague: Universita Karlova.

BRICKER, P. D. (1955a) 'Information measurement and reaction time: a review', in *Information Theory in Psychology* (ed. Henry Quastler). Glencoe, Illinois: The Free Press, pp. 350–359.

BRICKER, P. D. (1955b) 'The identification of redundant stimulus patterns', *J. exp. Psychol.*, **49**, 73–81.

BRIGGS, G. E., FITTS, P. M., and BAHRICK, H. P. (1957) 'Effects of force and amplitude cues on learning and performance in a complex tracking task', *J. exp. Psychol.*, **54**, 262–268.

BRIGGS, G. E., and WATERS, L. K. (1958) 'Training and transfer as a function of component interaction', *J. exp. Psychol.*, **56**, 492–500.

BROADBENT, D. E. (1952) 'Speaking and listening simultaneously', *J. exp. Psychol.*, **43**, 267–273.

BROADBENT D. E. (1952) 'Failures of attention in selective listening', *J. exp. Psychol.*, **44**, 428–433.

BROADBENT, D. E. (1954) 'The role of auditory localisation in attention and memory span', *J. exp. Psychol.*, **47**, 191–196.

BROADBENT, D. E. (1956) 'Listening between and during practised auditory distractions', *Brit. J. Psychol.*, **47**, 51–60.

BROADBENT, D. E. (1957a) 'Immediate memory and simultaneous stimuli', *Quart J. exp. Psychol.*, **9**, 1–11.

BROADBENT, D. E. (1957b) 'A mechanical model for human attention and immediate memory', *Psychol. Rev.*, **64**, 205–215.

BROADBENT, D. E. (1958) *Perception and Communication*. London: Pergamon Press.

BROADBENT, D. E., and GREGORY, MARGARET (1961) 'On the recall of stimuli presented alternately to two sense-organs', *Quart. J. exp. Psychol.*, **13**, 103–109.

BROADBENT, D. E., and GREGORY, MARGARET (1962) 'Donders' B- and C-reactions and S-R compatibility', *J. exp. Psychol.*, **63**, 575–578.

BROADBENT, D. E., and GREGORY, MARGARET (1963a) 'Division of attention and the decision theory of signal detection', *Proc. Roy. Soc. B.*, **158**, 222–231.

BROADBENT, D. E., and GREGORY, MARGARET (1963b) 'Vigilance considered as a statistical decision', *Brit. J. Psychol.*, **54**, 309–323.

BROADBENT, D. E., and GREGORY, MARGARET (1964) 'Stimulus set and response set: the alternation of attention', *Quart. J. exp. Psychol.*, **16**, 309–317.

BROADBENT, D. E., and GREGORY, MARGARET (1965) 'On the interaction of S-R compatibility with other variables affecting reaction time', *Brit. J. Psychol.*, **56**, 61–67.

BROADBENT, D. E., and GREGORY, MARGARET (1967) 'Psychological refractory period and the length of time required to make a decision', *Proc. Roy. Soc. B.*, **168**, 181–193.

BROADBENT, D. E., and HERON, A. (1962) 'Effects of a subsidiary task on performance involving immediate memory by younger and older men', *Brit. J. Psychol.*, **53**, 189–198.

BROADHURST, P. L. (1957) 'Emotionality and the Yerkes-Dodson Law', *J. exp. Psychol.*, **54**, 345–352.

BROWN, C. H. (1937) 'The relation of magnitude of galvanic skin responses and resistance levels to the rate of learning', *J. exp. Psychol.*, **20**, 262–278.

BROWN, I. D. (1960) 'Many messages from few sources', *Ergonomics*, **3**, 159–168.

BROWN, I. D. (1962) 'Measuring the "spare mental capacity" of car drivers by a subsidiary auditory task', *Ergonomics*, **5**, 247–250.

BROWN, I. D. (1965a) 'A comparison of two subsidiary tasks used to measure fatigue in car drivers', *Ergonomics*, **8**, 467–473.

BROWN, I. D. (1965b) 'Effect of a car radio on driving in traffic', *Ergonomics*, **8**, 475–479.

BROWN, I. D., and POULTON, E. C. (1961) 'Measuring the spare "mental capacity" of car drivers by a subsidiary task', *Ergonomics*, **4**, 35–40.

BROWN, J. (1954) 'The nature of set-to-learn and of intra-material interference in immediate memory', *Quart. J. exp. Psychol.*, **6**, 141–148.

BROWN, J. (1958) 'Some tests of the decay theory of immediate memory', *Quart. J. exp. Psychol.*, **10**, 12–21.

BROWN, J. (1959) 'Information, redundancy and decay of the memory trace', in *Mechanisation of Thought Processes*. National Physical Laboratory Symposium, No. 10. London: H.M.S.O.

BROWN, RUTH A. (1957) 'Age and paced work', *Occupational Psychol.*, **31**, 11–20.

BROWN, R. L., GALLOWAY, W. D., and SAN GIULIANO, R. A. (1965) 'Effects of time-sharing and body positional demands on cutaneous information processing', *Percep. mot. Skills*, **20**, 1021–1026.

BRUCE, D. J. (1958) 'The effect of listeners anticipation on the intelligibility of heard speech', *Lang. and Speech*, **1**, 79–97.

BRYAN, W. L., and HARTER, N. (1897) 'Studies in the physiology and psychology of the telegraphic language', *Psychol. Rev.*, **4**, 27–53.

BRYAN, W. L., and HARTER, N. (1899) 'Studies on the telegraphic language. The acquisition of a hierarchy of habits', *Psychol. Rev.*, **6**, 345–375.

BUCK, L. (1963) 'Errors in the perception of railway signals', *Ergonomics*, **6**, 181–192.

BUCK, L. (1966) 'Reaction time as a measure of perceptual vigilance', *Psychol. Bull.*, **65**, 291–304.

BURKE, D., and GIBBS, C. B. (1965) 'A comparison of free-moving and pressure levers in a positional control system', *Ergonomics*, **8**, 23–29.

BURSILL, A. E. (1958) 'The restriction of peripheral vision during exposure to hot and humid conditions', *Quart. J. exp. Psychol.*, **10**, 113–129.

CALLANTINE, M. F., and WARREN, J. M. (1955) 'Learning sets in human concept formation', *Psychol. Rep.*, **1**, 363–367.

CAMERON, C. G. (1964) Unpublished B.A. Thesis. University of Adelaide.

CARDOZO, B. L., and LEOPOLD, F. F. (1963) 'Human code transmission: letters and digits compared on the basis of immediate memory error rates', *Ergonomics*, **6**, 133–141.

CARMICHAEL, L., HOGAN, H. P., and WALTER, A. A. (1932) 'An experimental study of the effect of language on the reproduction of visually perceived form', *J. exp. Psychol.*, **15**, 73–86.

CARPENTER, A. (1946) 'The effect of room temperature on performance of resistance box test', *Med. Res. Coun. Appl. Psychol. Res.*, Unit Rep. No. 50.

CARPENTER, A. (1951) 'A case of absolute pitch', *Quart. J. exp. Psychol.*, 3, 92–93.

CARTERETTE, E. C., and COLE, M. (1963) 'Repetition and confirmation of messages received by ear and eye', *Quart. J. exp. Psychol.*, 15, 155–172.

CASTANEDE, A., and LIPSITT, L. P. (1959) 'Relation of stress and differential position habits to performance in motor learning', *J. exp. Psychol.*, 57, 25–30.

CATTELL, J. M. (1893) 'On errors of observation', *Amer. J. Psychol.*, 5, 285–293.

CATTELL, R. B. (1946) *Description and Measurement of Personality.* London: G. G. Harrap & Co.

CHAMBERS, E. G. (1961) 'Industrial fatigue', *Occupational Psychol.*, 35, 44–57.

CHANEY, F. B., and TEEL, K. S. (1967) 'Improving inspector performance through training and visual aids', *J. appl. Psychol.*, 51, 311–315.

CHASE, R. A., CULLEN, J. K., OPPENSHAW, J. W., and SULLIVAN, S. A. (1965) 'Studies on sensory feedback: III. The effects of display gain on tracking performance', *Quart. J. exp. Psychol.*, 17, 193–208.

CHASE, R. A., HARVEY, S., STANDFAST, SUSAN, RAPIN, ISABELLE, and SUTTON, S. (1961a) 'Studies on sensory feedback: I. Effect of delayed auditory feedback on speech and keytapping', *Quart J. exp. Psychol.*, 13, 141–152.

CHASE, R. A., RAPIN, ISABELLE, GILDEN, L., SUTTON, S., and GUILFOYLE, G. (1961b) 'Studies on sensory feedback: II. Sensory feedback influences on keytapping motor tasks', *Quart. J. exp. Psychol.*, 13, 153–167.

CHEATHAM, P. G. (1952) 'Visual perceptual latency as a function of stimulus brightness and contour shape', *J. exp. Psychol.*, 43, 369–380.

CHERRY, C. (1953) 'Some experiments on the recognition of speech with one and with two ears', *J. Acoust. Soc. Amer.*, 25, 975–979.

CHINN, R. MCC., and ALLUISI, E. A. (1964) 'Effect of three kinds of knowledge-of-results information on three measures of vigilance performance', *Percep. mot. Skills*, 18, 901–912.

CHOCHOLLE, R. (1940) 'Variation des temps de réaction auditifs en fonction de l'intensité a diverses fréquences', *Année Psychol.*, 40–41, 65–124.

CHOCHOLLE, R. (1943) 'Relation de la latence d'une sensation auditive différentielle avec l'amplitude d'une variation brusque de fréquence: . . . d'intensité', *Bull. biol.*, 137, 643–644, 751–752.

CHOWN, SHEILA M. (1960) 'A factor analysis of the Wesley Rigidity Inventory: its relationship to age and nonverbal intelligence', *J. abn. Psychol.*, 61, 491–494.

CHOWN, SHEILA, BELBIN, EUNICE, and DOWNS, SYLVIA (1967) 'Programmed instruction as a method of teaching paired associates to older learners', *J. Gerontol.*, **22**, 212–219.

CHRISTIE, L. S., and LUCE, R. D. (1956) 'Decision structure and time relations in simple choice behaviour', *Bull. math. Biophys.*, **18**, 89–111.

CLARIDGE, G. S., and HERRINGTON, R. N. (1960) 'Sedation threshold, personality and the theory of neurosis', *J. ment. Sci.*, **106**, 1568–1583.

CLARK, H. J. (1965) 'Recognition memory for random shapes as a function of complexity, association value and delay', *J. exp. Psychol.*, **69**, 590–595.

CLAY, HILARY M. (1954) 'Changes of performance with age on similar tasks of varying complexity', *Brit. J. Psychol.*, **45**, 7–13.

CLAY, HILARY M. (1957) 'The relationship between time, accuracy and age on similar tasks of varying complexity', *Gerontologia*, **1**, 41–49.

CLAY, HILARY M. (1964) *Research in Relation to Operator Training.* Monograph available from the Librarian, Science Research Council, London, W.C.1.

COHEN, B. H. (1963) 'An investigation of recoding in free recall', *J. exp. Psychol.*, **65**, 368–376.

COHEN, L. H., and LINDLEY, S. B. (1936) 'The relationship of muscle tonus changes to vibratory sensibility', *Psychol. Monogr.*, **47**, No. 212, pp. 83–93.

COLQUHOUN, W. P. (1960) 'Temperament, inspection efficiency, and time of day', *Ergonomics*, **3**, 377–378.

COLQUHOUN, W. P. (1961) 'The effect of "unwanted" signals on performance in a vigilance task', *Ergonomics*, **4**, 41–51.

COLQUHOUN, W. P. (1962) 'Effects of hyoscine and meclozine on vigilance and short-term memory', *Brit. J. industr. Med.*, **19**, 287–296.

COLQUHOUN, W. P. (1966) 'The effect of "unwanted" signals on performance in a vigilance task: a reply to Jerison', *Ergonomics*, **9**, 417–419.

COLQUHOUN, W. P. (1967) 'Sonar target detection as a decision process', *J. appl. Psychol.*, **51**, 187–190.

COLQUHOUN, W. P., and BADDELEY, A. D. (1964) 'Role of pretest expectancy in vigilance decrement', *J. exp. Psychol.*, **68**, 156–160.

COLQUHOUN, W. P., and BADDELEY, A. D. (1967) 'Influence of signal probability during pretraining on vigilance decrement', *J. exp. Psychol.*, **73**, 153–155.

COLQUHOUN, W. P., and CORCORAN, D. W. J. (1964) 'The effects of time of day and social isolation on the relationship between temperament and performance', *Brit. J. soc. clin. Psychol.*, **3**, 226–231.

CONRAD, R. (1951) 'Speed and load stress in sensori-motor skill', *Brit. J. industr. Med.*, **8**, 1–7.

CONRAD, R. (1954a) 'Missed signals in a sensorimotor skill', *J. exp. Psychol.*, **48**, 1–9.

CONRAD, R. (1954b) 'Speed stress', in *Symposium on Human Factors in*

Equipment Design (ed. W. F. Floyd and A. T. Welford). London: H. K. Lewis & Co. for The Ergonomics Research Society, pp. 95–102.

CONRAD, R. (1956) 'Performance of telephone operators relative to traffic level', *Nature*, **178**, 1480–1481.

CONRAD, R. (1957) 'Decay theory of immediate memory', *Nature*, **179**, 831–832.

CONRAD, R. (1958) 'Accuracy of recall using keyset and telephone dial, and the effect of a prefix digit', *J. appl. Psychol.*, **42**, 285–288.

CONRAD, R. (1960a) 'Serial order intrusions in immediate memory', *Brit. J. Psychol.*, **51**, 45–48.

CONRAD, R. (1960b) 'Letter sorting machines – paced, "lagged" or unpaced?', *Ergonomics*, **3**, 149–157.

CONRAD, R. (1960c) 'Very brief delay of immediate recall', *Quart. J. exp. Psychol.*, **12**, 45–47.

CONRAD, R. (1962a) 'Practice, familiarity and reading rate for words and nonsense syllables', *Quart. J. exp. Psychol.*, **14**, 71–76.

CONRAD, R. (1962b) 'An association between memory errors and errors due to acoustic masking of speech', *Nature*, **193**, 1314–1315.

CONRAD, R. (1963) 'Acoustic confusions and memory span for words', *Nature*, **197**, 1029–1030.

CONRAD, R. (1964a) 'Acoustic confusions in immediate memory', *Brit. J. Psychol.*, **55**, 75–84.

CONRAD, R. (1965) 'Order error in immediate recall of sequences', *J. verb. Learn. verb. Beh.*, **4**, 161–169.

CONRAD, R., FREEMAN, P. R., and HULL, AUDREY, J. (1965) 'Acoustic factors versus language factors in short-term memory', *Psychon. Sci.*, **3**, 57–58.

CONRAD, R., and HILLE, BARBARA A. (1957) 'The decay theory of immediate memory and paced recall', *M.R.C. Applied Psychology Research Unit Report* No. 307.

CONRAD, R., and HULL, A. J. (1964) 'Information, acoustic confusion and memory span', *Brit. J. Psychol.*, **55**, 429–432.

CONRAD, R., and HULL, AUDREY, J. (1966) 'The role of the interpolated task in short-term retention', *Quart. J. exp. Psychol.*, **18**, 266–269.

COOK, T. W. (1937) 'Amount of material and difficulty of problem solving', *J. exp. Psychol.*, **20**, 288–296.

CORBALLIS, M. C. (1966) 'Memory span as a function of variable presentation speeds and stimulus durations', *J. exp. Psychol.*, **71**, 461–465.

CORBALLIS, M. C. (1967) 'Serial order in recognition and recall', *J. exp. Psychol.*, **74**, 99–105.

CORCORAN, D. W. J. (1964) 'The relation between introversion and salivation', *Amer. J. Psychol.*, **77**, 298–300.

CORCORAN, D. W. J. (1965) 'Personality and the inverted-U relation', *Brit. J. Psychol.*, **56**, 267–273.

CORCORAN, D. W. J. (1966) 'Prediction of responses to multidimensional from responses to unidimensional stimuli', *J. exp. Psychol.*, **71,** 47–54.

COSTA, I. D., VAUGHAN, H. G., and GILDEN, L. (1965) 'Comparison of electromyographic and microswitch measures of auditory reaction time', *Percep. mot. Skills*, **20,** 771–772.

COULES, J., AVERY, D. L., and MESKIL, A. (1965) 'Information transmission in a pattern discrimination task as a function of initial task difficulty', *Percep. mot. Skills*, **21,** 927–939.

COURTS, F. A. (1939) 'Relations between experimentally induced muscular tension and memorization', *J. exp. Psychol.*, **25,** 235–256.

COURTS, F. A. (1942) 'Relations between muscular tension and performance', *Psychol. Bull.*, **39,** 347–367.

CRAFTS, L. W., and GILBERT, R. W. (1935) 'The effect of knowledge of results on maze learning and retention', *J. educ. Psychol.*, **26,** 177–187.

CRAIK, F. I. M. (1967) Personal communication.

CRAIK, K. J. W. (1943) *The Nature of Explanation.* Cambridge Univ. Press.

CRAIK, K. J. W. (1947) 'Theory of the human operator in control systems. I. The operator as an engineering system', *Brit. J. Psychol.*, **38,** 56–61.

CRAIK, K. J. W. (1948) 'Theory of the human operator in control systems. II. Man as an element in a control system', *Brit. J. Psychol.*, **38,** 142–148.

CRANNELL, C. W., and PARRISH, J. M. (1957) 'A comparison of immediate memory span for digits, letters and words', *J. Psychol.*, **44,** 319–327.

CRAWFORD, A. (1961) 'Fatigue and driving', *Ergonomics*, **4,** 143–154.

CRAWFORD, JUNE, HUNT, E., and PEAK, G. (1966) 'Inverse forgetting in short-term memory', *J. exp. Psychol.*, **72,** 415–422.

CREAMER, L. R. (1963) 'Event uncertainty, psychological refractory period, and human data processing', *J. exp. Psychol.*, **66,** 187–194.

CROSSMAN, E. R. F. W. (1953) 'Entropy and choice time: The effect of frequency unbalance on choice-response', *Quart. J. exp. Psychol.*, **5,** 41–51.

CROSSMAN, E. R. F. W. (1955) 'The measurement of discriminability', *Quart. J. exp. Psychol.*, **7,** 176–195.

CROSSMAN, E. R. F. W. (1956) 'The information capacity of the human operator in symbolic and non-symbolic control processes', in *Information Theory and the Human Operator.* Min. of Supply Publication WR/D2/56.

CROSSMAN, E. R. F. W. (1957) 'The speed and accuracy of simple hand movements', in *The Nature and Acquisition of Industrial Skills*, by E. R. F. W. Crossman and W. D. Seymour. Report to M.R.C. and D.S.I.R. Joint Committee on Individual Efficiency in Industry.

CROSSMAN, E. R. F. W. (1959) 'A theory of the acquisition of speed-skill', *Ergonomics*, **2,** 153–166.

CROSSMAN, E. R. F. W. (1960a) 'The information-capacity of the human motor-system in pursuit tracking', *Quart. J. exp. Psychol.*, **12**, 1–16.

CROSSMAN, E. R. F. W. (1960b) *Automation and Skill*. D.S.I.R. Problems of Progress in Industry No. 9. London: H.M.S.O.

CROSSMAN, E. R. F. W. (1961) 'Information and serial order in human immediate memory', in *Information Theory* (ed. C. Cherry). London: Butterworth & Co., pp. 147–159.

CROSSMAN, E. R. F. W., and GOODERE, P. J. (1963) *Feedback control of hand-movement and Fitts' Law*. Communication to the Experimental Psychology Society.

CROSSMAN, E. R. F. W., and SZAFRAN, J. (1956) 'Changes with age in the speed of information intake and discrimination', *Experientia Suppl.*, **4**, 128–135.

CROWDER, R. G. (1967) 'Reciprocity of retention and interpolated-task scores in short-term memory', *Percep. mot. Skills*, **24**, 903–909.

DALE, H. C. A. (1964) 'Retroactive interference in short-term memory', *Nature*, **203**, 1408.

DALE, H. C. A. (1967) 'Familiarity and free recall', *Quart. J. exp. Psychol.*, **19**, 103–108.

DALE, H. C. A., and GREGORY, MARGARET (1966) 'Evidence of semantic coding in short-term memory', *Psychon. Sci.*, **5**, 75–76.

DALLETT, K. M. (1964) 'Effects of a redundant prefix on immediate recall', *J. exp. Psychol.*, **67**, 296–298.

DARCUS, H. D. (1954) 'The range and strength of joint movement', in *Human Factors in Equipment Design* (ed. W. F. Floyd and A. T. Welford). London: H. K. Lewis & Co. Ltd.

DARDANO, J. F. (1962) 'Relationships of intermittent noise, intersignal interval, and skin conductance to vigilance behaviour', *J. appl. Psychol.*, **46**, 106–114.

DARROW, C. W. (1935) 'Emotion as relative functional decortication: the role of conflict', *Psychol. Rev.*, **42**, 566–578.

DAVIES, D. R., and HOCKEY, G. R. J. (1966) 'The effects of noise and doubling the signal frequency on individual differences in visual vigilance performance', *Brit. J. Psychol.*, **57**, 381–389.

DAVIES, M. H., CLARIDGE, G. S., and WAWMAN, R. J. (1963) 'Sedation threshold, autonomic lability and the excitation-inhibition theory of personality: III. The blood pressure response to an adrenaline antagonist as a measure of autonomic lability', *Brit. J. Psychiat.*, **109**, 558–567.

DAVIS, D. R. (1948) *Pilot Error.* Air Ministry Publication A.P.3139A. London: H.M.S.O.

DAVIS, D. R. (1949) 'The disorder of skill responsible for accidents', *Quart. J. exp. Psychol.*, **1**, 136–142.

DAVIS, D. R. (1958) 'Human errors and transport accidents', *Ergonomics*, **2**, 24–33.

DAVIS, D. R. (1966) 'Railway signals passed at danger: the drivers, circumstances and psychological processes', *Ergonomics*, **9,** 211–222.

DAVIS, R. (1956) 'The limits of the "psychological refractory period" ', *Quart J. exp. Psychol.*, **8,** 24–38.

DAVIS, R. (1957) 'The human operator as a single channel information system', *Quart. J. exp. Psychol.*, **9,** 119–129.

DAVIS, R. (1959) 'The role of "attention" in the psychological refractory period', *Quart. J. exp. Psychol.*, **11,** 211–220.

DAVIS, R. (1965) 'Expectancy and intermittency', *Quart. J. exp. Psychol.*, **17,** 75–78.

DAVIS, R., MORAY, N., and TREISMAN, ANNE (1961a) 'Imitative responses and the rate of gain of information', *Quart. J. exp. Psychol.*, **13,** 78–89.

DAVIS, R., SUTHERLAND, N. S., and JUDD, B. R. (1961b) 'Information content in recognition and recall', *J. exp. Psychol.*, **61,** 422–429.

DAVIS, R. C. (1940) 'Set and muscular tension', *Indiana U. Publ. Sci. Ser. No.* 10.

DAVIS, S. W. (1955) 'Auditory and visual flicker-fusion as measures of fatigue', *Amer. J. Psychol.*, **68,** 654–657.

DEANE, G. E. (1961) 'Human heart rate responses during experimentally induced anxiety', *J. exp. Psychol.*, **61,** 489–493.

DEES, VALERIE, and GRINDLEY, G. C. (1951) 'The effect of knowledge of results on learning and performance: IV. The direction of the error in very simple skills', *Quart. J. exp. Psychol.*, **3,** 36–42.

DEESE, J. (1955) 'Some problems in the theory of vigilance', *Psychol. Rev.*, **62,** 359–368.

DEESE, J., and KAUFMAN, R. A. (1957) 'Serial effects in recall of un-organised and sequentially organised verbal material', *J. exp. Psychol.*, **54,** 180–187.

DENENBERG, V. H., and KARAS, G. G. (1960) 'Supplementary report: The Yerkes-Dodson law and shift in task difficulty', *J. exp. Psychol.*, **59,** 429–431.

DENNY, J. P. (1966) 'Effects of anxiety and intelligence on concept formation', *J. exp. Psychol.*, **72,** 596–602.

DENNY, M. R., ALLARD, M., HALL, E., and ROKEACH, M. (1960) 'Supplementary report: Delay of knowledge of results, knowledge of task and intertrial interval', *J. exp. Psychol.*, **60,** 327.

DENNY-BROWN, D. (1949) 'Interpretation of the electromyogram', *Arch. Neurol. Psychiat.*, **61,** 99–128.

DEUTSCH, J. A., and DEUTSCH, D. (1963) 'Attention: Some theoretical considerations', *Psychol. Rev.*, **70,** 80–90.

DIMOND, S. J. (1966) 'Facilitation of performance through the use of the timing system', *J. exp. Psychol.*, **71,** 181–183.

DOHERTY, M. E. (1966) 'Response bias and Murdock's D Scale', *Psychol. Bull.*, **66,** 289–290.

DONDERS, F. C. (1868) 'Die Schnelligkeit psychischer Processe' *Arch. Anat. Phys.*, 657–681.

DOOLEY, R. P., and NEWTON, J. M. (1965) 'Transfer of training between quickened and unquickened displays', *Percep. mot. Skills*, **21**, 11–15.

DOUGLAS, C. G., and KOCH, A. C. E. (1951) 'Carbohydrate metabolism and muscular exercise', *J. Physiol.*, **114**, 208–221.

DRAZIN, D. H. (1961) 'Effects of foreperiod, foreperiod variability, and probability of stimulus occurrence on simple reaction time', *J. exp. Psychol.*, **62**, 43–50.

DUDLEY, N. A. (1958) 'Output pattern in repetitive tasks', *Inst. Prod. Engrs. J.*, **37**, 303–313.

DUFFY, E. (1957) 'The psychological significance of the concept of "arousal" or "activation" ', *Psychol. Rev.*, **64**, 265–275.

DUNCAN, C. P. (1958) 'Transfer after training with single versus multiple tasks', *J. exp. Psychol.*, **55**, 63–72.

DYAL, J. A. (1964) 'Effects of delay of knowledge of results in a line-drawing task', *Percep. mot. Skills*, **19**, 433–434.

DYAL, J. A. (1966) 'Effects of delay of knowledge of results and subject response bias on extinction of a simple motor skill', *J. exp. Psychol.*, **71**, 559–563.

DYAL, J. A., WILSON, W. J., and BERRY, K. K. (1965) 'Acquisition and extinction of a simple motor skill as a function of delay of knowledge of results', *Quart. J. exp. Psychol.*, **17**, 158–162.

EAGLE, M. N. (1967) 'The effect of learning strategies upon free recall', *Amer. J. Psychol.*, **80**, 421–425.

EASON, R. G., BEARDSHALL, ANN, and JAFFEE, S. (1965) 'Performance and physiological indicants of activation in a vigilance situation', *Percep. mot. Skills*, **20**, 3–13.

EASON, R. G., and BRANKS, J. (1963) 'Effect of level of activation on the quality and efficiency of performance of verbal and motor tasks', *Percep. mot. Skills*, **16**, 525–543.

EASON, R. G., and WHITE, C. T. (1961) 'Muscular tension, effort and tracking difficulty: studies of parameters which effect tension level and performance efficiency', *Percep. mot. Skills*, **12**, 331–372.

EASTERBY, R. S. (1967) 'Perceptual organization in static displays for man/machine systems', *Ergonomics*, **10**, 195–205.

EAYRS, J. T. (1964) 'Effects of thyroid hormones on brain differentiation', in *Brain-Thyroid Relationships* (ed. Margaret P. Cameron and Maere O'Connor). Ciba Foundation Study Group No. 18. London: J. & A. Churchill, pp. 60–71.

ECCLES, J. C. (1953) *The Neurophysiological Basis of Minds*. Oxford University Press.

EDWARDS, E. (1963) 'The integration of spaced signals', *Ergonomics*, **6**, 143–152.

EDWARDS, H. T., MARGARIA, R., and DILL, D. B. (1934) 'Metabolic

M

rate, blood sugar and the utilization of carbohydrate', *Amer. J. Physiol.*, **108**, 203–209.

EDWARDS, W. (1961) 'Behavioural decision theory', *Ann. Rev. Psychol.*, **12**, 473–498.

EGAN, J. P., CARTERETTE, E. C., and THWING, E. J. (1954) 'Some factors affecting multi-channel listening', *J. Acoust. Soc. Amer.*, **26**, 774–782.

EGAN, J. P., SCHULMAN, A. I., and GREENBERG, G. Z. (1959) 'Operating characteristics determined by binary decisions and by ratings', *J. Acoust. Soc. Amer.*, **31**, 768–773.

ELITHORN, A. (1961) 'Central intermittency: some further observations', *Quart. J. exp. Psychol.*, **13**, 240–247.

ELITHORN, A., and BARNETT, T. J. (1967) 'Apparent individual differences in channel capacity', in *Attention and Performance* (ed. A. F. Sanders). Amsterdam: North-Holland Publishing Co.

ELITHORN, A., and LAWRENCE, CATHERINE (1955) 'Central inhibition – some refractory observations', *Quart. J. exp. Psychol.*, **7**, 116–127.

ELLIOT, P. B. (1964) 'Tables of *d''*, in *Signal Detection and Recognition by Human Observers* (ed. J. A. Swets). New York: Wiley.

ELLIOTT, R. (1965) 'Reaction time and heart rate as functions of magnitude of incentive and probability of success', *J. Pers. soc. Psychol.*, **2**, 604–609.

EL-TEMAMY, M. A. A. (1966) Unpublished Ph.D. Thesis. University of Birmingham.

EMMERICH, D. S., GOLDENBAUM, D. M., HAYDEN, D. L., HOFFMAN, LINDA S., and TREFTS, JEANNE L. (1965) 'Meaningfulness as a variable in dichotic hearing', *J. exp. Psychol.*, **69**, 433–436.

ERIKSEN, C. W., and HAKE, H. W. (1955) 'Multidimensional stimulus differences and accuracy of discrimination', *J. exp. Psychol.*, **50**, 153–160.

ERIKSEN, C. W., and JOHNSON, H. J. (1964) 'Storage and decay characteristics of nonattended auditory stimuli', *J. exp. Psychol.*, **68**, 28–36.

ERIKSEN, C. W., and LAPPIN, J. S. (1967) 'Selective attention and very short-term recognition memory for nonsense forms', *J. exp. Psychol.*, **73**, 358–364.

ERIKSEN, C. W., and STEFFY, R. A. (1964) 'Short-term memory and retroactive interference in visual perception', *J. exp. Psychol.*, **68**, 423–434.

ESTES, W. K., and POLITO, F. DA (1967) 'Independent variation of information storage and retrieval processes in paired-associate learning', *J. exp. Psychol.*, **75**, 18–26.

EVANS, S. H. (1967) 'Redundancy as a variable in pattern perception', *Psychol. Bull.*, **67**, 104–113.

EYSENCK, H. J. (1947) *Dimensions of Personality*. London: Kegan Paul.

EYSENCK, H. J. (1952) *The Scientific Study of Personality*. London: Routledge & Kegan Paul.

FINE, B. J. (1963) 'Introversion-extraversion and motor vehicle driver behaviour', *Percep. mot. Skills*, **16**, 95–100.

FISHER, R. A., and YATES, F. (1938) *Statistical Tables for Biological Agricultural and Medical Research*. London: Oliver & Boyd.

FITTS, P. M. (1954) 'The information capacity of the human motor system in controlling the amplitude of movement', *J. exp. Psychol.*, **47**, 381–391.

FITTS, P. M. (1966) 'Cognitive aspects of information processing: III. Set for speed versus accuracy', *J. exp. Psychol.*, **71**, 849–957.

FITTS, P. M., and BIEDERMAN, I. (1965) 'S-R compatibility and information reduction', *J. exp. Psychol.*, **69**, 408–412.

FITTS, P. M., and DEININGER, R. L. (1954) 'S-R compatibility: correspondence among paired elements within stimulus and response codes', *J. exp. Psychol.*, **48**, 483–492.

FITTS, P. M., and PETERSON, J. R. (1964) 'Information capacity of discrete motor responses', *J. exp. Psychol.*, **67**, 103–112.

FITTS, P. M., PETERSON, J. R., and WOLPE, G. (1963) 'Cognitive aspects of information processing: II. Adjustments to stimulus redundancy', *J. exp. Psychol.*, **65**, 423–432.

FITTS, P. M., and RADFORD, BARBARA K. (1966) 'Information capacity of discrete motor responses under different cognitive sets', *J. exp. Psychol.*, **71**, 475–482.

FITTS, P. M., and SEEGER, C. M. (1953) 'S-R compatibility: spatial characteristics of stimulus and response codes', *J. exp. Psychol.*, **46**, 199–210.

FITTS, P. M., and SWITZER, G. (1962) 'Cognitive aspects of information processing: I. The familiarity of S-R sets and subsets', *J. exp. Psychol.*, **63**, 321–329.

FITTS, P. M., WEINSTEIN, M., RAPPAPORT, M., ANDERSON, NANCY, and LEONARD, J. A. (1956) 'Stimulus correlates of visual pattern recognition: a probability approach', *J. exp. Psychol.*, **51**, 1–11.

FLEISHMAN, E. A., and PARKER, J. F. (1962) 'Factors in the retention and relearning of perceptual-motor skill', *J. exp. Psychol.*, **64**, 215–226.

FLEISHMAN, E. A., and RICH, S. (1963) 'Role of kinesthetic and spatial-visual, abilities in perceptual-motor learning', *J. exp. Psychol.*, **66**, 6–11.

FLOYD, W. F., and WELFORD, A. T. (eds.) (1953) *Symposium on Fatigue*. London: H. K. Lewis & Co. for the Ergonomics Research Society.

FORREST, D. W. (1958) 'Influence of length of task on rate of work and level of muscular tension', *Occupational Psychol.*, **32**, 253–257.

FORRIN, B., and MORIN, R. E. (1966) 'Effect of contextual associations upon selective reaction time in a numeral-naming task', *J. exp. Psychol.*, **71**, 40–46.

FORRIN, B., and MORIN, R. E. (1967) 'Effects of context on reaction time to optimally coded signals', in *Attention and Performance* (ed. A. F. Sanders). Amsterdam: North-Holland Publishing Co.

FOSTER, HARRIET (1962) 'The operation of set in a visual search task', *J. exp. Psychol.*, **63**, 74–83.

FOWLER, B. (1964) Unpublished B.A. Thesis. University of Adelaide.

FOX, R. H., GOLDSMITH, R., HAMPTON, I. F. G., and WILKINSON, R. T. (1963) 'The effects of raised body temperature on the performance of mental tasks', *J. Physiol.*, **167**, 22–23.

FRAISSE, P. (1942) 'Etudes sur la memoire immédiate: II. La réproduction des formes rhythmiques', *Année Psychol.*, **43**, 103–143.

FRAISSE, P. (1944) 'Etudes sur la memoire immédiate: III. L'influence de la vitesse de presentation et de la place des elements. La nature du present psychologique', *Année Psychol.*, **45**, 29–42.

FRAISSE, P. (1957) 'La Période réfractoire psychologique', *Année Psychol.*, **57**, 315–328.

FRAISSE, P., and BLANCHETEAU, M. (1962) 'The influence of the number of alternatives on the perceptual recognition threshold', *Quart. J. exp. Psychol.*, **14**, 52–55.

FRASER, D. C. (1953) 'The relation of an environmental variable to performance in a prolonged visual task', *Quart. J. exp. Psychol.*, **5**, 31–32.

FRASER, D. C. (1958) 'Decay of immediate memory with age', *Nature*, **182**, 1163.

FREEDMAN, N. L., HAFER, BRENNA M., and DANIEL, R. S. (1966) 'EEG arousal decrement during paired-associate learning', *J. comp. physiol. Psychol.*, **61**, 15–19.

FREEMAN, G. L. (1931) 'Mental activity and the muscular processes', *Psychol. Rev.*, **38**, 428–449.

FREEMAN, G. L. (1933) 'The facilitative and inhibitory effects of muscular tension upon performance', *Amer. J. Psychol.*, **45**, 17–52.

FREEMAN, G. L. (1938) 'The optional muscular tensions for various performances', *Amer. J. Psychol.*, **51**, 146–150.

FREEMAN, G. L. (1940) 'The relationship between performance level and bodily activity level', *J. exp. Psychol.*, **26**, 602–608.

FRIEDMAN, M. J., and REYNOLDS, J. H. (1967) 'Retroactive inhibition as a function of response-class similarity', *J. exp. Psychol.*, **74**, 351–355.

FURNEAUX, W. D. (1962) 'The psychologist and the university', *Univ. Quart.*, **17**, 33–47.

GARNER, W. R. (1962) *Uncertainty and structure as Psychological Concepts*. New York: John Wiley & Sons.

GARNER, W. R., and HAKE, H. W. (1951) 'The amount of information in absolute judgements', *Psychol. Rev.*, **58**, 446–459.

GARVEY, W. D., and KNOWLES, W. B. (1954) 'Response time patterns associated with various display-control relationships', *J. exp. Psychol.*, **47**, 315–322.

GARVEY, W. D., and MITNICK, L. L. (1955) 'Effect of additional spatial references on display-control efficiency', *J. exp. Psychol.*, **50,** 276–282.

GARVEY, W. D., and TAYLOR, F. V. (1959) 'Interactions among operator variables, system dynamics and task-induced stress', *J. appl. Psychol.*, **43,** 79–85.

GATES, A. I. (1917) 'Recitation as a factor in memorizing', *Arch. Psychol. N.Y.*, **6,** No. 40.

GAUDRY, E., and CHAMPION, R. A. (1962) 'The identification of learning-curve parameters with intelligence and motivation', *Austral. J. Psychol.*, **14,** 87–94.

VAN DE GEER, J. P., and LEVELT, W. J. M. (1963) 'Detection of visual patterns disturbed by noise: an exploratory study', *Quart. J. exp. Psychol.*, **15,** 192–204.

GIBBS, C. B. (1951) 'Transfer of training and skill assumptions in tracking tasks', *Quart. J. exp. Psychol.*, **3,** 99–110.

GIBBS, C. B. (1954) 'The continuous regulation of skilled response by kinaesthetic feed back', *Brit. J. Psychol.*, **45,** 24–39.

GIBBS, C. B., and BROWN, I. D. (1956) 'Increased production from information incentives in an uninteresting repetitive task', *Manager*, **24,** 374–379.

GIBSON, J. J. (1950) *The Perception of the Visual World*. Boston, Mass.: Houghton Mifflin.

GIBSON, J. J., and RAFFEL, GERTRUDE, (1936) 'A technique for investigating retroactive and other inhibitory effects in immediate recall', *J. gen. Psychol.*, **15,** 107–116.

GLICKMAN, S. E. (1961) 'Perseverative neural processes and consolidation of the memory trace', *Psychol. Bull.*, **58,** 218–233.

GLUCKSBERG, S., KARSH, R., and MONTY, R. A. (1967) 'Sequential memory: keeping track performance as a function of information exposure time and interstimulus noise', *Percep. mot. Skills*, **24,** 651–656.

GOLDMAN-EISLER, FRIEDA (1956) 'The determinants of the rate of speech output and their mutual relations', *J. Psychosomatic Res.*, **2,** 137–143.

GOLDMAN-EISLER, FRIEDA (1958) 'Speech production and the predictability of words in context', *Quart. J. exp. Psychol.*, **10,** 96–106.

GOLDMAN-EISLER, FRIEDA (1961) 'Hesitation and information in speech', in *Information Theory* (ed. C. Cherry). London: Butterworth, pp. 162–174.

GOLDMAN, JOSEPHINE (1912) *Fatigue and Efficiency: A Study in Industry*. New York: Survey Associated Inc.

GOLDSTEIN, D. A., and NEWTON, J. M. (1962) 'Transfer of training as a function of task difficulty in a complex control situation', *J. exp. Psychol.*, **63,** 370–375.

GOLDSTEIN, M., and RITTENHOUSE, C. H. (1954) 'Knowledge of results in the acquisition and transfer of a gunnery skill', *J. exp. Psychol.*, **48,** 187–196.

GOTTSDANKER, R., BROADBENT, L., and VAN SANT, C. (1963) 'Reaction time to single and to first signals', *J. exp. Psychol.*, **66,** 163–167.

GOULD, J., and SMITH, K. U. (1963) 'Angular displacement of visual feedback in motion and learning', *Percep. mot. Skills*, **17,** 699–710.

GOULD, J. D. (1965) 'Differential visual feedback of component motions', *J. exp. Psychol.*, **69,** 263–268.

GOULD, J. D., and SCHAFFER, AMY (1965) 'Partial visual feedback of component motions as a function of difficulty of motor control', *J. exp. Psychol.*, **70,** 564–569.

GRANDJEAN, E., and PERRET, E. (1961) 'Effects of pupil aperture and of the time of exposure on the fatigue induced variations of the flicker fusion frequency', *Ergonomics*, **4,** 17–23.

GRAY, J. A., and WEDDERBURN, A. A. I. (1960) 'Grouping strategies with simultaneous stimuli', *Quart. J. exp. Psychol.*, **12,** 180–184.

GREEN, D. M., and BIRDSALL, T. G. (1964) 'The effects of vocabulary size on articulation score', in *Signal Detection and Recognition by Human Observers* (ed. J. A. Swets). New York: Wiley.

GREEN, D. M., BIRDSALL, T. G., and TANNER, W. P. (1957) 'Signal detection as a function of signal intensity and duration', *J. Acoust. Soc. Amer.*, **29,** 523–531.

GREEN, D. M., and SWETS, J. A. (1966) *Signal Detection Theory and Psychophysics.* New York: Wiley.

GREENSPOON, J., and FOREMAN, SALLY (1956) 'Effect of delay of knowledge of results on learning a motor task', *J. exp. Psychol.*, **51,** 226–228.

GREGORY, R. L. (1956) 'An experimental treatment of vision as an information source and noisy channel', in *Information Theory* (ed. C. Cherry). London: Butterworth & Co.

GRIEW, S. (1958a) 'Age changes and information loss in performance of a pursuit tracking task involving interrupted preview', *J. exp. Psychol.*, **55,** 486–489.

GRIEW, S. (1958b) 'Information gain in tasks involving different stimulus-response relationships', *Nature*, **182,** 1819.

GRIEW, S. (1958c) 'Uncertainty as a determinant of performance in relation to age; *Gerontologia*, **2,** 284–289.

GRIEW, S. (1959) 'Set to respond and the effect of interrupting signals upon tracking performance', *J. exp. Psychol.*, **57,** 333–337.

GRIEW, S. (1964) 'Age, information transmission and the positional relationship between signals and responses in the performance of a choice task', *Ergonomics*, **7,** 267–277.

GRIEW, S., and TUCKER, W. A. (1958) 'The identification of job activities associated with age differences in the engineering industry', *J. appl. Psychol.*, **42**, 278–282.

GRIM, P. F., and WHITE, S. H. (1965) 'Effects of stimulus change upon the GSR and reaction time', *J. exp. Psychol.*, **69**, 276–281.

GRUBER, H. E., and DINNERSTEIN, A. J. (1965) 'The role of knowledge in distance-perception', *Amer. J. Psychol.*, **78**, 575–581.

GULLAHORN, J. T., and GULLAHORN, J. E. (1963) 'A computer model of elementary social behavior', in *Computers and Thought* (ed. E. Feigenbaum and J. Feldman). New York: McGraw-Hill.

HABER, R. N. (1965) 'Effect of prior knowledge of the stimulus on word-recognition processes', *J. exp. Psychol.*, **69**, 282–286.

HABER, R. N., and HERSHENSON, M. (1965) 'Effects of repeated brief exposures on the growth of a percept', *J. exp. Psychol.*, **69**, 40–46.

HAIDER, M., and DIXON, N. F. (1961) 'Influences of training and fatigue on the continuous recording of a visual differential threshold', *Brit. J. Psychol.*, **52**, 227–237.

HALE, D. J. (1967) 'Sequential effects in a two-choice serial reaction task', *Quart. J. exp. Psychol.*, **19**, 133–141.

HALLIDAY, A. M., KERR, M., and ELITHORN, A. (1960) 'Grouping of stimuli and apparent exceptions to the psychological refractory period', *Quart. J. exp. Psychol.*, **12**, 72–89.

HAMMERTON, M. (1962) 'An investigation into the optimal gain of a velocity control system', *Ergonomics*, **5**, 539–543.

HAMMERTON, M., and TICKNER, A. H. (1966) 'An investigation into the comparative suitability of forearm, hand and thumb controls in acquisition tasks', *Ergonomics*, **9**, 125–130.

HARCOURT, R. A. F. (1959) Personal communication.

HARCUM, E. R., and FRIEDMAN, S. M. (1963) 'Reproduction of binary visual patterns having different element-presentation sequences', *J. exp. Psychol.*, **66**, 300–307.

HARDESTY, D., TRUMBO, D., and BEVAN, W. (1963) 'Influence of knowledge of results on performance in a monitoring task', *Percep. mot. Skills*, **16**, 629–634.

HARRIS, C. S., THACKRAY, R. I., and SCHOENBERGER, R. W. (1966) 'Blink rate as a function of induced muscular tension and manifest anxiety', *Percep. mot. Skills*, **22**, 155–160.

HARRISON, G. J. (1967) 'Some additive results in short term memory', in *Attention and Performance* (ed. A. F. Sanders). Amsterdam: North-Holland Publishing Co.

HARTLINE, H. K. (1938) 'The response of single optic nerve fibres of the vertebrate eye to illumination of the retina', *Amer. J. Physiol.*, **121**, 400–415.

HAUTY, G. T., TRITES, D. K., and BERKLEY, W. J. (1965) *Biomedical survey of ATC facilities: 2. Experience and age.* Federal Aviation Agency,

Office of Aviation Medicine, Civil Aeromedical Res. Inst., Oklahoma City. Rep. No. AM 65–6.

HAYWOOD, H. C., and SPIELBERGER, C. D. (1966) 'Palmar sweating as a function of individual differences in manifest anxiety', *J. Pers. Soc. Psychol.*, **3**, 103–105.

HEBB, D. O. (1949) *The Organization of Behavior*. New York: John Wiley & Sons. London: Chapman & Hall.

HEBB, D. O. (1955) 'Drives and the C.N.S. (Conceptual Nervous System)', *Psychol. Rev.*, **62**, 243–254.

HEBRON, MIRIAM E. (1966) *Motivated Learning: a Developmental Study from Birth to the Senium*. London: Methuen & Co. Ltd.

HELMSTADTER, G. C., and ELLIS, D. S. (1952) 'Rate of manipulative learning as a function of goal-setting techniques', *J. exp. Psychol.*, **43**, 125–129.

HELSON, H. (1947) 'Adaptation-Level as frame of reference for prediction of psychophysical data', *Amer. J. Psychol.*, **60**, 1–29.

HELSON, H., and STEGER, J. A. (1962) 'On the inhibitory effects of a second stimulus following the primary stimulus to react', *J. exp. Psychol.*, **64**, 201–205.

HEMINGWAY, A. (1953) 'The Physiological background of fatigue', in *Symposium on Fatigue* (ed. W. F. Floyd and A. T. Welford). London: H. K. Lewis & Co., for the Ergonomics Research Society.

HENDERSON, A., GOLDMAN-EISLER, FRIEDA, and SKARBEK, A. (1965) 'The common value of pausing time in spontaneous speech', *Quart. J. exp. Psychol.*, **17**, 343–345.

HENDERSON, J. G. (1959) 'The estimation of the transfer function of a human operator by a correlation method of analysis', *Ergonomics*, **2**, 274–286.

HENMON, V. A. C. (1906) 'The time of perception as a measure of differences in sensation', *Arch. Philos. Psychol. Sci. Meth.*, No. **8**.

HENRY, F. M. (1952) 'Independence of reaction and movement times and equivalence of sensory motivators of faster response', *Res. Quart.*, **23**, 43–53.

HENRY, F. M. (1961) 'Reaction time-movement time correlations', *Percep. mot. Skills*, **12**, 63–66.

HENRY, F. M., and ROGERS, D. E. (1960) 'Increased response latency for complicated movements and a "memory drum" theory of neuromotor reaction', *Res. Quart.*, **31**, 448–458.

HENSHAW, E. M., and HOLMAN, P. (1933) 'Manual dexterity – effects of training II, distribution of practice in manual dexterity', *Indust. Hlth. Res. Bd. Rep.* No. 67. London: H.M.S.O.

HERON, A. (1962) 'Immediate memory in dialling performance with and without simple rehearsal', *Quart. J. exp. Psychol.*, **14**, 94–103.

HICK, W. E. (1948) 'The discontinuous functioning of the human operator in pursuit tasks', *Quart. J. exp. Psychol.*, **1**, 36–51.

HICK, W. E. (1949) 'Reaction time for the amendment of a response', *Quart. J. exp. Psychol.*, **1**, 175–179.

HICK, W. E. (1952a) 'On the rate of gain of information', *Quart. J. exp. Psychol.*, **4**, 11–26.

HICK, W. E. (1952b) 'Why the human operator?', *Trans. Soc. Instrum. Technol.*, **4**, 67–77.

HICK, W. E., and WELFORD, A. T. (1956) 'Comment on the paper "Central inhibition: some refractory observations" by Alick Elithorn and Catherine Lawrence', *Quart. J. exp. Psychol.*, **8**, 39–41.

HILGENDORF, LINDEN (1966) 'Information input and response time', *Ergonomics*, **9**, 31–37.

HILLIX, W. A. (1960) 'Visual pattern identification as a function of fill and distortion', *J. exp. Psychol.*, **59**, 192–197.

HILLIX, W. A., and MARX, M. H. (1960) 'Response strengthening by information and effect in human learning', *J. exp. Psychol.*, **60**, 97–102.

HIRSH, I. J. (1950) 'The relation between localization and intelligibility', *J. Acoust. Soc. Amer.*, **22**, 196–200.

HOCHBERG, J., and BROOKS, VIRGINIA (1960) 'The psychophysics of form: reversible-perspective drawings of spatial objects', *Amer. J. Psychol.*, **73**, 337–354.

HOCHBERG, J. E., and MCALISTER, E. (1955) 'Relative size versus familiar size in the perception of represented depth', *Amer. J. Psychol.*, **68**, 294–296.

HOCHBERG, J., and MCALISTER, E. (1953) 'A quantitative approach to figural "goodness"', *J. exp. Psychol.*, **46**, 361–364.

HODGE, M. H., and POLLACK, I. (1962) 'Confusion matrix analysis of single and multidimensional auditory displays', *J. exp. Psychol.*, **63**, 129–142.

HOGAN, J. A. (1961) 'Copying redundant messages', *J. exp. Psychol.*, **62**, 153–157.

HOGAN, M. J. (1966) 'Influence of motivation on reactive inhibition in extraversion-introversion', *Percep. mot. Skills*, **22**, 187–192.

HOHLE, R. H. (1965) 'Detection of a visual signal with low background noise: an experimental comparison of two theories', *J. exp. Psychol.*, **70**, 459–463.

HOLDING, D. H. (1962) 'Transfer between difficult and easy tasks', *Brit. J. Psychol.*, **53**, 397–407.

HOLDING, D. H., and MACRAE, A. W. (1964) 'Guidance, restriction and knowledge of results', *Ergonomics*, **7**, 289–295.

HOLDING, D. H., and MACRAE, A. W. (1966) 'Rate and force of guidance in perceptual-motor tasks with reversed or random spatial correspondence', *Ergonomics*, **9**, 289–296.

HOWARD, K. I., and DIESENHAUS, H. I (1965) 'Personality correlates of change-seeking behavior', *Percep. mot. Skills*, **21**, 655–664.

HOWARD, T. C. (1963) 'The relation between psychological and mathematical probability', *Amer. J. Psychol.*, **76**, 335.

HOWARTH, C. I., and ELLIS, K. (1961) 'The relative intelligibility threshold for one's own name compared with other names', *Quart. J. exp. Psychol.*, **13**, 236–239.

HOWARTH, C. I., and TREISMAN, M. (1961) 'Lowering of an auditory threshold by a near threshold warning signal', *Quart. J. exp. Psychol.*, **13**, 12–18.

HOWE, M. J. A. (1965) 'Intra-list differences in short-term memory', *Quart. J. exp. Psychol.*, **17**, 338–342.

HOWE, M. J. A. (1966) 'A note on order of recall in short-term memory', *Brit. J. Psychol.*, **57**, 435–436.

HOWELL, W. C., and KREIDLER, D. L. (1963) 'Information processing under contradictory instructional sets', *J. exp. Psychol.*, **65**, 39–46.

HOWLAND, D., and NOBLE, M. E. (1953) 'The effect of physical constants of a control on tracking performance', *J. exp. Psychol.*, **46**, 353–360.

HUBEL, D. H. and WIESEL, T. N. (1962) 'Receptive fields, binocular interaction and functional architecture in the cat's visual cortex', *J. Physiol.*, **160**, 106–154.

HUBEL, D. H. and WIESEL, T. N. (1968) 'Receptive fields and functional architecture of the monkey striate cortex', *J. Physiol.*, **195**, 215–243.

HUGHES, I. M. (1963) *Studies in unidimensional Discrimination*. Ph.D. Dissertation at Cambridge University Library.

HULBERT, S. F. (1957) 'Drivers' GSRs in traffic', *Percep. mot. Skills*, **7**, 305–315.

HULICKA, IRENE M., STERNS, H., and GROSSMAN, J. (1967) 'Age-group comparisons of paired-associate learning as a function of paced and self-paced association and response times', *J. Gerontol.*, **22**, 274–280.

HULL, C. L. (1943) *Principles of Behavior*. New York: Appleton-Century.

HUNT, D. P. (1964) 'Effects of nonlinear and discrete transformations of feedback information on human tracking performance', *J. exp. Psychol.*, **67**, 486–494.

HURWITZ, L. J., and ALLISON, R. S. (1965) 'Factors influencing performance in psychological testing of the aged', in *Behavior, Aging and the Nervous System* (ed. A. T. Welford and J. E. Birren). Springfield, Illinois: Charles C. Thomas.

HYMAN, R. (1953) 'Stimulus information as a determinant of reaction time', *J. exp. Psychol.*, **45**, 188–196.

INGLIS, J. (1965) 'Immediate memory, age and brain function', in *Behavior, Aging and the Nervous System* (ed. A. T. Welford and J. E. Birren). Springfield, Illinois: Charles C. Thomas.

INGLIS, J., and ANKUS, MARY N. (1965) 'Effects of age on short-term storage and serial rote learning', *Brit. J. Psychol.*, **56**, 183–195.

INGLIS, J., and CAIRD, W. K. (1963) 'Age differences in successive responses to simultaneous stimulation', *Canad. J. Psychol.*, **17**, 98–105.

IRION, A. L. (1966) 'A brief history of research on the acquisition of skill', in *Acquisition of Skill* (ed. Edward A. Bilodeau). London and New York: Academic Press.

JACOBS, J. (1887) 'Experiments in prehension', *Mind*, **12**, 75–79.

JACOBSON, E. (1929) *Progressive Relaxation*. University of Chicago Press.

JAQUES, E. (1956) *Measurement of Responsibility*. London: Tavistock Publications.

JARRARD, L. E. (1960) 'The role of visual cues in the performance of ergographic work', *J. exp. Psychol.*, **60**, 57–63.

JEEVES, M. A. (1957) Unpublished Ph.D. Thesis. University of Cambridge.

JEEVES, M. A. (1961) 'Changes in performance at a serial-reaction task under conditions of advance and delay of information', *Ergonomics*, **4**, 329–338.

JENKINS, W. L., and CONNOR, MINNA B. (1949) 'Some design factors in making settings on a linear scale', *J. appl. Psychol.*, **33**, 395–409.

JENKINS, W. L., and OLSON, M. W. (1952) 'The use of levers in making settings on a linear scale', *J. appl. Psychol.*, **36**, 269–271.

JENKINS, W. O. (1947) 'The discrimination and reproduction of motor adjustments with various types of aircraft controls', *Amer. J. Psychol.*, **60**, 397–406.

JEROME, E. A. (1962) In *Aging around the World*: Proc. 5th Cong. Internat. Ass. Gerontol., San Francisco, 1960, Vol. 1 (ed. C. Tibbitts and W. Donahue). New York: Columbia Univ. Press., pp. 808–823.

JOHN, I. D. (1964) 'The role of extraneous stimuli in responsiveness to signals: refractoriness or facilitation?', *Austral. J. Psychol.*, **16**, 87–96.

JOHN, I. D. (1966) 'Intensity of non-key stimuli in the Donders' c-type reaction', *Austral. J. Psychol.*, **18**, 148–153.

JOHN, I. D. (1967a) 'A statistical decision theory of simple reaction time', *Austral. J. Psychol.*, **19**, 27–34.

JOHN, I. D.. (1967b) 'Sequential effects of stimulus characteristics in a serial reaction time task', *Austral. J. Psychol.*, **19**, 35–40.

JOHNSTON, W. A., HOWELL, W. C., and GOLDSTEIN, I. L. (1966) 'Human vigilance as a function of signal frequency and stimulus density', *J. exp. Psychol.*, **72**, 736–743.

JOHNSTON, W. A., HOWELL, W. C., and ZAJKOWSKI, M. M. (1967) 'Regulation of attention to complex displays', *J. exp. Psychol.*, **73**, 481–482.

JONES, A., WILKINSON, H. JEAN, and BRADEN, INA (1961) 'Information deprivation as a motivational variable', *J. exp. Psychol.*, **62**, 126–137.

JONG, J. R. DE (1957) 'The effects of increasing skill on cycle time and its consequences for time standards', *Ergonomics*, **1**, 51–60.

KALIL, R. E., and FREEDMAN, S. J. (1966a) 'Intermanual transfer of compensation for displaced vision, *Percep. mot. Skills*, **22**, 123–126.

KALIL, R. E., and FREEDMAN, S. J. (1966b) 'Persistence of ocular rotation following compensation for displaced vision', *Percep. mot. Skills*, **22**, 135–139.

KALSBEEK, J. W. H. (1964) 'On the measurement of deterioration in performance caused by distraction stress', *Ergonomics*, **7**, 187–195.

KALSBEEK, J. W. H. (1965) 'Mesure objective de la surcharge mentale: nouvelles applications de la méthode des doubles tâches', *Travail Humain*, **1–2**, 122–132.

KALSBEEK, J. W. H., and ETTEMA, J. H. (1964) 'Physiological and psychological evaluation of distraction stress', Proc. 2nd Internat. Cong. Ergonomics, Dortmund. Suppl. to *Ergonomics*, pp. 443–447.

KALSBEEK, J. W. H., and SYKES, R. N. (1967) 'Objective measurement of mental load', in *Attention and Performance* (ed. A. F. Sanders). Amsterdam: North-Holland Publishing Co.

KAPLAN, IRA T., and CARVELLAS, T. (1965) 'Scanning for multiple targets', *Percep. mot. Skills*, **21**, 239–243.

KAPLAN, I. T., CARVELLAS, T., and METLAY, W. (1966) 'Visual search and immediate memory', *J. exp. Psychol.*, **71**, 488–493.

KAPPAUF, W. E., and POWE, W. E. (1959) 'Performance decrement at an audio-visual checking task', *J. exp. Psychol.*, **57**, 49–56.

KARLIN, L. (1959) 'Reaction time as a function of foreperiod duration and variability', *J. exp. Psychol.*, **58**, 185–191.

KARLIN, L. (1965) 'Effects of delay and mode of presentation of extra cues on pursuit-rotor performance', *J. exp. Psychol.*, **70**, 438–440.

KARLIN, L. (1966) 'Development of readiness to respond during short foreperiods', *J. exp. Psychol.*, **72**, 505–509.

KASSUM, D. A. (1967) Unpublished report. Psychological Laboratory, University. of Cambridge.

KASWAN, J., and YOUNG, S. (1965a) 'Effect of luminance, exposure duration, and task complexity on reaction time', *J. exp. Psychol.*, **69**, 393–400.

KASWAN, J., and YOUNG, S. (1965b) 'Effect of stimulus variables on choice reaction times and thresholds', *J. exp. Psychol.*, **69**, 511–514.

KATZ, D. (1935) *The World of Colour*. London: Kegan Paul, Trench Trubner & Co. Ltd.

KATZ, D. (1949) 'Gestalt laws of mental work', *Brit. J. Psychol.*, **39**, 175–183.

KATZ, L. (1964) 'Effects of differential monetary gain and loss on sequential two-choice behaviour', *J. exp. Psychol.*, **68**, 245–249.

KATZ, M. S. (1967) 'Feedback and accuracy of target positioning in a homogeneous visual field', *Amer. J. Psychol.*, **80**, 405–410.

KAUFMAN, H., and LEVY, R. M. (1966) 'A further test of Hick's law with unequally likely alternatives', *Percep. mot. Skills*, **22**, 967–970.

KAY, H. (1951) 'Learning of a serial task by different age groups', *Quart. J. exp. Psychol.*, **3**, 166–183.

KAY, H. (1953) *Experimental studies of adult learning*. Unpublished Ph.D. thesis – Cambridge University Library.

KAY, H. (1954) 'The effects of position in a display upon problem solving', *Quart. J. exp. Psychol.*, **6**, 155–169.

KAY, H. (1955) 'Some experiments on adult learning', in *Old Age in the Modern World*: Rep. 3rd Cong. Internat. Ass. Gerontol., London 1954. Edinburgh: Livingstone, pp. 259–267.

KAY, H., and POULTON, E. C. (1951) 'Anticipation in memorizing', *Brit. J. Psychol.*, **42**, 34–41.

KAY, H., and WEISS, A. D. (1961) 'Relationship between simple and serial reaction times', *Nature*, **191**, 790–791.

KELLER, F. S. (1943) 'Studies in international Morse code: I. A new method of teaching code reception', *J. appl. Psychol.*, **27**, 407–415.

KENDON, A. (1967) 'Some functions of gaze-direction in social interaction', *Acta Psychol.*, **26**, 22–63.

KERR, M., MINGAY, ROSEMARY, and ELITHORN, A. (1963) 'Cerebral dominance in reaction time responses', *Brit. J. Psychol.*, **54**, 325–336.

KERR, M., MINGAY, ROSEMARY, and ELITHORN, A. (1965) 'Patterns of reaction time responses', *Brit. J. Psychol.*, **56**, 53–59.

KIMOTSUKI, K. (1967) 'On the measurement of the speed of finger motion', *J. Sci. Lab.*, **43**, 244–251.

KING, PEARL H. M. (1948) 'Task perception and interpersonal relations in industrial training: II', *Human Relations*, **1**, 373–412.

KIRCHNER, W. K. (1958) 'Age differences in short-term retention of rapidly changing information', *J. exp. Psychol.*, **55**, 352–358.

KIRK, R. E., and HECHT, ELIZABETH (1963) 'Maintenance of vigilance by programmed noise', *Percep. mot. Skills*, **16**, 553–560.

KLEINSMITH, L. J., and KAPLAN, S. (1963). 'Paired-associate learning as a function of arousal and interpolated interval', *J. exp. Psychol.*, **65**, 190–193.

KLEINSMITH, L. J., and KAPLAN, S. (1964) 'Interaction of arousal and recall interval in nonsense syllable paired-associate learning', *J. exp. Psychol.*, **67**, 124–126.

KLEMMER, E. T. (1956) 'Time uncertainty in simple reaction time', *J. exp. Psychol.*, **51**, 179–184.

KLEMMER, E. T. (1957) 'Simple reaction time as a function of time uncertainty', *J. exp. Psychol.*, **54**, 195–200.

KLEMMER, E. T. (1961) 'The perception of all patterns produced by a seven-line matrix', *J. exp. Psychol.*, **61**, 274, 282.

KLEMMER, E. T. (1964) 'Does recoding from binary to octal improve the perception of binary patterns?', *J. exp. Psychol.*, **67**, 19–21.

KLEMMER, E. T., and FRICK, F. C. (1953) 'Assimilation of information from dot and matrix patterns', *J. exp. Psychol.*, **45**, 15–19.

KLING, J. W., and SCHLOSBERG, H. (1961) 'The uniqueness of patterns of skin-conductance', *Amer. J. Psychol.*, **74**, 74–79.

KNAPP, BARBARA (1963) *Skill in Sport: the Attainment of Proficiency*. London: Routledge & Kegan Paul.

KNIGHT, A. A. (1967) Unpublished Ph.D. Thesis. University of Birmingham.

KNIGHT, A. A., and DAGNALL, P. R. (1967) 'Precision in movements', *Ergonomics*, **10**, 321–330.

KNOWLES, W. B., GARVEY, W. D., and NEWLIN, E. P. (1953) 'The effect of speed and load on display-control relationships', *J. exp. Psychol.*, **46**, 65–75.

KOPLIN, J. H., FOX, R., and DOZIER, F. (1966) 'A failure to replicate the inhibitory effects of a second stimulus following the primary stimulus to react', *J. exp. Psychol.*, **72**, 914–916.

KORN, J. H., and LINDLEY, R. H. (1963) 'Immediate memory for consonants as a function of frequency of occurrence and frequency of appearance', *J. exp. Psychol.*, **66**, 149–154.

KORNBLUM, S., and KOSTER, W. G. (1967) 'The effect of signal intensity and training on simple reaction time', in *Attention and Performance* (ed. A. F. Sanders). Amsterdam: North-Holland Publishing Co.

KOSTER, W. G., and BEKKER, J. A. M. (1967) 'Some experiments on refractoriness', in *Attention and Performance* (ed. A. F. Sanders). Amsterdam: North-Holland Publishing Co.

KRUEGER, W. C. F. (1937) 'The influence of amount limits and time limits upon the rate of work', *J. appl. Psychol.*, **21**, 113–118.

LABERGE, D., and TWEEDY, J. R. (1964) 'Presentation probability and choice time', *J. exp. Psychol.*, **68**, 477–481.

LACEY, J. I., BATEMAN, DOROTHY E., and VAN LEHN, RUTH (1953) 'Autonomic response specificity: an experimental study', *Psychosomatic Med.*, **15**, No. 1.

LACEY, J. I., and LACEY, BEATRICE C. (1958) 'The relationship of resting autonomic activity to motor impulsivity', in *The Brain and Human Behavior*. Res. Pub. Assn. Nerv. Dis. Baltimore: Williams & Wilkins.

LACHMAN, R., and TUTTLE, ABIGAIL, V. (1965) 'Approximations to English (AE) and short-term memory: construction or storage?', *J. exp. Psychol.*, **70**, 386–393.

LAMB, J., and KAUFMAN, H. (1965) 'Information transmission with unequally likely alternatives', *Percep. mot. Skills*, **21**, 255–259.

LAMBERT, W. E., and JAKOBOVITS, L. A. (1960) 'Verbal satiation and changes in the intensity of meaning', *J. exp. Psychol.*, **60**, 376–383.

LAMING, D. R. J. (1962) 'A statistical test of a prediction from information theory in a card-sorting situation', *Quart. J. exp. Psychol.*, **14**, 38–48.

LAMING, D. R. J. (1966) 'A new interpretation of the relation between choice-reaction time and the number of equiprobable alternatives', *Brit. J. math. statist. Psychol.*, **19**, 139–149.

LASZLO, JUDITH I. (1966) 'The performance of a simple motor task with kinaesthetic sense loss', *Quart. J. exp. Psychol.*, **18**, 1–8.

LAUER, A. R., and SUHR, V. W. (1958) *Road adaptation of a laboratory technique for studying driving efficiency with and without a refreshment pause.* Chicago, Illinois: National Safety Council.

LAVERY, J. J. (1964) 'The effect of one-trial delay in knowledge of results on the acquisition and retention of a tossing skill', *Amer. J. Psychol.*, **77**, 437–443.

LAVERY, J. J., and SUDDON, FLORENCE H. (1962) 'Retention of simple motor skills as a function of the number of trials by which KR is delayed', *Percep. mot. Skills*, **15**, 231–237.

LAWRENCE, D. H., and LABERGE, D. L. (1956) 'Relationship between recognition accuracy and order of reporting stimulus dimensions', *J. exp. Psychol.*, **51**, 12–18.

LAWSON, EVERDINA A. (1961) 'A note on the influence of different orders of approximation to the English language upon eye-voice span', *Quart. J. exp. Psychol.*, **13**, 53–55.

LAWSON, EVERDINA A. (1966) 'Decisions concerning the rejected channel', *Quart. J. exp. Psychol.*, **18**, 260–265.

LEE, L. CHARLOTTE (1961) 'The effects of anxiety level and shock on a paired-associate verbal task', *J. exp. Psychol.*, **61**, 213–217.

LEONARD, J. A. (1953) 'Advance information in sensori-motor skills', *Quart. J. exp. Psychol.*, **5**, 141–149.

LEONARD, J. A. (1958) 'Partial advance information in a choice reaction task', *Brit. J. Psychol.*, **49**, 89–96.

LEONARD, J. A. (1959) 'Tactual choice reactions: I', *Quart. J. exp. Psychol.*, **11**, 76–83.

LEONARD, J. A., NEWMAN, R. C., and CARPENTER, A. (1966) 'On the handling of heavy bias in a self-paced task', *Quart. J. exp. Psychol.*, **18**, 130–141.

LESHNER, S. L. (1961) 'Effects of aspiration and achievement on muscular tensions', *J. exp. Psychol.*, **61**, 133–137.

LEUBA, H. R. (1967) *Measuring the size of an ergonomics problem.* Paper to 3rd. Internat. Cong. Ergonomics, Birmingham.

LEVIN, I. P. (1967) 'Induced muscle tension and response shift in paired-associate learning', *J. exp. Psychol.*, **73**, 422–426.

LEVY, P., and LANG, P. J. (1966) 'Activation, control, and the spiral after movement', *J. Pers. soc. Psychol.*, **3**, 105–112.

LEWIS, M. (1965) 'Psychological effect of effort', *Psychol. Bull.*, **64**, 183–190.

LEWIS, R. E. F. (1954) 'Consistency and car-driving skill', *Brit. J. industr. Med.*, **13**, 131–141.

LICKLIDER, J. C. R. (1948) 'The influence of interaural phase relations upon the masking of speech by white noise', *J. Acoust. Soc. Amer.*, **20**, 150–159.

LIDDELL, H. S. (1944) 'Conditioned reflex method and experimental neurosis', in *Personality and Behavior Disorders*, Vol. II (ed. J. Mc V. Hunt). New York: Ronald Press.

LINCOLN, R. S. (1956) 'Learning and retaining a rate of movement with the aid of kinesthetic and verbal cues', *J. exp. Psychol.*, **51**, 199–204.

LINDLEY, R. H. (1963) 'Association value, familiarity and pronounciability ratings as predictors of serial verbal learning', *J. exp. Psychol.* **65**, 347–351.

LINDSLEY, D. B. (1951) 'Emotion', in *Handbook of Experimental Psychology* (ed. S. S. Stevens). New York: John Wiley & Sons. London: Chapman & Hall, pp. 473–516.

LIPPOLD, O. C. J., REDFEARN, J. W. T., and VUCO, J. (1960) 'The electromyography of fatigue', *Ergonomics*, **3**, 121–131.

LIPSITT, L. P., and ENGEN, T. (1961) 'Effects of presentation of paired and single-stimulus on discrimination of length', *Amer. J. Psychol.*, **74**, 274–277.

LLOYD, D. P. C. (1942) 'Stimulation of peripheral nerve terminations by active muscle', *J. Neurophysiol.*, **5**, 153–165.

LLOYD, K. E., REID, L. S., and FEALLOCK, J. B. (1960) 'Short-term retention as a function of the average number of items presented, *J. exp. Psychol.*, **60**, 201–207.

LOCKE, E. A. (1967) 'Motivational effects of knowledge of results: knowledge or goal setting?', *J. appl. Psychol.*, **51**, 324–329.

LOCKE, E. A., and BRYAN, JUDITH, F. (1967) 'Performance goals as determinants of level of performance and boredom', *J. appl. Psychol.*, **51**, 120–130.

LOEB, M., and BINFORD, J. R. (1964) 'Vigilance for auditory intensity changes as a function of preliminary feedback and confidence level', *Human Factors*, **6**, 445–458.

LOEB, M., and SCHMIDT, E. A. (1963) 'A comparison of the effects of different kinds of information in maintaining efficiency on an auditory monitoring task', *Ergonomics*, **6**, 75–81.

LOEHLIN, J. C. (1965) ' "Interpersonal" experiments with a computer model of personality', *J. Pers. soc. Psychol.*, **2**, 580–584.

LONG, E. R., HENNEMAN, R. H., and GARVEY, W. D. (1960) 'An experimental analysis of set: The role of sense-modality', *Amer. J. Psychol.*, **73**, 563–567.

LORGE, I. (1930) 'The influence of regularly interpolated time intervals upon subsequent learning', *Teach. Coll. Contr. Educ.* No. 438.

LORGE, I., and THORNDIKE, E. L. (1935) 'The influence of delay in the after-effect of a connection', *J. exp. Psychol.*, **18**, 186–194.

LOVAAS, O. I. (1960a) 'The relationship of induced muscle tension, tension level and manifest anxiety in learning', *J. exp. Psychol.*, **59**, 145–152.

LOVAAS, O. I. (1960b) 'Supplementary report: the relationship of induced muscle tension to manifest anxiety in learning', *J. exp. Psychol.*, **59**, 205–206.

LOVELESS, N. E. (1962) 'Direction-of-motion stereotypes: a review', *Ergonomics*, **5**, 357–383.

LUNDERVOLD, ARNE (1958) 'Electromyographic investigations during typewriting', *Ergonomics*, **1**, 226–233.

MCALLISTER, DOROTHY E. (1953) 'The effects of various kinds of relevant verbal pretraining on subsequent motor performance', *J. exp. Psychol.*, **46**, 329–336.

MCCALL, R. J. (1963) 'Invested self-expression: a principle of human motivation, *Psychol. Rev.*, **70**, 289–303.

MCCORMACK, P. D. (1962) 'A two-factor theory of vigilance', *Brit. J. Psychol.*, **53**, 357–363.

MCCORMACK, P. D., BINDING, F. R. S., and MCELHERAN, W. G. (1963) 'Effects on reaction time of partial knowledge of results of performance', *Percep. mot. Skills*, **17**, 279–281.

MCCORMACK, P. D., and MCELHERAN, W. G. (1963) 'Follow-up of effects on reaction time with partial knowledge of results', *Percep. mot. Skills*, **17**, 565–566.

MCCOY, W. K. (1963) 'Test of the accuracy of Crossman's Confusion-Function', *Percep. mot. Skills*, **17**, 303–320.

MACE, C. A. (1935) *Incentives: some experimental studies*. Industrial Health Research Board (Great Britain) Report No. 72.

MCFARLAND, R. A., and MOSELEY, A. L. (1954) *Human Factors in Highway Transport Safety*. Boston: Harvard School of Public Health.

MCGEOCH, J. A., and IRION, A. L. (1952) *The Psychology of Human Learning*. New York: Longmans.

MCGHIE, A., CHAPMAN, J., and LAWSON, J. S. (1965) 'Changes in immediate memory with age', *Brit. J. Psychol.*, **56**, 69–75.

MCGUIGAN, F. J. (1959) 'The effect of precision, delay, and schedule of knowledge of results on performance', *J. exp. Psychol.*, **58**, 79–84.

MCGUIGAN, F. J., and MACCASLIN, EUGENE, F. (1955) 'Whole and part methods in learning a perceptual motor skill', *Amer. J. Psychol.*, **68**, 658–661.

MACKAY, D. M. (1965) 'Visual noise as a tool of research', *J. gen. Psychol.*, **72**, 181–197.

MACKWORTH, JANE F. (1959) 'Paced memorizing in a continuous task', *J. exp. Psychol.*, **58**, 206–211.

MACKWORTH, J. F. (1964a) 'Interference and decay in very short-term memory', *J. verb. Learn. verb. Beh.*, **3**, 300–308.

MACKWORTH, J. F. (1964b) 'The effect of true and false knowledge of results on the detectability of signals in a vigilance task', *Canad. J. Psychol.*, **18**, 106–117.

MACKWORTH, J. F. (1964c) 'Performance decrement in vigilance, threshold and high-speed perceptual motor tasks', *Canad. J. Psychol.*, **18**, 209–223.

MACKWORTH, J. F. (1965) 'Decision interval and signal detectability in a vigilance task', *Canad. J. Psychol.*, **19**, 111–117.

MACKWORTH, J. F., and MACKWORTH N. H. (1956) 'The overlapping of signals for decisions', *Amer. J. Psychol.*, **69**, 26–47.

MACKWORTH, J. F., and TAYLOR, M. M. (1963) 'The d' measure of signal detectability in vigilance-like situations', *Canad. J. Psychol.*, **17**, 302–325.

MACKWORTH, N. H. (1950) *Researches on the Measurement of Human Performance*. Medical Research Council Special Report Series No. 268. London: H.M.S.O.

MACKWORTH, N. H., KAPLAN, I. T., and METLAY, W. (1964) 'Eye movements during vigilance', *Percep. mot. Skills*, **18**, 397–402.

MACKWORTH, N. H., and MACKWORTH, JANE F. (1958) 'Visual search for successive decisions', *Brit. J. Psychol.*, **49**, 210–221.

MACKWORTH, N. H., and MACKWORTH, J. F. (1959) 'Remembering advance cues during searching', *Brit. J. Psychol.*, **50**, 207–222.

MCNICOL, D. (1967) Unpublished Ph.D. Thesis. University of Cambridge.

MACPHERSON, S. J., DEES, VALERIE, and GRINDLEY, G. C. (1949) 'The effect of knowledge of results on learning and performance: III. The influence of the time interval between trials', *Quart. J. exp. Psychol.*, **1**, 167–174.

MACRAE, A. W., and HOLDING, D. H. (1965) 'Guided practice in direct and reversed serial tracking', *Ergonomics*, **8**, 487–492.

MACRAE, A. W., and HOLDING, D. H. (1966) 'Transfer of training after guidance or practice', *Quart. J. exp. Psychol.*, **18**, 327–333.

MCREYNOLDS, P., and ACKER, MARY (1959) 'Serial learning under conditions of rapid presentation of stimuli', *Amer. J. Psychol.*, **72**, 589–592.

MCRUER, D. T., and KRENDEL, E. S. (1959) 'The human operator as a servo system element. Parts I and II', *J. Franklin Inst.*, **267**, 381–403 and 511–536.

MALMO, R. B. (1959) 'Activation: a neuropsychological dimension', *Psychol. Rev.*, **66**, 367–386.

MARGRAIN, SUSAN A. (1967) 'Short-term memory as a function of input modality', *Quart. J. exp. Psychol.*, **19**, 109–114.

MARILL, T. (1957) 'The psychological refractory phase', *Brit. J. Psychol.*, **48**, 93–97.

MARKS, M. R., and JACK, OLLIE (1952) 'Verbal context and memory span for meaningful material', *Amer. J. Psychol.*, **65**, 298–300.

MARTIN, P. R., and FERNBERGER, S. W. (1929) 'Improvement in memory span', *Amer. J. Psychol.*, **41**, 91–94.

MARTZ, R. L. (1966) 'Signal presentation rate, auditory threshold and group vigilance', *Percep. mot. Skills*, **23**, 463–469.

MARTZ, R. L. (1967) 'Auditory vigilance as affected by signal rate and intersignal interval variability', *Percep. mot. Skills*, **24**, 195–203.

MELTON, A. W., and IRWIN, J. McQ. (1940) 'The influence of degree of interpolated learning on retroactive inhibition and the overt transfer of specific responses', *Amer. J. Psychol.*, **53**, 173–203.

MERKEL, J. (1885) 'Die zeitlichen verhältnisse der sillensthätig-keit', *Philos. Stud.*, **2**, 73–127.

MERTON, P. A. (1956) 'Problems of muscular fatigue', *Brit. med. Bull.*, **12**, 219–221.

MICHAELS, R. M. (1960) 'Tension responses of drivers generated on urban streets', *Bull. Higw. Res. Bd. Wash.*, No. 271, 29–44.

MICHON, J. A. (1964a) 'Temporal struction of letter groups and span of perception', *Quart. J. exp. Psychol.*, **16**, 232–240.

MICHON, J. A. (1964b) 'A note on the measurement of perceptual motor load', *Ergonomics*, **7**, 461–463.

MICHON, J. A. (1966) 'Tapping regularity as a measure of perceptual motor load', *Ergonomics*, **9**, 401–412.

MICHON, J. A., and VAN DOORNE, H. (1967) 'A semi-portable apparatus for the measurement of perceptual motor load', *Ergonomics*, **10**, 67–72.

MICHOTTE, A. (1946) *La Perception de la Causalité.* Louvain: Institut Supérieur de Philosophie.

MICHOTTE, A. (1963) *The Perception of Causality.* London: Methuen.

MICKO, H. C. (1966) 'Vigilance – arousal *vs.* reinforcement', *Quart. J. exp. Psychol.*, **18**, 39–46.

MILLER, G. A. (1956) 'The magical number seven, plus or minus two: some limits on our capacity for processing information', *Psychol. Rev.*, **63**, 81–97.

MILLER, G. A., GALANTER, E., and PRIBRAM, K. H. (1960) *Plans and the Structure of Behavior.* New York: Henry Holt & Co.

MILLER, G. A., HEISE, G. A., and LICHTEN, W. (1951) 'The intelligibility of speech as a function of the context of the test materials', *J. exp. Psychol.*, **41**, 329–335.

MILLER, G. A., and SELFRIDGE, JENNIFER A. (1950) 'Verbal context and the recall of meaningful material', *Amer. J. Psychol.*, **63**, 176–185.

MILLER, I. (1957) 'Perception of nonsense passages in relation to amount of information and speech-to-noise ratio', *J. exp. Psychol.*, **53**, 388–393.

MIRA, E. (1944) *Psychiatry in War.* London: Chapman & Hall.

MITCHELL, M. J. H., and VINCE, MARGARET A. (1951) 'The direction of movement of machine controls', *Quart. J. exp. Psychol.*, **3**, 24–35.

MONTPELLIER, G. DE (1935) *Les Altérations Morphologiques des Mouvements Rapides*. Louvain: Institut Supérieur de Philosophie.

MONTY, R. A., KARSH, R., and TAUB, H. A. (1967a) 'Pacing of rehearsal in sequential short-term memory', *J. exp. Psychol.*, **74**, 300–302.

MONTY, R. A., KARSH, R., and TAUB, H. A. (1967b) 'Keeping track of sequential events: irrelevant information and paced rehearsal', *Percep. mot. Skills*, **24**, 99–103.

MONTY, R. A., TAUB, H. A., and LAUGHERY, K. R. (1965) 'Keeping track of sequential events: effects of rate, categories, and trial length', *J. exp. Psychol.*, **69**, 224–229.

MORAY, N. (1959) 'Attention in dichotic listening: affective cues and the influence of instructions', *Quart. J. exp. Psychol.*, **11**, 56–60.

MORAY, N. (1960) 'Broadbent's filter theory: Postulate H and the problem of switching time', *Quart. J. exp. Psychol.*, **12**, 214–220.

MORAY, N., and TAYLOR, A. M. (1958) 'The effect of redundancy in shadowing one of two dichotic messages', *Lang. and Speech*, **3**, 7–10.

MORGAN, C. T. (1965) *Physiological Psychology*. New York: McGraw-Hill.

MORGAN, C. T., COOK, J. S., CHAPANIS, A., and LUND, M. W. (eds.) (1963) *Human Engineering Guide to Equipment design*. New York: McGraw-Hill Book Co., Inc.

MORIKIYO, Y., and IIDA, H. (1967) 'Choice behaviour and reaction times', *J. Sci. Lab.*, **43**, 461–467.

MORIN, R. E. (1955) 'Factors influencing rate and extent of learning in the presence of misinformative feedback', *J. exp. Psychol.*, **49**, 343–351.

MORIN, R. E., DEROSA, D. V., and STULTZ, V. (1967) 'Recognition memory and reaction time', in *Attention and Performance* (ed. A. F. Sanders). Amsterdam: North-Holland Publishing Co.

MORIN, R. E., FORRIN, B., and ARCHER, W. (1961) 'Information processing behaviour: The role of irrelevant stimulus information', *J. exp Psychol.*, **61**, 89–96.

MORIN, R. E., KONICK, A., TROXELL, NOLA, and MCPHERSON, SANDRA (1965) 'Information and reaction time for "naming" responses', *J. exp. Psychol.*, **70**, 309–314.

MORRISETT, L., and HOVLAND, C. I. (1959) 'A comparison of three varieties of training in human problem solving', *J. exp. Psychol.*, **58**, 52–55.

MORTENSON, F. J., and LOESS, H. (1964) 'Effect of very brief interpolated activity on short-term retention', *Percep. mot. Skills*, **18**, 797–803.

MOTTRAM, V. H. (1944) *The Physical Basis of Personality*. Harmondsworth: Penguin Books.

MOWBRAY, G. H. (1952) 'Simultaneous vision and audition: the detection of elements missing from overlearned sequences', *J. exp. Psychol.*, **44,** 292–300.

MOWBRAY, G. H. (1953) 'Simultaneous vision and audition: the comprehension of prose passages with varying levels of difficulty', *J. exp. Psychol.*, **46,** 365–372.

MOWBRAY, G. H. (1954) 'The perception of short phrases presented simultaneously for visual and auditory reception', *Quart. J. exp. Psychol.*, **6,** 86–92.

MOWBRAY, G. H. (1960) 'Choice reaction times for skilled responses', *Quart. J. exp. Psychol.*, **12,** 193–202.

MOWBRAY, G. H. (1964) 'Subjective expectancy and choice reaction times', *Quart. J. exp. Psychol.*, **16,** 216–223.

MOWBRAY, G. H., and RHOADES, M. V. (1959) 'On the reduction of choice reaction times with practice', *Quart. J. exp. Psychol.*, **11,** 16–23.

MUNSON, W. A., and KARLIN, J. E. (1954) 'The measurement of human channel transmission characteristics', *J. Acoust. Soc. Amer.*, **26,** 542–553.

MURDOCK, B. B. (1960a) 'The Distinctiveness of stimuli', *Psychol. Rev.*, **67,** 16–31.

MURDOCK, B. B. (1960b) 'The immediate retention of unrelated words', *J. exp. Psychol.*, **60,** 222–234.

MURDOCK, B. B. (1961) 'The retention of individual items', *J. exp. Psychol.*, **62,** 618–625.

MURDOCK, B. B. (1962) 'The serial position effect of free recall', *J. exp. Psychol.*, **64,** 482–488.

MURDOCK, B. B. (1963a) 'Short-term retention of single paired associates', *J. exp. Psychol.*, **65,** 433–443.

MURDOCK, B. B. (1963b) 'Interpolated recall in short-term memory', *J. exp. Psychol.*, **66,** 525–532.

MURDOCK, B. B. (1965a) 'A test of the "limited capacity" hypothesis', *J. exp. Psychol.*, **69,** 237–240.

MURDOCK, B. B. (1965b) 'Effects of a subsidiary task on short-term memory', *Brit. J. Psychol.*, **56,** 413–419.

MURDOCK, B. B. (1965c) 'Signal-detection theory and short-term memory', *J. exp. Psychol.*, **70,** 443–447.

MURDOCK, B. B. (1966a) 'The criterion problem in short-term memory', *J. exp. Psychol.*, **72,** 317–324.

MURDOCK, B. B. (1966b) 'Visual and auditory stores in short-term memory', *Quart. J. exp. Psychol.*, **18,** 206–211.

MURDOCK, B. B. (1967) 'Auditory and visual stores in short term memory', in *Attention and Performance* (ed. A. F. Sanders). Amsterdam: North-Holland Publishing Co.

MURDOCK, B. B., and VOM SAAL, W. (1967) 'Transpositions in short-term memory', *J. exp. Psychol.*, **74,** 137–143.

MURRAY, D. J. (1965) 'Vocalization-at-presentation and immediate recall, with varying presentation-rates', *Quart.   exp. Psychol.*, **17**, 47–56.

MURRAY, D. J. (1966) 'Vocalization-at-presentation and immediate recall, with varying recall methods', *Quart. J. exp. Psychol.*, **18**, 9–18.

MURRELL, K. F. H. (1957) 'Data on human performance for engineering designers: Controls', *Engineering*, **184**, 308–310.

MURRELL, K. F. H. (1965) *Ergonomics*. London: Chapman & Hall.

MURRELL, K. F. H., and ENTWISLE, D. G. (1960) 'Age differences in movement pattern', *Nature*, **185**, 948.

NAKAMURA, C. Y., and KASWAN, J. W. (1962) 'Effect of stimulus condition and reaction time information on spatial stimulus generalization', *J. exp. Psychol.*, **64**, 67–76.

NAKAMURA, C. Y., and KRUDIS, B. R. (1967) 'Evaluation of a response speed measure of incentive value of reward', *J. exp. Psychol.*, **74**, 44–49.

NAYLOR, J. C., and BRIGGS, G. E. (1963) 'Effects of task complexity and task organization on the relative efficiency of part and whole training methods', *J. exp. Psychol.*, **65**, 217–224.

NEISSER, U. (1963) 'Decision-time without reaction-time: experiments in visual scanning', *Amer. J. Psychol.*, **76**, 376–385.

NEISSER, U., and BELLER, H. K. (1965) 'Searching through word lists', *Brit. J. Psychol.*, **56**, 349–358.

NEUMANN, EVA (1960) 'Frequency and usefulness of verbal and non-verbal methods in the learning and transfer of a paired-associate serial motor task', *J. exp. Psychol.*, **60**, 103–110.

NEWMAN, E. B. (1966) 'Speed of reading when the span of letters is restricted', *Amer. J. Psychol.*, **79**, 272–278.

NICKERSON, R. S. (1965a) 'Response times for "same"–"different" judgments', *Percep. mot. Skills*, **20**, 15–18.

NICKERSON, R. S. (1965b) 'Response time to the second of two successive signals as a function of absolute and relative duration of intersignal interval', *Percep. mot. Skills*, **21**, 3–10.

NICKERSON, R. S. (1966) 'Response times with a memory-dependent decision task', *J. exp. Psychol.*, **72**, 761–769.

NICKERSON, R. S. (1967a) 'Categorization time with categories defined by disjunctions and conjunctions of stimulus attributes', *J. exp. Psychol.*, **73**, 211–219.

NICKERSON, R. S. (1967b) 'Expectancy, waiting time and the psychological refractory period', in *Attention and Performance* (ed. A. F. Sanders). Amsterdam: North-Holland Publishing Co.

NICKERSON, R. S. (1967c) 'Psychological refractory phase and the functional significance of signals', *J. exp. Psychol.*, **73**, 303–312.

NICKERSON, R. S., and FEEHRER, C. E. (1964) 'Stimulus categorization and response time', *Percep. mot. Skills*, **18**, 785–793.

NISHIOKA, A., AKIBA, N., and YAMAHIRA, J. (1960) 'Experiments on the prolonged vigilance task (I)', *Institute for Science of Labour, Tokyo, Rep.* No. 17, pp. 23–30.

NOBLE, M., FITTS, P. M., and WARREN, C. E. (1955) 'The frequency response of skilled subjects in a pursuit tracking task', *J. exp. Psychol.*, **49,** 249–256.

NOBLE, M., TRUMBO, D., and FOWLER, F. (1967) 'Further evidence of secondary task interference in tracking', *J. exp. Psychol.*, **73,** 146–149.

NORMAN, D. A. (1966) 'Acquisition and retention in short-term memory', *J. exp. Psychol.*, **72,** 369–381.

NORMAN, D. A. (1967) 'Temporal confusions and limited capacity processors', in *Attention and Performance* (ed. A. F. Sanders). Amsterdam: North-Holland Publishing Co.

NORMAN, D. A., and WICKELGREN, W. A. (1965) 'Short-term recognition memory for single digits and pairs of digits', *J. exp. Psychol.*, **70,** 479–489.

NORTH, J. D., and LOMNICKI, Z. A. (1961) 'Further experiments on human operators in compensatory tracking tasks', *Ergonomics*, **4,** 339–353.

NORTH, J. D., LOMNICKI, Z. A., and ZAREMBA, S. K. (1958) 'The design and interpretation of human control experiments', *Ergonomics*, **1,** 314–327.

OLDFIELD, R. C. (1954) 'Memory mechanisms and the theory of schemata', *Brit. J. Psychol.*, **45,** 14–23.

OLDFIELD, R. C. (1955) 'Apparent fluctuations of a sensory threshold', *Quart. J. exp. Psychol.*, **7,** 101–115.

OLDFIELD, R. C. (1966) 'Things, words and the brain', *Quart. J. exp. Psychol.*, **18,** 340–353.

OLDFIELD, R. C., and WINGFIELD, A. (1965) 'Response latencies in naming objects', *Quart. J. exp. Psychol.*, **17,** 273–281.

OOSTLANDER, A. M., and DE SWART, H. (1966) 'Search-discrimination time and the applicability of information theory', *J. exp. Psychol.*, **72,** 423–428.

OSBORNE, E. E. (1919) *The output of women workers in relation to hours of work in shell-making.* Industrial Fatigue Research Board Report No. 2. H.M.S.O., London.

PAILLARD, J. (1960) 'The patterning of skilled movements', in *Handbook of Physiology – Neurophysiology.* III (ed. J. Field, H. W. Magoun and V. E. Hall). Washington: American Physiological Society, pp. 1679–1708.

PAILLARD, J. (1968) Lecture at the Cambridge University Psychological Laboratory.

PARDUCCI, A. (1965) 'Category judgement: a range-frequency model', *Psychol. Rev.*, **72,** 407–418.

PARKS, T. E. (1965) 'Post-retinal visual storage', *Amer. J. Psychol.*, **78**, 145–147.

PETERS, R. W. (1954a) *Competing messages: the effect of interfering messages upon the reception of primary messages.* U.S.N. School of Aviation Medicine. Project NM00106401, Rep. No. 27.

PETERS, R. W. (1954b) *Message reception as a function of the time of occurrence of extraneous messages.* U.S.N. School of Aviation Medicine. Project NM 00106401, Rep. No. 33.

PETERS, W., and WENBORNE, A. A. (1936) 'The time pattern of voluntary movements', *Brit. J. Psychol.*, **26**, 388–396 and **27**, 60–73.

PETERSON, L. R. (1966a) 'Short-term verbal memory and learning', *Psychol. Rev.*, **73**, 193–207.

PETERSON, L. R. (1966b) 'Reminiscence in short-term retention', *J. exp. Psychol.*, **71**, 115–118.

PETERSON, L. R., and KROENER, SUSAN (1964) 'Dichotic stimulation and retention', *J. exp. Psychol.*, **68**, 125–130.

PETRIE, A., COLLINS, W., and SOLOMON, P. (1960) 'The tolerance for pain and for sensory deprivation', *Amer. J. Psychol.*, **73**, 80–90.

PEW, R. W. (1966) 'Acquisition of hierarchical control over the temporal organization of a skill', *J. exp. Psychol.*, **71**, 764–771.

PIERCE, J. R., and KARLIN, J. E. (1957) 'Reading rates and the information rate of a human channel', *Bell System Tech. J.*, **36**, 497–516.

PIÉRON, H. (1920) 'Nouvelles recherches sur l'analyse du temps de latence sensorielle et sur la loi qui relie ce temps à l'intensité de l'excitation', *Année Psychol.*, **22**, 58–142.

PIÉRON, H. (1936) 'Recherches sur la latence de perception des accroissements de luminosité', *Année Psychol.*, **37**, 1–16.

PIERREL, ROSEMARY, and MURRAY, CATHERINE S. (1963) 'Some relationships between comparative judgment, confidence and decision-time in weight-lifting', *Amer. J. Psychol.*, **76**, 28–38.

PIERSON, W. R. (1961) 'Body size and speed', *Res. Quart.*, **32**, 197–200.

PILLSBURY, W. B., and SYLVESTER, ANNE (1940) 'Retroactive and proactive inhibition in immediate memory', *J. exp. Psychol.*, **27**, 532–545.

PINNEO, L. R. (1961) 'The effects of induced muscle tension during tracking on level of activation and on performance', *J. exp. Psychol.*, **62**, 523–531.

PINNEO, L. R. (1966) 'On noise in the nervous system', *Psychol. Rev.*, **73**, 242–247.

PITZ, G. F., and DOWNING, L. (1967) 'Optimal behaviour in a decision-making task as a function of instructions and payoffs', *J. exp. Psychol.*, **73**, 549–555.

POLLACK, I. (1952) 'The information of elementary auditory displays', *J. Acoust. Soc. Amer.*, **24**, 745–749.

POLLACK, I. (1953a) 'The information of elementary auditory displays: II', *J. Acoust. Soc. Amer.*, **25**, 765–769.

POLLACK, I. (1953b) 'Assimilation of sequentially encoded information', *Amer. J. Psychol.*, **66**, 421–435.

POLLACK, I. (1963a) 'Message-uncertainty and message-reception: III. Effect of restriction of verbal context', *J. verb. Learn. verb. Beh.*, **1**, 392–395.

POLLACK, I. (1963b) 'Speed of classification of words into superordinate categories', *J. verb. Learn. verb. Beh.*, **2**, 159–165.

POLLACK, I. (1963c) 'Verbal reaction times to briefly presented words', *Percep. mot. Skills*, **17**, 137–138.

POLLACK, I., and DECKER, L. R. (1958) 'Confidence ratings, message reception and the receiver operating characteristics', *J. Acoust. Soc. Amer.*, **30**, 286–292.

POLLACK, I., and FICKS, L. (1954) 'Information of elementary multidimensional auditory displays. II', *J. Acoust. Soc. Amer.*, **26**, 155–158.

POLLACK, I., and JOHNSON, L. (1963A) 'Monitoring of sequential binary patterns', *Percep. mot. Skills*, **16**, 911–913.

POLLACK, I., and JOHNSON, L. (1963b) 'Continuing memory span for digits', *Percep. mot. Skills*, **17**, 731–734.

POLLACK, I., and JOHNSON, L. B. (1965) 'Memory-span with efficient coding procedures', *Amer. J. Psychol.*, **78**, 609–614.

POLLACK, I., JOHNSON, L. B., and KNAFF, P. R. (1959) 'Running memory span', *J. exp. Psychol.*, **57**, 137–146.

POSNER, M. I (1963) 'Immediate memory in sequential tasks', *Psychol. Bull.*, **60**, 333–349.

POSNER, M. I. (1964a) 'Rate of presentation and order of recall in immediate memory', *Brit. J. Psychol.*, **55**, 303–306.

POSNER, M. I. (1965) 'Memory and thought in human intellectual performance', *Brit. J. Psychol.*, **56**, 197–215.

POSNER, M. I. (1967a) 'Short term memory systems in human information processing', in *Attention and Performance* (ed. A. F. Sanders). Amsterdam: North-Holland Publishing Co.

POSNER, M. I. (1967b) 'Characteristics of visual and kinesthetic memory codes', *J. exp. Psychol.*, **75**, 103–107.

POSNER, M. I., and KONICK, A. F. (1966) 'On the role of interference in short-term retention', *J. exp. Psychol.*, **72**, 221–231.

POSNER, M. I., and MITCHELL, R. F. (1967) 'Chronometric analysis of classification', *Psychol. Rev.*, **74**, 392–409.

POSNER, M. I., and ROSSMAN, ELLEN (1965) 'Effect of size and location of informational transforms upon short-term retention', *J. exp. Psychol.*, **70**, 496–505.

POSTMAN, L., and BRUNER, J. S. (1949) 'Multiplicity of set as a determinant of perceptual behaviour', *J. exp. Psychol.*, **39**, 369–377.

POSTMAN, L., and GOGGIN, JUDITH (1964) 'Whole versus part learning of serial lists as a function of meaningfulness and intralist similarity', *J. exp. Psychol.*, **68**, 140–150.

POSTMAN, L., and GOGGIN, JUDITH (1966) 'Whole versus part learning of paired-associate lists', *J. exp. Psychol.*, **71**, 867–877.

POSTMAN, L., KEPPEL, G., and STARK, KAREN (1965) 'Unlearning as a function of the relationship between successive response classes', *J. exp. Psychol.*, **69**, 111–118.

POSTMAN, L., TURNAGE, T. W., and SILVERSTEIN, A. (1964) 'The running memory span for words', *Quart. J. exp. Psychol.*, **16**, 81–89.

POULTON, E. C. (1950) 'Perceptual anticipation and reaction time', *Quart. J. exp. Psychol.*, **2**, 99–112.

POULTON, E. C. (1953) 'Two-channel listening', *J. exp. Psychol.*, **46**, 91–96.

POULTON, E. C. (1954) 'Eye-hand span in simple serial tasks', *J. exp. Psychol.*, **47**, 403–410.

POULTON, E. C. (1958a) 'Copying behind during dictation', *Quart. J. exp. Psychol.*, **10**, 48–55.

POULTON, E. C. (1958b) 'Measuring the order of difficulty of visual-motor tasks', *Ergonomics*, **1**, 234–239.

POULTON, E. C. (1960) 'The optimal perceptual load in a paced auditory inspection task', *Brit. J. Psychol.*, **51**, 127–139.

POULTON, E. C. (1963) 'Sequential short-term memory: some tracking experiments', *Ergonomics*, **6**, 117–132.

POULTON, E. C. (1964) 'Postview and preview in tracking with complex and simple inputs', *Ergonomics*, **7**, 257–266.

POULTON, E. C. (1966) 'Tracking behavior', in *Acquisition of Skill* (ed. E. A. Bilodeau). New York and London: Academic Press, pp. 361–410.

PRICE, R. H. (1966) 'Signal-detection methods in personality and perception', *Psychol. Bull.*, **66**, 55–62.

PROVINS, K. A. (1957) 'Sensory factors in the voluntary application of pressure', *Quart. J. exp. Psychol.*, **9**, 28–41.

PROVINS, K. A. (1958) 'The effect of peripheral nerve block on the appreciation and execution of finger movements', *J. Physiol.*, **143**, 55–67.

PUGH, L. A., OLDROYD, C. R., RAY, T. S., and CLARK, M. L. (1966) 'Muscular effort and electrodermal responses', *J. exp. Psychol.*, **71**, 241–248.

RAAB, D. H. (1962) 'Effect of stimulus-duration on auditory reaction-time', *Amer. J. Psychol.*, **75**, 298–301.

RAAB, D. H., and GROSSBERG, M. (1965) 'Reaction time to changes in the intensity of white noise', *J. exp. Psychol.*, **69**, 609–612.

RABBITT, P. M. A. (1959) 'Effects of independent variations in stimulus and response probability', *Nature*, **183**, 1212.

RABBITT, P. M. A. (1962) 'Short-term retention of more than one aspect of a series of stimuli', *Nature*, **195**, 102.

RABBITT, P. M. A. (1964) 'Ignoring irrelevant information', *Brit. J. Psychol.*, **55**, 403–414.

RABBITT, P. M. A. (1965) 'Response-facilitation on repetition of a limb movement', *Brit. J. Psychol.*, **56**, 303–304.

RABBITT, P. M. A. (1966a) 'Errors and error correction in choice-response tasks', *J. exp. Psychol.*, **71**, 264–272.

RABBITT, P. M. A. (1966b) 'Times for transitions between hand and foot responses in a self-paced task', *Quart. J. exp. Psychol.*, **18**, 334–339.

RABBITT, P. M. A. (1966c) 'Error correction time without external error signals', *Nature*, **212**, 438.

RABBITT, P. M. A. (1967a) 'Learning to ignore irrelevant information', *Amer. J. Psychol.*, **80**, 1–13.

RABBITT, P. M. A. (1967b) 'Time to detect errors as a function of factors affecting choice response time', in *Attention and Performance* (ed. A. F. Sanders). Amsterdam: North-Holland Publishing Co.

RABBITT, P. M. A., and PHILLIPS, SHIRLEY (1967) 'Error-detection and correct latencies as a function of S-R compatibility', *Quart. J. exp. Psychol.*, **19**, 37–42.

RAPOPORT, A. (1959) 'A study of disjunctive reaction times', *Behavioural Sci.*, **4**, 299–315.

RAY, W. S. (1965) 'Mild stress and problem-solving', *Amer. J. Psychol.*, **78**, 227–234.

REICHARD, SUZANNE, LIVSON, FLORINE, and PETERSEN, P. G. (1962) *Ageing and Personality.* New York: John Wiley & Sons.

REID, C. (1928) 'The mechanism of voluntary muscular fatigue', *Quart. J. exp. Physiol.*, **19**, 17–42.

REID, L. S., HENNEMAN, R. H., and LONG, E. R. (1960) 'An experimental analysis of set: The effect of categorical restriction', *Amer. J. Psychol.*, **73**, 568–572.

RESTLE, F., and DAVIS, J. H. (1962) 'Success and speed of problem solving by individuals and groups', *Psychol. Rev.*, **69**, 520–536.

RESTLE, F., and EMMERICH, D. (1966) 'Memory in concept attainment: effects of giving several problems concurrently', *J. exp. Psychol.*, **71**, 794–799.

REY, P., and REY, J.-P. (1963) 'Les effets comparés de deux éclairages fluorescents sur une tache visuelle et des tests de "fatigue"', *Ergonomics*, **6**, 393–401.

REYNOLDS, B. (1952) 'The effect of learning on the predictability of psychomotor performance', *J. exp. Psychol.*, **44**, 189–198.

REYNOLDS, B., and ADAMS, J. A. (1953) 'Motor performance as a function of click reinforcement', *J. exp. Psychol.*, **45**, 315–320.

REYNOLDS, D. (1964) 'Effects of double stimulation: temporary inhibition of response', *Psychol. Bull.*, **62**, 333–347.

REYNOLDS, D. (1966) 'Time and event uncertainty in unisensory reaction time', *J. exp. Psychol.*, **71**, 286–293.

RICHARDS, J. M. (1962) 'The cue additivity principle in a restricted social interaction situation', *J. exp. Psychol.*, **63**, 452–457.

RICHARDSON, PATRICIA, and VOSS, J. F. (1960) 'Replication report: Verbal context and the recall of meaningful material', *J. exp. Psychol.*, **60**, 417–418.

RIEDEL, W. W. (1965) 'Anxiety level and the "doubtful" judgement in a psychophysical experiment', *J. abn. Psychol.*, **70**, 462–464.

ROBINSON, G., and LOESS, H. (1967) 'Short-term retention of individual paired associates as a function of conceptual category', *J. exp. Psychol.*, **75**, 133–135.

ROBINSON, J. S., BROWN, L. T., and HAYES, W. H. (1964) 'Test of effects of past experience on perception', *Percep. mot. Skills*, **18**, 953–956.

RODWAN, A. S., and HAKE, H. W. (1964) 'The discriminant-function as a model for perception', *Amer. J. Psychol.*, **77**, 380–392.

ROSENQUIST, H. S. (1965) 'Visual response component of rotary pursuit tracking', *Percep. mot. Skills*, **21**, 555–560.

ROSS, HELEN E., and GREGORY, R. L. (1964) 'Is the Weber fraction a function of physical or perceived input?', *Quart. J. exp. Psychol.*, **16**, 116–122.

RUBIN, G., VON TREBRA, PATRICIA, and SMITH, K. U. (1952) 'Dimensional analysis of motion: 3. Complexity of movement pattern', *J. appl. Psychol.*, **36**, 272–276.

RUBINSTEIN, L. (1964) 'Intersensory and intrasensory effects in simple reaction time', *Percep. mot. Skills*, **18**, 159–172.

RUCH, T. C. (1951) 'Motor systems', in *Handbook of Experimental Psychology* (ed. S. S. Stevens). New York: John Wiley & Sons. London: Chapman & Hall, pp. 154–208.

RUSSELL, W. R. (1959) *Brain Memory Learning*. Oxford University Press.

RYAN, J. (1967) Unpublished Ph.D. Thesis. University of Cambridge.

SALDANHA, E. L. (1955) 'An investigation into the effects of prolonged and exacting visual work', *M.R.C. Applied Psychology Research Unit Report* No. 243.

SALDANHA, E. L. (1957) 'Alternating an exacting visual task with either rest or similar work', *M.R.C. Applied Psychology Research Unit Report* No. 289.

SALTZMAN, I. J., KANFER, F. H., and GREENSPOON, J. (1955) 'Delay of reward and human motor learning', *Psychol. Rep.*, **5**, 139–152.

SAMPSON, H. (1964) 'Immediate memory and simultaneous visual stimulation', *Quart. J. exp. Psychol.*, **16**, 1–10.

SAMPSON, H., and SPONG, P. (1961a) 'Binocular fixation and immediate memory', *Brit. J. Psychol.*, **52**, 239–248.

SAMPSON, H., and SPONG, P. (1961b) 'Handedness, eye-dominance and immediate memory', *Quart. J. exp. Psychol.*, **13**, 173–180.

SANDERS, A. F. (1961a) 'Rehearsal and recall in immediate memory', *Ergonomics*, **4**, 29–34.

SANDERS, A. F. (1961b) 'Aandachtsverschuiving en lawaaihinder', *Ned. Tijd. Psychol.*, **16**, 460–474.

SANDERS, A. F. (1964) 'Selective strategies in the assimilation of successively presented signals', *Quart. J. exp. Psychol.*, **16**, 368–372.

SANDERS, A. F. (1967) 'Some aspects of reaction processes', in *Attention and Performance* (ed. A. F. Sanders). Amsterdam: North-Holland Publishing Co.

SARASON, I. G., and PALOLA, E. G. (1960) 'The relationship of test and general anxiety, difficulty of task and experimental instructions to performance', *J. exp. Psychol.*, **59**, 185–191.

SAUFLEY, W. H., and BILODEAU, INA MCD. (1963) 'Protective self-pacing during learning', *J. exp. Psychol.*, **66**, 596–600.

SCHAUB, G. R., and LINDLEY, R. H. (1964) 'Effects of subject-generated recoding cues on short-term memory', *J. exp. Psychol.*, **68**, 171–175.

SCHIFF, W. (1961) 'The effect of subliminal stimuli on guessing-accuracy', *Amer. J. Psychol.*, **74**, 54–60.

SCHOUTEN, J. F., and BEKKER, J. A. M. (1967) 'Reaction time and accuracy', in *Attention and Performance* (ed. A. F. Sanders). Amsterdam: North-Holland Publishing Co.

SCHOUTEN, J. F., KALSBEEK; J. W. H., and LEOPOLD, F. F. (1962) 'On the evaluation of perceptual and mental load', *Ergonomics*, **5**, 251–260.

SCHWAB, R. S. (1953) 'Motivation in measurements of fatigue', in *Symposium on Fatigue* (ed. W. F. Floyd and A. T. Welford). London: H. K. Lewis & Co., for the Ergonomics Research Society.

SEARLE, L. V., and TAYLOR, F. V. (1948) 'Studies of tracking behavior. I. Rate and time characteristics of simple corrective movements', *J. exp. Psychol.*, **38**, 615–631.

SEIBEL, R. (1963) 'Discrimination reaction time for a 1,023-alternative task', *J. exp. Psychol.*, **66**, 215–226.

SEIBEL, R., CHRIST, R. E., and TEICHNER, W. H. (1965) 'Short-term memory under work-load stress', *J. exp. Psychol.*, **70**, 154–162.

SEIDENSTEIN, S., CHERNIKOFF, R., and TAYLOR, F. V. (1960) *The relationship of a retinal-gain index to system performance*, U.S. Naval Res. Lab., Rep. No. 5548.

SELYE, H. (1950) *The physiology and Pathology of Exposure to Stress.* Montreal: Acta.

SENGSTAKE, C. B. (1965) 'Perception of deviations in repetitive patterns', *J. exp. Psychol.* **70**, 210–217.

SEYFFARTH, H. (1940) 'The behaviour of motor units in voluntary contraction', *Skr. Norke Vidensk akad. I Mat-Nat Kl.*, No. 4.

SEYMOUR, W. D. (1954a) *Industrial Training for Manual Operations.* London: Pitman.

SEYMOUR, W. D. (1954b) 'Experiments on the acquisition of industrial skills', *Occupational Psychol.*, **28**, 77–89. (1955) Part 2. *Ibid.*, **29**, 82–98. (1956) Part 3. *Ibid.*, **30**, 94–104. (1959) Part 4, assembly tasks. *Ibid.*, **33**, 18–35.

SHALLICE, T., and VICKERS, D. (1964) 'Theories and experiments on discrimination times', *Ergonomics*, **7**, 37–49.

SHANNON, C. E., and WEAVER, W. (1949) *The Mathematical Theory of Communication*. Urbana, IK: University of Illinois Press.

SHELLY, M. W. (1961) 'Learning with reduced feedback information', *J. exp. Psychol.*, **62**, 209–222.

SHEPARD, R. W., and SHEENAN, MAUREEN M. (1965) 'Immediate recall of numbers containing a familiar prefix or postfix', *Percep. mot. Skills*, **21**, 263–273.

SHERRINGTON, C. (1906) *The Integrative Action of the Nervous System.* Cambridge University Press (Reset Edition 1947).

SHERWOOD, J. J. (1965) 'A relation between arousal and performance', *Amer. J. Psychol.*, **78**, 461–465.

SIDOWSKI, J. B., and EASON, R. G. (1960) 'Drive, verbal performance and muscle action potential', *J. exp. Psychol.*, **60**, 365–370.

SIDOWSKI, J. B., and NUTHMANN, C. (1961) 'Induced muscular tension, incentive and blink rate in a verbal learning task', *J. exp. Psychol.*, **61**, 295–299.

SIEGEL, A. I., and WOLF, J. J. (1962) 'A model for digital simulation of two-operator man-machine systems', *Ergonomics*, **5**, 557–572.

SIMON, H. A., and KOTOVSKY, K. (1963) 'Human acquisition of concepts for sequential patterns', *Psychol. Rev.*, **70**, 534–546.

SIMON, J. R. (1960) 'Changes with age in the speed of performance on a dial setting task', *Ergonomics*, **3**, 169–174.

SIMON, J. R., and SIMON, BETTY P. (1959) 'Duration of movements in a dial setting task as a function of the precision of manipulation', *J. appl. Psychol.*, **43**, 389–394.

SIMONSON, E. (1965) 'Performance as a function of age and cardiovascular diseases', in *Behavior, Ageing and the Nervous System* (ed. A. T. Welford and J. E. Birren). Springfield, Illinois: Charles C. Thomas, pp. 401–434.

SIMONSON, E., and BROZEK, J. (1952) 'Flicker Fusion frequency. Background and applications', *Physiol. Rev.*, **32**, 349–378.

SINGLETON, W. T. (1953) 'Deterioration of performance on a short-term perceptual-motor task', in *Symposium on Fatigue* (ed. W. F. Floyd and A. T. Welford). London: H. K. Lewis & Co. for the Ergonomics Research Society.

SINGLETON, W. T. (1954) 'The change of movement timing with age', *Brit. J. Psychol.*, **45**, 166–172.

SINGLETON, W. T. (1955) 'Age and performance timing on simple skills', in *Old Age in the Modern World*: Rep. 3rd Cong. Internat. Ass. Gerontol., London, 1954. Edinburgh: Livingstone, pp. 221–231.

SINGLETON, W. T. (1957) 'An experimental investigation of sewing-machine skill', *Brit. J. Psychol.*, **48**, 127–132.

SINGLETON, W. T. (1959) 'The training of shoe-machinists', *Ergonomics*, **2**, 148–152.

SINGLETON, W. T., EASTERBY, R. S., and WHITFIELD, D. J. (1967) 'The human operator in complex systems', *Ergonomics*, **10**, 99–292 (also published in book form).

SIPOWICZ, R. R., WARE, J. R., and BAKER, R. A. (1962) 'The effects of reward and knowledge of results on the performance of a simple vigilance task', *J. exp. Psychol.*, **64**, 58–61.

SLACK, C. W. (1953) 'Learning in simple one-dimensional tracking', *Amer. J. Psychol.*, **66**, 33–44.

SLAMECKA, N. J. (1963) 'Choice reaction-time as a function of meaningful similarity', *Amer. J. Psychol.*, **76**, 274–280.

SLAMECKA, N. J. (1967) 'Recall and recognition in list-discrimination tasks as a function of the number of alternatives', *J. exp. Psychol.*, **74**, 187–192.

SLATER-HAMMEL, A. T. (1958) 'Psychological refractory period in simple paired responses', *Res. Quart. Amer. Ass. Hlth. Phys. Educ. Rec.*, **29**, 468–481.

SMITH, E. E. (1967) 'Effects of familiarity on stimulus recognition and categorization', *J. exp. Psychol.*, **74**, 324–332.

SMITH, K. U. (1966) 'Cybernetic theory and analysis of learning', in *Acquisition of Skill* (ed. E. A. Bilodeau). New York and London: Academic Press, pp. 425–482.

SMITH, K. U., and SMITH, W. M. (1962) *Perception and Motion*. Philadelphia: Saunders.

SMITH, L. A. (1965) 'Individual differences in maximal speed of muscular contraction and reaction time', *Percep. mot. Skills*, **21**, 19–22.

SMITH, M., and WILSON, EDNA A. (1953) 'A model of the auditory threshold and its application to the problem of the multiple observer', *Psychol. Monogr.*, **67**, No. 9.

SMITH, MARILYN C. (1967a) 'Theories of the psychological refractory period', *Psychol. Bull.*, **67**, 202–213.

SMITH, MARILYN C. (1967b) 'Reaction time to a second stimulus as a function of intensity of the first stimulus', *Quart. J. exp. Psychol.*, **19**, 125–132.

SMITH, MARILYN C. (1967c) 'The psychological refractory period as a function of performance of a first response', *Quart. J. exp. Psychol.*, **19**, 350–352.

SMITH, S., and MYERS, T. I. (1966) 'Stimulation seeking during sensory deprivation', *Percep. mot. Skills*, **23**, 1151–1163.

SMITH, S., MYERS, T. I., and MURPHY, D. B. (1967) 'Vigilance during sensory deprivation', *Percep. mot. Skills*, **24,** 971–976.

SMITH, W. M., MCCRARY, J. W., and SMITH, K. U. (1960) 'Delayed visual feedback and behavior', *Science*, **132,** 1013–1014.

SMITH, W. M., SMITH, K. U., STANLEY, R., and HARLEY, W. (1956) 'Analysis of performance in televised visual fields: preliminary report', *Percep. mot. Skills*, **6,** 195–198.

SOLOMONS, L. M. (1900) 'A new explanation of Weber's law', *Psychol. Rev.*, **7,** 234–240.

SPENCE, K. W., FARBER, I. E., and MCFANN, H. H. (1956a) 'The relation of anxiety (drive) level to performance in competitional and non-competitional paired-associates learning', *J. exp. Psychol.*, **52,** 296–305.

SPENCE, K. W., TAYLOR, J., and KETCHEL, RHODA (1956b) 'Anxiety (drive) level and degree of competition in paired-associates learning', *J. exp. Psychol.*, **52,** 306–310.

SPENCER, J. (1961) 'Estimating averages', *Ergonomics*, **4,** 317–328.

SPENCER, J. (1963) 'A further study of estimating averages', *Ergonomics*, **6,** 255–265.

SPENCER, J. (1965) 'Experiments on engineering drawing comprehension', *Ergonomics*, **8,** 93–110.

SPERLING, G. (1960) 'The information available in brief visual presentations', *Psychol. Monogr.*, **74,** No. 11.

SPERLING, G. (1963) 'A model for some kinds of visual memory tasks', *Human Factors*, **5,** 19–31.

SPERLING, G. (1967) 'Successive approximations to a model for short term memory', in *Attention and Performance* (ed. A. F. Sanders). Amsterdam: North-Holland Publishing Co.

SPIELBERGER, C. D., BERNSTEIN, IRA H., and RATLIFF, R. G. (1966) 'Information and incentive value of the reinforcing stimulus in verbal conditioning', *J. exp. Psychol.*, **71,** 26–31.

SPIELBERGER, C. D., and DENNY, J. P. (1963) 'Visual recognition thresholds as a function of verbal ability and word frequency', *J. exp. Psychol.*, **65,** 597–602.

SPITZ, H. H. (1967) 'Information transmission in an absolute judgment task with feedback, using normal and retarded subjects', *J. comp. physiol. Psychol.*, **64,** 85–92.

STABLER, J. R., and DYAL, J. A. (1963) 'Discriminative reaction-time as a joint function of manifest anxiety and intelligence', *Amer. J. Psychol.*, **76,** 484–487.

STAGER, P. (1966) 'Note on use of information concepts in the assessment of group structure', *Percep. mot. Skills*, **23,** 239–242.

STANILAND, A. C. (1966) *Patterns of Redundancy*. Cambridge University Press.

STAUFFACHER, J. C. (1937) 'The effect of induced muscular tension upon various phases 'of the learning process', *J. exp. Psychol.*, **21**, 26–46.

STEFFY, R. A., and ERIKSEN, C. W. (1965) 'Short-term, perceptual-recognition memory for tachistoscopically presented nonsense forms', *J. exp. Psychol.*, **70**, 277–283.

STEINMAN, ALBERTA R. (1944) 'Reaction time to change compared with other psychophysical methods', *Arch. Psychol., N.Y.*, **41**, No. 292.

STENNETT, R. G. (1957) 'The relationship of performance level to level of arousal', *J. exp. Psychol.*, **54**, 54–61.

STONE, G. C., and CALLAWAY, E. (1964) 'Effects of stimulus probability on reaction time in a number-naming task', *Quart. J. exp. Psychol.*, **16**, 47–55.

STONE, M. (1960) 'Models for reaction time', *Psychometrika*, **25**, 251–260.

STROUD, J. B. (1931) 'The role of muscular tensions in stylus maze learning', *J. exp. Psychol.*, **14**, 606–631.

SUCI, G. J., DAVIDOFF, M. D., and SURWILLO, W. W. (1960) 'Reaction time as a function of stimulus information and age', *J. exp. Psychol.*, **60**, 242–244.

SURWILLO, W. W., and QUILTER, R. E. (1964) 'Vigilance, age and response-time', *Amer. J. Psychol.*, **77**, 614–620.

SWETS, J. A. (1959) 'Indices of signal detectability obtained with various psychophysical procedures', *J. Acoust. Soc. Amer.*, **31**, 511–513.

SWETS, J. A. (ed.) (1964) *Signal Detection and Recognition by Human Observers.* New York: Wiley.

SWETS, J. A., and SEWALL, SUSAN T. (1963) 'Invariance of signal detectability over stages of practice and levels of motivation', *J. exp. Psychol.*, **66**, 120–126.

SWETS, J. A., SHIPLEY, ELIZABETH F., MCKEY, MOLLY J., and GREEN, D. M. (1959) 'Multiple observations of signals in noise', *J. Acoust. Soc. Amer.*, **31**, 514–521.

SWETS, J. A., TANNER, W. P., and BIRDSALL, T. G. (1961) 'Decision processes in perception', *Psychol. Rev.*, **68**, 301–340.

SYMONDS, SIR CHARLES (1966) 'Disorders of memory', *Brain*, **89**, 625–644.

SYMONS, J. R., and MACKAY, C. K. (1962) 'An investigation of changes in auditory sensitivity during the performance of a mental task', *Quart. J. exp. Psychol.*, **14**, 104–108.

SZAFRAN, J. (1963) 'Age differences in choice reaction time and cardiovascular status among pilots', *Nature*, **200**, 904–906.

SZAFRAN, J. (1966) 'Age, cardiac output and choice reaction time', *Nature*, **209**, 836.

SZAFRAN, J., and WELFORD, A. T. (1950) 'On the relation between transfer and difficulty of initial task', *Quart. J. exp. Psychol.*, **2**, 88–94.

TAKAKUWA, E. (undated) *The function of concentration maintenance (TAF) – as an evaluation of fatigue.* Hokkaido University School of Medicine.

TANNER, W. P., and SWETS, J. A. (1954) 'A decision-making theory of visual detection', *Psychol. Rev.*, **61**, 401–409.

TAUB, H. A., MONTY, R. A., and LAUGHERY, K. R. (1967) 'Keeping track of sequential events: effects of stimulus on-time and inter-stimulus off-time', *Percep. mot. Skills*, **24**, 159–166.

TAUB, H. A., and MYERS, J. L. (1961) 'Differential monetary gains in a two-choice situation', *J. exp. Psychol.*, **61**, 157–162.

TAYLOR, D. H. (1964) 'Drivers' galvanic skin response and the risk of accident', *Ergonomics*, **7**, 439–451.

TAYLOR, D. H. (1966) 'Latency components in two-choice responding', *J. exp. Psychol.*, **72**, 481–487.

TAYLOR, F. V. (1957) 'Simplifying the controller's task through display quickening', *Occupational Psychol.*, **31**, 120–125.

TAYLOR, F. V., and BIRMINGHAM, H. P. (1948) 'Studies of tracking behavior. II. The acceleration pattern of quick manual corrective responses', *J. exp. Psychol.*, **38**, 783–795.

TAYLOR, F. V., and GARVEY, W. D. (1959) 'The limitations of a "Procrustean" approach to the optimization of man-machine systems', *Ergonomics*, **2**, 187–194.

TAYLOR, JANET A. (1956) 'Drive theory and manifest anxiety', *Psychol. Bull.*, **53**, 303–320.

TAYLOR, M. M. (1965) 'Detectability measures in vigilance: comment on a paper by Wiener, Poock and Steele', *Percep. mot. Skills*, **20**, 1217–1221.

TAYLOR, M. M., LINDSAY, P. H., and FORBES, S. M. (1967) 'Quantification of shared capacity processing in auditory and visual discrimination', in *Attention and Performance* (ed. A. F. Sanders). Amsterdam: North-Holland Publishing Co.

TECCE, J. J. (1965) 'Relationship of anxiety (drive) and response competition in problem solving', *J. abn. Psychol.*, **70**, 465–467.

TECCE, J. J., and TESTA, D. H. (1965) 'Effects of heightened drive (shock), on 2-, 4- and 8-choice card-sorting', *Percep. mot. Skills*, **20**, 715–716.

TELFORD, C. W. (1931) 'The refractory phase of voluntary and associative responses', *J. exp. Psychol.*, **14**, 1–36.

THIESSEN, D. D., and RODGERS, D. A. (1961) 'Population density and endocrine function', *Psychol. Bull.*, **58**, 441–451.

THIESSEN, D. D., ZOLMAN, J. F., and RODGERS, D. A. (1962) 'Relation between adrenal weight, brain cholinesterase activity and hole-in-wall behavior of mice under different living conditions', *J. comp. physiol. Psychol.*, **55**, 186–190.

THOMAS, E. A. C. (1967) 'Reaction-time studies: the anticipation and interaction of responses', *Brit. J. math. statist. Psychol.*, **20**, 1–29.

THORNDIKE. E. L. (1931) *Human Learning*. New York: Appleton-Century.

THOULESS, R. H. (1931) 'Phenomenal regression to the "real" object. II', *Brit. J. Psychol.*, **22**, 1–30.

THURSTONE, L. L. (1927a) 'A law of comparative judgment', *Psychol. Rev.*, **34**, 273–286.

THURSTONE, L. L. (1927b) 'Psychophysical Analysis', *Amer. J. Psychol.*, **38**, 368–389.

THYLEN, J. O. (1966) 'The effect of initial pointer position relative to the control on directional relationships in the presence of two conflicting stereotypes', *Ergonomics*, **9**, 469–474.

TOPPEN, J. T. (1965) 'Effect of size and frequency of money reinforcement on human operant (work) behaviour', *Percep. mot. Skills*, **20**, 259–269.

Training Made Easier: A Review of Four Recent Studies. D.S.I.R. Problems of Progress in Industry No. 6. London: H.M.S.O.

TREBRA, PATRICIA VON, and SMITH, K. U. (1952) 'The dimensional analysis of motion: 4. Transfer effects and direction of movement', *J. appl. Psychol.*, **36**, 348–353.

TREISMAN, ANNE M. (1960) 'Contextual cues in selective listening', *Quart. J. exp. Psychol.*, **12**, 242–248.

TREISMAN, ANNE M. (1964a) 'Verbal cues, language and meaning in selective attention', *Amer. J. Psychol.*, **77**, 206–219.

TREISMAN, ANNE M. (1964b) 'The effect of irrelevant material on the efficiency of selective listening', *Amer. J. Psychol.*, **77**, 533–546.

TREISMAN, ANNE M. (1965) 'The effects of redundancy and familiarity on translating and repeating back a foreign and a native language', *Brit. J. Psychol.*, **56**, 369–379.

TREISMAN, ANNE M. (1966) 'Our limited attention', *Adv. Sci.*, **22**, 600–611.

TREISMAN, ANNE, and GEFFEN, GINA (1967) 'Selective attention: Perception or response?' *Quart. J. exp. Psychol.*, **19**, 1–17.

TREISMAN, M. (1964) 'Noise and Weber's law: The discrimination of brightness and other dimensions', *Psychol. Rev.*, **71**, 314–330.

TREISMAN, M., and WATTS, T. R. (1966) 'Relation between signal detectability theory and the traditional procedures for measuring sensory thresholds: Estimating d′ from results given by the method of constant stimuli', *Psychol. Bull.*, **66**, 438–454.

TRESSELT, M. E., and MAYZNER, M. S. (1965) 'Anagram solution times: a function of individual differences in stored diagram frequencies', *J. exp. Psychol.*, **70**, 606–610.

TRESSELT, M. E., and VOLKMANN, J. (1942) 'The production of uniform opinion by non-social stimulation', *J. abn. soc. Psychol.*, **37**, 234–243.

TROWBRIDGE, M. H., and CASON, H. (1932) 'An experimental study of Thorndike's theory of learning', *J. gen. Psychol.*, **7**, 245–258.

TRUMBO, D., NOBLE, M., and SWINK, J. (1967) 'Secondary task interference in the performance of tracking tasks', *J. exp. Psychol.*, **73**, 232–240.

TSAO, J. C. (1948) 'Studies in spaced and massed learning: I. Time period and amount of practice', *Quart. J. exp. Psychol.*, **I**, 29–36.

TULVING, E., and ARBUCKLE, T. Y. (1966) 'Input and output interference in short-term associative memory', *J. exp. Psychol.*, **72**, 145–150.

TULVING, E., and GOLD, CECILLE (1963) 'Stimulus information and cortextual information as determinants of tachistoscopic recognition of words', *J. exp. Psychol.*, **66**, 319–327.

TUNE, G. S. (1964) 'Sequential errors in a time-sharing task', *Brit. J. Psychol.*, **55**, 415–419.

TUNTURI, A. R. (1944) 'Audio frequency localization in the acoustic cortex of the dog', *Amer. J. Physiol.*, **141**, 397–403.

TURVEY, M. T. (1967) 'Repetition and the perceptual information store', *J. exp. Psychol.*, **74**, 289–293.

TUSTIN, A. (1947) 'The nature of the operator's response in manual control and its implications for controller design', *J. Instn. elect. Engrs.*, **94** (IIA), 190–202.

UHR, L., and MILLER, J. G. (eds.) (1960) *Drugs and Behavior*. New York: John Wiley & Sons Inc.

ULEHLA, Z. J. (1966) 'Optimality of perceptual decision criteria', *J. exp. Psychol.*, **71**, 564–569.

ULICH, E. (1967) 'Some experiments on the function of mental training in the acquisition of motor skills', *Ergonomics*, **10**, 411–419.

UNDERWOOD, B. J. (1961) 'Ten years of massed practice on distributed practice', *Psychol. Rev.*, **68**, 229–247.

VERNON, H. M. (1919) *The influence of hours of work and of ventilation on output in tinplate manufacture*. Industrial Fatigue Research Board Report No. 1. H.M.S.O., London.

VERNON, H. M. (1920a) *Fatigue and efficiency in the iron and steel industry*. Industrial Fatigue Research Board Report No. 5. H.M.S.O., London.

VERNON, H. M. (1920b) *The speed of adaptation of output to altered hours of work*. Industrial Fatigue Research Board Report No. 6. H.M.S.O., London.

VERNON, H. M. (1924) *On the extent and effects of variety in repetitive work*. Industrial Fatigue Research Board Report No. 26. H.M.S.O., London.

VERNON, H. M., and BEDFORD, T. (1924) *Two studies on rest pauses in industry*. Industrial Fatigue Research Board Report No. 25. H.M.S.O., London.

VERVILLE, E., and CAMERON, N. (1946) 'Age and sex differences in the perception of incomplete pictures by adults', *J. genet. Psychol.*, **68**, 149–157.

VICKERS, D. (1967) Unpublished Ph.D. Thesis. University of Cambridge.

VINCE, MARGARET A. (1948a) 'The intermittency of control movements and the psychological refractory period', *Brit. J. Psychol.*, **38**, 149–157.

VINCE, MARGARET A. (1948b) 'Corrective movements in a pursuit task', *Quart. J. exp. Psychol.*, **1**, 85–103.

VINCE, MARGARET A. (1949) 'Rapid response sequences and the psychological refractory period', *Brit. J. Psychol.*, **40**, 23–40.

VINCE, MARGARET A. (1950) *Some exceptions to the psychological refractory period in unskilled manual responses.* Medical Research Council Applied Psychology Research Unit Report No. 124/50.

VINCE, MARGARET A., and WELFORD, A. T. (1967) 'Time taken to change the speed of a response', *Nature*, **213**, 532–533.

VITELES, M. (1932) *Industrial Psychology.* New York: W. W. Norton & Co.

WALD, A. (1947) *Sequential Analysis.* New York: John Wiley & Sons. London: Chapman & Hall.

WALD, A. (1950) *Statistical Decision Functions.* New York: John Wiley & Sons. London: Chapman & Hall.

WALKER, E. L., and TARTE, R. D. (1963) 'Memory storage as a function of arousal and time with homogeneous and heterogeneous lists', *J. verb. Learn. verb. Beh.*, **2**, 113–119.

WALLACE, JEAN G. (1956) 'Some studies of perception in relation to age', *Brit. J. Psychol.*, **47**, 283–297.

WALLACE, J. (1966) 'An abilities conception of personality: some implications for personality measurement', *Amer. Psychologist*, **21**, 132–138.

WALLIS, C. P., and AUDLEY, R. J. (1964) 'Response instructions and the speed of relative judgments: II. Pitch discrimination', *Brit. J. Psychol.*, **55**, 121–132.

WALLIS, D., and SAMUEL, J. A. (1961) 'Some experimental studies of radar operating', *Ergonomics*, **4**, 155–168.

WARD, N. (1950) 'Speed as a function of distance: An analysis of road-cycling performances', *Brit. J. Psychol.*, **40**, 212–216.

WARRINGTON, ELIZABETH K., KINSBOURNE, M., and JAMES, M. (1966) 'Uncertainty and transitional probability in the span of apprehension', *Brit. J. Psychol.*, **57**, 7–16.

WAUGH, N. C. (1960) 'Serial position and the memory span', *Amer. J. Psychol.*, **73**, 68–79.

WAUGH, NANCY C. (1967) 'Presentation time and free recall', *J. exp. Psychol.*, **73**, 39–44.

WAUGH, N. C., and NORMAN, D. A. (1965) 'Primary memory', *Psychol. Rev.*, **72**, 89–104.

WEBSTER, R. G., and HASLERUD, G. M. (1964) 'Influence on extreme peripheral vision of attention to a visual or auditory task', *J. exp. Psychol.*, **68**, 269–272.

WEENE, P. L. (1965) 'Effects of random and orderly presentations of visual sequences', *Percep. mot. Skills*, **20**, 897–903.

WEHRKAMP, R., and SMITH, K. U. (1952) 'Dimensional analysis of motion: 2. Travel-distance effects', *J. appl. Psychol.*, **36**, 201–206.

WEINER, B., and WALKER, E. L. (1966) 'Motivational factors in short-term retention', *J. exp. Psychol.*, **71**, 190–193.

WEISS, A. D. (1965) 'The locus of reaction time change with set, motivation and age', *J. Gerontol.*, **20**, 60–64.

WEISS, B. (1954) 'The role of proprioceptive feedback in positioning responses', *J. exp. Psychol.*, **47**, 215–224.

WEISS, R. L., and SILVERMAN, J. (1966) 'Anxiety and response stereotypy: an experimental critique', *Percep. mot. Skills*, **22**, 95–104.

WELFORD, A. T. (1951) *Skill and Age: An experimental Approach*. Oxford University Press for the Nuffield Foundation.

WELFORD, A. T. (1952) 'The "psychological refractory period" and the timing of high-speed performance – a review and a theory', *Brit. J. Psychol.*, **43**, 2–19.

WELFORD, A. T. (1958) *Ageing and Human Skill*. Oxford University Press for the Nuffield Foundation.

WELFORD, A. T. (1959) 'Evidence of a single-channel decision mechanism limiting performance in a serial reaction task', *Quart. J. exp. Psychol.*, **11**, 193–210.

WELFORD, A. T. (1960a) *Ergonomics of Automation*. D.S.I.R. Problems of Progress in Industry – 8. London: H.M.S.O.

WELFORD, A. T. (1960b) 'Administrative work and human relations from the standpoint of an experimental psychologist' (abstract), *Ergonomics*, **3**, 179.

WELFORD, A. T. (1960c) 'The measurement of sensory-motor performance: survey and reappraisal of twelve years' progress', *Ergonomics*, **3**, 189–230.

WELFORD, A. T. (1962a) 'Arousal, channel-capacity and decision', *Nature*, **194**, 365–366.

WELFORD, A. T. (1962b) 'Experimental psychology and the study of social behaviour', in *Society: Problems and Methods of Study* (ed. A. T. Welford, M. Argyle, D. V. Glass and J. N. Morris). London: Routledge & Kegan Paul, pp. 153–168.

WELFORD, A. T. (1962c) 'Changes in the speed of performance with age and their industrial significance', *Ergonomics*, **5**, 139–145.

WELFORD, A. T. (1962d) 'Changes of performance time with age: a correction and methodological note', *Ergonomics*, **5**, 581–582.

WELFORD, A. T. (1965) 'Performance, biological mechanisms and age: a theoretical sketch', in *Behavior, Ageing and the Nervous System* (ed. A. T. Welford and J. E. Birren). Springfield, Illinois: Charles C. Thomas, pp. 3–20.

WELFORD, A. T. (1966) 'Individual capacity and social demands: a new look at social psychology', in *Operational Research and the Social Sciences* (ed. J. R. Lawrence). London: Tavistock Publications, pp. 531–542.

WELFORD, A. T., BROWN, RUTH A., and GABB, J. E. (1950) 'Two experiments on fatigue as affecting skilled performance in civilian aircrew', *Brit. J. Psychol.*, **40**, 195–211.

WELFORD, A. T., NORRIS, A. H., and SHOCK, N. W.(1963) 'Movement, time and age: a preliminary report' (abstract), *Ergonomics*, **6**, 310.

WEST, L. J. (1967) 'Vision and kinesthesis in the acquisition of typewriting skill', *J. appl. Psychol.*, **51**, 161–166.

WESTHOFF, J. M. (1964) 'In search of a measure of perceptual work', *Philips Tech. Rev.*, **25**, 56–64.

WESTON, H. C. (1953) *Visual fatigue – with special reference to lighting*, in Symposium on Fatigue (ed. W. F. Floyd and A. T. Welford). London: H. K. Lewis & Co. for the Ergonomics Research Society.

WHITE, R. W. (1959) 'Motivation reconsidered: the concept of competence', *Psychol. Rev.*, **66**, 297–333.

WHITTENBURG, J. A., ROSS, S., and ANDREWS, T. G. (1956) 'Sustained perceptual efficiency as measured by the Mackworth "clock" test', *Percep. mot. Skills*, **6**, 109–116.

WICKELGREN, W. A. (1964) 'Size of rehearsal group and short-term memory', *J. exp. Psychol.*, **68**, 413–419.

WICKELGREN, W. A. (1965a) 'Acoustic similarity and intrusion errors in short-term memory', *J. exp. Psychol.*, **70**, 102–108.

WICKELGREN, W. A. (1965b) 'Short-term memory for phonemically similar lists', *Amer. J. Psychol.*, **78**, 567–574.

WICKELGREN, W. A. (1966a) 'Short-term recognition memory for single letters and phonemic similarity of retroactive interference', *Quart. J. exp. Psychol.*, **18**, 55–62.

WICKELGREN, W. A. (1966b) 'Numerical relations, similarity and short-term recognition memory for pairs of digits', *Brit. J. Psychol.*, **57**, 263–274.

WICKELGREN, W. A. (1966c) 'Phonemic similarity and interference in short-term memory for single letters', *J. exp. Psychol.*, **71**, 396–404.

WICKELGREN, W. A. (1966d) 'Consolidation and retroactive interference in short-term recognition memory for pitch', *J. exp. Psychol.*, **72**, 250–259.

WICKELGREN, W. A. (1967a) 'Exponential decay and independence from irrelevant associations in short-term memory for serial order', *J. exp. Psychol.*, **73**, 165–171.

WICKELGREN, W. A. (1967b) 'Rehearsal grouping and hierarchical organization of serial position cues in short-term memory', *Quart. J. exp Psychol.*, **19**, 97–102.

WIENER, E. L. (1965) 'Tables of the function $1 - (1 - p)^N$', *Percep. mot. Skills*, **21**, 887–891.

WIENER, E. L., POOCK, G. K., and STEELE, M. (1964) 'Effect of time-sharing on monitoring performance: simple mental arithmetic as a loading task', *Percep. mot. Skills*, **19**, 435–440.

WIENER, N. (1948) *Cybernetics*. New York: Technological Press of M.I.T. and John Wiley & Sons.

WILKINSON, R. T. (1961) 'Comparison of paced, unpaced, irregular and continuous display in watchkeeping', *Ergonomics*, **4**, 259–267.

WILKINSON, R. T. (1962) 'Muscle tension during mental work under sleep deprivation', *J. exp. Psychol.*, **64**, 565–571.

WILKINSON, R. T. (1964) 'Artificial "signals" as an aid to an inspection task', *Ergonomics*, **7**, 63–72.

WILKINSON, R. T. (1965) 'Sleep deprivation', in *The Physiology of Human Survival* (ed. O. G. Edholm and A. L. Bacharach). London & New York: Academic Press, Ch. 14.

WILKINSON, R. T. (1967) 'Evoked response and reaction time', in *Attention and Performance* (ed. A. F. Sanders). Amsterdam: North-Holland Publishing Co.

WILLIAMS, A. C., and BRIGGS, G. E. (1962) 'On-target versus off-target information and the acquisition of tracking skill', *J. exp. Psychol.*, **64**, 519–525.

WILLIAMS, H. L., KEARNEY, O. F., and LUBIN, A. (1965) 'Signal uncertainty and sleep loss', *J. exp. Psychol.*, **69**, 401–407.

WILLIAMS, JUDITH A. (1966) 'Sequential effects in disjunctive reaction time: implications for decision models', *J. exp. Psychol.*, **71**, 665–672.

WINNICK, WILMA A., LURIA, J., and ZUKOR, W. J. (1967) 'Two signal detection approaches to tachistoscopic recognition', *Percep. mot. Skills*, **24**, 795–803.

WOODHEAD, MURIEL M. (1959) 'Effect of a brief loud noise on decision-making', *J. Acoust. Soc. Amer.*, **31**, 1329–1331.

WOODHEAD, MURIEL M. (1964a) 'Searching a visual display in intermittent noise', *J. Sound Vib.*, **1**, 157–161.

WOODHEAD, MURIEL M. (1964b) 'The effect of bursts of noise on an arithmetic task', *Amer. J. Psychol.*, **77**, 627–633.

WOODHEAD, MURIEL M. (1966) 'Varying the number of alternatives in short-term recall', *Brit. J. Psychol.*, **57**, 45–52.

WOODROW, H. (1914) 'The measurement of attention', *Psychol. Monogr.*, **17**, No. 76.

WOODWORTH, R. S. (1899) 'The accuracy of voluntary movement', *Psychol. Rev. Monogr. Suppl.*, **3**, No. 3.

WOODWORTH, R. S. (1958) *Dynamics of Behavior*. New York: Henry Holt & Co. London: Methuen.

WOODWORTH, R. S., and SCHLOSBERG, H. (1954) *Experimental Psychology*. New York: Henry Holt & Co. London: Methuen.

WRIGHT, J. M. VON (1957a) *An Experimental Study of Human Serial*

Learning. Soc. Sci. Fennica Commentationes Humanorum Litterarum, **23**, No. 1.

WRIGHT, J. M. VON (1957b) 'A note on the role of "guidance" in
learning', *Brit. J. Psychol.*, **48**, 133–137.

WYATT, S. (1927) *Rest-pauses in industry.* Industrial Fatigue Research
Board Report No. 42. H.M.S.O., London.

WYATT, S., and FRASER, J. A. (1925) *Studies in repetitive work with
special reference to rest-pauses.* Industrial Fatigue Research Board
Report No. 32. H.M.S.O., London.

WYATT, S., and FRASER, J. A. (1928) *The comparative effects of variety
and uniformity in work.* Industrial Fatigue Research Board Report
No. 52. H.M.S.O., London.

WYATT, S., FRASER, J. A., and STOCK, F. G. L. (1929) *The effects of
monotony in work.* Industrial Fatigue Research Board Report No. 56.
H.M.S.O., London.

WYATT, S., and LANGDON, J. N. (1932) *Inspection processes in industry.*
M.R.C. Industrial Health Research Board Report No. 63. H.M.S.O.,
London.

WYATT, S., and LANGDON, J. N. (1937) *Fatigue and boredom in repetitive
work.* M.R.C. Industrial Health Research Board Report No. 77.
H.M.S.O., London.

YATES, A. J. (1965a) 'Delayed auditory feedback and shadowing',
Quart. J. exp. Psychol., **17**, 125–131.

YATES, A. J. (1965b) 'Effects of delayed auditory feedback on morse
transmission by skilled operators', *J. exp. Psychol.*, **69**, 467–475.

YENSEN, R. (1965) 'A factor influencing motor overflow', *Percep. mot.
Skills*, **20**, 967–968.

YERKES, R. M., and DODSON, J. D. (1908) 'The relation of strength of
stimulus to rapidity of habit formation', *J. comp. Neurol. Psychol.*, **18**,
459–482.

YNTEMA, D. B., and MUESER, G. E. (1960) 'Remembering the present
states of a number of variables', *J. exp. Psychol.*, **60**, 18–22.

YNTEMA, D. B., and MUESER, G. E. (1962) 'Keeping track of variables
that have few or many states', *J. exp. Psychol.*, **63**, 391–395.

YNTEMA, D. B., and TRASK, FRANCES P. (1963) 'Recall as a search
process', *J. verb. Learn. verb. Beh.*, **2**, 65–74.

ZANGWILL, O. L. (1937) 'An investigation of the relationship between the
processes of reproducing and recognizing simple figures, with special
reference to Koffka's trace theory', *Brit. J. Psychol.*, **27**, 250–276.

ZANGWILL, O. L. (1939) 'Some relations between reproducing and
recognizing prose material', *Brit. J. Psychol.*, **29**, 370–382.

ZANGWILL, O. L. (1956) 'A note on immediate memory', *Quart. J. exp.
Psychol.*, **8**, 140–143.

ZEAMAN, D., and DENEGRE, J. (1967) 'Variability of irrelevant discriminative stimuli', *J. exp. Psychol.*, **73**, 574–580.

ZIMNY, G. H. (1965) 'Effect of flicker-periodicity and arousal during a rotary-pursuit task', *Amer. J. Psychol.*, **78**, 75–82.

ZUBEK, J. P. (1964) 'Effects of prolonged sensory and perceptual deprivation', *Brit. med. Bull.*, **20**, (1), 38–42.

ZUCKERMAN, M., and HABER, M. M. (1965) 'Need for stimulation as a source of stress response to perceptual isolation', *J. abn. Psychol.*, **70** 371–377.

Appendix

TABLE A.I *Crossman's Confusion Function*

Smaller discriminand (S_L) as proportion of greater (S_G)	$\log_2 S_G - \log_2 S_L$	$\dfrac{1}{\log_2 S_G - \log_2 S_L}$	Smaller discriminand (S_L) as proportion of greater (S_G)	$\log_2 S_G - \log_2 S_L$	$\dfrac{1}{\log_2 S_G - \log_2 S_L}$
·99	·015	68·97	·49	1·029	·970
·98	·029	34·31	·48	1·059	·945
·97	·044	22·75	·47	1·089	·918
·96	·059	16·98	·46	1·120	·893
·95	·074	13·51	·45	1·152	·868
·94	·089	11·20	·44	1·184	·844
·93	·105	9·52	·43	1·218	·821
·92	·120	8·13	·42	1·252	·799
·91	·136	7·35	·41	1·286	·777
·90	·152	6·58	·40	1·322	·756
·89	·168	5·95	·39	1·358	·736
·88	·184	5·42	·38	1·396	·716
·87	·201	4·98	·37	1·434	·697
·86	·218	4·60	·36	1·474	·678
·85	·234	4·27	·35	1·515	·660
·84	·252	3·98	·34	1·556	·643
·83	·269	3·72	·33	1·599	·625
·82	·286	3·49	·32	1·644	·608
·81	·304	3·29	·31	1·690	·592
·80	·322	3·11	·30	1·737	·576
·79	·340	2·94	·29	1·786	·560
·78	·359	2·78	·28	1·837	·544
·77	·377	2·65	·27	1·889	·529
·76	·396	2·53	·26	1·943	·514
·75	·415	2·41	·25	2·000	·500
·74	·435	2·30	·24	2·059	·486
·73	·455	2·20	·23	2·120	·472
·72	·474	2·11	·22	2·184	·458
·71	·495	2·02	·21	2·252	·444
·70	·515	1·94	·20	2·322	·430
·69	·535	1·87	·19	2·396	·417
·68	·556	1·80	·18	2·474	·404
·67	·578	1·73	·17	2·556	·391
·66	·599	1·67	·16	2·644	·378
·65	·621	1·61	·15	2·737	·365
·64	·644	1·55	·14	2·837	·353
·63	·667	1·50	·13	2·943	·340
·62	·690	1·45	·12	3·059	·327
·61	·713	1·40	·11	3·184	·314
·60	·737	1·36	·10	3·322	·301
·59	·761	1·31	·09	3·474	·288
·58	·786	1·27	·08	3·644	·274
·57	·811	1·23	·07	3·837	·261
·56	·837	1·19	·06	4·059	·246
·55	·863	1·16	·05	4·322	·231
·54	·889	1·13	·04	4·644	·215
·53	·916	1·09	·03	5·059	·198
·52	·943	1·06	·02	5·644	·177
·51	·971	1·03	·01	6·644	·151
·50	1·000	1·00	0·0	∞	0

TABLE A.2 *Normal deviates and ordinates for calculating d' and β when the variances of the distributions being compared are equal*

p	Normal deviate	Ordinate	p	Normal deviate	Ordinate
·01	2·326	·027	·26	·643	·325
·02	2·054	·048	·27	·613	·331
·03	1·881	·068	·28	·583	·337
·04	1·751	·086	·29	·553	·342
·05	1·645	·103	·30	·524	·348
·06	1·555	·119	·31	·496	·353
·07	1·476	·134	·32	·468	·358
·08	1·405	·149	·33	·440	·362
·09	1·341	·162	·34	·412	·367
·10	1·282	·176	·35	·385	·371
·11	1·227·	·188	·36	·358	·374
·12	1·175	·200	·37	·332	·378
·13	1·126	·212	·38	·305	·381
·14	1·080	·223	·39	·279	·384
·15	1·036	·233	·40	·253	·386
·16	·994	·243	·41	·228	·389
·17	·954	·253	·42	·202	·391
·18	·915	·263	·43	·176	·393
·19	·878	·272	·44	·151	·394
·20	·842	·280	·45	·126	·396
·21	·806	·288	·46	·100	·397
·22	·772	·296	·47	·075	·398
·23	·739	·304	·48	·050	·398
·24	·706	·311	·49	·025	·399
·25	·674	·318	·50	·000	·399

To obtain d' add the normal deviates corresponding to the proportions (p) of misses and false positives, i.e.

$$d' = ND \text{ for } p\text{NO}_{SN} + ND \text{ for } p\text{YES}_N$$

To obtain β divide the ordinate corresponding to the proportion (p) of misses by the ordinate corresponding to the proportion (p) of false positives, i.e.

$$\beta = \frac{\text{Ordinate for } p\text{NO}_{SN}}{\text{Ordinate for } p\text{YES}_N}$$

TABLE A.3 *Log₂ n for numbers from 1 to 100*

n	$\log_2 n$	n	$\log_2 n$	n	$\log_2 n$	n	$\log_2 n$
1	0·000	26	4·700	51	5·672	76	6·248
2	1·000	27	4·755	52	5·700	77	6·267
3	1·585	28	4·807	53	5·728	78	6·285
4	2·000	29	4·858	54	5·755	79	6·304
5	2·322	30	4·907	55	5·781	80	6·322
6	2·585	31	4·954	56	5·807	81	6·340
7	2·807	32	5·000	57	5·833	82	6·358
8	3·000	33	5·044	58	5·858	83	6·375
9	3·170	34	5·087	59	5·883	84	6·392
10	3.322	35	5·129	60	5·907	85	6·409
11	3·459	36	5·170	61	5·931	86	6·426
12	3·585	37	5·209	62	5·954	87	6·443
13	3·700	38	5·248	63	5·977	88	6·459
14	3·807	39	5·285	64	6·000	89	6·476
15	3·907	40	5·322	65	6·022	90	6·492
16	4·000	41	5·358	66	6·044	91	6·508
17	4·087	42	5·392	67	6·066	92	6·524
18	4·170	43	5·426	68	6·087	93	6·539
19	4·248	44	5·459	69	6·109	94	6·555
20	4·322	45	5·492	70	6·129	95	6·570
21	4·392	46	5·523	71	6·150	96	6·585
22	4·459	47	5·555	72	6·170	97	6·600
23	4·524	48	5·585	73	6·190	98	6·615
24	4·585	49	5·615	74	6·209	99	6·629
25	4·644	50	5·644	75	6·229	100	6·644

TABLE A.4 $p \log_2\left(\dfrac{1}{p}\right)$ and $p \log_2\left(\dfrac{1}{p} + 1\right)$

p	$p \log_2\left(\dfrac{1}{p}\right)$	$p \log_2\left(\dfrac{1}{p} + 1\right)$	p	$p \log_2\left(\dfrac{1}{p}\right)$	$p \log_2\left(\dfrac{1}{p} + 1\right)$
·01	·066	·067	·51	·495	·799
·02	·113	·114	·52	·491	·805
·03	·152	·153	·53	·485	·811
·04	·186	·188	·54	·480	·816
·05	·216	·220	·55	·474	·822
·06	·244	·249	·56	·468	·828
·07	·269	·275	·57	·462	·833
·08	·292	·300	·58	·456	·839
·09	·313	·324	·59	·449	·844
·10	·332	·346	·60	·442	·849
·11	·350	·367	·61	·435	·854
·12	·367	·387	·62	·427	·859
·13	·383	·406	·63	·420	·864
·14	·397	·423	·64	·412	·869
·15	·411	·441	·65	·404	·874
·16	·423	·457	·66	·396	·878
·17	·435	·473	·67	·387	·883
·18	·445	·488	·68	·378	·888
·19	·455	·503	·69	·369	·892
·20	·464	·517	·70	·360	·896
·21	·473	·531	·71	·351	·901
·22	·481	·544	·72	·341	·905
·23	·488	·556	·73	·331	·909
·24	·494	·569	·74	·321	·913
·25	·500	·581	·75	·311	·917
·26	·505	·592	·76	·301	·921
·27	·510	·603	·77	·290	·925
·28	·514	·614	·78	·280	·929
·29	·518	·624	·79	·269	·932
·30	·521	·635	·80	·258	·936
·31	·524	·645	·81	·246	·940
·32	·526	·654	·82	·235	·944
·33	·528	·664	·83	·223	·947
·34	·529	·673	·84	·211	·951
·35	·530	·682	·85	·199	·954
·36	·531	·690	·86	·187	·957
·37	·531	·699	·87	·175	·960
·38	·530	·707	·88	·162	·964
·39	·530	·715	·89	·150	·967
·40	·529	·723	·90	·137	·970
·41	·527	·731	·91	·124	·973
·42	·526	·738	·92	·111	·977
·43	·524	·745	·93	·097	·980
·44	·521	·752	·94	·084	·983
·45	·518	·759	·95	·070	·986
·46	·515	·766	·96	·057	·989
·47	·512	·773	·97	·043	·992
·48	·508	·780	·98	·029	·994
·49	·504	·786	·99	·014	·997
·50	·500	·793	1·00	0·0	1·000

TABLE A.5 *Probabilty of response (R) in paced tasks with differing signal rates and amounts of storage*

$\bar{x}$	Without storage	With storage over 1 stage	With storage over 2 stages	With storage over 3 stages
·1	·909	·995	·9998	·9999
·2	·833	·982	·998	·9995
·3	·769	·961	·994	·9992
·4	·714	·934	·986	·997
·5	·667	·904	·973	·992
·6	·625	·870	·953	·982
·7	·588	·836	·928	·966
·8	·556	·800	·897	·941
·9	·526	·765	·862	·909
1·0	·500	·731	·824	·870
1·1	·476	·698	·784	·826
1·2	·455	·666	·745	·781
1·3	·435	·636	·707	·737
1·4	·417	·607	·670	·694
1·5	·400	·580	·635	·654
1·6	·385	·555	·602	·617
1·7	·370	·531	·572	·683
1·8	·357	·509	·544	·553
1·9	·345	·488	·518	·524
2·0	·333	·468	·494	·499
2·1	·323	·450	·472	·475
2·2	·313	·432	·451	·454
2·3	·303	·417	·432	·434
2·4	·294	·402	·415	·416
2·5	·286	·387	·399	·400
2·6	·278	·374	·384	·385
2·7	·270	·361	·369	·370
2·8	·263	·350	·356	·357
2·9	·256	·338	·344	·345
3·0	·250	·328	·3330	·3333

Use of this table.

1. To find R when time per item t, signal frequency and λ are known: the product of t and signal frequency gives $\bar{x}$ against which R may be read directly. For example, if $t = \cdot5$ sec and signal frequency $= 4$ per sec, $\bar{x} = 2$ and R with storage over one stage ($\lambda = 1$) is ·468: i.e. responses will be made to ·468 of the signals presented, and the remaining ·532 will be missed.
2. To find t when signal frequency, λ and R are known: find R in the appropriate λ column; divide the $\bar{x}$ corresponding to this by the signal frequency to obtain t.
3. To find signal frequency when t, λ and R are known: find R in the appropriate λ column; divide the $\bar{x}$ corresponding to this by t to obtain the signal frequency.
4. When λ is not known it may be inferred provided values of R are obtainable over a fairly wide range of $\bar{x}$. At high and very low values of $\bar{x}$, R is practically independent of λ provided at least one signal can be stored. If signal frequency, t and R can be calculated for one or both extremes, the λ may be chosen which gives the best fit for intermediate values.

For values not given in the table interpolation is accurate enough for most purposes. When $\lambda = 2$ or more, R for values of $\bar{x}$ above 3·0 can be calculated approximately as $R = 1/\bar{x}$.

THE DERIVATION OF TABLE A.5

The model on which Table A.4 is based assumes (i) a single channel which, whenever a response is made, is occupied for a fixed length of time t during which it cannot deal with other signals, and (ii) that in certain circumstances signals arriving during the time the channel is busy can be held in some form of short-term storage until the channel is free.

The case when there is no storage

Let us consider first the case when no signals can be stored. This is shown diagrammatically in Figure A(1). The first signal (S_1) initiates the first response which occupies the single channel for a time interval t_1. S_2 occurs during this interval and is missed. At the end of t_1, the subject has to wait during an interval w_1 until a further signal, S_3, arrives. He then initiates a second response, and so on. Every response will be followed by a waiting time and thus the subject's whole time can be regarded as divided into two categories t and w and the total time over the task will thus be

$$(t_1 + w_1) + (t_2 + w_2) \ldots + (t_n + w_n)$$

and since $t_1 = t_2 = t_n$, the proportion of time spent making responses (T) may be expressed:

$$T_{(\lambda=0)} = \frac{t}{t + \bar{w}} \qquad (A1)$$

where λ is the number of signals that can be stored and $\bar{w}$ is the mean w. All signals occurring during the time spent making responses will be missed.

The proportion of signals responded to (R) may be calculated thus:

$$R_{(\lambda=0)} = \frac{T_{(\lambda=0)}}{\bar{x}} \qquad (A2)$$

when $\bar{x}$ is the average number of signals falling within a period t.

The case when one signal can be stored

An example of the case when one signal, but not more than one, can be stored is shown in Figure A(2). S_1 initiates the first response and occupies the channel for a time t_1, during which S_2 occurs. Because of the storage, S_2 is responded to in a time t_2, which follows immediately after the end of t_1 without any waiting time. S_3 and S_4 occur during t_2

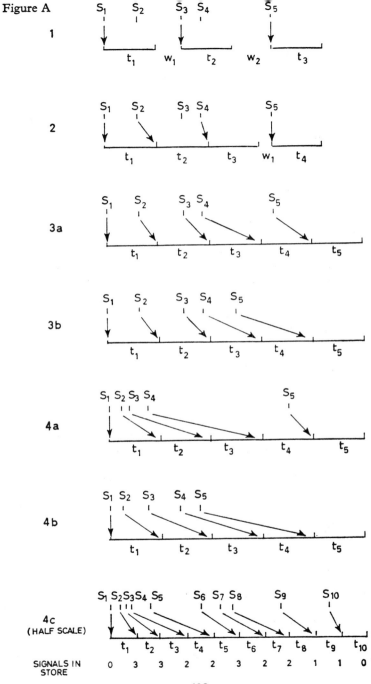

Figure A

and of these one (say S_3) is missed, and one (say S_4) is stored to be responded to during t_3, again without any waiting time intervening. No further signal occurs during t_3 so that a waiting time intervenes between the end of t_3 and the occurrence of S_5 which initiates t_4. It is clear that, with storage, less waiting times will occur and the proportion of signals responded to will be higher.

To calculate the proportion of responses when there is storage we need to calculate first the average length of chain of times t which occur without an intervening waiting time. When one signal can be stored, t_2 will follow t_1 without a waiting time whenever one or more signals occur during t_1. Let us call the probability of this $p(x_1 \geqslant 1)$ where x_1 is the number of signals occurring during t_1. The probability of t_3 following t_2 again without a waiting time will be the probability of one or more signals occurring both in t_1 and t_2, i.e.

$$p(x_1 \geqslant 1, x_2 \geqslant 1)$$

The probability of further responses following without a waiting time may be calculated in a similar manner. The total length of chain will thus be:

$$1 + p(x_1 \geqslant 1) + p(x_1 \geqslant 1, x_2 \geqslant 1) \ldots p(x_1 \geqslant 1 \ldots x_n \geqslant 1)$$

We will for future convenience denote this type of summation by the symbol ψ; followed by the basic term, in this case $(x \geqslant 1)$. We will also for future convenience write a for $(x \geqslant 1)$ so that we may denote the whole summation by $\psi(a)$.

We can think of the subject's time as being taken up with chains of responses of an average length $t \times$ mean $\psi(a)$ each followed by a waiting time $\bar{w}$. Putting A for mean $\psi(a)$ the proportion of time during which the single channel is busy may, by analogy with Eq. A1, be written

$$T_{(\lambda=1)} = \frac{tA}{tA + \bar{w}} \tag{A3}$$

and by analogy with Eq. A2 the proportion of signals responded to may be written

$$R_{(\lambda=1)} = \frac{T_{(\lambda=1)}}{\bar{x}} \tag{A4}$$

The case when two signals can be stored

When two signals can be stored the average length of the chains of responses which follow one another without an intervening waiting time will be increased. This is because responses can be made to both of two signals which occur during an interval t which is followed by an interval t during which no signals occur. An example is shown in Figure A(3a). S_1 initiates t_1, and S_2 is stored until t_2, as in the case with one stage of storage. During t_2, two further signals occur: S_3 is responded to during t_3, during which no further signals occur. S_4 is still in store, however, and is responded to during t_4, which follows immediately upon t_3. The whole cycle may be repeated without a waiting time intervening if further signals occur during t_4.

In Figure A(3a) the blank interval t_3 is shown as following immediately upon the interval t_2 during which two signals occur. The example in Figure A(3b) shows that this need not necessarily be the case and that the second signal during t_2 will not be missed if one or more intervals with one signal intervene. Thus in Figure A(3b), t_3 has one signal which can be carried over the blank interval t_4 until t_5.

This means that in the summation for determining the average length of chain two possibilities have to be considered: firstly, as before, a; secondly, and additionally, the probability that two or more signals will occur and that a blank interval will follow immediately or after one or more intervals in which one signal occurs. In the same notation as before we may write this possibility

$$p(x \geqslant 2).\psi(x = 1).p(x = 0)$$

Let us call this expression b. Then the whole ψ summation will be

$$\psi(a + b)$$

and if we call the mean for this expression B, we can by analogy with Eq. A3 write

$$T_{(\lambda=2)} = \frac{tB}{tB + \bar{w}} \tag{A5}$$

and

$$R_{(\lambda=2)} = \frac{T_{(\lambda=2)}}{\bar{x}} \tag{A6}$$

The case when three signals can be stored

When three signals can be stored, the storage capacity may be filled in one of two ways: either when an interval t occurs during which there are three signals or if two intervals occur with two signals and no blank interval between. In either case stored responses will fill two subsequent blank intervals. Figure A(4) illustrates these possibilities. In Figure A(4a) three signals occur during t_1. Two of these are responded to during two subsequent blank intervals t_2 and t_3, the third during t_4. In Figure

A(4b) two signals occur in each of t_1 and t_2, being worked off during the subsequent blank intervals t_3, t_4 and t_5. We should note that any number of intervals with one signal could be inserted between any of the intervals in Figure A(4a) and A(4b) without overloading the storage, and after the first blank interval the store will not be overloaded if an interval with two signals occurs. A possible more complex sequence of this kind is shown in Figure A(c) together with the numbers of signals in store at the end of each period t.

In the same notation as before we may thus write these two possibilities

$$p(x \geqslant 3).\psi(x = 1).p(x = 0).\psi(x = 1)$$
$$\times \psi[p(x = 2).\psi(x = 1).p(x = 0).\psi(x = 1)]p(x = 0)$$

and

$$px(= 2).\psi(x = 1).p(x \geqslant 2).\psi(x = 1).p(x = 0).\psi(x = 1)$$
$$\times \psi[p(x = 2).\psi(x = 1).p(x = 0).\psi(x = 1)]p(x = 0)$$

Summing and simplifying we obtain

$$[p(x \geqslant 3) + p(x = 2).p(x \geqslant 2).\psi(x = 1)]\psi^2(x = 1).p^2(x = 0)$$
$$\times \psi[p(x = 2).\psi^2(x = 1).p(x = 0)]$$

Let us call this expression c. The whole ψ summation thus becomes

$$\psi(a + b + c)$$

and if we call the mean for this expression C, then by analogy with Eq. A5 we may write

$$T_{(\lambda=3)} = \frac{tC}{tC + \bar{w}} \qquad (A7)$$

and

$$R_{(\lambda=3)} = \frac{T_{(\lambda=3)}}{\bar{x}} \qquad (A8)$$

Expressions for storage of more than three signals are cumbersome but similar in principle to the foregoing.

APPLICATION OF THE MODEL TO THE RANDOM CASE

We shall now consider the model as applied to the case where the signals arrive at strictly random intervals.

No storage

During each interval $(t + \bar{w})$ one signal will be responded to and $\bar{x}$

will be missed. The duration of $\bar{w}$ is therefore the average interval during which one signal occurs i.e.

$$\bar{w} = \frac{t}{\bar{x}} \tag{A9}$$

For the proportion of time spent responding, Eq. A1 may be rewritten

$$T_{(\lambda=0)} = \frac{t}{t + t/\bar{x}}$$

$$= \frac{\bar{x}}{\bar{x} + 1} \tag{A10}$$

and for the proportion of signals responded to Eq. A2 becomes

$$R_{(\lambda=0)} = \frac{1}{\bar{x} + 1} \tag{A11}$$

With storage

The calculation of $\bar{w}$ enables Eqs. A4, A6 and A8 to be rewritten respectively

$$R_{(\lambda=1)} = \frac{A}{\bar{x}A + 1} \tag{A12}$$

$$R_{(\lambda=2)} = \frac{B}{\bar{x}B + 1} \tag{A13}$$

$$R_{(\lambda=3)} = \frac{C}{\bar{x}C + 1} \tag{A14}$$

One stage of storage: calculation of A

Since in the random case $p(x_1) = p(x_2) \ldots = p(x_n)$,

$$A = 1 + p(x \geqslant 1) + p^2(x \geqslant 1) \ldots + p^n(x \geqslant 1)$$

or approximately (exactly if $n = \infty$):

$$A = \frac{1}{1 - a} \tag{A15}$$

Substituting according to the expression for a Poisson distribution, i.e.

$$p = \frac{\bar{x}^x}{x!}e^{-\bar{x}}$$

we obtain

$$A = \frac{1}{1 - (1 - e^{-\bar{x}})} = e^{\bar{x}} \tag{A16}$$

Two stages of storage: calculation of B

By analogy with Eq. A15 we may write

$$B = \frac{1}{1 - (a + b)} \tag{A17}$$

Substituting as before we obtain after reduction

$$B = e^{\bar{x}}(e^{\bar{x}} - \bar{x}) \tag{A18}$$

Three stages of storage: calculation of C

By analogy with Eq. A15 we may write

$$C = \frac{1}{1 - (a + b + c)} \tag{A19}$$

Substituting and reducing as before we obtain

$$C = e^{\bar{x}}[(e^{\bar{x}} - \bar{x})^2 - \tfrac{1}{2}\bar{x}^2] \tag{A20}$$

Table A3 gives $R_{(\lambda=0)}$, $R_{(\lambda=1)}$, $R_{(\lambda=2)}$ and $R_{(\lambda=3)}$ for various values of $\bar{x}$. By means of this table it is possible, knowing any three of the quantities, signal frequency, t, R and λ, to calculate the fourth. Strictly speaking, it only applies to the case where signals occur at random intervals and the task is of infinite length, but when storage is present moderate departures from randomness seem to make very little difference, and the inaccuracy due to assuming infinite length is small with tasks of moderate duration. A number of trials were made using a random signal generator with an electronic recording machine* acting as 'subject'. The recorder could be set to respond with a constant t and with 0, 1 or 2 stages of storage. Recorded results for a range of signal frequencies from below $\bar{x} = \cdot5$ to about $\bar{x} = 3\cdot0$ showed agreement with Table A5 to within 2 or 3%. The recorded figures tended to be a little too high, probably owing to the signal generator producing a series which was not quite random, having itself a short resolving time which would cause signals at the very shortest intervals to be run together and thus treated by the recorder as one.

The effect of variability in t

If t is not fixed but has appreciable variance the foregoing model will require modification. Firstly the mean probabilities of different frequencies of x will be affected since $\bar{x}$ will vary linearly with t. Consider

---

* N. T. Welford (1952) 'An electronic digital recording machine – the SETAR', *J. sci. Instrum.*, **29**, 1–4.

the probability of obtaining $x = 0$ in the random case. Since when $x = 0$, $p(x = 0) = e^{-x}$

$$\text{mean } \bar{x} = \text{mean } (- \log p_{(x=0)}) \tag{A21}$$

so that the arithmetic mean of $\bar{x}$ will correspond to the geometric mean of $p(x = 0)$. Since $p(x = 0)$ is less than 1, mean $p(x = 0)$ will be greater than if t had no variance. As the probability of a chain ending increases with $p(x = 0)$, the mean length of chain will decrease.

Secondly the product of t and length of chain will tend to be increased. Let us consider the case when there is one stage of storage. In place of tA in Eq. A3 we have to use mean $(t'.\psi(a))$ where t' is the mean t for any particular chain $\psi(a)$. We cannot usually calculate this since we do not know the individual t's and $\psi(a)$s. We can however estimate rough limits since

$$\text{mean } (t'.\psi(a)) = \bar{t}A + \sigma_{t'}.\sigma_{\psi(a)}.r_{t'.\psi(a)} \tag{A22}$$

where $\bar{t}$ is the overall mean t, $\sigma_{t'}$ is the standard deviation of t' $(= \sigma_t/\sqrt{\overline{\psi(a)}})$, $\sigma_{\psi(a)}$ is the standard deviation of $\psi(a)$ and $r_{t'.\psi(a)}$ is the product-moment correlation between t' and $\psi(a)$. Mean $(t'.\psi(a))$ will thus vary between $\bar{t}A$ when either $\sigma_{t'}$, $\sigma_{a(\psi)}$ or $r_{t'.\psi(a)} = 0$, and $\bar{t}A \pm \sigma_{t'}.\sigma_{\psi(a)}$ when $\sigma_{t'}$ and $\sigma_{\psi(a)}$ are greater than 0 and $r_{t'.\psi(a)} = \pm 1$. Since $r_{t'.\psi(a)}$ is likely to be positive, mean $(t'.\psi(a))$ is likely to be greater than $\bar{t}A$.

The overall result of these effects on T and thus on R can be seen if we express $\bar{t}$ and mean $\psi(a)$ as proportions of t and A in Eq. A3 – say $\bar{t} = t/\tau$ and mean $\psi(a) = A/\alpha$. Eq. A3 then becomes

$$
\begin{aligned}
T_{(\lambda = 1)} &= \frac{t/\tau.A/\alpha}{t/\tau.A/\alpha + \bar{w}} \\
&= \frac{tA}{tA + \tau\alpha\bar{w}}
\end{aligned}
\tag{A23}
$$

The overall effect will therefore diminish as tA rises relatively to $\bar{w}$. In other words, it will become relatively smaller as $\bar{x}$ and λ increase.

Author Index

Subject Index